THE HEART OF FATHER DAMIEN

THE HEART OF

Father Damien

1840-1889

VITAL JOURDAN, SS.CC.

Translated from the French by
REV. FRANCIS LARKIN, SS.CC.
AND CHARLES DAVENPORT

REVISED EDITION

An Angelus Book
GUILD PRESS, PUBLISHERS
Distributed by Golden Press, New York

First Edition:
NIHIL OBSTAT: Reverend Vincent Davis, ss.cc., s.t.l.—IMPRIMI
POTEST: William J. Condon, ss.cc., *Provincialis.*—NIHIL OBSTAT:
John A. Schulien, s.t.d., *Censor librorum.*—IMPRIMATUR: ✠ Al-
bert G. Meyer, *Archiepiscopus Milwauchiensis.*—Die 11ᵃ Augusti,
1955.

Nihil obstat of the
CONGREGATION OF RITES
Nicolaus Ferraro, s.c.r., Adsessor
Fidei Sub-Promotor Generalis
Rome, Mar. 14th, 1957
Prot. n. 1501/168

Revised Edition:
NIHIL OBSTAT: Austin B. Vaughan, s.t.d., *Censor Deputatus*
IMPRIMATUR: ✠ Francis Cardinal Spellman
Archbishop of New York
September 8, 1960

In obedience to the decree of Pope Urban VIII and in conform-
ity with the Apostolic Constitution *Officiorum ac munera* of Pope
Leo XIII, we declare that we claim no more than purely human
consideration for the extraordinary gifts of grace reported in this
book, and that we submit at all times unreservedly to the judgment of the Catholic Church.

The Translators

Foreword

THE official publication of the Holy See, in the July, 1955, issue, announced that on April 26, 1955, in the Apostolic Palace of the Vatican, a meeting of the Sacred Congregation of Rites was held to discuss the introduction of the Cause of the Servant of God, Damien de Veuster, missionary priest of the Congregation of the Sacred Hearts of Jesus and Mary (cf. *Acta Apostolicae Sedis,* Vol. 47, p. 525). That meeting signified that the heroic virtues and sanctity of Father Damien had already been carefully considered in the previous diocesan process with hopeful results and that the Cause has been taken up by the Holy See. We fervently pray that full apostolic approval may soon be given and that this humble priest may be elevated to the glory of the altars.

The world suffers contradiction when it sees pious men or women deliberately seeking to live their lives among trying difficulties and burdensome oppositions; yet it cannot restrain its admiration. This has been verified in the case of Father Damien. As soon as his decision to separate himself from the world to serve the lepers was known, not few were the voices raised in expressions of high regard and joyous astonishment, although others commented unfavorably. And when it became known that he had contracted leprosy and again later on the occasion of his death, from all quarters of the earth and from all peoples arose a tumult extolling his name while authors vied with one another in penning articles and books to describe his extraordinary life. This was the voice of the people pronouncing approval and rendering meaningless the objections and accusations hurled by a few misinformed and vile individuals. Their empty tinklings were lost in the extensive and powerful clamor of admiration that arose from all good men, whose voice were lifted up not due to imagination or sentimentality or emotion but because they knew the facts.

And here are the facts. A young man belonging to a rural, well-to-do family, the pride and joy of his good parents, endowed with splendid health, handsome in appearance, sane and without defect, at the age of eighteen years thinks about embracing the religious life; he goes to consult his brother, Pamphile, who had already made his profession in the Congregation of the Sacred Hearts; he studies and examines that religious institute, is attracted to it, and decides to enter and to consecrate himself entirely to God; he enters (February 2, 1859) and makes his religious profession (October 7, 1860) choosing the name of Damien, the name of the physician-saint invoked in the Canon of the Mass, an indication of his future apostolate. It seems that he does not think then of advancing to the priesthood but rather is content to remain hidden as a lay brother in the service of God. The inspiring words of a bishop who visits his religious house inflame him with a love for the missions beyond the ocean, where his own brother is preparing to go. But when Father Pamphile is suddenly struck ill and is unable to depart for the missions, Damien with daring generosity writes to his

Father General saying that he is disposed and prompt to substitute for his brother. The permission is granted, the ticket ready, and the departure so imminent that only a short interval remains for Damien to say good-by to his relatives at Tremeloo. At the Shrine of Our Lady at Scherpenheuvel he embraces his mother for the last time realizing that he probably would not see her again. In fact, before embarking he writes these words to his dear ones: "Good-by, dearest parents, henceforth we shall not have the happiness of seeing one another, but we shall always be united by that tender love which we bear for one another." After four and a half months of arduous travel he arrives at Honolulu (March 19, 1864). Following ordination to the priesthood and very strenuous labors as a missionary in difficult posts, Damien deliberately chooses to live practically alone in almost impossible surroundings amid miseries of every kind among the outcasts of humanity, the lepers of Molokai. Out of love of Jesus Christ he dedicates to the service of these derelicts his life, his mind, his heart, his energies, and his talents, foreseeing, as it was easy to foresee, that he himself would likewise die of their malady, leprosy: *Charitas Christi urget nos* (II Cor. V, 14).

Because of these facts the world calls him a hero and he was; but at the same time by his life of sacrifice most emphatically he manifested that he was a holy man for "who lives in charity, lives in God, and God in him" (I John IV, 16) and "greater love than this no man hath, that a man lay down his life for his friends" (John XV, 13). This Damien did, for at the age of forty-nine the Apostle of Molokai died, a victim of love and of sacrifice; because of his love for the souls of his lepers he was sacrificed.

How welcome is this book, THE HEART OF FATHER DAMIEN; it brings new light to the well-known facts and draws from previously unpublished sources additional information about our beloved hero. Through his own letters, now exhumed from the archives of the mother house of the Congregation of the Sacred Hearts, he reveals better than ever before his own heart, generous, sincere, and candid, a heart formed in the school of Christ, inspired by the high ideals of the Congregation of the Sacred Hearts, and dedicated entirely to God and neighbor. The author of THE HEART OF FATHER DAMIEN, Father Vital Jourdan, SS.CC., and the translators, Father Francis Larkin, SS.CC., and Charles Davenport, are to be congratulated and thanked for presenting a deep and keen insight into the noble and magnificent soul of the saintly Father Damien.

✠A. G. CICOGNANI
Archbishop of Laodicea
Apostolic Delegate

The Feast of Christ the King, 1955
Washington, D. C.

Preface

THIRTY years ago, Father Vital Jourdan, priest of the Congregation of the Sacred Hearts of Jesus and Mary, published in French his biography of Father Damien under the title of *Le Père Damien de Veuster, apôtre des lépreux.* At that time an English translation was contemplated but never made. Later, in 1937, John Farrow wrote his *Damien the Leper,* which is still popular today.

Both Father Jourdan and Mr. Farrow were handicapped by lack of access to important documents in the archives of the generalate of the Congregation of the Sacred Hearts. However, in recent years these sources have been made available. Father Jourdan decided therefore to revise and augment his book in order to present as authentic and detailed a biography as possible.

Even before the French original was published, work on the translation was begun. The translators have endeavored to achieve two things: to remain faithful to the author's ideas, and to present them in a pleasing style. Therefore they have not hesitated to translate freely his often difficult idiom, and to adapt, augment, and delete (with permission, of course) whenever it was deemed necessary.

The result is, they believe, the most complete biography on Father Damien in English yet published. Moreover, although footnotes have been omitted, to avoid reference-cluttered pages, this biography is as authoritative as the author and the translators could make it.

We wish to express our sincere thanks to the following: His Excellency, the Most Reverend Amleto G. Cicognani, Apostolic Delegate to the United States, for his graciousness in writing the inspiring Foreword; the Very Reverend William J. Condon, SS.CC., Provincial of the Fathers of the Sacred Hearts in the United States, for his encouragement and co-operation; Father Vital Jourdan, SS.CC., who, despite his arduous duties as curate of the Church of St. Gabriel in Paris, managed to find time to write the book and to help the translators; Father Simon Pease, SS.CC., M.A., of the faculty of the Sacred Hearts Seminary, Wareham, Mass., for reading the manuscript and for helpful comments; Frater Marion Mangin, SS.CC., M.A., Queen of Peace Mission Seminary, Jaffrey, N. H., who retyped a good portion of the manuscript; Mr. Raphael Brown for bringing up to date the section on Hansen's disease and also for writing the Epilogue; Mrs. Lola Benedict for helping with the translation and for invaluable research in the Library of Congress; Father Peter d'Orgeval, SS.CC., veteran Molokai missionary; Brother Jules Haagen, SS.CC., Sacred Hearts Seminary, Washington, D. C., former missionary of Molokai, for invaluable information about Father Damien's present-day spiritual influence; and, finally, Brother Patrick Hughes, SS.CC., who, before being sent to Honolulu, was stationed at Molokai for a number of years.

FRANCIS LARKIN, SS.CC.

Contents

PART III *CALVARY*

EPILOGUE

APPENDIX

PART I

Formative Years

1 Boyhood

HOUSES with sharp-pointed roofs and bold windows cutting the north wind . . . fog swirling around old towers . . . a rolling generous countryside . . . a lively, colorful people with a soul that is exuberant and yet calm and with a humor that is just a trifle heavy . . . this is a stranger's first vision of Flanders.

The powerfully built lion symbolizes the Fleming's candor, his ardor, his courage, his robust health, and even more robust will that is ready for the noblest deeds. He likes very simple things, the essentials. His motto is: "Be what you are. Do what you are supposed to do."

The soul of the Flemings lies not only in their power to observe the world as we find it in the heavy sumptuous tones of their tapestries, in the strident cries of their poetry, in the strong speech of the people. It is the form of life that has been enriched little by little by their very hesitations, their failures, their efforts at reform. Paul Valery says: "This race is a strange mixture of impetuosity and langor, of violent activity and a bent toward contemplation that is ardent and patient, furiously sensual at times and yet detached from the material world."

The characteristic traits of the Flemings come from the fact that they are a race of peasants. Only scattered handfuls are city-folk. Through centuries of outrages, robberies, and cruelties from Burgundians, French, Spaniards, Austrians, and Germans the Flemings have remained unmoved. As Cyril Verschaeve writes: "We feel something at the bottom of our nature like a solid foundation that will never give way under our feet, something that makes us face all kinds of death, go into the future, go against all history that tries to impose itself on us, go along with the history that is in us. It is nature and not will or geopolitics that governs history. That deep, inexhaustible nature whose past buries itself in God and whose future spreads out in endless glories, that is what we bear in the depths of our life. This is the Flemish in us. It makes our nature Flemish. It makes Flanders."

The changeable climate has made the Flemish peasant outwit the earth. His combat with the capricious elements has developed in him a shrewdness of his own and a feeling for colors and the appearance of things. It has given him a realism and a sensitivity for the slightest variations of nature; the smells, habits, colors of flowers, trees, insects, animals.

There is a sense of the beautiful, of the good and wholesome that can be acquired only under the sun in the midst of green things. For a real peasant his health naturally blossoms into holiness. For him, by an understanding with creation and the help of its Creator, a human personality develops. Man plants and waters, but God gives the increase. Nature offers a unique background for prayer to men of the earth. The religious sense of creation has always assured them a Christian balance, strong and unshaken, in their lives.

This story of Damien de Veuster is the story of a typical Flemish peasant.

A man of robust temperament, of loyal and energetic character, he gave himself with the spontaneity of a tree giving its fruit. His soul contained a life that was clear and unified. His was a life of young and vigorous realism. He was not buried in the clouds. He was a man of action. In him we stand face to face with one of those beautiful examples produced by a soil and a race penetrated by centuries of hard work, honesty, and faith.

A language frontier splits Belgium in two — Flanders on the north and Wallony in the south. In Flanders, a few miles north of Louvain, between Aerschot and Malines, is a flat region where little vegetable gardens and fields of grain alternate with evergreens, scrubs, and waste patches. Here are the well-kept farmhouses of the hamlet of Ninde in the town of Tremeloo. On the left is the Dyle with its two meandering tributaries, the Demer and the Laak. Generations of peasants have stubbornly worked this ungrateful soil. Their life has remained sober and rough from it.

In 1840 Tremeloo became a town. With its ten hamlets and dependencies it had some 1600 inhabitants. They never spared themselves to better this land. Their character shows it. It sets them apart from their neighbors. They are stubborn, patient, tenacious, vindictive. They laugh at mockery just as they do at privation, fatigue, and bad weather. Despite these and other knocks, they stay on their feet. Far from the more polished centers of life, they have a contempt for all formality, a positive repugnance for delicate language and manners. Their spirit is a little quarrelsome. But their openhearted joviality makes you like them. They are a strong, hardy race — and thanks be to God — full of the Christian spirit. Faith is deeply rooted in these patriarchal families. Nothing dispenses from the complete observance of the divine law in these blessed homes of Flanders where God chooses more of His ministers and His apostles than from almost anywhere else.

Such was the de Veuster family at the beginning of the past century. Francis de Veuster, the father, was born in 1800. He married Anne Catherine Waustere, a young peasant girl originally from Haecht, a nearby village. Hand in hand they fulfilled the duties of man and wife and of Christian parents. In time they had eight children: Auguste and Joseph became priests; Eugenie and Pauline entered the Ursulines; Leonce, Gerard, and Constance married; Mary died when she was fourteen.

Joseph, the future Father Damien, was the next to last child. He was baptized on the day of his birth, January 3, 1840, and was named after his godfather, Joseph Goovaerts.

The de Veusters were fairly well-to-do peasants who raised and sold grain. This business required Joseph's father to go to the market at Louvain, Malines, Antwerp, and Brussels every other day. Then he would return to a little one-story red-brick house on the road to Haecht, where the barn stood on the other side of a yard in which the chickens scratched for food and a dog barked once in a while and eight children played.

Today the house is almost as it was then. In 1901 the Fathers of the Sacred Hearts acquired the property for a shrine and museum. Later they built a scholasticate next to the de Veuster home. When it burned down after World War II, it was replaced by a modern seminary. A plaque at the shrine reads:

HERE WAS BORN
FATHER DAMIEN
JOSEPH DE VEUSTER
APOSTLE OF THE LEPERS

Surrounded by her large family, the mother was proud of her little "Jef" who was so fat and full of life. He was

going on four when God began to ask of this good woman
half of her children for His exclusive service. Eugenie, the
oldest girl, took her vows with the Ursulines at Thildonck
in October, 1845. Six years later she died of typhus at their
school in Uden, Holland, where she had been one of the
students' favorite teachers.

Three others would follow Eugenie into religious life.
This is not surprising. Their mother was behind it all.
Almost as soon as they learned to talk she taught them
their prayers. And if the little de Veusters were good, she
would take down the big book written in Old Flemish
with Gothic type and beautiful pictures, and which she
alone could read, and lay it across her knees to read them
The Lives of the Holy Martyrs and Hermits. Their wide
eyes revealed the enthusiasm and admiration of their young
souls. They were going to grow up and be just like the
saints in the big book!

At five, Jef was having his own spiritual adventures. A
Flemish fair, *Kermesse* as they call it, was in full swing at
Werchter. It was one of those Kermesses the Flemish
painters have immortalized on their canvases — simple fun,
noisy celebration, eating and drinking. Jef slipped through
the crowd and vanished. Where in the world had he gone?
Finally, grandfather, a little wiser than the rest, suggested
the church. There he was, his tiny body hidden under the
pulpit.

At seven he started to a school which was conducted at
Werchter by Arnold Bols and his son Auguste. With his
brothers and sisters and cousins, he walked the two good
miles from Ninde to Werchter. Rain or shine, he picked
up his wax-covered canvas bag with his sandwiches and
fruit and went off to school. The only extant document
bearing on this period says his teacher found him "very
bright."

Jef kept thinking about all the things his mother read

him from the big book. One day on the way home from school he decided to turn his companions into hermits. They stopped in the woods to practice silence, recollection, and prayer until nightfall. When the tardy anchorites finally got home, their worried parents gave them further material for their spiritual consideration.

Jef carefully kept his Guardian Angel busy. With typical Flemish passion he went in for ice skating until he was one of the best skaters on the Dyle. But no matter how good he was, he couldn't skate on water. One day he was going along as fast as he could, enjoying the exhilaration that comes from good hard ice and sharp skates. A light whip across the face of the ice and you fly. Suddenly, Jef felt the ice cracking. It was thin where the Dyle meets the Laak. He cut with one of his skates and made for solid ice and safety. As naturally as he breathed in the frosty air, he thanked his Guardian Angel. Even when he was alone on the ice, he knew he was part of a skating team. And he knew who was the better one.

Another time he owed his Angel even more. They were coming home from school, and, as children will do, held hands and stretched out across the road. When they were approaching a sharp turn, a cart suddenly bore down on them. They screamed and scattered. But not quickly enough. The driver tried to stop, but before he could, the cart hit Jef. A wheel struck his head; he lay there in the dirt. But fortunately, he got up with only a bump on his head and a bruised back. He must have been a very solid little Fleming indeed.

They used to call him "the little shepherd." For hours he would caress the sheep, tease them, make them run. One day a ewe didn't quite agree with his carryings-on with her offspring. With one good butt she knocked him flat. He bounced easily, however; he was back on his feet laughing.

Since we have almost no documents of this period, we are forced to conjecture what must have been the boy's good and bad points. Probably he was no different from the other boys — the same spontancity, the same enthusiasm, the same petulance. Jef couldn't miss the atmosphere of Tremeloo where voices could be raised, peasants could be rough and brutally frank, words were not softened when contradictions arose, and fists sometimes flew freely.

Only religion could tame him down and humanize him. He made his First Communion at Tremeloo on Palm Sunday when he was ten. Did he understand the meaning of this great religious act? Perhaps he did. Perhaps he didn't. Later he would look back and see the workings of his divine Master.

One story of his pity and generosity has come down to us. His mother had stuffed the children's lunch bag with good Flemish cookies. Just when they were opening their watering mouths, a young beggar appeared on the scene with a good story — wonderful news, in fact. He had brought a little bird for each of them and had left it at their homes, since they were at school. Wasn't he nice? The children looked at each other . . . a bird for them! ! . . . they looked at the beggar . . . at the cookies . . . at each other again. Why, of course, he must have part of their cookies. Then Jef got an even better idea. "Let's give him all of them. The poor are always in need." They did. When they got home, no birds!

By the time he was thirteen, he had learned about all he could at Werchter, so he shut his books, stuffed his tablets into his schoolbag, and went home. Along with Leonce and Gerard, he helped his father in the fields, took care of the animals, and worked around the house. Work was practically a game for him. He was growing tall and strong. Soon he was taller than his older brother Leonce and so strong he could lift hundred-kilo bags "as though they were nothing." His father used to say he was handy and smart enough to be four boys.

For four years the apprentice farmhand worked the small piece of land at Ninde, spaded, ran the harrow, planted, harvested. During the day he drove the wagon, worked in the orchard. When he worked down at the barn, apparently he didn't mind the choking smell of manure that penetrated everywhere. Going along at the even keel of his character, he was simply conscious that he was doing the duties of his state in life.

He had a helping hand for anyone. Alert and enterprising, the young man inspired confidence. One old lady loved to recall how he had cured her entire fortune — her cow. The veterinarian had given up hope. But the lad felt sorry for the old lady. He told the butcher, who was taking such excellent care of the cow, that he could go home. Jef sat up all night, and the next morning his patient was out of danger.

In August, 1853, Auguste, his brother, entered the minor seminary at Malines. As a student, he was above average; he was fifth in a class of forty and remained one of the upper ten throughout. In 1857, he went to the Sacred Hearts Fathers novitiate at Louvain. Meanwhile, Eugenie died and Pauline, Jef's favorite, took her place with the Ursulines two years later.

Would you call this time lost? It was a long time at home. Twenty years later he would say that all the things he had learned at home had helped him in his work time and again. Trust in Divine Providence is wisdom. But the boy kept thinking.

A peasant's life is rough. There are no holidays. Animals have to be fed and cleaned every day. At grips with the natural elements, an ungrateful soil, unpredictable seasons, the peasant wrests the necessary food from the earth. But the earth that grows his thorns also grows his roses —

austere but manly and healthy joys of work that is personal and little mechanized. A servant of creation, he works along with the power of God.

Without knowing this, Jef somehow must have sensed it. He was a descendant of the old Flemish families who have been baptized for centuries. He was part of those peaceful solitudes that gave birth to the mysticism of which Ruysbroeck is the most famous representative. He naturally united himself to God, held to the plow with a firm grip, without turning up his nose in disgust . . . simply . . . with silent, stubborn courage . . . quiet strength . . . patience . . . never suspecting the sublimity of it all. This co-operation with the work of God formed his conscience and revealed his dignity to him.

This farmer boy sowed no wild oats. His deep piety helped him, but that does not mean virtue cost him less than it did others. He was an adolescent and he knew what it meant to be tempted. He had to fight to master his strong body. He decided to sleep on a board which he carefully hid each morning. But as mothers always do, his mother soon discovered the mortification of this latest disciple of the Fathers of the Desert.

Farming the small de Veuster homestead did not require so many hands. Leonce and Gerard plus their father's days at home were enough. Jef's capabilities and enterprising spirit seemed to demand a better outlet.

His father thought of making him an associate in the grain business. He decided Jef would be a grain trader as he was at Tremeloo and as Joseph Goovaerts, Jef's godfather, was at Antwerp. He would make his apprenticeship at Antwerp. But on thinking it over, they saw that the smattering of education received at Werchter was not enough. He'd better learn French first. So they changed their plans and sent him to a Wallon school.

Joseph entered the school at Braine-le-Comte as a

boarder on May 15, 1858. Luckily, M. Deure-L'Hoir, the director, liked this eighteen-year-old boy whose intellectual life had lain fallow for four years but who was as robust and goodhearted as they came.

Somewhat lost in his Wallon surroundings, where along with some other Flemings he cut a strange figure, the newcomer quickly acclimated himself and got resolutely down to his studies. A month hadn't gone by before he was writing home of how much he liked the place. The daily menu at Ninde must have been pretty temperate for him to say that at school they ate as though every day were a fair. The beer, he said, was excellent. But his heart remained Flemish; he went to fairs, wrote that all the quarrels over language could be settled by whacks of a ruler, and had a few quarrels of his own. Being of a volcanic mold, he wouldn't put up with any Wallon jibbing. "My second pair of pants were torn at the knees the first day I got here."

The ten letters the folks at home received showed how busy Jef was at Braine-le-Comte. He was happy to be up to his ears in studies that were enriching his soul. Hoped they'd forgive him for not writing more often . . . wasn't forgetting any of them for a moment . . . owed much, so much to them, especially this chance to go on with his education that would be useful to him for the rest of his life. Even vacations had no attraction for him. They seemed to break up "the furrow he was plowing with the plodding perseverance of a peasant in the field of knowledge." Very probably he spent his vacations at Louvain with Auguste as his French teacher.

In this Belgian school of 1858, religious education was not forgotten. In his penmanship book he wrote such sayings as: "Christian knowledge is love applied to the measurement of God's greatness and our own littleness." "You must not only be religious and love devotion, but you have to make it pleasant, useful, and agreeable to everyone."

At Braine-le-Comte he went through a trial on which his fidelity to his vocation and his whole future depended. There is no doubt about it, at this time he heard the call of God. He tackled this problem just as he had gone to work on the farm and had plunged into his studies — with that same ardor and drive.

But he didn't breathe a word of it to anybody; any premature confidences might compromise everything. Characteristically, he turned to prayer. His cousin and M. Deure-L'Hoir say he used to stay up nights and pray while the rest were asleep. There was so much against his vocation. He was behind in his studies, and, besides, his father the grain merchant thought the credit side of his balance sheet looked pretty good as it was. Eugenie had become an Ursuline and died. Pauline had followed Eugenie; and now Auguste was in the seminary. Jef was supposed to help him carry on the grain business. They were counting on him. It would probably be better if he stuck to the grain trade.

But this powerful Fleming was used to moving big obstacles. Pauline's profession furnished him his chance to make the first overture. He ended his letter of July 17: "She told me that she left home for good on June 8th. How happy she must be! She has had the chance to take on the hardest job you can have. My turn to choose the way I should follow will come soon, I hope. Would it be possible for me to join my brother Pamphile?" Pamphile was Auguste's name in religion.

The excitement Pauline's departure had caused at home, to which he cleverly added his own request, made his parents realize that something was going on at Braine-le-Comte. Jef was clearly directing his thoughts toward a life more perfect than that of a good Christian layman. At home they were a little alarmed to see the hopes his father

had nurtured so tenderly now slipping away. But on thinking it over, if God wanted him, well, they couldn't say no.
The grain dealer wisely took the tack — "we'll see . . . let's
be sure first."

For months, long months Jef let the idea ripen. He tried
to find out God's will and promised to do it down to the
last detail. His generosity grew with each of his long night
vigils of prayer. Then in October a Redemptorist came to
Braine-le-Comte to preach a mission. This strengthened
Jef's resolution more than ever.

"Foolish sinner," the missionary cried, "who for a fleeting
moment of pleasure damns himself to an eternity of pain!"
The whole parish got into the spirit of the mission. "Big
fish" came back to the Sacraments, the ordinary good
people resolved to be better, the real good to try even
harder. The soul of this Flemish peasant was a fertile field
for the divine word. Interiorly he renewed his sacrifice
and searched for the way to answer the divine call most
perfectly.

At first he wanted to go to the Trappists, since the idea
of penance and manual labor appealed to him. He was
used to it. But Auguste, now Brother Pamphile, as a novice
in the Sacred Hearts Congregation, talked him out of it.
Pamphile's argument was that after all if the Holy See
approved any Congregation as an infallible way of attain-
ing sanctity, you could become a saint in that Congregation as well as in any other. It was up to you. That decided
Jef.

Considering his age and scanty cultural baggage, he'd
better hurry. Hurrying to carry out his small and large
projects was to be Jef's fate all his life. To break the last
barriers, his soul burst into words of lightning and thunder
on Christmas, 1858: "Don't think this idea of entering the
religious life is my idea! It's Providence, I tell you, that is
inspiring me. Don't put any obstacles in the way. God is

calling me. I must obey. If I refuse I run the risk of going to hell. As for you, God will punish you terribly for standing in the way of His will."

Strong words, yes. But they got results. He could go. Around the first of January, Jef left Braine-le-Comte where he had stayed about seven months. Accompanied by his father, he joined Pamphile at Louvain. His parents thought it was just a visit to look the place over. But the brothers had been working faster than anyone at Tremeloo suspected. Father Wenceslas Vincke, SS.CC., the superior of the house at Louvain, agreed to take Joseph as a postulant. And his father went home alone.

2   The Fathers of the Sacred Hearts

THE religious institute Joseph de Veuster was to enter in January, 1859, bears a canonical name that is a bit long but quite specific: Congregation of the Sacred Hearts of Jesus and Mary and of Perpetual Adoration of the Most Blessed Sacrament of the Altar. Its members are popularly known as the Fathers of the Sacred Hearts. One of its best known members is Father Mateo Crawley-Boevey, SS.CC., founder and apostle of the Enthronement of the Sacred Heart in the Home.

The founder of this Congregation (known in Europe as the "Picpus Fathers" from the Rue de Picpus, on which the mother house was located) was Father Marie-Joseph Coudrin, a French diocesan priest. Ordained secretly on March 4, 1792, in the Irish Seminary in Paris, he went about in disguise, risking his life administering the Sacraments to the faithful.

In September, 1792, while hiding in a barn, during his thanksgiving after Mass, he had a vision of white-clad missionaries going to all parts of the world, spreading love for the Sacred Hearts, at the same time he saw religious kneeling day and night at the foot of the tabernacle making reparation for the crimes committed against the Blessed

Sacrament and praying for the missionaries. This vision became a reality when, arriving at Poitiers, he met a member of a noble family, Countess Henriette de la Chevalerie, whom he recognized as one he had seen in the vision. Saved from death at the hands of the revolutionaries, she had joined a group of women in making adoration day and night in a private home in reparation for the terrible crimes of the French Revolution.

Father Coudrin became her spiritual director and later, with her collaboration, founded the Congregation of the Sacred Hearts. Together they took their vows of poverty, chastity, and obedience on Christmas eve, 1800. Perpetual adoration was begun in 1803, near the famous Picpus Cemetery where are buried some 1700 victims of the guillotine. This adoration, despite revolutions and persecutions, has never ceased to this day.

As its title indicates, the primary purpose of the Congregation is to "practice and propagate devotion to the Sacred Heart of Jesus and the Immaculate Heart of Mary" and to carry on round-the-clock adoration. Each member makes a half hour of day adoration, daily, and one hour of night adoration, weekly. Father Damien remained faithful to this practice, even during his busiest days at Molokai.

The Congregation was approved by Pope Pius VII in 1817. In 1825 the Fathers were asked to undertake the conversion of the Polynesians of the South Seas. Missionaries left for Hawaii in 1827. In 1833 the evangelization of the Marquesas and Tahiti groups of islands was begun. Since then the Congregation has spread to 27 countries, with headquarters in Rome.

The members of the Congregation are pledged to imitate these four periods of our Lord's life, in keeping with the general aim of practicing and spreading devotion to the Sacred Hearts of Jesus and Mary: His childhood, by education; His hidden life, by perpetual adoration; His apostolic life, by preaching and missionary work; His crucified life, by mortification and penance. The spirit of the Congregation is that of the family: simplicity and charity.

The Superior-General of the Congregation at the time Joseph de Veuster applied for entrance had established a house of formation at Louvain. The famous university of the same name was recalling the good old days when it had been the well-known Alma Mater (1425-1795) both because of the orthodoxy and learning of its professors and the number of its students. The seminarians of the Sacred Hearts Fathers attended the university lectures and continued the spiritual formation proper to their Congregation in their own religious house, now the provincial house of the Belgian Province of the Congregation.

Without the support of his brother Pamphile, who had already joined the community and whose abilities were known, one might wonder if Joseph would have been received. Certainly the Superior could not be blamed for hesitating in the presence of this young man. He was eager and willing, there was no doubt about that. But he did not even know the first declension in Latin and subjected the French language to exquisite tortures.*

At most the applicant might make a choir Brother. He could take care of the chapels, the infirmary, or act as a secretary. It was a little higher than being a missionary

---

* An interesting side light on young de Veuster's lack of training is furnished by Father Gerard Schellinger, former vice-rector of the American College at Louvain. He states in a letter: "Msgr. Jules De Becker, former Rector, told me that young Damien, then an ignorant Flemish boy, applied for admission to the American College, 'because he desired to go to the Missions in America' and was refused admission because 'of his rudeness in manner and appearance and his gross ignorance of Latin or any other language.' Little was it realized at that time that a saint was sent from the door . . ." *(Trans. note).*

Brother.* This was a heavy blow for the newcomer, who had counted on becoming a priest. Disappointed but submissive, he bowed . . . yet not without plans of his own. He took the habit of a choir Brother in February as Brother Damien. His humility at least would not be lost within this narrowed horizon. Nonetheless, he was still thinking of his original idea, as we shall see many times later. Deep down he hadn't given up his plans.

In the course of the day, he had several chances of seeing his brother who was living under the same roof. His tenacity, his terrific drive, his determination to get things done showed he could overcome the difficulties a nineteen-year-old boy might have when he begins Latin. He tried to remember rules, expressions, and phrases of that somewhat difficult tongue. Just as a game, he and Pamphile used to play around with translating and writing. Before long the older brother was marveling at the ease with which his younger brother picked up his offhand lessons.

This huge Fleming's power of mind was equal to his physical strength. He was getting along so well that Brother Pamphile reported it to the Superior. From then on, he began a regular course with the Superior's knowledge and supervision. In six months Brother Damien could pick up a fifth-year Latin text and translate it at sight.

But the Superior did not have to wait that long to see the obvious finger of God on his young novice whose ability equaled his application. With the approval of his council, he decided to have Brother Damien enter the class of student novices. If these beginnings were justified by re-

* Originally a postulant could be admitted in the Congregation either as a candidate for the priesthood, as a choir Brother, or as a missionary Brother. The principal duties of a choir Brother were the daily singing of the office, teaching, or manual labor. This rank has now been suppressed. A novice is now admitted either as a candidate for the priesthood or as a missionary Brother.

sults, nothing would stand in his way to the priesthood.

The Latinist was even more determined than ever and worked doubly hard. Also during that time he made an intensive study of the Rule and prescriptions of the Congregation. His superiors did not think it necessary to extend his time of probation beyond twenty months, the regular period being eighteen months. The novice was on his way to final profession which took place at first vows. These final vows were made at Issy in France where novices trained elsewhere had to spend the last three months of their probation. Brother Damien went there at the end of June, 1860.

It goes without saying that the main work and the hardest one in a novice's orientation to a life of perfection that has to go on until his death, no matter what the obstacles are, is his religious education and formation. With his mind made up to give his whole being to God, Brother Damien employed all the resources of a will that was already mature. But there was still plenty for him to do to get his balance — being a little more gentle here, stepping things up a bit there, being moderate at all times.

Father Caprais Verhaege, SS.CC., was in charge of the seminarians' training. A man of exceptional virtue and author of a work on mystical theology, he also was spiritual director of a good number of diocesan priests. To him the bishop of Tournai had entrusted the delicate assignment of studying the case of the famous stigmatic of Bois d'Haine, Louise Lateau.

If a novice's perfection consisted solely in keeping himself in a state of passivity and receptivity in blind obedience to his director without any personal initiative on his part, Brother Damien was assuredly not good novice material. For to these things he added his own outlook, his own turn of mind, his own style of thinking and acting. No up-in-the-clouds spirituality for him. He was original enough to settle difficulties by means of his own rich imagination. Coming late to the religious life, with bits of the material world clinging to him and a newly acquired spirituality, he set about ridding himself of an awkwardness, a clumsy way of expressing his best feelings that sometimes brought him grief. However, it was that originality, the initiative cultivated on the edges of the beaten path, that was going to make his life such a tremendous success.

To aid his memory he carved the three points of a conference on his desk with his pocketknife: silence, recollection, prayer. This curious document, which drew down upon him public correction, is now in the museum at Tremeloo.

A fellow novice said that his zeal for night adoration was incomparable. His robust constitution won for him the privilege of habitually taking the hour from two to three o'clock in the morning. He never bothered going back to bed. "How often I was edified by his recollection and fervor! Like St. Paul the first hermit he had the habit of emitting little sighs at prayer which struck the ear sweetly and excited one to devotion." This testimony is goodhearted, but neither the Rule nor the novice master prescribed such music, light though it was.

His liking for some of the Fathers of the Desert made Brother Damien go beyond the demands of the community practices. "One night," his brother tells us, "when we were sleeping in the same room, I thought I saw a big bundle at the foot of his bed. I got up to see what it was. It was my brother sleeping on the floor, since he didn't bring his board from Tremeloo."

Discipline was austere but it was in no way gloomy. Brother Damien was always in good humor. His confreres called him *le bon gros Damien* — "big good-natured Damien." His joviality and happy chatter or Flemish humor relaxed their nerves. But these bursts of exuberant fun often brought him reproaches from his brother Pamphile: "No doubt about it. We laugh too much." Father Verhaege declared that in his long experience he had never come across a more sociable or lovable character.

Stray remembrances of his zeal, it is clear, do not reveal much about the profound change taking place in his soul. That was God's secret.

At the end of June, 1860, Brother Damien left Louvain for the French novitiate at Issy. Then he went to the mother house at 31, Rue de Picpus in Paris to take his vows on October 7, 1860. The symbolism of the burial cloth under which he lay during the ceremony of the vows will come back to him thirteen years later, and we will be amazed to learn to what point his generosity had carried him. One small detail that might be overlooked: on opening the register containing the professed and witnesses of the October 7 ceremony, one can see a thick signature scrawled out in pen — that of Brother Damien. The stylus cut an irrevocable oath into marble.

At the birthplace of his Congregation, he stayed for some time to breathe in the atmosphere of piety and simplicity and of heartfelt friendliness. He studied scholastic philosophy for a year, keeping up with his Latin and Greek at the same time.

A classmate described him as being at this period a big-boned man with broad shoulders, a huge head, high forehead, and full jowls. Therefore, his professor felt justified in nicknaming him *mon gros Damien* — "my big Damien." His nearsighted eyes slightly marred his otherwise happy and appealing features . . . a typical Flemish face, filled out, radiant with health and smiling all over.

He had not the slightest trouble adapting himself to his new French surroundings. His Superior's testimony on this point is clear. "A lot of them used to run around in circles as though they had a fever. It was hard for them to get the spirit of the Community. Not Brother Damien. From the first day he acted like a fish in water, as though he'd always lived here. He went with ease from study to prayer to recreation, and he worked furiously. He wanted to make up for lost time and his robust health sustained him in those long hours of study. He had terrific drive. He was all but bursting. A little moderation wouldn't have hurt him."

"Many a time," another witness said, "I saw him come out of the classroom, his mind burning with some idea, impulsively grab a pen and jot down the idea or observation which he thought important." But we must not be too quick to put him in the category of the merely intellectual. "If he did lose himself a little in the books, he was never abstract or theoretical, as is so often the case with that kind of people."

Inordinate desire of knowledge might be nothing more than dissipation of spirit and a mere illusion if it feeds one's vanity. What good is it to know all the theories in philosophy, if one neglects grace and charity? To forestall such dangers the superiors at Picpus had established the courses in philosophy in their own community at the mother house. His stay there left the stamp of the Congregation on Brother Damien's soul. Three letters written home at the time are loaded down with pious reflections that reveal the future missionary but one still very much attached to his parents.

His grandmother had just died and he felt it keenly. A fellow religious had also died suddenly. Impressed by these events, he preached in what might seem to us an old-fashioned style: "All that God does is best. She was ripe for heaven. There she will have the heart of a mother for us. Hope of finding her again with Eugenie encourages us, stimulates us to prepare ourselves for a happy death.

We who long only for the moment of the dissolution of our body are walking along the way of justice and holiness. We shall have the happiness of hearing: 'Come, ye blessed of my Father.'"

There is no doubt that Brother Damien had the community spirit. He affirmed that differences in taste, education, character, and nationality disappear in the face of the same aspirations, the same religious and intellectual efforts. "We get along with one another marvelously!" As a matter of fact, confined as the students were, their life at Picpus flowed along in the monotonous regularity of prayer, classes, recreation.

Monotonous yes, but never boring. How could the young seminarians be bored? They were fervent in church, studied hard, and at recreation or on walks had a good time with their gay bantering. Damien's description is typical of a Flemish peasant: "We're as busy as rabbits." The thought of the priesthood dominated everything. "In our community we live in perfect understanding with one another. We're all beaming with health. Everything is going along wonderfully." This is his constant refrain.

For those in the little hamlet of Ninde, Paris was the capital of the world and what went on in it interested them, especially now that they had a correspondent there. But Paris of 1860 scarcely figures in Damien's life. Wholly given over to the austere joys of his religious vocation now that he was a full-fledged member, he cared precious little about the sensation of the hour. What if Napoleon III's France was experiencing an intoxicating sensation of well-being, bathed in brilliant luxury and fine living? Haussmann could tear down the old sections of the city, lay out wide boulevards, construct sewers, build theaters, and touch up the whole face of gay Paris. Sarah Bernhardt could identify herself with the suffering Andromache, and Gounod could assist in Faust's triumph. Brother Damien wasn't interested in these historical crumbs. If behind the iron gates of the Tuileries he watched the Zouaves returning from Solferino, no one heard about it.

We know only that each Wednesday a group of seminarians went in all directions through the new elegant park of Vincennes. "I know every drive in the place," he wrote. "A thousand workmen are beautifying it." If we are wondering about the seduction the capital of the world exercised on him, we are in for a disappointment. "We didn't like it there. Had no peace. All you saw were gentlemen and ladies, riders and carriages. It distracted and bored us. Walks through the city don't appeal to me the way they used to. They give me the blues. When we're making up our minds where to go, I leave it up to those who are more curious than I." The sights of the Paris streets troubled and annoyed the young seminarian's pure soul.

Thus quickly settled in the austere cloisters of the Rue de Picpus, Brother Damien, liked for his willing spirit and good humor, was preparing himself for his future apostolate — especially from the time His Excellency Tepano Jaussen, SS.CC., Bishop of Tahiti, gave a conference on the mission field to a wide-eyed community.

A great missionary figure, Bishop Tepano Jaussen was then in his prime. For thirteen years he had been Vicar Apostolic of Tahiti, playing an important part in the rapid progress of the faith in those regions. He had returned temporarily to publish a Tahitian dictionary, thanks to subsidies from the Navy Department. During his prolonged stay at Picpus he had frequent talks with the students.

Polynesians sunk in paganism and needing to be brought to the God of truth . . . Queen Pomare and her broken-down mechanical piano . . . long rows of coconut trees on white coral islands . . . Brother Damien, more sensitive to these concrete details of religious expansion than to metaphysical abstractions, drank in all these tales with great enthusiasm. In this frame of mind, he ended one of his letters: "The Bishop is returning to his mission in Oceania soon, and I think he will take one of us with him. . . . Wouldn't you be happy if I were the one?"

While waiting for the hour when he would take upon himself the role of a fisher of men and go to convert infidels, he got the idea of trying his hand on someone who was not a pagan by any means. As we look back on it, it strikes us as the indiscretion of a dreamer. The first drag of his fisher's net fell on his father. Francis de Veuster was a good man, a good Christian. He went to Communion four times a year, which was considered devout in those days. But our young missionary was impatient to exercise his unused zeal. His father spent his days thinking about his grain . . . did he give enough thought to storing up merit in heaven?

Damien dared tell him:

It would be better to let up a little on material worries and think more of your salvation. This is a sacred duty I am fulfilling by giving you this advice. In order to work out your salvation more efficaciously, go to the Sacraments often, avoid the slightest fault, say your morning and evening prayers faithfully, don't do anything without first raising your heart to God and saying: "Lord, I am doing this for Your greater glory."

I urge you to meditate every day on the love of God, on death, the last judgment, eternity, the gravity of sin, or on some other great truth. You can be helped in this practice by reading some pious book such as the *Imitation of Christ* or the lives of the saints.

Forgive me for recommending to you things that may seem to you to be hard or impossible. But the experience I have had of God's mercy makes me believe that with His grace you will succeed.

We may believe that the program of perfection the son outlined left the father skeptical, but happy to learn at his own expense that Jef was really better cut out to touch men's hearts than to develop the grain business.

Subsequently, Mr. de Veuster enrolled — without being asked — in the Confraternity of the Scapular, as did the rest of the family. It happened at Father Pamphile's first Mass. All the family were gathered around the new priest at the banquet. At the end of the dinner, Brother Damien pulled a package of scapulars of Our Lady of Mt. Carmel out of his pocket and gave one to each member of the family. "This is the best remembrance you can take away from the celebration!"

Damien returned to Louvain at the end of September, 1861. The Superior of the seminary where he would spend his last two years in Europe was Father Wenceslas Vincke, who had accepted him two years before as a postulant. Father Vincke was a zealous priest who strongly encouraged studies and who had extended his influence outside the seminary by founding organizations to help the sick, orphans, and poor children.

Brother Damien buried himself in theology and was more impatient than ever to get going. You would think he suspected his days were numbered, for he got things done in a hurry and utilized every spare moment. His Superior says the future missionary studied his theology eagerly and successfully. At that time study was his main business; he even surprised everyone by taking several elective courses at the university. However, he was never swamped by his studies, but managed to keep his notes up to date. Still, there must have been a lot of good will in the statement made thirty years later that "his ability to go to the heart of a question and the encouragement his answers brought him from the professors made some surmise he was headed for a brilliant teaching career!"

This was certainly not his desire. "Rare as was his ability to work," Msgr. Van Veddingen states, "he did not study for the pleasure of studying nor to become a professor. He was studying to become an apostle."

Among his effects are two manuscripts containing notes on tracts in theology; on the True Religion, the Church, Tradition, Scripture, the Incarnation, the Blessed Mother. His name and address on the cover leave no doubt that they were his. These two large notebooks, which he may have gotten from a classmate, never left him. Although they were merely summaries of the tracts as they were explained at the time, later on they were a tremendous help in controversies with heretics.

From all we can learn of him we are convinced that his mind and imagination were borne more to practical action than to speculation. In the realm of ideas he was eminently a conformist. His late vocation forced him to be.

A few facts and documents reveal certain traits of his character. He wasn't one to lose his head easily, as sometimes happens to those who go to a university. Moreover, he was a realist with no illusions about his small stock of erudition. "When I'm in the classroom," he humbly admitted to his brother, "with so many capable young men around me, I really feel ashamed to be there."

The student knew how to practice mortification. Some of the students had to eat at the second table after the others had finished; sometimes they ran short of meat or the leftovers were rather scanty. Brother Damien never said a word about it. In fact, he used to give his portion to his neighbor who, having a big appetite, took it gladly while Damien stuck to soup and vegetables which were always plentiful. His generous acts won him a rebuke from Pamphile.

Father Vincke said his regularity was such that even the sharpest eye could not find fault with him. He also added that God put this beginner's soul through the most trying duties of the common life. He was like one of those sleds that glide rapidly through northern streets when the snow is heavy.

According to Father Vincke, who should know, Damien was one of the best-liked students. However, students can often get into heated discussions. But Damien was not one to put up with bitter and cutting remarks. When this happened one day, he shouted: "That's unworthy of a child of the Sacred Hearts!" and brusquely strode off. But almost before he'd said it, he was sorry. His lively nature played these tricks on him, even though he watched himself so he wouldn't offend anybody. "If there was any fault in this matter," the Superior added, "he was man enough to make up for it. With the help of God's grace, he constantly tried to suppress these outbursts of his character."

Naturally impulsive as he was, Damien suffered all his life from these explosions which came in spite of himself and over which he wept bitterly. Masters of the spiritual life say that God permits imperfections in His chosen ones to keep them humble, to leave them something to struggle with so their virtue will come out like gold from the fire.

Brother Damien kept his love for manual labor and could keep up with the hardest worker. If the community had anything to be done, he was there to help. In fact, when the chapel next to the seminary was being restored, he was around almost too much.

Rebuilt in the fourteenth century and dedicated to St. Anthony the Hermit, this chapel had been put to various uses in the course of the centuries. After the Revolution it was made into a store until Protestants bought it for a church in 1847. The Sacred Hearts Fathers were finally able to buy it and restore it to its original purpose. Bishop Jaussen reblessed the church probably in January, 1863.

Damien, who was present, had no idea that one day his remains would be interred there to be visited by admiring crowds.

He was not satisfied with being an interested bystander when there was work to be done. Once he surprised both fellow religious and laborers alike. They had decided a very tall chimney attached to the chapel was useless and simply taking up room, but they also agreed they were not the ones to wreck it. Brother Damien hunted up a long ladder, climbed to the top and calmly took the unwanted chimney apart brick by brick. The masons themselves, accustomed as they were to dizzy heights, shouted, "Brother Damien is a wonder!" As a matter of fact, he was.

He received minor orders at Malines, September 19, 1863.

3 *Westward Ho!*

IN 1863 the Sacred Hearts Fathers decided to send missionary reinforcements to the Hawaiian Islands where Bishop Louis Maigret, SS.CC., the Vicar Apostolic, badly in need of men, was loudly demanding them. They agreed that six Sacred Hearts priests and Brothers and ten Sisters would leave for Oceania by the end of October. Father Pamphile was one of them. Had it not been the moving stories about their foreign missionaries stationed in the South Seas for thirty years that made him leave the seminary at Malines to join the Sacred Hearts Fathers? Now, to his great joy, he himself was ordered to those missions!

But while man may propose, God disposes. An epidemic of typhus broke out at Louvain and while visiting the sick Father Pamphile himself caught the disease. Right at the beginning of October when the sailing date was approaching! Upon the doctor's advice, his orders were returned to the mother house.

Sadly the sick man watched his dream shatter. He told Damien what a disappointment this was. A sudden inspiration flashed in Damien's mind. If he could get permission to take Pamphile's place! Pamphile nodded.

Accustomed to quick action, even if it entailed a future

full of tremendous consequences, Brother Damien leaped up, grabbed pen and paper. He carefully saw to it that the letter did not pass through Father Vincke's hands, for he would have opposed the idea. Damien took advantage of his Rule and wrote straight to the Father General. If his request were accepted, his life was settled.

His letter has been lost but we can guess its contents — the empty place in the mission band and its lost reward . . . how much it might help in Pamphile's recovery to have this consolation . . . his own robust health and above all that interior compulsion, that obvious calling which was an evident sign of God's will . . . you just couldn't refuse to let him go. His appeal won. The General answered at once.

Even though Canon Law no longer allows such an exception, the younger brother's noble offer, considering the circumstances of time and persons, seemed to justify this one exception. The answer was yes.

Brother Damien was eating when the Superior threw the answer from Paris in front of him. "You're acting with foolish recklessness," he said looking at him sternly, "wanting to get out to the missions so fast!" Damien hurriedly read the letter. His face suddenly beamed with joy. He could go to the missions in Hawaii! Amid the cheers of his confreres, he rushed from the table, brandishing his orders and disappeared. He burst into Pamphile's room with the good news.

There wasn't much time — just enough for a farewell to his relatives and then a hurried trip to Paris for the retreat before leaving. Hastily, he went to Ninde for the final good-by. It was a heavy, unexpected blow to his parents. They would never be seeing their affectionate, good-natured son again. Leave-taking like this was brutal, and Damien with his warm heart did not feel it least. But he had accepted this one-way journey and found supernatural motives to build up their courage and bring them to submit to God's will, which would make their separation less frightful. When it was time to go, his eyes took in at a single glance all the memories of his childhood — and how much he loved his family! With a forced smile he walked out of Ninde forever.

He didn't have the heart to say good-by to his mother again, so they agreed to meet him the next day at the shrine of Our Lady of Montaigu. For years this shrine had had a special place in his devotion and he wanted to go there just once more.

Montaigu, near Diest, is one of the places in Flanders where crowds of pilgrims have come to pray to the Mother of God for centuries. At the present time, about a hundred thousand visit it each year. Formerly, our Lady's statue was venerated in the trunk of an oak. Since 1627 a large beautiful Renaissance church, crowned with a majestic dome and heavily ornamented with gold, has held the miraculous image. Around the statue you see giant candles casting their light over thousands of crutches and other ex-votos left by grateful pilgrims. Often as a young man, St. John Berchmans came from his native Diest to kneel there in prayer to our Lady. Each year the Sacred Hearts students made the pilgrimage. At that time there were no trains or streetcars, so about midnight the pilgrims started out on a walk that lasted until sunrise, when they reached the sanctuary to hear Mass and receive Holy Communion.

That night Damien walked alone. At daybreak he met his mother and sister-in-law, Marie. Our Lady of Montaigu looked down on a touching sight that morning. The two of them spent a few hours in prayer, in silence, in resignation. Nothing was said. Nobody did anything that would betray their feelings but you could hear the nervous rustling of the beads as their hands slipped along the rosary, and there was a mist of tears glasses didn't hide. She prayed for him; he prayed for her. The mother was asking the Queen of the Apostles to protect the son whom God was calling from her mother's care. The son entrusted his mother to the Consoler of the afflicted. And the Mother of God must have given these simple hearts a special smile of love, knowing that they were being crushed, as she had been, by the cruel demands of souls to be saved.

Marie, his sister-in-law, never forgot that day. Forty years later, it was vivid in every detail.

"When we finished our prayers, we had to hurry. We left the church. His mother and I went ahead, he lagged behind and kept looking back.

" 'Why so slow?' his mother asked.

" 'It's the last time I'll see this beloved shrine. Let me fill my eyes with it. I asked our Blessed Mother to let me work on the missions for twelve years.'

"I saw he had a handkerchief in his hand to wipe away his tears. Then we heard the wheels and horses. The coach for Louvain was coming. Seeing the cleric turn around, the driver thought he wanted to ride, so he stopped his horses.

" 'Well, then, let's say good-by,' his mother said.

"Damien embraced us, climbed up into the coach and the horses started off. He waved again and that was the last we saw of him.

"We felt bad, especially since he'd gone so quickly. Walking back we said the Rosary and felt better after a while. We couldn't think of anything to do but pray to our Blessed Mother for our missionary who'd just left us. But we had no idea of what would happen to him at Molokai."

At Paris, Brother Damien made the three-day retreat which the Father General himself preached to the missionaries.

Before sailing he wrote a long letter to Tremeloo, full of faith and confidence in God which the retreat had stirred up in him. At Picpus his soul was glowing white-hot and he poured it out. We cannot expect of him at this time the discretion and tact not to turn the red-hot iron in his family's wound. He seemed to have no idea whatsoever of the impression his words would make: "We are ready to embark on a sea that is often stormy and ready to swallow us." He added: "But it is Jesus Christ who preserves His missionaries from all dangers, who commands the winds to be still, the sea to be calm, wild beasts to flee, spiritual enemies, the demons, the world, and the flesh to leave us in peace. It is He who will make us enjoy unsuspected happiness in the midst of tribulations, sufferings, and contradictions."

Today we don't like to hear youngsters preaching sermons to their parents, as though they had the right to doubt their conduct. "Always lead a Christian life, keep your soul from the slightest fault. Walk the narrow path. This is what I ask of you as a last favor." And again:

> Be brave in doing God's will always and everywhere. Desire, I beg you, to accept that adorable will, manifested by the commandments of God and the Church, as also by the voice of the priest whom God has given you as the infallible rule of your life, of all your actions, and of all your words. This is the will described in the Gospel as the narrow but sweet path that leads to heaven.

Before leaving, Damien had his picture taken, posing like St. Francis Xavier with a large crucifix in his hand. He has a full face, very Flemish; the pose is too studied but it is one that he kept even in the prosaic reality of apostolic work. However, it reveals his candor and good will. With the picture, he sent along his well-known exhortation to Ninde. "Be careful to keep your soul free from the slightest voluntary fault. May heaven bless your old age! May the Blessed Mother grant you a holy death!" Decidedly, this is going a little too far.

Later, taught the hard lessons of life and faced with great sufferings, both his own and those of others, he will soften and find a lot more moderation, simplicity, naturalness, and kindness.

On October 29, 1863, a group of Sacred Hearts priests and religious poured into the East Station in Paris with a pile of trunks, suitcases, and boxes tied with string to catch the Paris-Cologne-Hamburg express. The party consisted of Father Chretien Willemsen, Brother Damien, two other students, Brothers Clement and Lievin, Brother Aymard with another missionary Brother, and the Sacred Hearts Sisters.

After twenty-nine hours of hard riding they entered Bremerhaven. They went down to the wharves of this old Hanseatic town which were swarming with freighters, flat barges of the Weser, and big three-masted ships. One ship was flying the red, white, and blue crescented flag of the Kingdom of Hawaii. It was the *R. M. Wood* waiting for the missionaries who would book passage on its eighth crossing.

Now air travel places Honolulu next door to Europe, but for Brother Damien it was a four and a half month trip. The long slow voyage made it possible for him to reflect on the life of the apostolate ahead of him and between seasicknesses to get his stomach used to the unvaried diet of corned beef and beans. The fare was set down as a round one thousand gold francs, which was reasonable enough. Comfort and meals suffer when compared to today's luxuries.

On board were Captain Geerken, his wife, cousin, and sixteen sailors, all German Protestants. From the beginning, the Captain invited the religious to eat at his table, and friendship sprang up between them and the crew. Of course, since this was the first time Brother Damien had come in contact with non-Catholics his fiery zeal had to go into action. He discussed the true religion with them in the hope of converting them. Vain hope. He began to learn by experience that people aren't changed merely by arguments out of the book.

For their own good, the religious decided to establish a regular schedule, so that all this time on board would not be wasted. A detailed horarium was outlined for Mass, prayer, study, manual labor, and recreation. Father Chretien was superior and all permissions were to be given by him, but he suffered from seasickness more than the rest. The rule ran into many a snag.

Their ship was to steer a course across the Atlantic to Cape Horn, fight its way through the Straits of Magellan, sail toward the equator and the eastern Pacific. We have parts of the journey described in Father Chretien's diary and Brother Damien's letters.

From the outset their stomachs experienced queer sensations; they felt miserable all over as seasickness hit them. In a joking mood Brother Damien said, "Little Fr. Chretien as Superior of our floating Community has paid his price. He kept losing everything he'd eaten and choked until it seemed his chest would burst. This lasted for over a month. Brother Aymard was the same way."

Father Chretien spoke pleasantly about Brother Damien and added: "But why speak only of him as though the rest did not have their merits." Less subject to seasickness than the rest, he quietly took up the duties left by the victims. As the need arose, he was sacristan, host-maker, ingenious discoverer of ways to keep the chalice from turning over, infirmarian, student with his theology courses to keep up. He was the Superior's right-hand man who said of him: "He's really been the man of the hour." Being in charge of clothing, Damien got the idea of turning over his wardrobe to the expert hands of the Sisters so they could complete it and patch up some of his confreres' clothes.

As a pinch-hitting infirmarian he was rather resourceful. Father Chretien fell into an alarming state of exhaustion. "Listen, Father," Brother Damien said, "your head is all stopped up. We've got to clear it out. You should take a little snuff. It'll clean out your head and you'll be able to see better." The patient obeyed, the remedy worked, and in a few days he was again saying his breviary.

For reasons such as these, Father Chretien's diary is studded with eulogies of Brother Damien. He constantly found chances to show his sociability and helpfulness. His strong personality was making more and more of an impression; the sailors were especially impressed by his strength when he worked with them . . . talking religion "which they didn't like too much." He asked permission for everything from the Superior, kept the rule, and studied theology furiously along with Brothers Clement and Lievin.

A Sister who had seen her Sisters off at Bremerhaven told Father Pamphile: "Your brother is another Aloysius Gonzaga. You couldn't hear Mass when he was serving without being struck by his devotion." He said the Divine Office although he didn't have to, since he was only in Minor Orders. Father Chretien hesitated to say Mass one day because of bad weather, but did so at Brother Damien's insistence. "That boy's zeal is contagious!" he remarked.

Once in a while they saw other ships in the distance and tried to pick out their nationality. One sailed by flying the French colors. "French! French!" the missionaries shouted at the top of their lungs. "Bretons! Bretons!" the answer came back.

On reaching the equator, the ship's crew began the traditional rites. However, the religious bought off the sailors to avoid being tossed into the water, and stood by as innocent spectators of the age-old tributes to King Neptune.

On New Year's day a brilliant sun found them some 22 degrees below the equator. There the crew caught several beautiful albatrosses which they stuffed, and also sharks "like that on Jef Van Rivieren's insignia," dolphins, and enormous porpoises, weighing up to three hundred pounds.

On January 19 they approached dangerous Cape Horn. As they neared it, they remembered the shipwreck of the *Marie-Joseph* which twenty years before had taken the lives of twenty-five Sacred Hearts missionaries — a bishop, seven priests, seven Brothers, and ten Sisters whom Bishop Rouchouze, SS.CC., was bringing out to the Hawaiian Islands. The group recited the Office of the Dead and two Rosaries for those whose places they were taking.

Everybody aboard was surprised to see how calm the Straits were. These so-called terrors were all imaginary! Two days of good weather and they would be in the Pacific, out of danger. But the next morning, a terrific storm blew up and drove them two hundred leagues to the south. For ten long days the ship was a plaything of a mad sea. A novena was begun, ending on the feast of the Purification. Our Lady of the Sea helped them, for the winds reversed and carried them in the opposite direction with the same violence — toward the Hawaiian Islands, but over 7000 miles still lay before them.

Another terrifying storm broke on February 5. During the night the churning, swelling sea lifted the little ship straight up into the air, but still kept them going in the right direction. Foreseeing what might happen, the Captain had hauled in his sails, otherwise the mast would have snapped. The storm was driving them along at a little over five knots an hour between heavy walls of waves that seemed as big as mountains. The waves would break on deck with an ear-splitting crash, the ship would list to the right and then to the left. All day long the rocking continued while the ship tossed like a fisherman's boat. One slight slip and a man would have been washed overboard.

After this nightmare, the *R. M. Wood* followed Magellan's course, driven northwest by the trade winds as he had been. They passed Juan Fernandez Island where Daniel Selkirk, known to us as Robinson Crusoe, had lived . . . Easter Island, then shrouded in a mystery stretching back to prehistoric times . . . Pitcairn where the descendants of the *Bounty* mutineers were living . . . then above the Marquesas they had beautiful sailing with serene skies and delightful evenings.

As though impatient, the ship crossed the equator in full sail. Soon the missionaries were gazing at the coasts of Panama, Costa Rica, Guatemala. Immense joy flooded the missionary band as they realized that soon their interminable journey would be over and they would be in the land of their dreams and desires. Forgotten were those agonizing hours of the storms. The diary reads: "Joy has been the keynote . . . how often we laughed heartily . . . I made the voyage joyfully . . . I have never laughed so much as at sea."

On March 17, "land ahead!" kept everybody awake and sent them up to the forward deck. A shapeless mass appeared in the distance, grew more definite, revealed its purple basalt cliffs ringed with coconut palms, and behind it all, the paradox of volcanoes capped with eternal snows. The Hawaiian Islands.

The ship sailed on past the islands of Maui and Molokai, and on March 19, at nine o'clock in the evening, they rounded Diamond Head to see Honolulu in the night.

4   The Paradise of the Pacific

"IT WOULD be impossible for me," Brother Damien wrote home, "to tell you of the immense joy a missionary has, after five months traveling, to see his new country that he must water with his sweat to gain poor souls for God."

The Hawaiian archipelago is a group of islands, reefs, and shoals strung out from southeast to northwest for 1600 miles between 154° 40' and 170° 75' W. longitude and 18° 54' to 28° 15' N. latitude. Hawaii is about 4000 miles from Japan. The archipelago comprises some twelve islands, the principal ones being Oahu, Maui, Kauai, Lanai, Molokai, and Hawaii. This last one, by far the largest of the islands, gives its name to the whole group. Honolulu, the capital, is on Oahu, not far from Pearl Harbor.

Geologically speaking, the islands are young, having arisen during the middle tertiary period. The islands are built up over a fissure 1600 miles long, in the ocean floor. They are really the tops of mountain peaks sticking up out of the ocean.

During the great Ice Age, the islands "rose up out of the sea." In reality, the ocean waters subsided and exposed larger areas of the mountaintops. During that period, Molokai, Lanai, and Maui were all one island. The Ice

Age was followed by a "submergence" period, when the melting icecaps filled the ocean with water and the sea rose as much as 2500 feet around the island peaks.

Next, a period of complex "submergences" and "emergences" occurred, during which there was little time for reefs to build. Geologists say that the Hawaiian Islands are now in one of the "submergence" periods with the islands covered about 1200 feet.

The islands are of basaltic lava, the outcropping of ancient volcanoes that were rocky and barren. But centuries of deposits have covered the hillsides and valleys with a layer of extremely fertile soil; giant palms, eucalypti, rose laurels, hibiscus, coconuts, bananas, orange trees, ferns, and vines grow luxuriantly. The climate is dry on the southwest coast, while on the northwest side rains are frequent. The temperature is even, averaging about 75 degrees the year around. The average daily range is about 9 degrees; constant trade winds from the northeast moderate the heat. Americans have well named it the "Paradise of the Pacific."

In 1545, a Spaniard, Mendana, first sighted the islands, but nothing was done until 1778 when the Pacific explorer Captain Cook landed at Maui and moved on to Hawaii. In honor of the Earl of Sandwich, who was the first lord of the British admiralty and his sponsor, he named the chain of islands the "Sandwich Islands." Since the natives had been waiting for the return of a chief — the god Lono — who had disappeared mysteriously, they received the strangers as gods. Captain Cook humorously accepted the honor, but when the English sailors had enough of this comedy, they made fun of the chiefs and priests, levied heavy taxes, and above all mistreated the Hawaiian women. Cook himself tore down a temple for firewood and took the idols on board ship. Then things got out of hand and the Captain and his crew were massacred.

This incident gave the natives a reputation in Europe of being savages. No one seemed to remember that the natives hadn't started the trouble, but for years sailors and traders avoided the islands.

The South Sea Islanders are a strong, handsome race with soft brilliant eyes that light up their bronze-colored features. If his history sometimes reveals him as brave, war-like, and even cruel, the Hawaiian was ordinarily calm and peaceful, timid, childlike, and inclined to be indolent by nature. He went along through life in what seemed a dreamland where a rich soil yielded a livelihood almost without his having to turn a hand. His hut was built against a tree, the branches serving as beams, and vines holding the entire construction together without a nail being used. His bed was a grass mat on the ground. Here and there bone fishhooks, spears, a bow and arrows, a club were thrown in disorder against the grass walls; his utensils were a calabash or gourd and some coconut shells. Outside, a palm leaf lean-to protected the hollow stones in which he pounded out the taro roots; beside it was his canoe.

From taro roots he made a sort of paste called *poi* which was his principal food. To it he added roast pig cooked over hot stones, sweet potatoes, and numerous kinds of tropical fish and fruit. He ate on the ground without the encumbrance of knives and forks. He drank water or *awa*, a homemade liquor of which he was passionately fond. After dinner, the men smoked and told endless stories. On feast days — and they were plentiful — and even on workdays, the men and women, adorned with garlands of flowers around their necks, arms, and legs, sang love songs to the accompaniment of a guitar and danced until they were out of breath — all this with a remarkable grace and languor. Pleasure being their main occupation, naturally their morals were loose and flabby.

In contrast with other Polynesians, the Hawaiians were never cannibals. Their songs, traditions, and other remnants of bygone days show that even in their savagery they appreciated, though in a confused way, the ideas of beauty, grandeur, and goodness; they even had a gentleness that is astonishing. The chief had a deep sense of honor, respect for the sworn pledge, and a loyalty to friends even unto death. Places of refuge were set aside for criminals fleeing from the anger of a chieftain. At times human sacrifices were offered to placate the gods, the victims always being either prisoners of war or those condemned to death.

Woman was not man's equal. She could not eat with him or go out with him in his canoe. But she was never sacrificed. Nobility was traced through her; illogical though it was, if she were noble she could ascend the throne and exercise sovereignty.

The people were divided into three strata: the chiefs who ruled, sorcerers who were priests and medicine men, and the little people whose one right was to obey. The whole ancient history of Hawaii is composed of tales and songs about friendships and wars among the chiefs. The strong man ruled — administering justice, imposing taxes in kind and in feathers with which he adorned his robes, and punishing lawbreakers.

The law was composed of taboos with detailed prescriptions enforced under pain of death or mutilation. Women, for instance, could not eat bananas, coconuts, pork, or poultry; these foods were dishes for gods and men.

Mrs. Thurston, the wife of an American missionary, met a little girl with one eye missing. "Why do you have only one eye?" she asked.

"Because I ate a banana," was the answer. It was a crime to sneeze at a religious ceremony.

Witch doctors were the sole interpreters of taboos. They had a monopoly on education — astrology, the secrets of the gods, and remedies for body and soul. Their knowledge, functions, and profits were family possessions. Wielding this amount of power, they were able to impose on the poor credulous people.

The natives had a confused idea of a God who created the world, a first man, and rewarder of the good and bad; however they also believed especially in evil gods who people the earth, sea, and sky. All the frightful forces of nature were the work of these supernatural beings who had to be placated. Any evil was traced back to them. The most terrible gods were *Pele* and *Maui* who as late as 1820 were still demanding human sacrifices. The goddess *Pele* was in charge of volcanoes.

The little we know of Hawaiian civil and religious history is connected with five kings, of whom the last three were Father Damien's contemporaries.

After Captain Cook had been killed with a spear, the white man's civilization and teaching stirred up Kamehameha, a local chieftain, to make an effort at dominating the entire archipelago. This brainy Polynesian, with an English navigator named Vancouver as his adviser, carried on his ventures in the era of Rivoli and Wagram. Vancouver brought him sheep and cattle, taught him the principles of foreign politics and how to build ships. At his death, Kamehameha designated his son Liholiho as his successor, stipulating that the most intelligent of his favorites should share the royal power with the boy.

This was a necessary precaution for the new monarch who lacked his father's know-how. The islanders were learning the classical history of the South Seas. Adventurers and South Sea whalers passed on to the natives their taste for brandy, firearms, cards, European clothes and ways, and a series of catastrophic diseases against which they were totally unprepared and which threatened to wipe them out of existence in a hurry.

Their Royal Majesties of Hawaii pushed the idea of grandeur to its limits. King Kalakaua went on a world tour in 1881 that looked like a vaudeville show. Queen Liliuokalani, who succeeded him and who, as shall be seen, was not entirely lacking in ability, wanted to make the foreign consuls address her on their hands and knees with their faces turned at right angles! Such carryings-on as these led to the republic of Sanford Dole, the pineapple king, and paved the way for U. S. annexation in 1898. Hawaii remained an Organized Territory of the U.S. until 1959. Today it is the fiftieth state of the Union.

Under King Liholiho taboo was abolished, the people demolished the temples, and the witch doctors took to the mountains, leaving the field wide open for a new religion. In 1820 Congregational and Presbyterian missionaries would arrive followed by Catholics.

The Protestant groups entrenched themselves solidly, though their rigorism had little in common with the free and easygoing ways of the natives. However, their religion became the state religion, and they used this advantage to the fullest extent.

In 1825 Pope Leo XII entrusted missionary efforts in the Hawaiian Islands to the Sacred Hearts Fathers. Six of them landed at Honolulu on July 7, 1827. Well received by the authorities, they were rapidly making converts; for besides being models of virtue, the missionaries had a religion to offer that fitted in more with the people's frame of mind and local customs. However, King Kamehameha, dominated by some American Protestants, persecuted Catholics and expelled the missionaries. The French frigate *L'Artemise* demanded and received reparations for injuries inflicted on the French priests. The King finally proclaimed freedom of religion.

The Sacred Hearts Fathers could then be legally established in the country. In 1840 Catholics numbered 2000. Five years later, the Pope elevated the islands to a Vicariate Apostolic and placed Bishop Maigret in charge. Catholics increased to 13,000. The number tripled under Kamehameha IV (1855-1863) who thought highly of the Bishop and tried to bring the Sacred Hearts Sisters there to teach the young ladies. There were forty missionaries in the field when Brother Damien arrived.

5   *Puna*

THE arrival of the missionaries and the ten Sisters all dressed in white impressed the crowd waiting to see them. While they were singing the *Te Deum* in the cathedral, Brother Damien could think of nothing else but when he would get out on the missions and how he must keep on preparing himself with all the strength of his will.

Like all newcomers to a strange land, he was constantly being astonished at the things he saw. Three days after they landed, he was writing home about "three big fish, so good that I've never tasted anything like them in all my life," about Father Hermann [later Bishop Hermann Koeckemann], and a large number of natives "who sang so well I've never heard anything like it." He still remembered the beautiful churches at Malines, Brussels, Paris, and he wrote: "Great was my astonishment when I saw the beautiful church here in the Islands." And handshakes — "I believe I must have shaken more than a thousand hands!" What was happening to him rarely happened to anyone. It was the price of his impressionable youth. Compared to the veterans, he had a lot to learn.

Brother Damien received subdiaconate on Holy Saturday, March 26, 1864. He was sent at once to the Sacred

Hearts Fathers College of Ahumanu, Oahu, to prepare for ordination to the priesthood in two months. There, without having to exaggerate, he could admire the enchanting sight of towering cliffs and deep-cut gorges, for out of the entire 216 acres of the college land 126 were inaccessible bluffs. Above all, he could finish up his truncated studies. He was doing them in a hurry, for he had been doing in four years what others would take ten to do. He learned quickly, but more than this, it was only too clear that the Bishop was impatient to use the recruits who should have been all prepared for the ministry before they left Europe.

Brother Damien was ordained deacon probably on the feast of The Patronage of St. Joseph, his patron, April 17. On May 21, along with Brothers Clement and Lievin, he was ordained to the priesthood in Honolulu. "Christians came from all over the Islands," he wrote, "to see their young spiritual Fathers who must protect them from ravening wolves." He continued in this same tone that seems a little redundant to us but which was the style of the times: "In spite of the hardness of my heart, it seemed to me that it would melt like wax the first time I distributed the Bread of Life."

He continued:

Here I am, dear parents, a missionary in a corrupt, heretical, idolatrous land. How great are my obligations! How immense my apostolic zeal should be! What purity of conduct, what correctness in judgment, what prudence must I have from now on! Alas! how can I, who have afflicted you so many times in the past by my whims, keep myself up to high level of my duties! Do not forget, I beg you, the poor priest who is now going out day and night on the volcanoes of the Hawaiian Islands in search of stray sheep. Pray for me day and night, get others to pray for me, for if God withdraws His grace from me, I will be plunged into that same mud of vice from which I am trying to draw others.

In this letter to Ninde, the first one he wrote after his ordination, he had a good idea of just what it meant to be a priest: an exalted honor, a terrible responsibility.

But, and we purposely stress this, it is regrettable that he was deprived of the chance of following the regular and complete course of studies and formation that Canon Law now requires. Father Damien did not have enough time to be subject to the spiritual training of experienced masters and seasoned fellow religious. Four years at Louvain and Paris were far too few. And hardly had the oil of ordination dried when he was thrown out into the mission field. Left alone with the natives, he had to be his own master. Alone, or practically alone, with only short and chance contacts with other missionaries, it was up to him to perfect himself, to better himself. And he was a Fleming from Tremeloo, explosive, bursting with life, preferring dangers, volcanic as the ground he rode his horse over. Such a man doesn't change by a flick of the wrist. We will have to remember this when we judge his sudden outbursts and the roughness of his impetuous nature. By himself how could he calm down, become mild, smooth off the rough edges? Years later he will come face to face with the leprosy victims whose terrible sufferings will touch his heart and make his soul gentle. But would even they be able to change him?

Bishop Maigret was at first annoyed at getting a replacement so young and only half formed, nor did he have time to discover the vigor, piety, zeal, and impetuosity of Father Damien. He assigned him and Father Clement to districts on the large island of Hawaii. Damien was beginning his missionary life. The Bishop himself decided to take the young priests to their mission and install them.

One June evening the three of them boarded a ship at Honolulu. Next morning the steamer stopped at Maui for a while, giving them an opportunity to go ashore and say Mass. By chance, three Sacred Hearts missionaries of the island were there: Fathers Aubert, Gregory, and Leonor. Father Damien would have liked to stay with them for a few days but as Mass was ending the steamer's whistle blew and they had to rush back on board.

From the bottom of his heart, Father Damien poured out his complaint to God. If only he could have stayed just a few days to profit from the experience and advice of these veterans. "A young missionary could know all the theology books by heart," he said, "but many times still wouldn't know how to act with new Christians recently emerged from barbarism."

His prayer was heard. They were scarcely out of the bay when an accident forced them ashore. A fire broke out and before it was discovered the hull and deck were blazing. The ship couldn't continue its voyage, so the missionaries would have to wait for the next boat.

Days passed. Bishop Maigret was in a hurry to get back to Honolulu to bless a chapel. Father Damien wasted no time; he started studying Hawaiian under Father Aubert. He was burning to get out and preach to some Christians about ten or fifteen miles away. Feeling that another boat might come by in the meantime, the Bishop hesitated but finally gave in. When Father Damien returned, the Bishop and Father Clement were gone. Undisturbed, he toured the island of Maui several times under a broiling June sun.

We suspect that Father Damien — like every beginner in the art of homiletic oratory and lacking adequate preparation — ran into snags and abrupt stops. He particularly got himself into trouble with a language he still knew very imperfectly. The goodnatured Hawaiians were highly amused when, as words failed him, he smiled a little, pulled out his handkerchief, and solemnly blew his nose.

He caught the first boat he could in hope of rejoining his

companions at the newly blessed chapel, but the Bishop hadn't waited for him. With a fellow missionary as his guide at first and then with divine Providence, Father Damien tramped up and down a couple hundred miles of mountains and valleys on foot and horseback in pursuit of his Bishop who was continuing his visitation. On July 24, he finally caught up with him and Fathers Charles and Celestin who had missions next to his. Four days later, after a last-minute briefing from his Bishop, he entered the district of Puna, his destination. Next day, Father Charles Pouzot, SS.CC., a veteran missionary, wrote to Father Modeste, SS.CC., the Provincial Superior of the Sacred Hearts Fathers in Honolulu: "Fr. Damien will stay at Puna when his house is finished. Looks like he's going to be an instrument of much good."

The island of Hawaii — "Big Island" — where Father Damien was to spend a third of his twenty-five years on the missions, has six districts: Kona, Hilo, Kau, Kohala, Hamakua, and Puna. The total area of the whole archipelago is 6435 miles, so Hawaii with 4030 miles takes up about two thirds of the entire area. Three towering mountains dominate its central massif: Mauna Kea (13,784 feet), Mauna Loa (13,679 feet), and Haulalai (8251 feet). In June, 1950, Mauna Loa, which is a volcano, again became active.

Mountains alternate with fertile valleys and virgin forests where all kinds of trees and vines grow luxuriantly. Long bands of cold black lava, sometimes miles wide, run from the craters into the sea. The island is par excellence the land of volcanoes; nowhere in the world can you find so many or such violent ones. Kilauea, the most extraordinary one, is right on the border of the district of Puna. It has no less than 1000 craters, is about ten miles in circumference, with walls some 600 feet high, and encloses Halemaumau, which is the pit of the Kilauea volcano.

Halemaumau is 750 feet deep and 3000 feet wide. The ancient Hawaiians thought this was the residence of Pele, the goddess of eternal fire.

Halemaumau unceasingly changes its shape. The hardened lava surrounding it varies in width and depth. One writer described it thus:

At present it is a lake of boiling, booming, incandescent lava with long tongues of fire crashing against the sides. The place seethes with an indescribable life. The heat and reverberations of this hellish furnace drive you away, yet you are fascinated and turn back to watch the flames shoot up to be lost in the molten mass pouring out from the depths of the earth. This marvel gets on your nerves, you are frightened, get dizzy watching this hell boil over, and yet you stay there and gaze. Some of the lava is so hot and fluid that it forms long strings which float in the air like gold filament. These are Pele's hair, the Hawaiians explained.

Countless writers have given us glowing accounts of the Hawaiian scenery, heaping one brilliant phrase on another to portray their wonder. Technicolor films have captured the beauty of these most fantastic of the Polynesian islands. Father Damien's pen scratches along prosaically. His lack of aesthetic training and complete absence of humanistic culture left him with his down-to-earth and unpolished nature. He never found any occasion to wax enthusiastic over such spectacles of nature or to sing of the glory and goodness of God as the Poverello of Assisi did. He was not a poet.

This was his report to his superior at Louvain:

I am stationed in a district near a large volcano, which our natives regard as a god and still worship. There is nothing to see here except the constant activity

of a fire with such immense heat that it melts everything, even the highest mountains. Also when it is active
our poor islanders are terribly afraid and hurry to offer
sacrifice to please the angry god. I myself witnessed this
idolatry one day when I went down into the interior of
the volcano.

He completed his report to the Father General: "I have
often seen this great volcano. One poor Hawaiian was just
on his way to offer sacrifice to the goddess. I took the
opportunity to give him a short sermon on hell."

To put his young and zealous missionary on guard
against some illusions, Bishop Maigret reminded him of
our Lord's words about those who reaped where they had
not sown and others who sowed with no hope of reaping.
"Make up your mind that the mission is beginning in
your district."

In reality, the situation at Puna was pitiful when Father
Damien went to work. The vast territory — it took three
days to get over it — had 350 Catholics scattered among
pagans and Protestants. They had no church and no
Catholic schools. For seven years no priest had lived
among them. This was what their faith was up against.
As for morals, they had fallen back into being just like the
rest of the Hawaiians. Then too there was intense competition from the Protestant missionaries.

The young apostle set to work joyfully. Overflowing
with activity, he found reasons for hope in his inveterate
optimism and brought in extenuating circumstances:
"With energy and good conduct, these people should be
excellent."

He said of his islanders in this secluded place:

They don't think about tomorrow. If they have taro to
eat that's all they ask. Clothes mean little to them.
Ordinarily the men wear a shirt and a pair of pants,

the women have dresses that hang straight down with
no waist line. Practically everybody goes barefoot and
bareheaded. They have no worries about robbers; everything is in common. If someone doesn't have anything
to eat, he goes over and eats with the neighbors. The
houses are straw huts; a mat covers the floor and on it
the whole family eats, sleeps, and works.

Gliding over their indolence, he gladly enumerated their
good points; their kindness, affability, their great goodness.
They had neither desire for wealth nor hankering after
luxury. They would even go without necessities to enter-
tain guests. Even the Protestants gave him a hearty welcome and treated him with respect.

In August, 1864, he slipped in a word about Hawaiian
politics. "The false ministers who ran the government have
been humiliated. The King and the whole government has
turned against them. This is exactly what we need." Kamehameha V was beginning his nine-year reign and was
modernizing the country. To help him in his work, he had
called in a famous Frenchman, M. Varigny, to be his prime
minister and factotum. Here and there in his letters, Father
Damien mentions that at Puna they had confidence in the
government, as, for example, in questions about land.

That no one thought of bothering Father Damien is
understandable. The young priest had everything to win
their sympathy. Young and wide awake, he had a handsome, smiling face, the strength of a bull, winning manners,
and a sweet, sonorous voice that seemed tailor-made for
Hawaiian with all its vowels. He was lively, good-humored,
forgetful of self, extremely devoted to his people. You
couldn't help being drawn to him.

One of the missionaries, Father Nicaise Ruault, SS.CC.,
who was an eyewitness of what he was doing, wrote to the
Provincial: "The Christians are completely enchanted with

him and he loves them." Damien himself wrote: "Our poor islanders are very happy when they see Kamiano [Damien] coming. And I, for my part, love them very much. I would gladly give my life for them as our Savior did. I don't spare myself when it's a question of going twelve or fifteen miles to visit the sick."

Making the rounds in his huge parish, preaching, giving instructions, baptizing, hearing confessions, winning converts, and administering the last Sacraments — this was his work. A neighboring missionary said of him: "His zeal won't let him stay a day in one place." On foot or horseback he was constantly attending to his people. "I'm acclimated to the place. I enjoy perfect health. Ordinarily I ride a horse and make all my trips without getting too tired."

Yet, he had to start from scratch in his district. The old chapels were falling apart or had caved in. At first, he said Mass in native huts. As soon as his superiors sent him the necessary funds, he began to build a series of chapels. All his life he was a builder and architect. In October, 1864, he was asking the Provincial for lay Brothers who were carpenters, and spoke to him about approaching the King in regard to long-term buying and selling of lands "without which authorization, the local Protestants will oppose it." His practical experience gained on the farm back home was becoming more and more helpful as the years went by. At Puna he put up four, maybe six, buildings that were modest but enough for his neophytes.

Considering himself the spiritual father of a family, he asked Father Modeste, his Provincial, for the spiritual helps his children needed:

Parents' first duty is to provide for their children. I have the obligation of giving my children, newly born of water and the Holy Spirit, the things that are neces-

sary for spiritual life. I humbly beg you to send me as
soon as possible Catholic textbooks, a large amount of
catechisms, Mysteries of the Rosary, and all other useful
books. The people of Puna are very poor, I will have to
give these things away free. I'll make up for it by living
at their expense. I seldom have to open my purse to buy
food . . . I especially want the Catholic textbooks since
I have arranged with a school teacher to put them in
the hands of Catholic children who are attending Protestant schools. They will use these books for readers and
thus will counteract the influence of the heretical schools
which they have to attend. Besides, they will learn their
prayers and catechism.

Although he was only a novice missionary, Father
Damien was soon reaping the fruits of his labor. Father
Charles wrote of his efforts: "He went around Puna once
and the first drag of his net brought in thirty fish — big
and little ones. That's the best proof the people have accepted him." Damien himself, however, attributed his
success to God and the prayers of others. "I consider myself an instrument in God's hands. How many times in the
past few months have I been providentially led out of my
way to little huts where I brought a new life to old folks
and prepared the dying for eternity. . . . In spite of privations and misery, God often gives me consolations I never
expected."

Along with his Hawaiians, he begged Father Modeste
for chapels, bells, priests — above all, for chapels. The
Provincial was already making the objection which he will
make repeatedly to him — that he should complain more
about the shortage of souls that have been converted than
about his shortage of chapels. "First of all, souls should be
won over and converted into spiritual temples. Then the
building and decorating of material temples will follow of
itself."

On this point Father Damien humbly observed that "hearts would be converted much faster here at Puna, if God would first grant the conversion of their pastor's heart." Evidently, far from letting up, the young missionary had his eye on progressing in the spiritual life, and when he wrote to his friends he begged for prayers that he might receive the graces he needed but felt unworthy of:

> If Providence had sent a Curé of Ars here, all the stray sheep would have returned to the fold in a hurry. . . . Pray that Fr. Damien will give himself completely to God and devote himself to His service to his last breath. To have begun is nothing, the hard thing is to persevere. This is the work of God's grace. That grace will never fail me, I am sure of that, provided I do not resist it. Pray for me. I will do all that depends on me. . . . Pray that I don't give in to temptations and that my words will be penetrated with the unction of the Holy Spirit.

Happy though he was at his first post, he stayed there only eight months. The real reason he had to leave was Father Clement's poor health. The later was in charge of two districts on Hawaii, Kohala, and Hamakua. In July, Father Stanislas Lebret, SS.CC., the ecclesiastical superior, wrote to Father Modeste:

> I'm very much afraid Fr. Clement's health isn't going to hold up and that soon he will be unable to work. He seems to us unable to endure the long hard work. It's much harder to take care of Kohala and Hamakua than Puna. It certainly would be good if a strong man like Fr. Damien were there. Pardon me if I am bold enough to make these observations which are outside my field.

The sprawling territory for which Father Clement was responsible took in about a third of the island. A moun-

tainous country, broken terrain, full of rocks, gorges and
precipices, thick thorn bushes, with no roads and often no
paths, it called for a robust man, a man of iron, who was
an excellent rider and who was ready for anything. Father
Clement's delicate constitution couldn't take the climate
and hard traveling and work. At the beginning of 1865
he said he thought his confrere was better cut out for this
double mission than he was. He proposed, if it was all
right with the Bishop — to exchange mission fields. "With
all my heart," Father Damien wrote, "I agreed and we
wrote the Bishop." The reasons were good so the Bishop
also agreed.

When he told the Father General of the change, the
priest of Puna confessed to him that this separation from
his Christians had been harder than leaving home; he had
already taken them so much to his heart.

6   *Kohala and Hamakua*

HIS new mission district — or better, districts — of Kohala and Hamakua were about two thousand square miles in extent and contained some three thousand souls. It took six weeks to get over it all.

Father Damien found out that everywhere in the field of souls, thorns and weeds were sticking their heads up above the good grain. The few Catholic families were scattered among the many non-Catholics and idolaters of the district. Fifteen chapels thatched with pala leaves had fallen down. Meetings were held in the natives' huts. However, a wooden church was still standing with its three altars, a bell tower and a bell; its three chandeliers were decorated with artificial flowers, and there was a five-room pala house for the priest. "Luxurious," he called it.

The job ahead of him was no small one, but his zeal thrived on opposition and his health was good. Father Damien would give eight years of his life to this mission.

He devoted all the strength he had to souls, leaving the rest to God. "As for the good that results from my external occupations for the salvation of souls, it's up to God, the Master of the Vineyard, to give the increase. The missionary is only a worker who plants and waters. Sometimes something comes up, sometimes it doesn't. But all I know is if you don't plant, nothing comes up."

His apostolate was inspired with that same love his Master had for men when He preached in Palestine. "I love my Hawaiians very much and I'm doing all I can for them. And they in turn love me as children love their father and mother. I hope this mutual affection will bring about their conversion. If they love their priest, they will easily love our Lord, since the priest is His minister."

He tried to be very close to his people to instruct them, to combat errors, to strengthen their wills which wavered so easily, and to buck up the weak and soft souls. As he was always on the go, he had plenty of opportunities to exercise his zeal and devotion. A European journalist received the following letter from one of his confreres:

I imagine you would like to hear conversion stories that are striking, miraculous, and numberless; however, I can't supply you with them. I'm only a professor of A B C's at the College of Ahuimanu and not a St. Francis Xavier. If you want a correspondent of that type, you will have to get in touch with Fr. Damien. When an Hawaiian asked him where he lived, he pointed to his saddle and answered: "There's my home."

Under the tropical sun he rode unceasingly, spurring his horse over broken ground where there were no trails at all. Often he had to climb mountains that went almost straight up; at times they were too steep for his horse. Then he would leave the horse, crawl up and over the obstacle and keep on going. Cost him what it would, he went miles and miles with one idea in mind — to do good, even if it were to only one soul.

His people in the Kohala district were perhaps the hardest to get to in the whole archipelago. The paths were so dangerous that no one dared run the risk of riding a mule. Figure it out for yourself; over a space of some ten or twelve miles there were ten deep ravines with rocky sides to climb. Horse and rider never knew what would happen next. A couple of miles from Damien's church was an elevation of 2000 feet. He could make it to the top in forty-five minutes, which to his delight considerably bettered the record of a Protestant missionary but he admitted he was exhausted when he reached the top.

Others of his parishioners were as hard to reach — he could do so only by canoe. In a letter of October 23, 1865, he describes a near-tragedy:

October 23, 1865

I have in my district a Christian settlement which is reached with great difficulty. No beaten road leads to it by land, and the sea is ordinarily very rough near the place. I was told that Father Eustace visited it only twice a year. As I love the Christians of the place very much, I wished to spend the first Sunday of October in their midst. On Saturday the sea was rather calm. Going down early in the morning to the coast I took a little boat, which was nothing more than a simple tree hollowed out. Before entering I recited a good act of contrition. We left the so-called port, and we were rowing at a rapid speed when all of a sudden one of the boatmen cried out: "We perish." Indeed, our canoe, which was about five feet broad, capsized, and we were all three soon swimming in the sea. Fortunately for me I had learned swimming when a boy. As neither of the boatmen knew any better than myself how to right the boat without letting in the water, we were obliged to reach the shore by swimming with one hand and propelling the boat, all filled with water, with the other. I lost none of my luggage, for I had, before starting, properly fastened everything to the boat. Only my fine little breviary, which I liked very much, because it was so complete and at the same time very light to carry about, was soaked all through with sea-water, so that I can no longer use it in my travels.

I had enough of it for the day, and deferred my intended visit till the following week, and then went by the mountains. After a four days' journey made now on horseback, now on foot, and after crossing an arm of the sea, I arrived at last at the place which I had so much longed to visit. God repaid me with many consolations in the midst of these Christians, who live there almost as recluses separated from the rest of mankind. With the exception of two or three, all had been baptized. I arrived just in time to administer baptism to a newly-born babe, who immediately afterward went off to heaven.

Going from one place to another didn't bother him too much, even if it meant being on the road six weeks at a time, for wherever he was, he was at home. He had no fear of robbers since he had no money. He stopped at the first hut he came to and received everything he wanted at no charge. Nor did fodder for his two horses and two mules cost him anything; he staked them out at night and let them graze.

Inevitably accidents happened on the road. One evening at the top of a mountain, his mule ran away with him, carried him about ten miles from home, and finally halted in the middle of a herd of wild cattle. He sat there in the darkness, wet and hungry. Luckily a dog barked in the distance. He made his way toward the sound and came to a Hawaiian hut where he was welcome. Such happenings were quickly forgotten, once the apostolic roughrider reached his destination. The hundred or so Christians he was visiting that day were about a four hours' ride from his house. They had a Catholic school taught by a government-paid teacher. Damien was to say Mass in the school-

house, which was a straw hut with a door about four feet
high through which the wind blew constantly. The candles
kept going out during Mass. When he arrived, he fixed up
the altar by driving four poles into the ground and putting
a cloth on top. A cloth covered it all, and he was ready
to begin Mass. All morning the faithful had been coming
to confession. At nine o'clock they were called to Mass by
the sound of a horn made from a large shell. Everybody
recited the Mass prayers aloud and by heart. The sermon
was on the Gospel and he tried to show them Christ's
great love for each of them. A number of the natives went
to Holy Communion. After services, they went to the hut
where he had spent the night and waited around to talk.
His host had prepared fish and bread. When dinner was
over, the horn blew again and all returned to church for
Rosary, catechism, and evening prayers. They then came
up to shake the missionary's hand and went home happy.

In other places, where there was no church or school,
the people gathered in some native's hut, at that one, for
example, where over a hundred sugar-cane workers on the
plantations came each Sunday to hear Mass. Most of them
were Christians. At several points on the island the faithful
who were unable to attend Mass would gather around a
prayer leader and join themselves in spirit with those who
were able to hear Mass.

Father Damien keenly felt the shortage of chapels; the
three or four he had built were not nearly enough. He
found out that his people were more recollected, happier,
prouder of their faith in their chapels. Besides, nothing
attracted the Hawaiians to the faith as much as the beautiful and colorful ceremonies in a church where their souls
sensed God's presence. Even non-Catholics and infidels
ended up by envying a religion that appealed so much to
their hearts. So the missionary continued the work he had
started at Puna — the construction of chapels wherever they

were needed. But where was he to find the resources, plans, help?

In August, 1865, Father Modeste wrote on this subject to the Father General:

> Fr. Damien is a *vir desideriorum* [a man of desires]. His visit was so short that we hardly had time to contemplate his noble face, radiant with health. Today in the letter I wrote to him I told him that we have to do good moderately, for it is easy to think up projects for doing good, but it is not so easy to put them into execution, especially when you have to untie purse strings.

We are touching on the first judgment of authority about the young (25-year-old) missionary. It seems they would always say of him that he lacked consideration and balance. Impatience ate him up. This Flemish "demon" wanted to put his plans through — willingly or by force. To assure the perseverance of his Christians and to bring others in, he needed chapels. Conclusion — get things moving to get more chapels. In December, 1865, Father Modeste again remarked to the Father General:

> Fathers Damien and Clement are asking for chapels and would certainly like to have the material helps necessary for their spiritual temples, but they have got to have patience. Chapels don't grow like mushrooms.

Little by little — too slowly to suit Father Damien — the money came in. Father Modeste, Bishop Maigret, and the Mother Superior of the Sacred Hearts Sisters in Honolulu sent it to him. With it the missionary builder bought wood of the tamanu, mango, and breadfruit trees which were indispensable for his projects. Around the first of the year, he himself wrote to the Queen to ask for a grant of land on which to build a church in the district of Hamakua. She gave him 600 acres. He could now go ahead.

When the chapel was completed, he described it in detail, obviously proud of his work:

October 23, 1865

Allow me to take you to another part of my district; it is about ninety miles from here. There had never been a chapel in the place. From my very first visit several catechumens had received baptism. I asked them, in return for the great favor Almighty God had that day done them, to build a chapel. They promised to do it and have faithfully kept their word. Some of them being wood-cutters, they went up the mountains and cut down some very fine trees, and sawed the branches into timber for the building, not of a sort of hut, as most of our chapels are, but of a regular chapel built entirely of wood. Here I had everything ready; but who was to raise a suitable chapel with these materials? To employ a carpenter from other parts would entail very great expense. So I made the plan as best I could, and commenced the construction myself with two natives. When these people have some one to guide them, they are not without ability. So far we have succeeded fairly well. We mounted the frame-work last Tuesday.

On the gable is a cross over six feet and a half high. At my next visit here, I hope to adorn it with wood carved by the natives themselves, and then to finish the interior of the chapel. If some generous American were to procure me the windows for it, we should have a beautiful little chapel in the midst of a very flourishing Christian community. I thank God for it with all my heart.

The architect and foreman (perhaps more ingenious than expert) was also an all-round worker, for with his powerful physique he was not at all afraid of hard labor. His chapels, humble as they were, were built one after the other, usually about one a year. Under the direction of this husky priest, those natives of good will were induced to take up this rough work. His example, more than his exhortations, stirred them out of their lethargy.

Bishop Maigret remarked: "The natives are everlastingly astonished at him. They shout as though it were a miracle when, they watch him carry a huge beam from the mountains which three or four of them could hardly lift."

Seeing that he took on himself the hardest work of all, men, women, and children gave him unbelievable support.

One church was to be situated on the mountain a few miles from the sea. The slope was so steep that three pairs of oxen could barely pull the cart up empty. There was not a sign of a road; you had to jump from one rock to the other, and all the time the sun beat down mercilessly on the hillside. In the evening he had the Christians go down to the beach where they slept in the open air with a stone for a pillow. At the break of day, after morning prayers in common, everyone shouldered his load of lumber and started the trek from shore to mountain. Since the Brother-carpenter of the missions had previously prepared each piece of lumber, Father Damien simply put the pieces in their proper place as they were brought up the mountain. Night prayers together would end the day; at last the chapel was finished and blessed. "If God wills it," wrote the foreman-priest, "I hope to build another next year about 20 miles away."

Above all, the missionary's main effort was to "build up spiritual temples" by the administration of the sacraments and especially by preaching. Putting first things first, he went with a straight simplicity toward his goal. There was no compromise of principle. He thundered against error, scourged vices, urged the people to repent and pray, and tried to get the Christians to make their morals agree with their beliefs. He had a strong voice, spoke in a lively, familiar way, so that only those who wanted to misunderstand him could do so. With all his soul he struck out against their intolerable abuses, their traditional and stupid recourse to witch doctors, sacrifices offered to idols, their ingrained vices. "I had quite a few people at Mass today," he said. "After reading the Gospel, I was, like St. John the Baptist, stirred up against sinners. I let them have it a little too much, it seems to me." He had to act sternly to make them be pure in the midst of pagans and to be sure they would hold on to the indissolubility of marriage.

"Let's suppose you marry a couple this year," he said:

> They live together in peace two or three months and then some little dispute will break out, and they separate for good. Each will take another partner. Now, the civil law forbids adultery. They will be taken before the judge and be fined 150 francs which means long years of slavery for them. They will get a divorce and then remarry. But how can a priest absolve them in a case like this?

He followed the Church's stand on the unity and indissolubility of marriage contracted by two Catholics married before a priest. But once principles were safeguarded, he instinctively tried to find a way to reconciliation. Later he gave his line of conduct: once doctrine and discipline are taken care of, to build up rather than destroy.

If Father Damien treated the witch doctors in actual practice the way he did in his letters, he certainly did not spare those charlatans who caused him so much trouble. As he saw it, the natives were like the Jews in the Old Testament. Now they served God, now they were lamentably lax and consented to acts of idolatry. Though the statues of the old gods had been destroyed, some of the people still clung to superstitious practices. Here and there a medicine man worked his cures by recourse to the devil, but with such skillful hypocrisy that even the shrewdest man could be fooled. Sudden cures were taken as miracles.

Here's what would happen. A Christian would get sick. With the neighbors' help he'd find out the best medicine man for his case, then they'd consult this specialist. But the latter wouldn't move precipitously for all the world. First of all, he recollected himself, said a prayer to the god he represented, thrust his hand into a bag containing black and white pebbles. The color of the pebble told him whether he should go or not, whether the case was worth it.

Once he arrived, the medicine man would hear the patient's confession and make him admit that the trouble all came from not keeping a vow. The offended deity was tormenting him until he made fitting reparation. A propitiatory sacrifice had to be made at once. This consisted of roast pig and strong liquor which were first presented to the god concerned and then shared by priest, patient, and neighbors. Once these rites were performed, the medicine man — who often knew no more about medicine than Father Damien's horse — would go out to pick herbs. The patient would take them and often was dead by morning. He would then — to the doctor's great shame — be buried. But the doctor's prestige did not suffer one bit.

Father Damien wrote to his brother Pamphile: "Apropos of these banquets, what would you as a theologian do if you heard the confessions of natives who took part in them? Mind you, they go there only for the meal."

Though the missionary's way of life was modest, he still needed money. Running over his annual financial reports, which were minutely kept and conscientiously submitted to his superiors, we can get an idea of his real spirit of religious poverty and appreciate it.

Then too it was not for nothing that he was the son of a Tremeloo merchant. His figures never ran very high. If he was no financial wizard, he was not without a business-

man's sense: "Your Excellency," he wrote to Bishop
Maigret, "I have bought a large tract of land. Later I will
plant coffee trees; in the meantime, I have borrowed 400
francs to pay my debts."

We have a stack of thirty or so letters that Father
Damien wrote at that time to order supplies from Honolulu for his building projects: detailed lists of planks,
shingles, glass, locks, kegs of nails, paint, brushes, putty.
Two barrels of cement, for example, to build a good cistern.
For his chapels he ordered crosses, pictures, candles, molds
to make candles from his beeswax, balls, ornaments, chal-
ices, patens, altar stones, candlesticks. But especially, he
asked for articles that would further religious education
and prayer; Catholic textbooks, catechisms, books on the
Rosary, religious books in Portuguese and Spanish. Father
Damien had to learn these two languages to speak with
the immigrants.

In regard to one of his chapels, he ingeniously presented
his case to his Provincial, Father Modeste, in November,
1868:

> You might note that by becoming a carpenter and
> handling the materials well, I was able to build a chapel
> for 250 dollars. It is a building of suitable size for the
> place and attractive both inside and out. We are waiting
> to pay the debt. I certainly don't want to be called "the
> ruination of the mission" as others have been. Besides,
> my confrere, Fr. Gulstan [Ropert] and I have to see
> to our upkeep and we have only 6 dollars left in the
> money box. Here is what I'm bold enough to propose
> to you — as a fine fellow but unfortunately as a bad re-
> ligious — I am undertaking to pay the 95 dollars, which
> I owe at Vaipio; besides I hope to be able to cover
> Fr. Gulstan's and my expenses for the coming year. As
> for the debt at Hilo, it's killing me.

Father Damien, then spoke admiringly of a Belgian compatriot who was with him. The man was even-tempered, active, and very capable. He cooked for Father and made his stay at Vaiapuka much more pleasant than it had been alone. He served his Mass in the morning and in the evenings they said their prayers together. After this preamble, Father Damien got down to the business he had in mind: "At Honolulu could you use any kidney or navy beans which we are growing quite successfully here? Would you ask the Sacred Hearts Sisters if they would take 300 pounds of them, and with the money you receive you might send us biscuits, wheat and rice. In this way we can live here from the fruit of our labor without being a drain on the mission."

"We are also planting a lot of tobacco." Tobacco was selling at a high price in Hawaii and could be harvested several times a year. His Belgian companion was bringing in good returns and he wanted to imitate him at least on a small scale, for we have a letter of his announcing a shipment of tobacco to Honolulu.

Also at Honolulu the Mother Superior of the Sacred Hearts Sisters, with whom Father Damien got along very well, often received shipments of potatoes from his Christians — unexpectedly. "People always need potatoes. Would she keep them . . . and pay for them? The price will pay a bill that's due." And again: "In order to paint the church at Kavaihae the Christians are thinking about sending a shipment of potatoes which will pay for the paint. Better get a supply before the whaling ships come in, for this will double the price." A true merchant!

In December, 1867, he listed the animals belonging to the mission in his districts: 5 horses, 2 mules, 2 colts — "my successor is not going to be without a mount as I was when I got here" — a cow, about 50 sheep. He also had some chickens, bees, pigs. "After taking care of the Lord's flock," he told Pamphile, "Joseph has to give his attention to his sheep." He bought 55 of them for two and a half francs a head. From time to time he killed one for eating. No doubt he got a good price for the others.

He did not forget what was owed him and steadfastly defended the balance of his books: "I owe a merchant in Hilo," he wrote the Provincial, "for the paint I bought. Couldn't you get Fr. Charles to pay for it? It seems to me that it would be only just, for when his mule starved to death waiting for him to get back from Honolulu, I replaced it with my best mule, not counting the many hogs he still owes me for."

On special occasions such as celebrating the completion of a new chapel on which everybody had worked, they had unimaginable Hawaiian banquets *(luaus)*. Their importance was in keeping with "the great efforts the people have made."

The day before, everybody would be there and all would be ready. They would go to the new church which was too small for the crowd. The priest's sermon, after he had dwelt on the meaning of the celebration, turned to welcoming their fellow Christians who had come a long way for the feast. Nothing was overlooked. Christians of the neighborhood furnished the food; the men brought cattle, and the women and children brought pigs. Close to a thousand people took part in the banquet that was held on the grass around the church. As was the custom they sat on the ground without tables or chairs, or even knives and forks. Even the most refined ate with their fingers.

There was another banquet a few months later when Bishop Maigret made a visit. Father Damien wrote:

I went to meet him on my mule. Together we covered 33 leagues and crossed 120 streams. Sunday we stopped at the chapel. Since the Bishop was in a hurry to get back, he wanted to proceed right away with the consecration. But our people would not hear of it. They asked him to give them ten days to invite the neighboring Christians and organize a decent celebration. The Bishop gave in and witnessed indescribable enthusiasm. My catechist asked each Christian to donate a pig. They slaughtered a whole herd, not counting the cattle needed to round out their menu. We had practically everything we could ask for. After the dinner the Bishop proceeded with the ceremony.

Education of the young people was of capital importance in a country where only too soon they became well acquainted with vice. For lack of funds the Catholic schools at Kohala had fallen into ruins. Catholic pupils were sent to schools conducted by Protestant teachers, and were exposed to the danger of receiving instructions contrary to their faith. But this unhappy state of things was soon changed.

In October, 1865, Father Damien wrote: "Our new government does not meddle in religion. It leaves everybody free and on equal footing. Now our teachers are paid. The head of education has even asked me to send some young women to the Sacred Hearts Sisters in Honolulu so they can become teachers." The following year Father Damien got four Catholic teachers from the school inspector. This enabled him to teach catechism to the children during the week since they were all in one place.

According to him, the little Hawaiians learned reading, arithmetic, and geography faster than their catechism. Only after repeating the same thing a hundred times and with limitless patience could he get across the essential points. Their precociousness in vice was enough to make him weep:

> They have hardly learned to talk when they know things young theologians still have to learn. Their par-

ents say all kinds of dirty things in front of them and initiate them into the most abominable practices of paganism. These irregularities cause our natives to contract diseases that make them old before their time and kill them off at the first hardship.

The number of Catholic schools increased, opening the way for a better future.

Father Damien couldn't be everywhere and doing everything, so he trained a group of assistants. When he ran across a promising young man, he carefully taught him to read and to explain the Sunday epistles and gospels, gave him further instructions so he could teach others. These he called catechists or prayer leaders. On Sundays, when Father wasn't there — which was pretty often — and in between his visits, it was the catechist's job to take care of the flock. He called the faithful to church, conducted the services, led the hymns, gave a little commentary on the word of God, and got the catechumens ready for baptism, keeping the community on its toes until Father returned. "Some of them are eloquent preachers," he affirmed. This organization was blessed by heaven.

The success of certain catechists was marvelous. "I've succeeded in training them to preach with eloquence and orthodoxy. Often larger crowds listen to them than to me, non-Catholics and unbelievers prefer their preaching to mine. They enjoy listening to them, while they are bored when I say Mass at which time they understand nothing."

They made conversions, and sometimes by astounding arguments:

My prayer leaders' zeal is a great help to me in the religious formation of my own new converts. Only little by little does the faith penetrate the souls of non-Catholics and unbelievers who prefer their preaching. Here's an example:

One day a Protestant on his way from church met one of my prayer leaders. As they walked along, the latter explained to him the parable of the Pharisee and the Publican. "You Protestants," he said, "who stand when you pray are like the proud Pharisee who refused to kneel down to ask pardon. But we Catholics pray on our knees, after the example of the Publican, who humbly prostrated himself before God and went back to his home forgiven." This observation was a ray of light and grace for the non-Catholic. He resolved to say his prayers from then on, on his knees, so he would be heard, and for that purpose he decided to join the Catholics. The next day he went to tell the teachers in the Protestant school that he was taking his son out of school because they were nothing but Pharisees and deceivers.

Since Father Damien began his missionary career when he was only twenty-four or twenty-five and was bursting to win souls, it's not surprising that he suffered a great deal over the slow progress and mounting difficulties of his work.

Weighed down with overwork and failures, he like so many others groaned interiorly. He was perfectly open with the Father General:

Generally, I have little consolation and plenty of trouble. Without divine grace it would be impossible for me to find the burden that lies on my shoulders sweet and light. So at times I am even led to be glad that my end is approaching.

When you're young, healthy, and confident as Father Damien was, you don't ask for death without good reasons. No doubt such attacks of depression lasted only momentarily. After describing the curriculum of his missionary life from 1864 to 1870, he frankly admitted to the Father

General: "Independently of the interior help of grace, the experience of four years [his stay at Kohala] has proved to me that a missionary needs the external help of a fellow missionary to dissipate a kind of gloomy thought caused by daily contact with the corruption of the Hawaiian world. Little by little it engenders a melancholy that is unbearable at times."

Yet we cannot question the delicateness of his conscience or the depth of his spiritual life. The work of God he was doing sustained him, his superiors understood him, his Hawaiians loved him, the heavy blows from spiteful human nature had not yet touched him to the quick, and if he was sensitive, he kept his habitual good humor.

However, the Father General had to realize his need for a companion. The soul of a priest could not be contented indefinitely surrounded solely by licentious natives. As the Sacred Hearts Rule prescribed, he went to confession regularly:

> Every two or three months I try to see Fr. Charles at Hilo or Fr. Regis at Kona. But that's not enough! Yet how can I do any more when each confession represents 50 or 60 leagues on the road? This is March 26, I haven't seen a fellow missionary since January. A couple of weeks ago I wanted to visit Hilo to go to confession, but because of the bad sailing I had to turn back without seeing anyone. So my only confessor is our Lord in the Blessed Sacrament.

Another urgent reason the Father General would understand: "I complain of being all alone in this huge district not so much for myself as for my children whose father I am in Jesus Christ. They are dying without receiving the sacraments because there are no priests, and they are too far away to visit."

"I am impatiently waiting for new missionaries," he

wrote. "We've heard that Fr. Gulstan and Brothers Boniface and Quentin are coming. But when are they going to get here? Will I have even just one to help me? I hope for it but without counting on it too much. Anyway we'd need a dozen to do the work."

Were his superiors deaf to his pleas? Evidently not. But reinforcements were being called for in other fields and there was always a shortage. They were doing the best they could.

In 1866 the Provincial forwarded to Father General Father Damien's request to have his brother Pamphile sent to the missions. His advice was: "He would fit in well here. As you think best, however!" His superiors thought it best for Father Pamphile to be a professor in Europe.

"Should I congratulate you on your promotion?" the missionary at Kohala asked him, very disappointedly. "There you're on your way to honors instead of being a poor missionary among savages. How impenetrable are the designs of Providence!"

Later Father Pamphile was sent to the University of Louvain to get his degree in theology. Father Damien was ironic, indignant, almost mean . . . as though his older brother's assignment was his own doing. "Do I have to give up the prospect forever of seeing you here?" he asked him in October, 1870. "Why get a doctor's cap at the expense of poor Hawaiians? It was to be a missionary, you will recall, that you became a religious. It was you who once censured me for lack of enthusiasm about the missions. I was hurt to learn that in 1867 you ducked the General's appeal and another had to take your place, as I had in 1863."

We shouldn't be surprised. Flemish brothers cruelly tell each other the truth without the slightest intention of causing any hard feelings. In this case, Father Damien had not been in on the superiors' plans and he was wrong. Anyhow right in the middle of the letter he suddenly changed his tone and became pleasant. At least Pamphile ought to come if only to taste their delicious Hawaiian cooking. "When you come I'll give you some good coffee, I make it really strong. No milk or beer; but honey and eggs. I have an oven where I can bake excellent bread. I've just bought a couple of horses. They'll be for you too. Come as quick as you can, you lazy fellow!"

Two years later he was still deploring Pamphile's professorial vocation. Pretty stiff irony, it seems to us — but not for a Fleming: "You seem somewhat sore at me, as you haven't deigned to write me for three years. Did you consider as insults the tiny reproaches I addressed to you in October, 1870? Pardon, I beg you, these slight impoliteness . . ." Alluding to the Franco-Prussian War which was still a current event for him, he asked: "Have you always been a professor at Versailles? The city was occupied by the Prussians. We got that from the newspapers. They reported the good work of several priests who distinguished themselves on that occasion, but they made no mention of you. Don't tell me you were scared of cannon balls? I never wanted to see that from a Belgian of Tremeloo!"

Pamphile never came — at least while Damien was alive. Later, in 1895, he tried to fulfill his brother's wish and went to take his place among the patients at Molokai. An idealist, a man at home with abstract studies, a theologian, philosopher, placid and somewhat distracted, Father Pamphile was no man of the wilds, and above all he was no Hawaiian missionary. Twenty months were enough to convince him and his superiors that he was much better off teaching religious sciences at his seminary in Europe.

It was Father Gulstan who landed at Kohala. In April, 1869, Father Damien told his friends the good news. "I must tell you that today I am no longer alone. Fr. Gulstan has come to help me take care of my little parish 20 leagues long. He preaches in Hawaiian very well and the natives have fallen in love with him!" We will meet him again later, for he will become the Vicar Apostolic of the Hawaiian Islands.

This eulogy he gave to his young companion reveals Father Damien's simplicity and sincerity. When we run across unfavorable judgments that accuse him of being touchy, jealous, and selfish, we have plenty of material to decide whether this is well founded or not. He said of Bishop Maigret: "Although he is old and feeble, when he is on a journey he is a challenge to the young missionaries, even the strongest. . . . He's one of our best riders, especially when he is on Kapakahi, his mule."

Here are other pen sketches he made at that time of some of his older comrades: Father Stanislas: "25 years a parish priest in Brittany, 25 years on the missions in heroic times. He's using what strength he has to build solid, beautiful churches, so that after his death his spiritual sons will have places where they can carry on the practice of religion." Father Celestin: "A young priest from the diocese of Rouen. Talks Hawaiian like a lawyer and is a very good missionary." Father Clement, who took over his old district of Puna: "A real missionary and soon he will have changed the district completely." Father Charles at Hilo: "Protestantism is very strong there and this priest has a lot of trouble keeping up and consolidating religion. At times he complains that the good he would like to do is going on so slow. It's then that you've got to have a missionary's courage and he's worked there for more than twenty years."

The missionary's life at Kohala ran along steadily between hope and disillusion, in the simple contacts with the natives whose mode of life he three quarters adopted, in the progressive discovery of their souls' resources and the endowments of their simple, gentle nature. He freely opened his soul to Pamphile and designedly gave him a few picturesque details of his work. The Fleming in him didn't forget the food:

Once my Sunday morning work is over, it's time to eat. We always have a gourd full of poi in reserve. Meat is always at hand and water more so. Coffee and bread we have at times, but beer and wine never. The dishes are not always washed. And as I've worked all week, my hands are not in as good a condition as yours — you who have nothing to do but page through books. But habit and hunger make us eat just the same. For dessert I smoke a pipe.

That done, time to get on your horse! I have to visit another group of Christians. If, as often happens, I have to say a second Mass, my breakfast is put off to about 2 or 3 o'clock. I finish the day either in the confessional or teaching theology to my catechists, who fill in for me. Obviously in the evening I can't do any more. But the wearier I am the happier I feel.

That's Sunday. During the week: first Mass; then often instructions; then breakfast — always poi! It's been at least seven months since I've had anything else to eat. Then, I take off my habit, pick up the saw and become a carpenter, for it's only at the price of plenty of sweat that I have pretty decent chapels throughout. I've also built some in good little Fr. Gulstan's district. A storm blew down his house and two of his chapels. The trouble I had rebuilding them!

This storm was not nearly as bad as those of 1865 and 1860. In March, tremors of the earth, at first slight and intermittent, then deeper and more accelerated, warned them of the coming catastrophe. On April 2, the southern part of the island trembled, shook violently, and cracked open, forests swayed, the bells in the churches rang of their own accord, the trees were uprooted and crashed on top of one another. The verse of the Psalm: "The mountains skipped like rams and the hills like the lambs of the flock," came true to the letter. Huge rocks avalanched into the valleys. The side of a mountain was torn loose and hurled like a meteor smashing men, beasts, and houses in a five-mile area. At Kaou the ground split open, releasing a stream of molten rocks and dirt six miles wide; it flowed on for three miles burying a herd of cattle and sheep along with thirty-one of their keepers who were petrified at the sight of the flaming river coming out of the earth.

More frightful still was what happened at Apoua where they thought the whole island was going to sink into the ocean. Disturbed by underwater volcanoes, the sea seemed to crouch for a leap then burst onto the shore, with churning waves 30 feet high. With a horrible crash it swallowed men, women and children, boats and houses that disappeared amid a confused mass of trees, rocks, boards, and animals. After two or three waves of this kind, not a trace was left of the fishing villages on the beach.

Finally, on April 7, the cataclysm entered its final stages. That day the volcano erupted in several places, belching enormous rocks and floods of lava down on the helpless natives.

About thirty people were killed by the volcano and another forty by a cyclone that struck so fast that no one had time to get out of the way. Some of the churches were destroyed entirely, while two stone churches fell apart from the earthquake.

Father Damien escaped death, but a number of his churches, rectories, and schools were destroyed. Many of his neophytes perished. He was not a man to weep in vain over the ruins. Loaded down with food and clothing, he went out looking for survivors to bring aid and comfort in their distress. He began to rebuild his churches with the same ardor which had built them in the first place.

In his disconnected letters which were a sort of animated conversation about his hour-to-hour occupations and preoccupations we discover the missionary as he was. He said to his more cultivated brother who mentioned it: "I'm neither a poet nor a good writer." We have fifty or so of his letters written at Kohala (March, 1865 to April, 1873), thirty-two of them to Father Modeste, his Provincial, six to his brother and relatives, four to Father General, and two to fellow priests at Louvain.

He wrote only when he had to; for example, to order lumber from Honolulu, report on the condition of his mission to his superiors, to give them the news at Tremeloo.

Here are a few short passages. On March 7, 1866, he pleaded his case for building a chapel on his mission rather than in Honolulu. Cavalierly he went straight to the point:

> I haven't had the patience to wait for your orders to start building here at Kahuahale. I told my Christians that they're building a church at Honolulu and this news made them go to work on ours. Kahuahale is a little hill next to a spring that has water even in the dry season. Christians live all around it. You can see the chapel from the sea. The ship going from Maui to Kona will see it. From Kona to Vaimea it is continually in view as you go through the terrible reefs of Kiholo. The land seemed a little narrow, so my Christians built a retaining wall to level it off, and on the platform we'll build the chapel. It will be 32 feet long and 20 wide.

Father Modeste couldn't say no.

December 29, 1867, he gave a financial report for the year and added: "I have to say *mea culpa* for having received something without entering it in the books, for I'm six dollars short."

January 5, 1869: "During the year 1868, in the double district of Hamakua and Kohala — 65 baptisms, about 50 of them adults; 16 marriages, 2 of them mixed. I haven't counted the dead."

June 21, 1869, he justified a failure in religious obedience:

> I must frankly confess that your letter hurt me deeply. In conscience I thought I could make expenditures that were absolutely necessary to finish the church at Vaimea. Without the help of my Christians and not being able to leave my lumber by the sea, I thought it was all right to rent a wagon. If I had received your prohibition before I would not have gone forward with the work, but it came too late. Now I have the unhappiness of learning that I have acted more or less contrary to obedience. Please have the goodness to pardon my error and pray for me that I will go astray in these matters no further.

March, 1871: "About 10 months ago an old man asked if he could stay with me so I could take care of him as long as he lived and bury him when he died. He has left me his entire fortune — a hundred dollars, 2 horses, and an iron stove." All the questions relative to inheritance were debated back and forth between the Provincial and Father Damien; the latter accepted the decision against inheriting which was based on very good reasons. Then he unceremoniously added: "The wind here is strong enough to blow the horns off a bull . . . To keep my body in servitude, I help my native spade the fields he is cultivating."

Father Damien had a very tender heart. Every year a letter went out to his dear ones at Tremeloo telling of his deep attachment to them. It is interesting to see how he went down into the details of every one of their lives to find out if they were happy — and good Christians. Often he complained that they weren't sending him any news:

> It will soon be two years since I've heard from you. How are you, mother and dad? How's your health? Is everything all right with the family? Is Leonce still living at La Croix? Are Constance and Victor still at the mill in Betecom? Is Gerard still farming at Ninde? Does uncle still come on Sundays to go to church with you? And I, thank God, am very well and hardly have time to get bored with my vast parish.

Later, when disease was ravaging his strong body, he continued to say that things weren't going too badly with him, so as not to disturb his aged parents.

His parents hardly ever wrote, naturally leaving that to Pamphile who, absorbed in studies and classes, kept putting it off too. The missionary was beside himself when he received a letter from Tremeloo after nine months' waiting:

> I received your letter with inexpressible joy. You were right, my dear father, to neglect your temporal business to think a little more about 'eternity. It is the thought of eternity that has made half of your children enter the cloister and which makes me apply myself to my duties more and more . . . I am happy to hear that my brothers have gone in together to run the steam mill and I hope they succeed. They will, if they stick together and don't quarrel. Dad, see to it that they do.

In 1872 two letters, one to Pamphile and the other to his parents, revealed the same anxiety about their letters. To Pamphile: "You must be pretty angry at me not to write for three years . . ." To the others: "What's happened, my dear parents? It's been three years since I've heard from you. Are you both still alive? Perhaps the Lord has called one of you? If so, His will be done, but at least deliver me from this uncertainty. Thank God, I am always strong and in good health, always happy among my Hawaiians." He then goes on to speak of his churches, of Janneke Roof, the carpenter, of the War of 1870, of each member of his family, of the progress of the faith in these distant islands which he would never leave. "Let's try to serve God well and we'll see each other together in heaven."

He wrote to his brothers:

Mother wrote me that each of you have three children. Jean, Leonce's son, should be big by now. Tell him to study hard and when he's fourteen have him take Latin. Tell him I'm expecting him here and that I have two saddle horses for him. As for you, my dear brothers, remember that out of the eight of us children, you alone can help our parents in their old age. I humbly beg you to take my place and give them the filial affection and care they had a right to expect from me. Show them great respect and never say anything that could hurt them. Live united, love one another, and raise your children in the fear of God. I'm expecting a letter from you. Your devoted brother. Joseph.

Pauline, his favorite sister, was a religious in Holland. Not a word from her . . . had she died? "It's more than three years and I haven't had a sign of life from you, my dear sister . . . Write me I beg you. Have mercy on your poor missionary brother who, forced to be forgotten among the natives, is soon going to become a native himself . . . But I think the reason is that you've gone to heaven." In fact, a few months later Pauline did die in her convent at Uden.

On receipt of letters from Flanders how easy it was for Father Damien to go back twenty years to his childhood days. "About twenty leagues from home, en route to Fr. Regis' to go to confession," he wrote to Pamphile,

> I got your letter at one of the ports. All night, as I crossed the lava of a new volcano, I thought over the news you had sent. Now I was at the mill in Betecom with Leonce and Gerard, now at the bedside of Henri Winckx on whom I hope God will have mercy, now with Pauline in her convent where tranquil happiness reigns, so different from the excitement of my missionary life. I accompanied you on your trip in Flanders . . . Where are those happy times, my dear brother, living under our parents' care, and when we went to school together at Werchter, and later to the University of Louvain? The beautiful times of our childhood and youth have passed! It is now the time of manhood when we have to work courageously in the vineyard of the Lord, you in Europe (perhaps), I in Hawaii. It doesn't make any difference! Let's march forward in our noble careers! If you can't join me here, at least form strong, virtuous, intrepid, charitable men among your students who will take our places when we are called to our eternal rest.

Just how great was Father Damien's success during these eight years at Kohala and Hamakua? It was the time for sowing; others would come to harvest. His missionary life before April, 1873 — when God was to fix his fate — was hardly different from any other foreign missionary's. We have been careful not to overestimate its apparent worth, and have based our own judgment on well-founded information, especially of the missionaries who were backed up by age, knowledge, their own experience in construction work and carrying on business with the capital, and who had also had their own successes.

From 26 to 32, young Father Damien did the very best

he could as a missionary, giving himself to his people body and soul. But his activity, with his limited spiritual training, his unbounded confidence and drive, the physical need of being constantly on the move, might have given him a feeling of inferiority in comparison with the veteran missionaries, if God hadn't encouraged him. We can pick up traces of success here and there in his letters.

In 1865:

A great number of crosses; but side by side with these painful hardships, come some sweet joys. On my first visit I had more than fifty baptisms entered in my book, besides a number of apostates reconciled.

The following year he noted:

As I had to prepare all my neophytes for their Christmas Communion, I spent the afternoon in the confessional. There the sincere conversion of some big sinners caused me a profound joy. Next day I celebrated two Masses — one the Communion Mass, the other was the high Mass. In the midst of his privations and sufferings the missionary at times experiences an abundance of joy of which you have no idea.

At the end of 1868 he wrote:

In one of our chapels my sweat has been repaid by the consolation God gave me there. Poor Hawaiians came to join the army of the Lord. Sixty adult baptisms have crowned my labor.

October of the following year:

The movement of conversions has increased despite the devil, despite heretics and unbelievers who are doing all in their power to turn souls off the road. Continue to pray for the conversion of unbelievers. Doubtless it is to you, to your prayers, that I owe the baptism of from forty to fifty people this year.

In 1872 he confided to his sister Pauline:

By instructing my people and keeping them close to me when they are sick, I have reason to believe that a good number have died with good dispositions. In general, they are very happy to receive the last sacraments.

For a great number then, thanks to a deathbed conversion, heaven was not closed forever. The missionary was not spending himself in vain.

Always an optimist, he reported to the Father General, with extreme confidence, the way conversions were taking place in the islands, and concluded that "if we had enough personnel to fill all the posts of the archipelago and to watch over the education of youth, the majority of the islanders would soon come under the banner of the Cross."

July 14, 1872, Father Damien seemed bursting with joy when he said:

Now I have enough chapels, rectories, animals and fields. I'm going to be able to apply myself to taking care of the sick and studying this year. At least, if Providence doesn't send me elsewhere.

A presentiment perhaps that before the year was over he would be on his real mission.

PART II

Molokai

7   The Leprosarium of Molokai

THERE is probably no disease known to modern medical science about which there exists so much confused misinformation as leprosy. Similarly, no other disease has such an obscure and little-studied history. Practically every statement found in standard encyclopedias and treatises on the subject has been challenged, if not disproved, in recent years.

It is often alleged that the disease originated in ancient Egypt, and that the first recorded description of its symptoms occurs in the Old Testament. However, a recent study concludes that "we have no definite proof that leprosy was common or even known in ancient Egypt," whereas the Hindu *Susruth Samhita,* written about 600 B.C. but containing much older traditional knowledge, "describes most of the signs and symptoms of leprosy . . . with which we are familiar today." As to so-called "biblical leprosy," a careful analysis of about thirty treatises and articles in medical and Bible encyclopedias discloses that experts are almost unanimous in declaring that the "leprosy" mentioned in the Book of Leviticus is not the disease now known as leprosy or Hansen's disease. This important fact is duly recognized by a footnote in the new translation of the Old Testament prepared by the Catholic Biblical Association of America which states that the Hebrew term used to designate so-called leprosy "does not refer to Hansen's disease, currently called leprosy."

In New Testament times true leprosy was familiar to Greek physicians under the name *elephantiasis Graecorum*. It is entirely possible that some of the victims of leprosy who were cured by our Lord actually had true leprosy. In any case, whatever their disease may have been, the miraculous character of the cure is guaranteed by its instantaneousness.

But until we have a thorough scientific study of the history of leprosy, it will be impossible to state with any certainty where it originated and how it spread across Asia, Africa, and the Near East in ancient times. Due to confusion in the terms used and to the absence of accurate descriptions in many instances, it is by no means certain that during the Middle Ages in Europe all cases of leprosy were correctly diagnosed. While it is frequently alleged that the Crusades were primarily responsible for spreading the affliction in Europe, Catholic scholars have proved that it was widely prevalent several centuries before the First Crusade.

Despite all the confusion surrounding the history of leprosy, it will ever remain an undeniable and a glorious fact that the Church of Christ took a decisive part in alleviating the tragic destiny of the many thousands of victims of leprosy in medieval Europe. Due to an erroneous conception of the contagiousness of the disease, society insisted on ostracizing those unfortunate men and women. The Church, however, remembering the compassion which its divine Founder had shown toward them, did all that it could for their material and spiritual welfare by instituting hospitals and by providing special facilities for the reception of the Sacraments, while many saintly persons, including a large number of canonized saints, contributed their own direct personal charity in nursing and caring for the outcasts.

For reasons which have not yet been clearly determined, leprosy declined sharply in Europe after the fifteenth century. Among the various factors responsible for its almost complete extinction were no doubt the strict measures taken to segregate its victims, the terrible epidemic of the Black Death in the fourteenth century, the relative advance in medical knowledge and hygiene, and the identification of syphilis and other skin diseases which had formerly been classed as so-called leprosy.

Again it is not known whether true leprosy existed in the Americas before the coming of European colonists. But it is certain that the slave trade resulted in the transporting of many cases from Africa to Latin America. Similarly in the nineteenth century infected Chinese laborers probably spread the disease in the islands of the Pacific Ocean.

It is utterly impossible to obtain an accurate count of the total number of cases of leprosy in the world today. Estimates range from three to ten million. India and China are said to have about one million victims apiece, with the largest concentration in the southern part of both countries. Southeast Asia is heavily infected, while a broad belt of infection stretches across all of central Africa. The northern part of South America and most of Brazil have many cases.

In the popular mind, leprosy has traditionally remained the most frightful of all diseases. This intense horror cannot reasonably be blamed on the so-called "leprosy" described in the Bible, because a careful reading of Chapters 13 and 14 of the Book of Leviticus shows very clearly, once we set aside our preconceptions, that the word as used therein was applied to various mild skin disorders that were con-

sidered noncontagious and curable. Probably our lepra-
phobia stems from highly colored and sensational descriptions of medieval leprosy. True leprosy is no doubt a very
serious affliction which can, in cases where no modern
drugs or vaccine are available, be disfiguring and crippling,
and it is infectious. But the popular idea of leprosy is
tragically false in attributing to it a high degree of contagiousness. Actually both the experience of thousands of
doctors and nurses and the formal conclusions of modern
medical science have established beyond a shadow of a
doubt that the disease is only "mildly contagious." Young
children are more susceptible than adults, and men are
usually more susceptible than women. Many leprosaria
include large numbers of children and frequently three
times as many male as female patients. But the disease is
not hereditary; a child born of a mother with leprosy will
not become infected if it is separated from her at birth;
hence the great importance of special nurseries or preventoria, as has been fully demonstrated by the splendid
achievements of these institutions in Brazil.

The exact mode of transmission remains the great un-
solved mystery of leprosy research. The bacillus probably
enters the body through the nose or throat or digestive
tract or through open skin wounds. The period of incubation may vary from a few months to several years.

The bacillus itself, known as *Mycobacterium leprae* or
Hansen's bacillus, was first identified in 1874 by the Nor-
wegian Dr. Gerhard A. Hansen. It is a rod-shaped microbe
which resembles the tuberculosis bacillus. But unlike the
latter, it cannot be artificially cultivated and it cannot be
transmitted experimentally to animals. It is also a striking
fact that a number of attempts to infect human volunteers
by inoculation have uniformly failed.

There are two principal types of Hansen's disease:

1. The *lepromatous* type (formerly called nodular) is

characterized by skin lesions or nodules, i.e., swelling sores. In advanced cases the skin of the face becomes so thickened that it produces the so-called leonine or lionlike aspect. Invasion of the nerve fibers results in anesthesia or loss of sensation. Patients with this type suffer from acute "lepra reactions" or "lepra fevers" which become increasingly frequent and debilitating. Many advanced cases are afflicted with blindness and difficulty in breathing. A characteristic hoarseness is caused by involvement of the vocal cords. Due to the presence of the bacilli in the open skin lesions, the lepromatous type is considered infectious.

2. The *tuberculoid* type (formerly called neural) presents a very different appearance. Patients with this type have a relatively smooth skin and can be recognized by the disappearance through absorption of the fingers and toes, due to the destruction of the nerves by the bacillus. Contraction and paralysis may also occur. Involvement of the deeper tissues produces large chronic ulcers, particularly in the feet. However, this type is also characterized by a tendency to self-repair, and in the majority of instances the disease spontaneously dies out (so-called "burn-out" cases) before an advanced stage is reached. Because the bacilli are only rarely discharged on the surface, the tuberculoid type is generally considered noninfectious.

As a rule Hansen's disease is not in itself fatal. The patient usually succumbs to some other sickness. Many victims live with the disease for twenty to forty years. The great majority of patients are relatively able-bodied and can perform light work, often with surprising skill.

From the point of view of the general public, it must be stressed that today the traditional journalistic picture of the leprosy patient is 90 per cent false. Most patients in leprosaria are not markedly disfigured. Visitors often mistake patients for other visitors. As to the so-called advanced cases, first, they number only about 10 per cent of the total in most institutions, and, second, a glance at the illustrations in any modern textbook of dermatology will show that serious disfigurement is found in numerous other diseases to a degree which surpasses that which is observed in Hansen's disease.

For centuries leprosy was rightly considered incurable, although some cases of natural or spontaneous recovery have been known. The traditional remedy was chaulmoogra oil, which did effect an improvement in a relatively small number of cases. But it was not until the discovery and use of the sulfone drugs after World War II that large numbers of "arrested" or apparently cured cases have been reported. Today the whole outlook of the world's leprosy researchers and patients has undergone a profound change. For the first time in history, that outlook is definitely optimistic. While the sulfone drugs have not yet proved to be an ideal specific remedy for the disease, it is now a demonstrated fact that they effect a rapid major improvement in appearance and consequently in morale in most patients treated, and that they have apparently destroyed the bacilli in thousands of patients.

Nevertheless in most parts of the world the leprosy patient still suffers grievously from an affliction which he tends to consider more cruel than the bacillus itself: the age-old unscientific popular stigma which brands him as a dangerous outcast. It is this demonstrably false legend, rooted in misinformation, which causes the greatest suffering to the patients and to their families. Throughout the world today these innocent victims of an unjust and unjustifiable prejudice are rising in protest against that legend.

Quite understandably, since Hansen's disease is actually very different from the concept of "leprosy" in the mass mind, the patients concentrate much of their legitimate resentment against the term "leprosy" and more especially

against the word "leper," which they consider nothing less
than libelous. Under the leadership of the Carville *Star,*
the monthly magazine published by the patients in the
famous American hospital, a campaign for the abandon-
ment of "leprosy" and "leper" has in recent years succeeded in bringing the expression "Hansen's disease" into
general use, culminating in its acceptance as a synonym
of "leprosy" by the American Medical Association. However, for various technical reasons, some of the world's
leading leprologists still insist on using "leprosy" although
they are now nearly unanimous — at least in the English-
speaking world — in eliminating the objectionable "leper."
In this connection, the Fifth International Congress on
Leprosy in Havana in 1948 passed a resolution advocating
that the use of the word "leper" and other undesirable
terms be avoided in all popular literature, while retaining
"leprosy" in scientific writing. This resolution was re-
affirmed at the Sixth International Congress in Madrid in
1953. Very significantly, the Havana Congress also dep-
recated "all publicity . . . in which leprosy and the
patient are dramatized, when the presentation does not
agree with modern knowledge."

Surely Father Damien would agree with modern Catholic missionaries that the Church should play a leading
role in this world-wide campaign of enlightenment.

In the Hawaiian Islands, this mysterious disease, hardly
suspected at least by its real name before 1850, suddenly
took on a terrifying expansion. In 1823 Rev. Steward, a
Protestant missionary, wrote: "Cases of ophthalmia, scrofula, and elephantiasis are very common." It seems certain
that the diseases he spoke of were really Hansen's disease.
About the same time, Chinese and Japanse began to im-
migrate to work on the plantations. Ten years later oriental
leprosy raged; the resentful natives called it *maipake* —
Chinese disease. A real epidemic swept the islands; it was

aggravated by smallpox and some have maintained was spread from arm to arm by vaccination. Around 1863, from 10 to 15 per cent were infected. In 1850, the government in Honolulu set up a Board of Health, charged with doing "everything that in their opinion ought to be done or undone, removed or procured, for the preservation and cure of contagious, epidemic and other diseases, and more especially of Cholera." No mention is made of leprosy and only one case was verified.

In 1863, Dr. Hillebrand, a Board member, vehemently pointed out that there were numerous cases of leprosy in the country, that it was spreading, and energetic measures were called for. His fear was considered exaggerated and they waited eight months before appointing a doctor to make an investigation.

But some of the foreigners sent up howls of alarm in the press. Disturbed, if not scared out of their wits, the royal officials then put through extremely severe measures that were reminiscent of the Middle Ages. A kind of penal colony was established. King Kamehameha V issued a decree on January 3, 1865, that leprosy victims were to make themselves known and the Board of Health was to examine suspects; incurables were to be sent to the Settlement on Molokai, the others were to be treated at the Kahili Hospital near Honolulu.

Dr. Arthur A. Mouritz, the physician of the lepers at the time of Father Damien, tells how the lands for the Settlement of Molokai were acquired. The royal decree had prescribed the purchase of lands in a section particularly suited for the purpose. In June, 1865, the site on Molokai was proposed to the Board; July 15, Mr. Rhodes, the Board president, was authorized to buy it, if inspection showed it to be suitable. On September 20, eight hundred acres were bought at Kalawao and Vailes plus some adjacent parts for $1,800 and other lands in exchange.

A notice of October 25, 1865, stated that patients were to go to Kalaupapa (Molokai) to the Settlement established by the Board. There "all possible care will be extended to them." Nothing less, but nothing more. There has been much discussion on this point.

It seems that the notice spoke of Kalaupapa because it was the point of debarkation. Mouritz does not mention that the Board had purchased land at Kalaupapa. On the contrary, he states that Ahupuaa at Kalaupapa was acquired by the officials only in 1873. Dr. G. L. Fitch, a physician at Kakaako and Molokai, is even more precise in his report of 1884: "In 1873 the westerly side of the promontory was annexed to the settlement, but there remained several *kuleanas*, or homesteads, which were not purchased by the government, and the owners of these *kuleanas* remain on their lands to this day." Therefore from 1866 to 1873 all of Kalaupapa was still owned by the *Kamaainas*, the original inhabitants. In 1873, part of Kalaupapa was purchased by the Board, and the inhabitants kept the rest. According to Mouritz, these Kamaainas lived at the Settlement twenty-nine years, from 1866 to 1895 when they were forced to leave. In the beginning, they numbered about forty. Not one of them contracted Hansen's disease.

Further, not only did the patients not live at Kalaupapa but they were forbidden to go there. Father Damien himself, in his report of 1886, says that on his arrival at Molokai all the patients lived at Kalawao and were not allowed to go to Kalaupapa except on the day the ship came in. This explains why they stayed at Kalawao when Kalaupapa offered so many advantages — better land, nearness to the harbor where provisions were unloaded once a week, and especially a better climate.

Molokai is the center of the Hawaiian archipelago, southeast of Oahu and northwest of Maui. It looks like a giant fish lying on its side. The natives called it "the land

of cliffs," for it had been torn up by volcanoes. Its harbor-
less coasts cut it off from the rest of the islands. Only in
the north were there any stretches of fertile land. Its geo-
graphic handicaps left it behind in the economic progress
of the archipelago. Of all the islands, it was the most for-
lorn. In 1873, it could count no more than 2000 inhabitants.

On the northern end, the Kalawao promontory runs into
the ocean. It is a tongue of land about six miles square,
walled off from the rest of the island by *palis* which are
gigantic cliffs from 2000 to 3600 feet high. In the center
is a crater about 100 feet high and 200 feet wide. A barren
plain is strewn with huge rocks, bunches of grass, cane,
and old pandanus trees. Surrounded on three sides by
water and hemmed in from the back by the *palis*, the
place had been prepared by nature for a leprosarium.

Apropos of the island's climate, we notice in an American biography of Brother Joseph Dutton that it is painted
as a veritable paradise. In the lives of Father Damien, the
bell tolls with a different tone — Molokai, land of horror,
wind-whipped, barren, desolate. Dr. Mouritz explains the
apparent contradiction. The Kalaupapa side is well protected and enjoys a delightful climate; if its soil is cultivated, it can become a kind of Eden. On the Kalawao
side, the mountain throws a shadow across everything in
the early hours of the afternoon, stops the prevailing wind
coming in over the beach, and consequently often causes
chilly rains. Mouritz says that during the winter, Kalawao
is very disagreeable — the climate is penetrating, cold,
rainy. Such conditions would not bother healthy people
too much, but inflict much pain and suffering on leprosy
victims. We can understand, then, why Father Damien,
though in a tropical climate, would ask for warm clothing
for his people.

In all good faith the government and Board of Health
believed they had solved the problem in every respect by

shipping the patients off to Molokai with daily rations, a pair of pants or a cotton dress, a two-room building that was supposed to be a hospital under the direction of an administrator and some assistants. Actually, however, it was a barbarous method of isolation and a frank admission that the disease was considered incurable. Some of the sufferers understood and gave themselves up voluntarily. There was Bill Ragsdale, for example, a cousin of Queen Emma, a capable lawyer, well-to-do, related to the best families, revered by the people and the foreign colony for his character and generosity. He reported and sailed for Molokai.

Despite such examples, families refused to hand over their sick, and the police had to hunt them out. Molokai quickly got the reputation of being a graveyard, a place of anarchy, a Sodom calling down a rain of fire and brimstone. There was no doctor, no nurse, no priest, no justice of the peace, no resident police, no work, no comfort — and no hope.

On the other hand, the natives had no repulsion for the disease nor the slightest fear of catching it. The sufferers continued to live among them just like anybody else. Rather than die alone in some far-off place, they preferred to suffer surrounded by their families and await the end in their poor huts. The refusal was general. Parents would not let their children be taken from them, husbands and wives would not be separated, and the old folks refused to leave the places where they had lived all their lives.

The officials resorted to force. Doctors were accompanied by the police, and bloodhounds were set loose in the fields to track down the sick like prey. A man would run away. He'd take refuge in some inaccessible place — in a ravine or a cave and come out only at night to receive aid from his friends.

This state of affairs was to go on for a long time. "All

the leprosy victims are far from being in the Settlement," Father Albert Montiton wrote in July, 1878. "You meet them everywhere — in the caves by the sea, in the middle of the forest, in huts in deserted places. They run and hide at the sight of a stranger." Two years later, Brother Poirier, a missionary, said: "As for leprosy sufferers condemned to Molokai, that's no longer a question here. As soon as they hear that they will be taken, they all hide themselves in the rocky cliffs of Hawaii where it's going to be very hard to find them. They are very numerous. I see them all the time. I know at least twenty, several of them Catholics."

The sufferers offered open resistance to this order which caused them so much trouble. On Kauai, Dr. Smith and several agents of the Board were massacred. Elsewhere policemen were fatally wounded. The first doctor of the Settlement, Dr. N. B. Emerson, was also killed. For years on Oahu, investigators were welcomed with Winchesters.

The royal decree appeared January 3, 1865. Eight months later, investigators in fifteen districts were unable to furnish any reports. In November, only sixty-two suspects were picked up; forty-three were found to be infected — thirty-two men and eleven women. Two months later, a miserable group of outcasts embarked at Honolulu. It was the first shipload in an endless series that went on until about 1900.

When the doctors read the cruel decree to the suspects in the Kalihi hospital, it was a heart-rending scene. "What a sight," writes an eyewitness. "The sick were accompanied by parents who clutched them in their arms, covered them with ceaseless kisses, mingled with tears. When the sick were torn from their arms to be put on board, the cries of despair and screams of pain were enough to tear your soul apart!"

At Molokai a so-called hospital — without doctors or beds — was reserved for the worst cases. They stretched out on mats spread on the floor. The others crowded into the huts left vacant by the natives. The Board of Health had the idea that once they were settled the stronger ones would farm enough to take care of their needs; regular shipments of meat and clothes would supply the rest. But the cold fact is that nobody worked. Medical supplies failed, food shipments were irregular and insufficient. Between 1866 and 1873 about 40 per cent of the outcasts died — 311 out of 797.

Ambrose Hutchinson, himself a patient, who spent a half-century in the hospital and who for some time was resident superintendent at the Settlement, tells us what went on there with pretty crude realism. The day after he came to the Settlement, he says:

My eyes caught sight of another object that attracted my attention. I was held spellbound on the spot to see clearly and to know what it was. A man, his face partly covered below the eyes with a white rag or handkerchief tied behind his head, came out from the house that stood near the road. He was pushing a wheelbarrow loaded with a bundle, which at first I mistook for soiled rags. He wheeled it across the yard to a small windowless shack that rested on the ground on the west side of the yard adjoining a jailhouse and stopped before the doorway opening to the west. The man half turned over the wheelbarrow and shook it. The bundle (instead of rags, it was a human being) rolled out on the ground with an agonized groan. The fellow turned the wheelbarrow around and wheeled it away, leaving the sick man lying there helpless. After a while, the dying man raised and pushed himself in the doorway; with his body in and his legs stretched out, he lay there face down.

This spectacle of inhumanity which I witnessed that day thrilled me with intense horror, and made a lasting impression on my mind with a foreboding sense . . . I may be a like victim, God only knows.

Except for a few rich persons, those who died at Molokai had neither coffin nor funeral. When anyone died, his companions rolled him up in a blanket, tied cords around his neck, waist, and ankles, passed a pole under the cords, and two men carted him off to his grave. The hole they buried him in was so shallow that the hogs came to devour the corpse.

The patients of this improvised hospital sank into despair and bestiality. They suffered from cold and hunger, lived in sordid promiscuity. No effort was made to treat their disease or stop its progress; visits from the doctor were rare. They were abandoned, without relatives, without home, without affection; no one thought of them except to repress their revolts. They were given no work, no distraction from their misery. No priest was there to console them, care for their souls, or pray for them. Decidedly, this was too much torment at one time — all hope was driven from these poor unfortunates on whom rested one of the most dreaded of curses.

The result, almost inevitable, was moral and mental breakdown. Preyed on by helpless rebellion and concentrated rage, they trampled underfoot all divine and human laws. With nothing to sustain them and no reason for living, they lost all human dignity and let themselves go. They had been treated as untouchables, they had been hunted down as contaminated animals. Very well then, they would become brutes, since they were no longer men and women. At least before they died they would extract some pleasures from their infected flesh. Lacking human joys, they grasped at those of beasts.

"Aole kanawai ma reia wahi" — "In this place there is no law!" This was the word of welcome the old-timers had for new arrivals. It was the maxim they followed. They idled away their time sleeping, playing cards, drinking, indulging in vice. This was main street in Sodom. Men,

women, single and married, lived together helter-skelter
with privacy always a matter of chance. They made
okolehao from *ki* roots (*Dracaena terminalis*): it was almost pure alcohol. Drunkenness rapidly sank into orgy,
naked dances, and other shameless games that took place
in front of the altars of Laka, the Hawaiian Venus, the only
divinity they consented to worship.

Here is the way Father Damien describes conditions in
a letter written years later:

June 1886

By special providence of our divine Lord, who during His public life showed a particular sympathy for
lepers, my way was traced toward Kalawao in May 1873.
I was then thirty-three years of age, enjoying robust
health.

About eighty of the lepers were in the hospital; the
others, with a very few *kokuas* [helpers], had taken
their abode further up toward the valley. They had cut
down the old pandanus or punhala groves to build their
houses, though a great many had nothing but branches
of castor-oil trees with which to construct their small
shelters. These frail frames were covered with ki leaves
or with sugar-cane leaves, the best ones with pili grass.
I myself was sheltered during several weeks under the
single pandanus-tree which is preserved up to the present in the churchyard. Under such primitive roofs were
living in the most revolting promiscuity, without distinction of age or sex, old or new cases, all more or less
strangers one to another, these unfortunate outcasts of
society. They occupied their time with playing cards,
hula (native dances), drinking fermented ki-root beer,
home-made alcohol, and with the sequels of all this.
Their clothes were far from being clean and decent, on
account of the scarcity of water, which had to be
brought at that time from a great distance. Many a time

in fulfilling my priestly duty at their domiciles I have been compelled to run outside to breathe fresh air. To counteract the bad smell I accustomed myself to the use of tobacco, and on many occasions the smell of the pipe was my preservation, and saved me from carrying in my clothes the noxious odor of the lepers. At that time the progress of the disease was fearful, and the rate of mortality very high.

Selfishness had its day. Boys and girls were abandoned, men "adopted" them. These innocents served as domestics and instruments of pleasure until they became too sick or useless. Women were forced to be prostitutes in order to have friends who would take care of them. When leprosy had done its work, they were unceremoniously thrown out. You could find them hiding behind some wall waiting for death.

To these immoral unions were added jealousy, fights, robberies. The Hawaiians, who ordinarily are so sensitive to others' miseries, were losing all feeling. Hardened to suffering, the healthier ones took food away from those too weak to stop them. They knew they could get by with it, for they had nothing to lose. Their overseers, themselves patients, were often no better and connived at these practices.

What did the authorities do about this anarchy? Were they aware of what was going on in the internment camp? Or were they absorbed by the difficulties of a native state that was coveted by foreigners, expert in intrigue and force? Or were they short of money? Things always went along as though the administration had no other desire than to take this dangerous element out of circulation without being able to suppress them.

The Board of Health appointed a resident superintendent to the Settlement who was to be assisted by some of

the better disposed patients. The first of these superinten-
dents was a Frenchman named Leprat; it is not stated
whether he had Hansen's disease or not. Unable to control
the anarchy in the Settlement, he confined himself to reports to the Board on the uprisings and excesses he witnessed, and the lack of food, clothing, and shelter which
the patients were complaining about. He did nothing to
remedy the situation.

His successor was an ex-officer of the British army named
Walsh; his wife came as a "nurse." Firmer and more enterprising, he made things a little better by backing up his
orders with a police force recruited from the husbands of
some of the women patients. Unfortunately, neither he nor
his wife understood Hawaiian. He built a cottage for himself, a school for the children, separate dormitories for the
boys and girls, bettered the hospital menu and brought
milch cows to the island. Without doubt he would have
done even more if he had not died unexpectedly. Mrs.
Walsh replaced her husband but could not keep order.
An old retired sailor was named as her assistant; however,
they didn't get along and soon mutinies started again. Then
Kahoohuli, a patient and former captain of the Hawaiian
Royal Guard, was appointed director. Kahoohuli ruled
with an iron hand, severely punished the leaders, quashed
the revolt and at least for a while brought peace to the
seething colony.

This was the state of affairs when Lunalilo ascended the
throne in 1873. People were learning more and more about
Molokai and public indignation was mounting. A feeling
of pity swept the islands. The best elements were able to
register their protests in the press.

New Board members put through measures to separate
the healthy from the sick. Some tolerance was granted to
admit uninfected husbands, wives, and parents. The patients were treated better. Each week they received five

pounds of meat or twelve pounds of salmon, twenty-one pounds of *paiai* (made from baked taro roots; if it is thicker, it is *poi,* the main food of the natives), or five pounds of rice, seven pounds of biscuits and flour, and five pounds of salt.

The healthier patients were encouraged to farm — a profitable and distracting exercise, even lucrative. They were paid the regular prices for their produce. The better class went to work, and some of them even built cottages and tried to make their lives more pleasant. The hospital rooms were enlarged; beds were substituted for mats on the floor.

But the improvements were far from enough. Did the government have the means to make the big sacrifices that were needed? The obstacle the undertaking ran into at the very beginning was real and had far-reaching consequences.

Public opinion, which had been growing indignant over the neglect of the leprosy sufferers, loudly applauded the improvements. It also approved the suggestion made by a newspaper that the King go to the Settlement and find out for himself how they were being treated. Lunalilo limited himself to a message of sympathy which the *Hawaiian Gazette* printed on May 14, 1873.

A month earlier, on April 15, an outstanding writer, Walter Murray Gibson, who was to become head of his Majesty's government, had written in *Nuhou,* a Hawaiian vernacular newspaper of which he was editor: "If a noble Christian priest, preacher or sister should be inspired to go and sacrifice a life to console these poor wretches, that would be a royal soul to shine forever on a throne reared by human love."

Soon that appeal would be heard and his desire magnificently realized.

8   *Forever!*

THE sufferers at Molokai continued their bitter complaints and stubborn resistance to all governmental measures regarding them, and looked for compensation in a mad chase after vice. Not all of them, however. If there was a group in an isolated place, nicknamed "the village of Fools," who let their passions run wild in games, dances, drunkenness, and debauchery, there was also a group of Catholics who were more restrained, more resigned and decent.

Mindful of his responsibilities, Bishop Maigret was very much concerned about them. Now and then he sent them a missionary from one of the neighboring islands. On the southern part of Molokai beyond the *palis* were two hundred Catholics scattered up and down the valleys. For two or three days a year a priest would come over from Oahu or Maui to give them the sacraments. With the increasing number of patients in the prison in the north, priests came oftener and stayed longer. In 1871 and 1872 Father Raymond stayed several weeks; Father Aubert also came.

All the natives had for religious services were miserable grass huts, so they kept after the Bishop for a decent church. He decided it would be better to build it at the Settlement, as the people there were in greater need and closer together.

Brother Bertrand, the improvised master-builder, tells us how they did it. Out of some four hundred leprosy patients, a hundred or so were Catholics. These Catholics among the patients appealed to their fellow Catholics throughout the archipelago for help. Natives and foreigners contributed. The mission added what was needed to the four hundred dollars the people had donated.

But who would do the building? The Sacred Hearts Brothers who knew anything about such work were busy on Hawaii or Maui. They lighted on Brother Bertrand, a humble printer, but happy to be helpful. He and a native assistant got the material together, and after a rough trip landed at Molokai. This was in 1872. Six weeks was all he needed to put up the chapel. Father Raymond blessed it in honor of St. Philomena. They had twelve baptisms that very day.

From then on the Catholic patients — without a priest — gathered in their church on Sundays to recite the Mass prayers and the Rosary. They even asked for the Stations of the Cross to learn patience from the contemplation of Christ's suffering.

While Brother Bertrand was building the chapel, the Christians kept saying: "Talk to *Lui Ka Epikopo* [Louis the Bishop]. Tell him it is isn't enough for us to see a priest once a year. We've got a lot of time to die between visits! How are we going to save our souls without a priest?"

Father Boniface came down to the Settlement the following Lent. Eighty-six Christians made their Easter duty and an old prayer leader from Oahu had such an edifying death that the Father sent details about it to his Provincial:

God seemed to have prolonged his life to give him a

priest and the consolations of religion. In spite of unspeakable sufferings, the dying man had perfect resignation. He clasped a crucifix, his rosary and prayerbook, which he kept saying were the most precious things he had in the world. While I was giving him Holy Viaticum, he held his prayerbook with the two fingers he had left to say the prayers before and after Communion. He asked me to help him to his last breath. His agony continued till the next day. Three old people were so touched that they asked to be baptized right away.

All this and many other things, the Bishop knew. He studied the problem of a resident priest and hesitated. Sacrifice a priest to them? Weren't they all indispensable in their important districts? And then . . . the post was really dangerous! A man could catch the disease. This is not to imply, however, that the missionaries were afraid of being sent there. Father Aubert, for example, had written to him in December, 1872, stating very firmly: "Since you lack the courage to put a priest there, I am going there without orders, if you do not forbid me." The Bishop's answer was clear: "Stay where you are." The prelate was taking his time. It was a hard decision.

May 4, 1873, he consecrated a beautiful large church at Wailuku, Maui, which had taken six years to build. Among the Sacred Hearts missionaries who attended from neighboring districts were Fathers McGinnis, Leonor, Rupert, Boniface, Gulstan, Gregory, and Aubert. Father Damien hurried from Kohala to join them and see his brother priests.

There are many versions of the scene of the Bishop's declaration that he had finally decided to send a priest to Molokai. We give the account of Father Aubert Bouillon, an eyewitness. During an informal conversation, the Bishop turned to the four young priests: Fathers Damien de Veuster, a Belgian; Gulstan Ropert, a Frenchman; Boniface Schaeffer and Rupert Lauter, Germans. He told them of his anxiety over the sufferers at the Settlement who were becoming more numerous every day. No one on the islands needed a pastor more than these poor, sick, and dying outcasts. He rather vaguely expressed his desire not to name any priest in particular.

"Bishop," the four priests answered, "say the word and any one of us will go to the Settlement."

"Couldn't you set up a sort of rotating system?" he asked. "Then you could take turns replacing each other."

The priests agreed. They would each stay three months at Kalawao and at the same time keep their districts on Hawaii and Maui.

Professor Charles Warren Stoddard of Notre Dame University* says Father Damien offered to remain there. Be that as it may, Father Damien went first. As Bishop Maigret had to get back to Honolulu, he went with Father Damien to Molokai which was on the way.

"Remembering that I was covered with a funeral pall the day of my religious profession, here I am, Bishop, ready to bury myself alive with those poor unfortunates. Moreover I know many of them personally." These words have been attributed to Father Damien. But even if he has not said them, they do express his inmost thoughts.

Proof of it can be found in two letters he wrote, one to his brother Pamphile in November, 1873, the other to Bishop Koeckemann in October, 1885:

> The Settlement absolutely had to have a priest, but it was a difficult thing. All contact was strictly forbidden, at least as far as staying with them was concerned. Having already lain under the funeral pall on

---

* Prof. Stoddard, a convert, visited the Settlement in 1868 and again in 1884. His book *The Lepers of Molokai* did much to establish Father Damien's true position in public esteem. He also wrote *Father Damien, a Sketch* (1903).

the day of my religious profession, I believed it my duty to offer myself to His Excellency "who did not have the cruelty," he said, "to command anyone to make this sacrifice."

Later, when Father Damien suffered keenly from his priestly solitude and was on the point of going to Honolulu to tell his troubles to his new Bishop, he reminded himself: It was due to the memory of having lain under the funeral pall 25 years ago, on the day of his vows, that he had the courage to face the danger of catching the terrible disease by doing his duty at Molokai and trying to die to himself more and more.

He was not like the relatives of the patients who felt no repulsion; he had to overcome himself and approach them at the risk of getting the disease.

Joseph Dutton later testified that when Father Damien gave leprosy patients the sacraments and took care of them at Kohala, and when he heard their confessions he felt his skin prickle and burn. Four years before coming to Molokai he had written to Tremeloo: "Leprosy is beginning to be widespread here. A great number of the natives are infected. It doesn't kill them, but cures are rare. This disease is very contagious." There's no doubt that he had heard the cries of despair, had watched the police take them away, and more than likely had even helped fugitives hide out. His interest in them had been growing day by day.

Even before the Bishop's invitation — an *invitation*, for it certainly was no order — he had heard already another compelling invitation within him assuring him of God's will. In April, 1873, he had told the Father General:

By order of the Board of Health all the leprosy victims they could collect have been sent to the Settlement of Molokai, as to a government prison. Many of our

Christians here at Kohala also had to go. I can only attribute to God an undeniable feeling that soon I shall join them. However, eight years of service among Christians you love and who love you have tied us by powerful bonds. Even just joking about my going to Molokai upsets them.

When I boarded ship for Wailuku, the same voice told me that I would not return to Kohala and that I would never again see our dear children or the four beautiful chapels I built. It was with tears in my eyes that I left my dear Christians.

Shortly after the Wailuku celebrations, Bishop Maigret and Father Damien boarded the *Kilauea* which was carrying fifty leprosy victims and some cattle to Molokai.

It was Saturday, May 10, 11:00 a.m. Here is a description of the arrival at Molokai: Leaning on the ship's rail, the Bishop and Father Damien caught sight of the gray cliffs of the *palis*, with its green patches of straight up-and-down undergrowth. Soon they could see the Kalaupapa beach and behind it some huts and the wooden landing pier. When the patients learned they had arrived, those who were able ran to meet them. "Our neophytes surrounded us," the Bishop related, "their rosaries hanging around their necks." The patients were not complaining now about their food or clothes which were somewhat better, thanks to the new Board of Health. The big thing they lacked was a priest to live with them. To make sure a priest would remain with them, during the few hours the Bishop was there, 200 Catholics presented a signed petition asking the prelate for a resident priest. Their joy was boundless when "Louis our Bishop" presented the priest who had offered to stay among them. Doubtless he would remain at the disposal of his superiors, but they would no longer be alone. Many of them threw themselves at the Bishop's feet, weeping. He was sick at heart.

Father Damien had come for a few months only. Others were to come to relieve him. This system of rotation would guarantee them a priest all the time. Yet, the mysterious assurance in his heart that urged Father Damien to stay at the Settlement necessitated his Superior's approval. This prudent scruple explains the letter that went out faithfully each week to the Provincial. On May 12, only two days after his arrival, he asked Father Modeste if he would get Father Gulstan to watch over his district at Kohala "until he returned," but eagerly added, "provided you have not found some one to replace me definitely, for I am willing to devote my life to the leprosy victims. It is absolutely necessary for a priest to remain here. The harvest is ripe. The sick are arriving by the boatloads. They die in droves!" He had left home with nothing but his breviary. "Send me some wine, hosts, religious books and some for study, rosaries, shirts, pants, shoes, a sack of flour, a bell and a razor."

Because of the circumstances, the living quarters in his mission were primitive to say the least. "While waiting for you to send me wood to build a house, I am living under a puhala [screwpine or pandanus] tree."

Eight days later he was hard at work, as though he were installed for life: "There's something to keep me busy from morning to night. On my list I have two hundred and ten Catholics and eighty catechumens. Yesterday, high Mass, superb singing, many Communions, and since I arrived crowds of confessions." And the burning question — "Tell me if you and the Bishop have picked out the lucky priest who is to stay here and gather this ripe harvest for the Lord. All repugnance toward the sufferers has disappeared."

Father Modeste answered the same day: "We haven't made a final decision yet. You can stay at Molokai as your devotion dictates until you receive new orders."

People have remarked on the frequency of Father Damien's letters to his Provincial from the time he got there. He was most obedient and wanted approval, but clearly, persistently, he kept reminding the superiors not to ignore or forget that he wanted to stay at Molokai. He announced to Father Modeste that in one of the valleys he had discovered a group of Catholics who hadn't seen a priest for ten years. "While giving Extreme Unction to a student from Ahuimanu, Zepherini, I found that his foot was being eaten by worms. Poor boy! He is suffering greatly; but I hope he will go straight to Heaven." That ought to soften the Provincial.

Some days later he had to make excuses for not yet visiting the natives beyond the *palis*. There were 200 Catholics outside the Settlement whom he was going to see later, but visiting the sick right now was "taking four or five days from morning to night."

It was May 28, only eighteen days after Father Damien had landed. During that time he had been causing quite a stir elsewhere — in Honolulu society — in the papers — with the major superiors. This, along with his insistence, and perhaps that of others, more or less forced the superiors to arrive at a decision.

Tuesday, May 13, *Nuhou*, Gibson's paper published an article:

A Christian Hero. We have often said that the poor outcast lepers of Molokai, without pastor or physician, afforded an opportunity for the exercise of a noble Christian heroism, and we are happy to say that the hero has been found. When the *Kilauea* touched at Kalawao last Saturday, Bishop Maigret and Father Damien, a Belgian priest, went ashore. The venerable Bishop addressed the lepers with many comforting words, and introduced to them the good father, who had volunteered to live with them and for them. Father Damien formed this resolution at the time and was left ashore among the lepers without a home or a change of clothing except such as the lepers offer. We care not what this man's theology may be, he is surely a Christian hero.

The following day, the *Hawaiian Gazette,* a newspaper favorable to Protestantism, editorialized: "What they need now are a faithful minister of the Gospel and a physician who are willing to sacrifice themselves for the good of this unfortunate community."

On his return to Honolulu, Bishop Maigret was thanked by some of the most prominent people. The news had gone all around the capital and the impression it made was profound. The papers played up the fact that Father Damien had gone there hurriedly and without resources: "Without a home or a change of clothing except such as the lepers offer." A collection to help him brought in $130 in one day. A notice to this effect appeared in *The Advertiser.* In less than a week he was "the hero of Molokai" throughout the islands. This was a title he never gloried in: "They are talking about me in the papers," he would say later on; "it would be better if they kept quiet. Things here are much more serious than any esteem they might give me." That was the way he looked at it.

"Hero of Molokai" was also a title that never ceased to gall some other people. The stir produced by his devotedness was interpreted by some non-Catholics as a reproach to them. In the May 24 and 31 editions of *The Advertiser,* letters were published from readers trying to prove that Protestant ministers had already been working among the lepers.

All this talk about his subordinate astounded Father Modeste. He could find no human explanation for it. In his important letter of May 28, to the Father General in Paris, he attributed it to divine Providence. Without going into any special eulogies over Father Damien he noted that, a short time before, the papers had not breathed a word about Fathers Boniface and Raymond's stay at the Settlement nor of Brother Bertrand who had built a chapel there. For them, silence; for Father Damien who had hardly gotten there — loud public admiration. "Everybody is talking of his devotedness, of the danger to which he is exposing himself. They admire his courage, praise his sacrifice of living with them without shelter and even basic necessities." To head off any suspicion of negligence, he hastened to mention that all the Hawaiian missionaries traveled without provisions. Besides, the chance had been too good to miss — the boat Damien sailed on had just taken on a shipment of cattle at Maui for the Settlement. Father Damien had not foreseen this, so he didn't have any baggage with him. But the fact had so struck everybody that they had taken up a collection.

Father Modeste was not easily given to admiration. In his eyes all his religious stood on equal footing and he had the same yardstick for measuring their worth. The rest he left to God. For him, at Molokai it was a question of suffering Christians, therefore of "Our Christians" who would no longer be abandoned. Father Damien — or someone else, it made no difference who — was going to take care of their souls. He would teach them, sanctify them, say Mass for them. If God did not think it wise to cure them of their physical ills, Christ had poured out His blood to cure them of their spiritual afflictions. "Note well," he added just to keep the record straight, "without underestimating Fr. Damien's devotion, I ought to tell you that several of our priests have asked for that post permanently." The Bishop and he had not wanted to leave a priest in residence there. They hadn't sent Damien to stay, but in view of the circumstances that brought him there, the good effect it had on the public, the need of helping the dying, they had thought it best to leave him there. He could come to Honolulu overnight when he wanted to go to confession.

The case was won! Moral necessity forced his superiors to agree to Father Damien's request. At the end of June or the beginning of July, he came to Honolulu. He saw the Bishop and very probably his Provincial who confirmed his orders in good and proper form. To pretend that Father Damien installed himself in this heroic spot against his superiors' wishes, that he had been obstinate and self-willed, is miles away from the real facts and sheer fantasy.

The man who invaded the lazaret of Molokai on May 10, 1873, had a physiognomy which demanded and well repaid attention. He had an energetic temperament and was impatient of any obstacle to his high and essential duties. He was neither fault finding nor repellent. He was "all things to all men." His flock had no servile fear of him. His was a jovial and pleasant disposition. He liked a bit of drollery and kindly raillery. On occasion, what a laugh he had! It was spontaneous, gargantuan, issuing forth from his heart. Yet, withal, he was extremely sensitive. Woe to the man who interfered with an affair which absorbed the fiery ardor of his heart. Truly, he did not have such a bad character. In a word, he was a man of action, filled with a pure and burning zeal for his lepers — at once his brethren and his children.

This sketch given to us by Dr. Mouritz stands in violent contrast to the portrait presented by other physicians, amateur and professional, who wrote from preconceived notions and with the air of distinguished "know-it-alls." These arbitrary and dogmatic opinions cannot stand up to the facts. Also, the practical results of the efforts expended at the leprosarium by these latter physicians were negligible in his opinion and in the opinion of others. Among these "others" was Gibson, the writer, statesman, diplomat, long-time president of the Board of Health, and head of the Hawaiian government, who declared publicly: "In order to cure the Hawaiian race of its ills it requires the spirit of divine love, not the stern, scientific methods of London, Berlin, Paris, New York or elsewhere."

The young 33-year-old missionary with nine years' experience to his credit could thank his lucky star for being sent to Molokai. He was fearless, energetic, unusually strong, full of drive and optimism, discounted his sacrifices, and was capable of carrying out the most difficult assignments. The future looked bright.

While being humble about it, Father Damien was convinced he had that spirit of divine love Gibson spoke about. It was precisely this divine love that had made him become a religious and missionary. It was this love that had urged him to come to the Settlement and had opened his heart, his eyes, and his arms to all the needs and sufferings of his pitiful charges. If goodness always communicates itself, the same virtue reveals itself in different ways in different people. The man who came to Molokai had a way of drawing people to himself, of warming and stealing their hearts. It is useless to say that he was a man of refinement, of sweet and delicate charms, because he was not. Enough to say that the arrival of this good-natured, healthy priest completely changed the atmosphere of the Settlement. The poor people quickly sensed that they had found a true friend. They were no longer orphans. A wave of hope swept through the colony.

Father Damien immediately started getting acquainted with the place and its occupants. Leprosy was not unknown to him. He had seen some of its victims at Kohala. But he had never been surrounded by hundreds of victims at all stages of the disease. Here a young girl tried to hide the ravages of the disease on her face. There an old man dragged his maimed body along like a begger in a Flemish painting. Everyone wanted to receive his handshake or alms. At times the frightening spectacle caused a rebellion of all his senses — his eyes meeting an array of deformed human beings . . . his ears split with their throaty cries . . . his touch frozen by the contact of rotting fingers . . . and the constant smell that seemed to come from the opened grave.

Every step he took revealed new miseries. Souls as well as bodies were suffering deep wounds. To relative material wretchedness was added complete moral misery; but we've waded through that already. It is easy to imagine that during the first weeks of his stay, he must have forced himself to tackle and retackle the tremendous task to which he was binding himself for the rest of his life. Edward Clifford, an enthusiastic biographer and eyewitness of his zeal, ascribes to him the words he used to repeat to himself in typical Flemish style: "Come on, Jef, my boy, this is your life's work!" Words that amounted to a vow of consecration to the inmates of the Settlement.

When Damien first arrived, he prudently refused to sleep in the patients' huts. He made his home under the branches of a puhala tree near his chapel. This initial prudence made Dr. Mouritz remark: "Now, had Damien maintained the same attitude toward contact with leprosy throughout his period of residence at Kalawao as he did on his arrival [when he declined to live in a room where lepers lived], the history of Damien, 'the martyr priest of Molokai,' would in all probability never have been written."

The same specialist tells, however, what to expect if you sleep under a puhala tree:

The puhala tree generally and by preference selects

rocky ground to germinate, its aerial roots and their surroundings afford a choice nidus (nest) for centipedes,
scorpions, ants, mosquitoes, roaches; and fleas carried
by mangy cats, dogs, and sheep, who seek shelter from
sun, wind and rain under its branches.

As if all this is not enough, sleep at night is also
interrupted by tree rats and noisy chattering birds, such
as the mynah and sparrow, and roosting poultry.

I once was compelled to spend the night under the
spreading branches of a puhala in the district of Puna,
Hawaii, whilst I did not have all the vermin companions
I have enumerated, I had some of them and hereafter
would always advise any traveler or wayfarer not to
camp under a puhala tree.

First night at Kalawao. All alone . . . his small crucifix
. . . his breviary . . . his spare shirt . . . all alone . . . camp-
ing out on the ground . . . on the threshold of his life's
penance . . . a night more beautiful than the vigil of a
crusader. . . .

Damien lay there and thought over all the demands
that would be made on him. His material job — daily visits
to the sick, getting them better food and shelter, medicine,
bandages, clothing, trying to get some semblance of sani-
tation in the place. And then his spiritual duties — his
words that could give them a spiritual shot in the arm, his
example (since he couldn't ask them to do anything he
wouldn't do), his priestly help to the sick and dying.

Before going into the history of what he did there, we
had better clear up Father Damien's juridical position at
the Settlement. Strictly speaking, he was only the Bishop's
delegate, sent there to be a priest and pastor of the Catholic population, whether patients or not. In civil law, he
was a non-patient bound to obtain official authorization to
stay in the forbidden area. Later, when his Provincial lost
his head and, carried away by some unknown motive

(we'll try to see why), said: "He acts as though he were director, doctor, factotum, and gravedigger of the Settlement . . . and he's none of them," he bolstered up his thesis by falling back on this abstract formulation of the law.

Nevertheless, we must clearly understand that in the material organization of the Settlement, Father Damien had to respect governmental administration. The resources of the Settlement plus help from the state treasury should have assured its upkeep and smooth functioning.

At King Lunalilo's ascent to the throne (January 8, 1873), the original Board of Health was dissolved. The efforts it had made were weak and practically negligible. The boards that were to succeed it were always composed of a president, chosen from the government, a secretary, and several other persons, among them doctors and Protestant ministers. The Board was in Honolulu and controlled the Settlement. Any important business had to go through it. It appointed the heads of different posts in the colony.

The immediate head of the Settlement was Superintendent R. W. Meyer, one of the big landowners of Molokai, who was in charge for some 30 years. He lived with his large family at Kalae on the other side of the *palis* in the southern part of the island and went over to the Settlement only now and then. He was in complete charge of administration and was assisted by a resident superintendent. The latter, often a patient himself, directed all the other employees both white or native. All were paid by the state and the salary was proportioned to their unenviable job. The patients, far from appreciating their good offices, especially at the beginning, poured out most of their wrath, recrimination, and rebellion on them. Most of the patients had little confidence in anyone or anything; and what little they did have was sparingly measured out to their state officials.

As has been mentioned, the new Board of Health in

1873 enacted strict measures to keep healthy persons away from the diseased. Husbands, wives, and parents had been given too much latitude in joining the sufferers. This was stopped on the pretext of preventing contagion. Persons who did not have leprosy were forbidden to go to that part of the island. As such a person, Father Damien's case came up.

How would the Board settle it? We must remember that the majority of this organization was then made up of Protestant ministers, some of whom were both apprehensive and jealous. They were apprehensive because being married they feared contagion (which is quite understandable) for themselves and their families. Very rarely did they get to the island. They were jealous because they found it hard to swallow the eulogies the newspapers poured out on the Catholic priest. In the course of our story we will be forced in a number of instances to mention the jealousy and antagonism of Protestants and Protestant ministers. This is an unpleasant phase of the story, but one that cannot be entirely overlooked. Yet, that this was not the reaction of all Protestants to Father Damien will be very evident from the wholehearted and generous support, and the admiration accorded him by Rev. H. B. Chapman and countless others of all faiths and of none.

On the grounds of civil legality, the priest had to get official authorization. On the grounds of religious legality, a priest has a right to exercise his ministry. As things worked out, it never occurred to Damien to ask for the civil authorization needed. Had the Board let it be known they were against him, they would have become the target of public ridicule since the whole archipelago was praising him and did not so much as suspect that the board might hesitate to throw the doors wide open to him. They hit on an acceptable, in fact an excellent, solution. They wouldn't chase him out but they would forbid him to leave "for fear of spreading the disease outside." The idea was that Damien would refuse to be a prisoner and would leave of his own accord.

Here is the official prohibition not to leave Kalawao:

Department of Interior
Honolulu, Sept. 1st, 1873

Rev. Fr. Damien,
Kalawao, Molokai
Sir,

At the latest meeting of the Board of Health it was reported that at different times you had left the Leper Settlement and visited other parts of the Island of Molokai, returning again to the Asylum.

The secretary was instructed to write to you that complaints had been made by natives whose homes had been purchased in the leper settlement by the Board for the use of the Asylum, that they were debarred from the privilege of visiting their old homes and friends, a privilege which others seemed to enjoy.

By the official notices of the "Board" as published on the 10th Febr. and 18th June, 1873, all communication with the settlement was strictly prohibited, as by law the Board was authorized to do by the Act to prevent the spread of leprosy, approved July 19th, 1870, excepting only such agents of the "Board" as it might find absolutely necessary to send from time to time to furnish supplies or to regulate the government of the settlement.

The "Board" however presents no objection to the permanent residence of any minister of religion who may be willing to minister to the spiritual wants of the lepers.

The prohibition above referred to has been fully carried out and with great benefit to the Settlement and general public; and I am directed to ask you not to embarrass the Board by disregarding their regulations which have been so strictly enforced in all cases except your own.

All ministers of religion who have made applications

for permits to visit the Asylum have been refused; and, when the reasons were given they fully and cheerfully acquiesced in the action of the Board.

> I have the honor to be
> your obedient servant
> Charles Gulick
> Secretary, Board of Health

From this stern command Damien suffered terribly. The prospect of not seeing his superiors or fellow missionaries any more was hard on him. But what bothered him most was not being able to go to confession. As he saw it, he was a weak man like everybody else. He couldn't stand for months to elapse between confessions. Most religious went to confession once a week, and he couldn't even go once a month. Father Damien had a very delicate conscience. We'll see that his cruelest and greatest sacrifice was to be continually deprived of a confessor.

About July 1, he had gone to Honolulu precisely to go to confession and to plead his case in person with influential people who understood what he was doing. He talked to his Bishop and then went to see Edwin O. Hall, then president of the Board of Health. In the course of the conversation, Hall in a polite way told him of the June 18 decree which forbade all contact with the Settlement. Then wanting to show that his was a princely nature, he decided to have the priest classified as a real leper. Since he had decided to stay at Molokai, then let him stay. "Since you've gone there, don't leave any more, so you won't spread leprosy elsewhere."

In September, the steamer stopped at Kalaupapa with the usual load of provisions and patients. Knowing how badly Father Damien wanted to see him, the Provincial had come. He started to land, but the captain told him: "I have formal orders to stop you." Damien came out in a boat and prepared to board: "Stay back! Stay back!" the captain shouted at him. "I've been strictly forbidden to let you see anyone!"

The poor priest felt this was an injustice. Suspicion was soiling the purity of his work. The two priests tried to carry on a conversation at a distance. No one on board knew French. Father Modeste leaned over the rail while Damien went to confession in French. Doubtless the Hawaiian sailors respectfully moved away and others made the sign of the cross as Damien received absolution down below.

Some weeks later Father Aubert wanted to come from his mission at Maui to visit his confrere. He put on secular clothes so he wouldn't be recognized and went to Kalawao from the south end of the island. "Around midnight," he wrote, "I slid down the mountainside on my hands and feet for about three hours." His mission accomplished, he went back the same way he came, believing he had passed unnoticed. But the Board's spies were awake. "When I got back home, I received a visit from the police. I'd been reported to the Government who in turn complained to the Bishop. It was known all over Honolulu, but public opinion was on our side."

Bishop Maigret was indignant and lodged a protest with the top authorities over his subordinate's confinement. He received a letter from the president of the Board in the following straightlaced terms:

Department of Interior
Honolulu, November 4, 1873

Rt. Rev. Louis Maigret
Bishop of Arathea
Rev. Sir,

Your communication of October 31st was received on the 3rd inst., in which you say you have heard that the

Rev. Damiano has been forbidden to leave the lands of Kalauao and Kalaupapa, and that if he did leave those lands, he would be arrested by the police as a criminal.

A letter was addressed to the Rev. Fr. Damien on the 1st of September of which the enclosed is a copy, and that is the only action the Board of Health has taken in regard to him individually.

You are aware that the Board of Health has set apart the places you name, as an Asylum for lepers, and that public notice of the fact has been continuously published in the Hawaiian and English languages, since the 18th of June, 1873. ISOLATION of those unfortunate persons afflicted with leprosy has been deemed by the medical faculty the only hopeful means of eradicating a disease which as you are aware has spread throughout the Kingdom to such an extent that over 800 cases have been gathered together on Molokai. ISOLATION therefore was the prominent object before the Board, as it doubtless was also in the legislature, which passed the law conferring such extensive powers upon the Board of Health.

As you may readily believe, to effect as complete isolation as possible and thus to eradicate the fatal disease has been most truly a heart-rending task to the Board of Health. Nothing in all the past experience of life has so taxed the feelings, or so deeply stirred the sympathy of the heart as the appeals of husbands and wives, parents and children, to be allowed to accompany their friends, or to visit them at the Asylum. And you will appreciate the difficulties of the situation, should exceptions be made to the general rule deemed necessary to effect the object so imperatively demanded by the public safety.

Complaints of partiality could not be met, should the Board consent to a violation of its rules in respect to the isolation of lepers. It is by persons NOT LEPERS that the most urgent appeals are made, to visit their friends, and the whole object of the Board of Health could be frustrated were they to make exceptions.

Trusting that those explanations will enlist your sympathies for the Board of Health in their endeavors to execute impartially the wishes of the legislature; and thanking you most cordially for the approbation for the rules adopted by the Board, and the benevolent action of the Hawaiian Government in regard to the unfortunate case under consideration.

> I have the honor to be
> your most obedient servant
> Edwin O. Hall
> President of the Board of Health

They had not been able to throw Father Damien out directly or indirectly. He accepted his confinement indefinitely. His cloister walls were still a little elastic, so to speak.

The Board of Health tried to confine him exclusively to the Settlement. Not only was he forbidden to leave the island but even to circulate beyond the *palis*. This would keep him from taking care of the Catholics in the south. They were joining absurdity to injustice. He hit on the idea of getting protection from the French consul.

Only eight days after his stiff letter to the Bishop, the president of the Board, under pressure from the French Consul, saw the Minister of Foreign Affairs who modified the rigor of the decree. Here are extracts from the official documents:

The Commissariate of France to the Bishop Maigret

> November 16, 1873

Your Excellency:

I have the honor of transmitting to you two extracts of dispatches that I received, November 15, and treating of prohibitions made against members of the Catholic mission, prohibitions against which Father Damien had protested to me.

As you will note, in the *First Extract,* even though the prohibitions are lifted, there is in the last two lines (of paragraph two) an important notification about what concerns the future. As for the *Second Extract,* it contains the terms of the new decision and the request that you be informed of it through my good offices.

Theo. Bailleu, Consul of France

Sir,

Your communication of the 13th inst. is at hand in which you bring to the notice of the Board of Health, through Monsieur Theo. Bailleu, commissioner and consul for France, a complaint made by the Rev. Father Damien, to which the Board of Health can alone reply.

Without entering, at present, into an explanation of the trying difficulties with which the Board of Health has to contend, and which are already known to some extent to your Excellency, in order to effect the isolation of the lepers, as by Law provided, I embrace the present occasion to notify you, that at a meeting of the Board of Health held on the morning of the 13th inst. the following resolution was unanimously adopted, to wit: — "Resolved . . . that from and after this date, the rule relating to the Leper Asylum on the Island of Molokai, dated June 18th, 1873, is so far modified as to admit the visits of medical men and ministers of religion for the exercise of their functions of their office; the special permission of the Board of Health having previously been obtained."

Under the operation of this resolution, I trust the wishes of Mons. Bailleu will be fully met, and I would thank you through him, to inform the Bishop of Arathea that applications from him for any of the clergy, or from individual clergymen on their own behalf will receive the permission demanded by the Board of Health.

Signed:
Hall

His Excellency, Chas. R. Bishop
Minister of Foreign Affairs

This modification will, I am sure, be very gratifying to you, and to the Reverend Father, whose difficulties and wishes you have so kindly and earnestly presented, and I trust that nothing will occur in consequence of the modification of the rule, to give the Board cause to regret the change made.

Signed:
Bishop

Monsieur Theo. Bailleu
Commissioner and consul of France.

Following this exchange of letters, Father Damien wrote to the Board of Health to obtain the necessary authorization. Through the French Consul he received from the Board's secretary the following lines:

Department of Interior
Honolulu, Dec. 18th, 1873

Rev. Fr. Damien
Kalawao
Sir,

I am directed by His Excellency the President of the Board of Health to acknowledge the receipt of your letter of the 11th inst., and to say that you are hereby permitted to visit the Leper Asylum on Molokai from time to time as circumstances require, and you can show this to the Superintendent of the Asylum as your authority for so doing.

I have the honor to be
your obedient servant
Charles Gulick
Secretary, Board of Health

Father Damien interpreted the letter in the widest possible sense. Any time he thought it necessary, for the good of his patients, he freely went outside of the restricted area.

What in fact — if not in law — really were the strict

limits of Father Damien's mission? Father Reginald Yzendoorn, SS.CC., historian of the Hawaiian missions, gives us the answer. The sufferers' pitiful condition forced him to go beyond their souls and to take care of their bodies too. He found 800 poor unfortunates living in abject misery, crowded into their grass huts. Once he came upon a bunch of hogs eating the corpse of a man who hadn't been buried deep enough.

Dr. Mouritz, a scientific and humanitarian soul, wanted to limit his activity: "As for myself, I often had to tell the priest in no uncertain tone and language, 'I want no advice nor interference; mind your own business, attend to your own proper sphere of work, to wit, the spiritual welfare of the lepers; do not listen to the tittle-tattle and inane gossip of the Settlement.'"

The daily contacts which — in his own affectionate and devoted way — he had with his flock from the time he got there gave him an understanding of their needs of which the authorities had no idea or concern. In so many instances the latter could offer no remedy. From the very beginning, the sufferers seemed so neglected and abandoned that he wrote: "If I only had a dozen hospital Sisters, how they would help!"

During his first few months, he thought it was his duty to beg public charity to get his patients the little things sick people crave and which help lighten their pains. The Sacred Hearts Sisters at Honolulu had particular pressure put on them. Sugar, tea, biscuits, linen, clothes flowed from these charitable souls at the capital. "There's no welfare bureau here," he said, "non-Catholics and unbelievers who are paid each month are running the place. I make up for it within my means and strength. When I was at Honolulu I begged for them and got enough to clothe 300!"

His role of disinterested benefactor quickly won him

esteem and influence. No one was mistaken. He was a good shepherd and not a hireling. Every day people's affection and confidence were growing. "Everybody," he wrote three months after his arrival, "is beginning to see that the Catholic priest is a common father of the poor and unfortunate."

Even the Board of Health was not slow to see that, whether they liked it or not, here was a man they would have to do business with.

The more Damien realized the extent of his mission and the work he had to do, the more he felt his will setting. He was not going to let anyone intimidate him. He was a Fleming — and therefore a hard fighter — nothing and nobody was going to stand in his way. He showed this in the long bitter fight he carried on against the perverse elements at the Settlement.

He had no fear of the good-for-nothings, clandestine moonshiners, card sharks, thieves, petty intriguers, liars, and women of questionable morals. Still less did he fear a learned and serious man who held views different from his own. Dr. Mouritz declared: "His unyielding attitude on many affairs outside his own proper sphere of work brought him in conflict with the Board of Health." Of course, Mouritz was pleading his own case and consequently exaggerated. It's strange that in all the piles of documents of Father Damien's relations with the Board we find so few of the alleged conflicts.

The harsh and unjust command not to put his foot outside the Settlement did not seem to bother him too much. "All right. You do your duty," he categorically told the Board officers, "but understand I will do mine." Professor Stoddard is our witness. Charles Dutton certifies that when they notified him that if he left the Settlement, he would be arrested, he answered in a short, firm letter that he would leave the island when he pleased.

Father Damien was not a leprosy patient and there was no danger of his infecting others. A number of Catholics lived at Molokai outside the settlement and were without a priest. There were chapels there too. It did not matter to him that he had received an order not to go there. Without fear, without reproach, without defiance he simply crossed the borders when his people needed him. He could hardly violate orders without being seen by Superintendent Meyer, the chief of police, who was supposed to watch over arrivals and departures at the Settlement. Father Damien even stopped at his house. Meyer laughed and said, "I guess you know I have orders to arrest you on the spot." But Meyer knew the orders were given out of spite and did nothing about them.

Superintendent Meyer unceasingly favored Father Damien's apostolate. It is only right to give him due praise. Meyer was a German Protestant, wise and strong, a stranger to jealousy and prejudice. He was really worthy of his office as director of the Settlement the 30 years he held it.

When Dr. Mouritz speaks of the differences between Meyer and Father Damien, he is certainly exaggerating. According to him, his long residence at the hospital had made the Catholic priest arrogant, imperious, excessively overbearing. He would brook no interference in his own affairs and constantly meddled in those of others. His frequent interference with Meyer's directions often caused arguments and strained relations. Now, we have a considerable number of Meyer's letters to the priest and they clearly show that misunderstandings were rare and were quickly settled. That the Catholic priest and the Lutheran official did not always agree is quite probable. Their viewpoints were not the same, and their judgments about the patients and some of the employees differed at times.

Nevertheless, the letters prove that both were intelligent and honest and both desired the patients' welfare. Their friendship was unbroken.

The patients, it is true, had no love for Meyer and he, for his part, was not overly interested in them. Yet he was a conscientious official who did his duty well and was paid for it. For the rest he trusted almost entirely in Father Damien to do all he could at the Settlement. In the midst of his hundred and one occupations, the Superintendent would write such significant phrases as: "I need your valuable help, for you're the only one I can trust . . . I hope your word will soon reassure me. If I could leave, I would join you right away and we would have some nice talks together."

By the time a year had gone by, Father Damien's position was cleared up and improved. For his superiors, his mission field was definitely the island of Molokai. His confreres, as well as his superiors, were no longer thinking of his difficult assignment in terms of its spectacular side. The patients had a friend who would never leave them. Meyer had an extremely valuable helper, on the spot.

As for the Board of Health, what are we to think of their relations with Damien? Charles Dutton in his book *The Samaritans of Molokai* explains the situation by quoting Brother Joseph Dutton's frank description of certain of Father Damien's character traits. Damien was, in the words of the latter:

. . . vehement and excitable in regard to matters that did not seem to him right, and sometimes said and did things which he afterward regretted. I am safe in saying that, in all the differences, he had a true desire to do right, to bring about what he thought was best. No doubt he erred sometimes in judgment, as all of us do.

These things make his relations with the Government officials more readily understood. With some they were better than with others; with all better at times than at other times. In certain periods he got along smoothly with everyone, and at all times he was urgent for improvements, or what he thought were such. The carrying out of things done by the Government was facilitated by his actions. In some cases he made for confusion, as the various authorities would not agree with him. I believe that his efforts for the people here for material improvements have been beneficial to the place. In spiritual matters he did great good.

Charles Dutton then goes on to say:

We must remember that he was an energetic, impulsive priest from the Belgian peasant class. It casts no discredit on his memory to admit that the time when he volunteered to take his brother's place as a missionary in the South Seas was a time when the Church did not insist that its missionaries have the long technical schooling that is required today . . . Indeed, Damien did not have even the training of the average priest of his own time. No doubt he was a poor theologian— and considering what he had to do, it is probably just as well that he was;* no Louvain scholar would have been contented at Molokai.

The long adjournments, the endless formalities of the Board exasperated Father Damien. He just could not understand them. All he saw was his beloved sufferers and their crying needs. He had no other motive for his actions. With this in mind we can understand why the authorities

* This is the opinion of Charles Dutton. It does not seem to be borne out by the facts. For one whose formal training had been so curtailed, he showed a remarkable grasp of theology. *Trans. note.*

found him a stubborn, hardheaded, brusque, "officious" fellow. He was certainly all these things, but if he was, it was only because he had his eyes on essential things — the good of his people.

The Board that at first had not been able to stomach his presence was soon endorsing him, favoring him, considering him indispensable. The time would come when that body, headed by generous and intelligent presidents, like Gibson and George Trousseau, would seek to help him and to back him up in every possible way.

In 1879, Father Damien wrote: "The government is very good to me. Though the mission takes care of my needs, every week the Board sends me my part of the provisions just as for the patients." Bishop Koeckemann, the Vicar Apostolic, without commenting on the depths of their feelings, says the Board really was courteous to Father Damien. They considered the Catholic priest as the most powerful moral force in the hospital, acting as Meyer's confidential agent though he didn't have the office. His intelligence and ceaseless activity were making him indispensable. As a permanent resident, he had an on-the-spot knowledge of the needs of all the patients. At times he was too loyal, too conscientious, too well informed, for he let the Board know what ought to be done in no uncertain terms. That happened to be his way of asking for more justice and generosity in provisions and in the colony organization. The Board co-operated within the limits of its power and funds. Meyer didn't get along with some of his employees; virtue, honesty, and discipline were not exactly the order of the day at the Settlement.

The Catholic priest made the government's work a good deal easier. In fact, the Board decided to appoint him resident superintendent in November, 1877, when the post became vacant. The salary offered him was $10,000 a year. Indignant, he sent back a letter:

"If you presented me with a hundred thousand, I would not want it. If I had profit only in view, I would not stay here five minutes. Only God and His service of souls keep me here. Do you think that my mother would still acknowledge me as her son, if I consented to receive a salary for this kind of work?"

All that he would consent to, was to act in a temporary capacity until a new resident superintendent was appointed. We have two letters he wrote while he was temporarily in charge; the first in Hawaiian, the second in English:

Kalaupapa; December 1, 1877

To Kalaola, at Honokohau

Greetings!

The Board of Health has temporarily put me in charge of the lepers. Therefore I am sending Wawiki Capena Keonopolu to get the barrels you have prepared. Send the poi at once so that it will not spoil; if it is already bitter, add five hundred barrels of fresh poi, so that we can mix the old poi with the fresh poi. If you hurry them, would not the people at Honokohau be able to prepare our next poi for Monday or Tuesday at the latest? Thus it would be possible to send it to **us** by the next boat.

Set to work right away. If you furnish us good poi, we will often send the boat to you. As for the price, it will be that which was agreed on with Pela Ragsdale [Bill Ragsdale, the former resident superintendent], and which we paid the last two times.

We will be able to buy 1,000 or 1,200 barrels of poi from you; see that it is of good quality. Take the trouble of watching over the shipping yourself.

Very devotedly yours,
J. Kamiano
Director ad interim

The second letter was on behalf of a Hawaiian who wanted to join his wife who was a patient:

Kalauao; 13th December, 1877

His Excellency J. M. Smith
President of the Honorable Board of Health
Sir:

The bearer of this letter arrived here with a permit to stay two weeks; he has behaved himself in a proper manner by assisting his blind wife. His time being expired I send him away. He wishes to return after he has settled his family matters to aid and assist his blind wife; also, to make himself useful to the Board. If possible, grant his request.

Your most obedient servant
Fr. Damien
Provisional superintendent of
the Leper Asylum

His temporary job ended on February 25, 1878. This was a relief for him. The work was too absorbing and could be harmful to the spiritual duties to which he wanted to limit himself.

An act of kindness on the part of the Board that greatly encouraged Father Damien is worth recording here. One day, Father Damien sent his old wagon to a repair shop in Honolulu. Gibson learned of this:

November 20, 1882

Reverend Father Damien
Dear Sir,

You sent to town some time ago a broken down, and rather worthless vehicle to be repaired for your use at the Leper settlement. The Board of Health, highly appreciating the value of your services rendered so faithfully for the benefit of the unfortunates at the settlement, have authorized me to procure a new vehicle for your use, which I send by this opportunity; and, I beg your acceptance of the same, along with my affectionate regard and high esteem.

Walter M. Gibson
President, Board of Health

All the bridges between him and his old mission of Kohala were not so thoroughly burned that he couldn't get news from his former parishioners now and then. This is a letter he kept:

To my previous pastor, Rev. Fr. Damien
Dear Father:

I would like to let you know that things are not going the way they did when you were here. You helped us in every way; this is no longer the case at present. We will never forget what you did for us, and we hope you will not forget us. You were a good father to us. Now, people no longer go to church. There is no other news.

Give our best regards to our good friends at Kalawao and Kalaupapa. Please have the goodness to answer me.

Very truly yours,
C. Halumaile

During the course of the year a word of encouragement came to him from the Father General. This always means a great deal to a religious:

I thank God for the favor that He has bestowed on you by entrusting to you the sublime mission of Molokai. Without doubt, it has nothing that is agreeable to nature; this you can understand and appreciate; but, with the eyes of faith, you consider yourself fortunate to have been chosen to comfort our Lord in those poor lepers. In your devotedness, always have unshakable courage.

In November of the year of his arrival, **Father** Damien had taken time out from his busy schedule to write a long letter to his brother, Pamphile, giving him a detailed description of his coming to Molokai, and the nature of his work. It is invaluable for the insight it gives us to what went on in his soul the first months of his arrival:

Kalawao, November, 1873

V.C.J.S.

My dear Brother — God has deigned to choose your unworthy brother to assist the poor people attacked by that terrible malady, so often mentioned in the Gospel — leprosy. For the last ten years this plague has been spreading in the islands, and at last the Government found itself obliged to isolate those affected with it. Shut up in a corner of the island of Molokai, between inaccessible cliffs and the sea, these unfortunate creatures are condemned to perpetual exile. Out of two thousand in all, who have been sent here, some eight hundred are still living, and among them a certain number of Catholics. A priest was wanted; but here was a difficulty. For, as all communication was forbidden with the rest of the islands, a priest who should be placed here must consider himself shut up with the lepers for the rest of his life; and Mgr. Maigret, our Vicar-Apostolic, declared that he would not impose this sacrifice on any of us. So, remembering that on the day of my profession I had already put myself under the funeral pall, I offered myself to his lordship to meet, if he thought it well, this second death. Consequently, on May 11, a steamer landed me here, together with a batch of fifty lepers, whom the authorities had collected in the island of Hawaii.

I found on my arrival a little chapel dedicated to St. Philomena, but that was all. No house to shelter me. I lived a long time under the shelter of a tree, not wishing to sleep under the same roof as the lepers. Later on the whites of Honolulu having assisted me with their donations, I was able to build myself a hut, sixteen feet long and ten wide, where I am now writing these lines. Well, I have been here six months, surrounded by lepers, and I have not caught the infection. I consider this shows the special protection of our good God and the Blessed Virgin Mary.

Leprosy, as far as is known, is incurable; it seems to begin by a corruption of the blood. Discoloured patches appear on the skin, especially on the cheeks; and the parts affected lose their feeling. After a time this discoloration covers the whole body; then ulcers begin to open, chiefly at the extremities. The flesh is eaten away, and gives out a fetid odour; even the breath of the leper becomes so foul that the air around is poisoned with it. I have had great difficulty in getting accustomed to such an atmosphere. One day, at the Sunday Mass, I found myself so stifled that I thought I must leave the altar to breathe a little of the outer air, but I restrained myself, thinking of our Lord when He commanded them to open the grave of Lazarus, notwithstanding Martha's words, *jam foetet*. Now my sense of smell does not cause me so much inconvenience, and I enter the huts of the lepers without difficulty. Sometimes, indeed, I still feel some repugnance when I have to hear the confessions of those near their end, whose wounds are full of maggots. Often, also, I scarce know how to administer Extreme Unction, when both hands and feet are nothing but raw wounds.

This may give you some idea of my daily work. Picture to yourself a collection of huts with eight hundred lepers. No doctor; in fact, as there is no cure there seems no place for a doctor's skill. A white man, who is a leper, and your humble servant do all the doctoring work.

Every morning, then, after my Mass, which is followed by an instruction, I go to visit the sick, half of whom are Catholics. On entering each hut, I begin by offering to hear their confession. Those who refuse this spiritual help are not, therefore, refused temporal assistance, which is given to all without distinction. Consequently, everyone, with the exception of a very few bigoted heretics, look on me as a father. As for me, I make myself a leper with the lepers, to gain all to Jesus Christ. That is why, in preaching, I say we lepers, not my brethren, as in Europe. You may judge by the following fact what a power the missioner has. Last Saturday some of the younger people, discontented with their lot, and thinking themselves ill-treated by the government, determined on an attempt at revolt. All, except two, were Calvinists or Mormons. Well, I only had to present myself and say a word or two, and all heads were bowed, and all was over!

I have baptized more than a hundred persons since my arrival. A good part of these have died with the white robe of baptismal grace. I have also buried a large number. The average of deaths is about one every day. Many are so destitute that there is nothing to defray their burial expenses. They are simply wrapt in a blanket. As far as my duties allow me time, I make coffins myself for these poor people.

Don't send me any more intentions for Masses. I have more than I can manage. It is well known that we do everything gratis. But our good Master knows how to repay us. Or rather He has already repaid us. If our Lord were to ask me: *Quando misi vos sine sacculo et pera et calceamentis, numquid aliquid defuit vobis?* (When I sent you without purse, or scrip, or shoes, was anything wanting to you?) I should certainly have to reply, *Nihil, Domine* (Nothing, Lord). In fact, after leaving all I had at Kohala for Father Fabian, I came here without anything. I have not a penny of income, yet *nihil mihi deest* (I want for nothing). I have even alms to give away. How is this to be explained? That is His secret, who promised to give a hundredfold to those who gave up all for Him.

I have just built another chapel, two miles from this, at the other end of the settlement. This chapel costs me 1,500 francs, without counting my work as carpenter; and I am only 25 francs in debt. St. Joseph is my procurator. Our Sisters at Honolulu send me clothes, and some charitable souls do the rest.

A few months back the Minister of the Interior forbade me to set foot outside the leper settlement. I was then a state prisoner. Today, a despatch of the French Consul announces my liberty. Blessed be God! I can now not only take care of my lepers, but labor also for the conversion of the rest of the island, in which there is not yet any other priest. I ought to have a companion, but where can I get one? Pray and get prayers that the Lord may bless my mission.

Your brother in the Sacred Hearts
Damien

9 Priest at Work

EVERY active priest has to devote a considerable amount of his time to works of mercy — feeding, clothing, visiting, consoling, pardoning, guiding poor unfortunates. Molokai constantly made these demands of Father Damien and constantly he took care of them. The patients had to have food, clothes, houses, medicine, work, games. He became their confidant and their lawyer, their beggar and their banker, their representative, their nurse, their justice of the peace, their carpenter and their recreational director, their policeman, their constant friend and companion.

Meyer's administration, under the Board's direction, had intelligent and devoted workers, but it also had a lot of second-rate help that connived at evil and fouled things up in general. Damien couldn't help clashing with them. He threw himself into the fight to straighten out their mistakes, make up for their negligence, resist their immorality, and fight for the rights of his people.

When he came, the Settlement had been in existence seven years. During that time the number of people varied from 200 to 400. In 1873, the number went up to 800 and stayed in that neighborhood as the table on page 146 shows.

The table accounts only for patients; employees and people who accompanied their relatives must be added to it and there were about 100 of these, so Father Damien had a thousand parishioners more or less.

Deaths were an everyday thing at Molokai. The places left by the dead were quickly taken by newcomers landing from the *Mokili,* a miserable boat that crawled along at six knots, pulling in at Kalaupapa.

Year	Patients Admitted	Deaths	Men	Women	Total
1873	415	142	515	285	800
1874	78	141	455	266	721
1875	178	149	465	279	744
1876	75	119	432	262	694
1877	122	129	433	251	684
1878	209	111	477	305	782
1879	92	204	414	254	668
1880	51	151	352	216	568
1881	195	129	398	236	634
1882	70	111	369	224	593
1883	300	150	453	290	743
1884	108	167	430	252	682
1885	103	142	422	221	643
1886	43	101	389	191	580
1887	220	111	449	239	688
1888	571	236	643	368	1011
1889	307	149	722	444	1166

Not having official responsibility for the Settlement, the priest intervened when and where he could according to circumstances. He felt bound to undertake only "the most urgent tasks" from day to day. Piecemeal he got his work done.

Joseph Dutton describes him at work:

Drive ahead at what he thought was most important until he thought something else was more important, when he would jump into that. Thus he always left a track of unfinished jobs, though a certain share would be completed. It seemed sometimes that he tried to do more than one person could do or ever expect to finish. ... As things first occurred to him he would take his cue, and off he was, to use his most frequent expression. "Off I am, Brother Joseph!" he said to me daily, almost hourly, and always with the request that I finish what he was doing when the new project was suggested that called him off; that is, if it was a thing I could do, as usually it was. He seldom came back to the old jobs. By the time he finished, or before, something different would be quite likely to carry him to fields not thought of before; and then would come the expression, "Brother Joseph, you are going to finish these" — referring to the previous jobs. And he would laughingly add, "I am the carpenter, Brother Joseph the joiner." With me it was an almost constant finishing of jobs he started — carpenter, joiner, and various sorts of things — everything. My boyhood familiarity with tools and my having been in charge of army construction work served me well in these busy years. Very useful to me (and to him). . . .

He always rushed about. Yet, in his rushing way, he almost always stayed long enough to get my views about any kind of building work. It should be added that very little of the work done by Father Damien was wholly useless, though it was taken up hurriedly and carried out with the help of others. He had a way with his own work and the aid of others — a way of making things turn out all right, at least so that a thing would work, though very often it would be far different from what he had first intended. Sometimes the result would be amusing, but he would say, "Well, we can use it!" He always had great zeal and was ready to pursue with vigor whatever it seemed to him ought to be done. And he rather expected others to take his view. It made no difference whether it was his duty to do it; anything that he thought was good to do was his immediate action — he considered that it became his duty.

A good down-to-earth peasant, he refused to let himself be imposed on, and he lost none of his precious time in useless discussions and formalities. Instinctively he got to the bottom of things, overcame obstacles, saw what was necessary and did it. What good was it to hesitate, to discuss and hold up the work? There was work to be done . . . and right away!

No important government business at the Settlement was undertaken without including him. Even if he had had no idea about it, his advice would still be sought. He added his example to his advice — an example that put life into the healthier patients, for it was well seasoned with good humor and happy spirits. One of his fellow priests said of him, "He was the soul of every improvement." This is something; for we shall see later that at times this same confrere was strangely silent about his work.

FOOD AND CLOTHING

The colony was miserable when he came. The patients absolutely had to have good food, if not special food. What they got left much to be desired; for a long time it was food of a poor grade, insufficient, and unequally distributed.

Damien had been at Molokai ten years when he was still receiving letters like this from Meyer:

Kalae, February 21, 1884

My dear Father Damien,

I received your letter this morning and I am exceedingly sorry to hear of the distress of the poor lepers; but, I hope that by Sunday or Monday, the *Mokili* will be dispatched with a supply of provisions.

The fault is beyond my control; twice now, the *Lihuei* has passed by on account of some other trouble and I have been unable to send mails or anything to Honolulu.

I can't buy anything for the store; have no money; and can't get thus far even a dollar for all the ration bills of the present year, and half of the last; and, have also been promised a month ago a supply, but still have not received any.

The store in question belonged to the Board of Health. Patients with money could buy their own food and clothing, but they were a small minority. From many angles the poor patients were at a disadvantage; nor could the administration, entangled in red tape, make any exceptions in special cases.

The patients' relatives did not receive rations, so the food ran short, thanks to the way it was generously shared and thanks also to negligence and waste. One supply, however, never ran short, and that was at the missionary's own warehouse. Father Damien had set up a store where they could get supplies free. He kept his stock up from gifts to the mission and the boxes of "good things" from Honolulu. In the end he was getting public charity from everywhere. But don't think public charity to the leprosy patients ever imperiled the Islands.

The better-off patients preferred to live at Makanalua, halfway between Kalawao and Kalaupapa. The poorer ones, in order to spare themselves long trips, built their houses as close as they could to Father Damien's generous hand and his wonderful warehouse. There were to be found his boxes, his jugs, his barrels, his supplies. And they quickly learned that from now on, all they had to do was to line up at the door and knock. They used to say: "If we need anything, we'll go to *Makua Kamiano* (Father Damien) and he'll help us." With his sleeves rolled up and sporting his best smile, he had a welcome word for everyone and then he gave . . . gave . . . again . . . gave always — bread, biscuits, rice, sugar, eggs, tobacco, candy, even chickens when he had them.

Sure, some of them fooled him with imaginary needs which he readily believed; but he made no investigations. Nor did he show any resentment, for it was his theory that kindness was the best way to stop their crookedness.

However, it was really the business of the Hawaiian government and the Board of Health to supply food and clothing at regular fixed intervals; his own stock and goodness only supplemented them. Damien never ceased reminding the Board of the sufferers' rights and its duties. Some pretty reliable witnesses say he did this with or without nice-sounding words and his usual bluntness. He denounced abuses and offered criticisms. In or out of season he presented those in charge with strong advice, congratulations, encouragement, plans, and suggestions. He was really the spokesman and best friend of the patients. "We lepers," he used to say when speaking to them or about them, and that even before' he contracted the disease himself.*

At the request of Gibson, then president of the Council and Board of Health, he submitted in 1886 a first-rate document which shows us his real role. We have to keep the date in mind and remember that the picture he paints is a considerable improvement over preceding years.

---

* Most popular lives of Father Damien describe the supposed dramatic scene in which Father Damien, now a leper himself, turns around after the Gospel at Mass and says, for the first time, "We lepers . . ." There is far more drama in the historical truth. The facts of the matter are these. In November, 1873 — only seven months after his arrival at Molokai — Father Damien wrote to his brother, Father Pamphile, as follows. "As for me, I make myself a leper with the lepers, to gain all to Jesus Christ. That is why, in preaching, I say we lepers, not my brethren, as in Europe." (Cf. p. 143) *Trans. note.*

Damien submitted the following pertinent observations:

FOOD

The food on which a leper has to live exercises a great influence on the disease. Our Hawaiian *taro*, containing a great quantity of starch, and being easy of digestion, is our (sic) best vegetable. So far, I have never seen any bad effects from it, even in fevers and other temporary ailments to which our lepers are so often subjected. Hawaiian people in general, but especially our lepers, cannot go well without it. I remember that, some ten years ago, the place having been about three months without *taro* on account of the scarcity of that vegetable, several deaths occurred in consequence of it, and the majority of the people looked emaciated, although they had plenty of rice and sweet potatoes.

The administration having to supply weekly from six to seven hundred people, each with twenty-one pounds of cooked *taro*, a few words concerning the manner how it is obtained may be desirable.

At the northern side of Molokai are three large valleys, viz. Halawa, Wailau, and Pelekunu, in which the cultivation of *taro* is the chief business of a considerable number of natives. On them especially we have to rely for our regular supply. The high cliffs preventing all overland road traffic, the cooked *taro*, or *paiai*, has to be brought by sea either in open boats or a small schooner, as was done from the beginning, or in a small steamer latterly.

The steamer's service has been highly appreciated by the public on account of its regularity, schooners and boats being often prevented by calm or rough weather from arriving when the food is wanted; unavoidably, our people are then deprived of their good *poi*, which is left to rot where it was cooked, causing great loss to all concerned. If *poi* cannot be obtained, the issue of rice or hard bread takes its place, of which there is always a certain quantity on hand, though it is recognized that, with the exception of the Chinese, neither native nor foreigner could live on rice as principal food.

A certain number of our people, with their more or less mutilated hands, succeed in raising a few sweet potatoes, which answer well for a change in the diet, or in case of emergency. Unfortunately, some of our Hawaiians are much addicted to the use of a certain beverage made of sweet potatoes, which they allow to ferment, and thus obtain an obnoxious, intoxicating drink. They are very fond of it, but it makes them excited, and has a bad effect on their system, as have all other alcohols; and I wish to express here my sincere thanks to our local administration for having wisely prohibited the use of it.

Besides their regular food, a pint of good milk provides them advantageously with a wholesome, nourishing beverage in the line of diet. The question naturally occurs to the mind of the reader, how can a sufficient quantity of milk to supply such a number of people be procured? May I be allowed to explain my views on this.

This Settlement, in the greatest part, affording the best kind of grazing for stock, I would suggest to the administration with all my might to increase as much as possible the number of good milch cows. Unfortunately, on account of the great amount of meat wanted, about five thousand pounds a week, and the frequent failure of the arrival at the regular time of beef cattle, our butchers are sometimes obliged to kill off more or less of our valuable milk stock, which keeps the latter on a decrease, and therefore lessens terribly the supply of milk.

Let me regretfully state, it is now several years, up to the present day, that not one-tenth of our lepers outside of the hospital yard have been enabled to enjoy the benefit of a small daily supply of milk.

I beg leave to be allowed to make here a suggestion for the benefit of the Board of Health and for the lepers. May it be proposed at the next Legislature to make, besides the regular appropriations for the support of the lepers, an additional one, such as to provide the necessary means for buying at once as many head of cattle as our beautiful plain for grazing can support — say from 500 to 1000 head, of which a certain number should be used for breeding and milk, and the rest for beef cattle. In regard to salmon, as a substitute for meat, I simply will state that it may do once in a while, but the less the better.

Father Damien's sensible advice which was the fruit of his own experience was listened to, and they put his suggestions into effect in order to relieve the sufferers as much as possible.

CLOTHING

Nor did Damien neglect the important question of clothing. He stated in his report:

The Settlement being situated at the northern side of the island, and backed at the south by very high and steep mountains, the climate is naturally cool. The winter season brings forth generally a long spell of cold weather. The disease, too, at a certain stage, interferes much with the free circulation of the blood, and therefore our lepers often complain of cold. Those who have suitable and warm clothes to protect themselves from the inclemency of the weather resist it generally very well, but for those who, through neglect or destitution, have barely enough to cover their nakedness, the cold and damp weather has a bad effect. They then begin to feel feverish and cough badly; swelling in the face and limbs sets in, and if not speedily attended to the disease generally settles on the lungs, and thus hastens them on the road to an early grave. On my arrival I found the lepers in general very destitute of warm clothing. So far they had received from the administration a suit of clothes and a blanket; but some of them being very neglectful and filthy, in a few months nothing remained but rags. Those who had friends in the outer world were fortunate in receiving from time to time a few articles of clothing, but the friendless and the poor suffered greatly. There was no store at the time within the limits of the Settlement where they could buy a few garments or other necessities, and those who received or could earn some money had to entrust it to the captain of the schooner to buy for them what they were in want of.

We all greatly felt the necessity of a suitable market store, and on a very sound principle, the Molokai store was inaugurated by the Board of Health in the summer of 1873. To start with, a thousand dollars out of the appropriation was invested to lay in the first stock, and with a certain percentage above the cost price to cover current expense, the store has since then been running on its own account, supplying our people with any article they may wish to buy. Each year the Board issues an order for six dollars to each leper to enable them to buy at the said store whatever they are in need of, especially in the line of clothing. So far this store has proved to be a success and a great convenience to the people here, and we could not do very well without it.

Besides the allowance by the Board of Health, Christian charity has given us a helping hand in the matter of clothing, and assisted us to our great satisfaction. In previous years it was nothing unusual to receive from time to time a cart-load of clothing for distribution to the needy; for instance, such as were received a year and a half ago from the hands of Her Majesty Queen Kapiolani, and those who assisted her in filling the leper subscription. Thanks for the aid in the past. May the future prove that untiring perseverance of charity continues to assist the Board of Health in supplying the unfortunates of Molokai with all their necessities; especially with warm clothing, because, may I here remark that the yearly allowance of six dollars to provide clothes and other indispensable articles is quite insufficient for those who have no private means, and no friends or relatives to give them a helping hand. I beg to lay this statement, based on a long experience, before the honorable Board of Health for future consideration.

The allowance granted by the Board, combined with Christian charity and some private industry, of which I intend to speak hereafter, has greatly ameliorated the condition of our lepers and provided them with comparatively good clothes.

WATER SUPPLY

Father Damien even became a water commissioner. At first he had carried water in buckets for his people, but later drew up plans for a reservoir and finally water was piped into the Settlement. The people could bathe and wash their clothes, which was no small improvement. The remarks he made to the Board in his report show that he had looked the situation over very carefully and had it well in hand:

From the landing place of Kalaupapa up to Kalauwao*
we have no regular water stream. Fortunately, at the upper part of the Kalauwao valley there is one, but the water is not very abundant, though sufficient if properly managed, to supply this one village. When I first arrived here the lepers were obliged to carry their water in oil cans from that gulch on their shoulders, or on horses, under the greatest difficulty; there also they used to wash their clothes. The scarcity of water at that time accounted, to some extent, for their living very dirty.

In the summer of A.D. 1873, we received some water pipes, and all our able lepers were only too willing to help in laying them, and in building a small reservoir.

* Father Damien uses the old spelling throughout his report.

Since then Kalauwao has been well supplied with good water for drinking, bathing, and washing, and has been proved to be a better place for living than Kalaupapa, where the people continue to resort to rain or brackish water, and in dry seasons they are obliged to come to Kalauwao for it.

On studying this question of water supply, I was informed that at the terminus of the valley called Waihanau (water arise), which valley is located a little more than one mile southeast of Kalaupapa, there is a natural reservoir. At one time in company with two of our intelligent white men and some of my boys, I went to investigate the truth of it, and, after two thousand feet of traveling in the gulch, we arrived at this truly beautiful reservoir, built by Nature's hand in the form of a circular basin; its diameter in one direction is 72 feet, and 55 in the other.

On sounding its depth we found twelve feet of water at a short distance from the bank, and eighteen feet toward the center. The water being ice-cold, none of my boys dared to swim across to ascertain its true depth close to the high cliff, where probably it is deeper. The water looks very clear and has an excellent taste. I should remark here the statement which a native, who, during the period of ten years, has made it his business to deliver water to any part of Kalaupapa for a certain fee, made to me, viz.: "If no other source in the vicinity affords any water during very dry seasons, this basin has never failed to furnish any amount needed." The above statement was acknowledged to be true by a great many more of the old residents who had seen that reservoir and confirmed it. This, and the large overflow in connection with the drainage from above, leaves me to conclude that there must be a large feeding source below. This reservoir is perfect and permanent in itself, without incurring any expense or labor.

Now, instead of going to Waikolu to obtain a water supply for Kalaupapa, as was intended, which would

involve besides the difficulty of labor of building a
reservoir and for laying from such a distance, say over
five miles, the amount of pipe required for that purpose,
a very large expense to the Government, therefore I
simply recommended the laying of good pipe from this
Waihanau reservoir. The question of supplying water
for Kalaupapa has been for a long time under discussion,
and never thoroughly investigated, under the impression
that it would cost too much, and there the matter rests
at present.

My desire being to see the work carried on without
any further delay once I was sure of getting this supply
of beautiful water at a comparatively short distance, and
wishing to give all information necessary, I have taken
the pains to measure the exact distance, which I found
to be from the reservoir to the Kalaupapa storehouse
thirteen thousand six hundred and eighty (13,680) feet.
All this distance is an uninterrupted, gradual decline;
and having on hand a better reservoir, and a surer supply
of water than we have at Kalawao with a 2-inch pipe
for half the distance, and 1½-inch for the remaining part,
without a doubt the Kalaupapa village can be abundantly supplied with good, pure water. And having
here a man capable of executing such a work, with
many hands to assist him, I think that the expense above
the cost of the pipe would be but a trifle.

HOUSING PROJECTS

Of all his material labors, Father Damien found his
greatest delight in carpentry. Dr. Mouritz says: "Fr.
Damien was a jack-of-all-trades, but carpenter work was
his mania and recreation. He did good work, his good
physical development enabled him to work for hours with
little fatigue. Bath tubs, window and door casings were
his specialty, and were at the disposal of all."

He could work at his "specialty" to his heart's content.
In his report he told the Board:

In previous years, having nothing but small, damp huts nearly the whole of the lepers were prostrated on their beds, covered with scabs and ugly sores, and had the appearance of very weak, broken-down constitutions. In the year 1874, the great question was how to improve the habitations of the unfortunate people, the Government appropriation being at that time barely enough to provide them with food?

During that winter a heavy south wind blew down the majority of their half-rotten abodes, and many a weak leper lay there in the wind and rain, with his blanket and clothes damp and wet. In a few days the old grass beneath their sleeping mats began to emit a very unpleasant vapor. I at once called the attention of our sympathizing agent to the fact, and very soon there arrived several schooner loads of scantling to build solid frames with. All the lepers who were in distress received, on application, the square laths to thatch the grass or sugar cane leaves to. Afterward rough N.W. boards arrived, and also the old material of the former Kalihi hospital. From private and charitable sources we received shingles and flooring. Those who had a little money hired their own carpenters; for those without the means the priest, with his leper boys, did the work of erecting a good many small houses.

In 1878, after the inspection of the Settlement by a special committee, of which Your Excellency [Gibson, then a member of the Assembly] was chairman, sent by the Legislature to Kalawao, the Board of Health having obtained a larger appropriation by a special recommendation of that committee, at once erected a good many comfortable houses, and also provided several other comforts for the lepers of which they were greatly in need.

Lime has always been supplied by the Board of Health gratuitously for whitewashing the cottages, and thus, little by little at comparatively small expense to the Government, combined with private and charitable re-

sources, were inaugurated the comfortable houses which
constitute today the two decent-looking villages of Kalawao and Kalaupapa. I estimate the number of houses at
present, both large and small, somewhat over three hundred, nearly all whitewashed and, so far, clean and neat,
although a number of them are not yet provided with
good windows. These houses, of course, cannot have the
proper ventilation they need, and naturally create an unpleasant and unhealthy smell; I therefore humbly pray
that the Board will be kind enough to take steps and
see that this still-existing evil be soon remedied. In conclusion, I am happy to remark that, if I compare the
present with the past, the unfortunate people of today
are not only more comfortable and better off in every
respect, but their disease in general is a great deal milder
and less progressive, and, in consequence, the death rate
is not so high. This is greatly due to the improvement
in the houses.

And the improvement was greatly due to him. He would
take off his cassock, roll up his sleeves, and start to work
with the leprosy sufferers around him like a master carpenter surrounded by his apprentices. "I have seen him under
a tropical sun," writes James Sinnet, "covered with sweat
and dust, sawing and hammering away with his lepers."
Back and forth they handed him the hammer, saw, mallets,
rule, and compasses. They looked admiringly at his powerful muscles as he pounded nails, sawed, planed. He looked
as if he was playing a game. But if it was a game, it was
a heroic one as he worked on, ignoring the smells and
sores of his fellow workers and ignoring too the danger of
contagion.

Of course, the building project was not completed overnight. At the end of 1877 he was putting in orders for
wood, nails, tools, paint. Acting as banker for his people,
he drew up plans for them and either with or without their

help built little whitewashed homes for them. He wrote: "Several of our leper families being more in want of a house than of clothes have deposited in my hands their little treasures." In picking up the carpenter's tools, he knew he was undertaking a work of Christian mercy, one of which he could be proud: "I am not ashamed to act as mason or carpenter, when it is for the glory of God."

WORK AND RECREATIONAL PROJECTS

The patients' main work was farming since it was the most feasible occupation for them. They had complete success in this. From 1869 to 1873 they had spent all their time at Kalawao sleeping, drinking, eating, and playing cards. Few farmed. Later on when a tract of land at Kalaupapa was annexed to the Settlement, they began to grow sweet potatoes. Damien told the Board:

In regard to the wholesome exercises obtained by cultivating the soil, a few facts showing how it has been and should continue to be encouraged, may here be brought under observation. Soon after that piece of land mentioned above had been put at the disposal of the lepers, many whose hands were not too much mutilated began at once to plant a patch of sweet potatoes, and very soon had an abundant crop.

During the winter when the boats which had to supply the Settlement with *taro* were prevented from arriving on account of the bad weather, the local administration was fortunate enough to get a weekly supply of sweet potatoes from those who had a quantity at their disposal, and thus not only prevented a temporary famine, but the money usually paid to the outsiders for *paiai* was paid into the hands of our lepers, and, little by little, money came into circulation among the poor people. This being a great encouragement, very soon the majority had some potatoes of their own planted and shortly afterward they petitioned the local administration to obtain instead of their weekly rations its equivalent in money. This having been granted, numbers of lepers availed themselves of this opportunity to obtain cash to buy their little necessaries with.

As the number of patients grew and because of the climate, the government turned Kalaupapa into a branch settlement. Kalaupapa consisted of only a few native huts, a poor harbor, and a miserable path that straggled over to Kalawao. Under Father Damien's direction, the people undertook to build a road out of the path and to make a good harbor by blasting the rocks with dynamite.

The work must have started and stopped several times, since he wrote to the Minister of the Interior in 1883:

> At your request we have started the repairing of the government road at the Molokai settlement. The work is about half done and to encourage the laborers — please forward me the amount due as shown in this enclosed voucher — If convenient please deposit the money at R. W. Meyer. With the balance left I will try to finish the repairing there remains to be done.

The money must have been slow in coming. He again let the Minister know about it, at the same time suggesting a new project that was urgently needed:

Sir

In January last I was requested by the late minister of interior to carry out the repairing of the government road from Kalaupapa to Kalawao which was in very bad condition; $300 was the estimate required — and promised, which please have the kindness to forward me by R. W. Meyer. This enclosed voucher shows $152.20 due at the affixed date, the balance will be about the end of this month.

Mr. Meyer and I, we had today a look at the bad

rocks in our harbor. I know a man living in Halava who might do the blasting and I would say the interior department might assist the agent of the board of Health to pay the necessary expenses. A few barrels of cement will be required too.

> Very truly yours,
> J. Damien, Catholic priest

With the road built and the rocks gone, Kalaupapa was soon a village of beautiful little cottages surrounded by gardens and flowers, looking out at a good harbor and enjoying a fine climate.

Father Damien encouraged his people to become landowners, work their own little plots, grow flowers, buy a horse, and play music. The natives loved celebrations, and Father Damien gave them plenty by organizing processions and public games. He revived their taste for music and singing. The Fleming who remembered the Kermesses of Belgium, with their bass drums, trombones, bugles, and clarinets, organized a band. Soon the fifes, flageolets, and flutes made "of old sheet iron with holes punched in them" were replaced by excellent instruments from Honolulu. These born musicians were fully equipped.

This band caused no little stir. Joseph Dutton recalls how during one performance he saw a musician lose a finger, while another had part of his lip fall off but went right on playing. The lady organ player of 1886 had only the fingers of her right hand, so she used a piece of wood on her left hand to get the lower notes.

Father Aubert wrote: "I'll never forget the serenade they gave us in the moonlight. After supper we went outside. A hundred or so lepers were waiting for us with a lot of flags, four drums and a dozen other musical instruments. For two long hours, lepers with only 2 or 3 fingers left on their hands and their lips swollen, played all kinds of music to perfection."

Lovers of music and loud celebrations, the patients were once more getting joy out of life. Their mournful lack of interest disappeared, and even the immorality in part. Egoism, jealousy, and fighting were giving way to a healthy joy, and sympathy was uniting sufferers of the same misfortune. Without doubt it was a relative happiness, but you have to remember the Hawaiian's carefree, indolent spirit. His conditions were getting better every day. Devotion was conquering his trials. Now he felt he was surrounded by consideration and affection. The Settlement was no longer just a prison where he was stuck, as an undesirable, until freed by death. This part of the island looked like a farming district, with villages of whitewashed cottages surrounded by flowers. Along the roads, horses galloped and people carried on their business. It looked like a normal land where people lived a normal social life.

Horseback riding was well suited to their tastes. It was a good pastime, and it was healthful for them, since it increased their circulation and slowed the progress of their disease. Father Damien explained to the Board:

Leprosy is a constitutional disease by which, generally, the circulation of the blood is partially obstructed, the nerves and muscles more or less paralyzed, and the limbs are often disabled, in one place or the other, which varies in almost every case.

A person afflicted with leprosy, who quietly gives himself up to the ravages of the disease and does not take exercise of any kind, presents a downcast and sloughly appearance, and threatens soon to become a total wreck. Therefore exercise, as a daily occupation, is highly commendable to invigorate the system, giving a fresh impetus to the general movement of the muscles and to the free circulation of the blood, thus averting many pains, sores, and other consequences of a prostrated constitution.

In former days (from 1866 to 1873), all the lepers being collected at the rather small village of Kalawao, the majority of them passed their time in sleeping, drinking, and playing cards, while only a few others cultivated the fields; and horses being limited at that time, a minimum number only of the inmates could enjoy the exercise of a horse-back ride.

Later on, all that tract of land at Kalaupapa having been annexed to the Leper Settlement, traveling was at once increased to a great extent; going from one village to the other became not only a healthful exercise and pleasure, but a frequent necessity; horses too have increased, and are easily procured. This tract includes a very fertile piece of cultivated land — over two hundred acres are fenced in along the foot of the mountains. Every leper is privileged to occupy any vacant portion of it he may choose to cultivate, as some were already accustomed to do in the Kalawao fields.

Traveling on foot, riding on horseback, and cultivating the soil are the most healthy occupations of our lepers. Let me, therefore, bring to notice that, up to the present date, about nine-tenths of the entire population are enjoying these invigorating occupations and exercise, while previously only about one-tenth could do so. Such daily exercise as can be obtained here does not only strongly aid in checking the disease in its rapid progress, but also averts many ailments which otherwise might befall the victim. Inducements of this kind, in regard to daily exercise for the welfare of all afflicted which this Settlement affords, cannot likely be gotten up in any other asylum in the world.

THE RECTORY

Most of the fun and celebrations took place at the rectory which at first had been a large leafy pandanus tree where Damien ate and slept. The large flat rock which he is said to have used for a table is still to be seen next to the church.

However, benefactors in Honolulu soon sent him material to build a little twelve-by-fifteen-foot house. In 1878, his Provincial gave him permission to build "a real house" that would cost from fifty to seventy dollars. It was twenty-one by twenty-four feet, two storied, and had an outside stairway leading to the second floor. "You just couldn't have anything nicer," he confided to his Provincial. "If one of my friends from Tremeloo comes to see me, I'll have a place to put him."

In a letter to his family he assured them:

I live alone. Don't be afraid, the lepers aren't living with me. As for my meals, I eat only two a day, which are prepared for me by a woman who is not a leper. In the morning, I eat rice, meat, coffee and rolls. In the evening, I eat what was left from morning plus a cup of tea that I have to warm over a lamp. See, I'm not starving, and in fact, I live quite well. My chickens furnish me with all the eggs I need. I have so much work to do that I'm hardly ever home. I have to sacrifice sleep to write you.

For a time, then, Father Damien had a non-leper cook; but later he had to get lepers to cook for him.

Professor Stoddard furnishes us with a description of his chicken yard:

He [Father Damien] brought from his cottage into the churchyard a handful of corn, and scattering a little of it upon the ground, he gave a peculiar cry. In a moment his fowls flocked from all quarters; they seemed to descend out of the air in clouds; they lit upon his arms, and fed out of his hands; they fought for footing upon his shoulders and even upon his head; they covered him with caresses and with feathers. He stood knee-deep among as fine a flock of fowls as any fancier

would care to see; they were his pride, his playthings;
and yet a brace of them he sacrificed upon the altar of
friendship, and bade us go in peace.

The royal hospitality of a Flemish peasant!

In 1876, Father Aubert sounded out several patients to
find out if they missed home. The answer was "no" . . .
and for a number of reasons. They were better treated than
at home. They were satisfied with the superintendent, and
besides they had the Catholic priest who built their cottages, gave them tea, biscuits, sugar, and clothes. No distinction was made between Catholics and Protestants. This
man was no hireling out for money and honor; he was a
shepherd ready to give his life for his flock.

His children's happiness made their Father happy. He
categorically stated that he was happy and wouldn't leave
them for anything.

Doctor and Nurse

Food, housing, and amusements were excellent things.
But leprosy gnawed away at their bodies inexorably. At
the risk of being infected, Father Damien combated it.
Dr. Mouritz stressed more than others Father Damien's
complete lack of precaution. He even held the priest up
as a shining example of what can happen to one who is
not careful:

> Fr. Damien took no precaution whatever. In the kind-
> ness of his nature, he never forbade lepers entering his
> house; they had access to it any time, night or day. I
> named his house "Kalawao Family Hotel and Lepers'
> Rest," free beds, free board for the needy; this desig-
> nation I believe could not be improved on, it exactly
> fitted the daily prevailing conditions.

But Father Damien went on without the slightest hesitation and without the least worry over the danger.

He made it a matter of conscience to visit all the patients each week, those in the hospital first of all. And except for forced absences — amounting to less than six months all together — Father Damien, according to Bishop Koeckemann, never failed to see them for a period of over fourteen years. If anyone told him of an urgent case, he would leave everything to help the body and soul in distress.

About a hundred of the more advanced cases were confined to the hospital. Visiting them, Father Damien never came with empty hands. He was always loaded down with medicine, sedatives, "good things" from Honolulu. The way he acted in the sick room could not fail to cheer up the natives and remove any distance between them. He was kind, joyful, confident, friendly. The natives took him in as though he were one of them.

He didn't seem to notice the corruption and stench that pervaded everything. Bishop Koeckemann says: "He was always ready to sit or kneel by the sick bed on a dirty mat," soothing them in their sorrows and helping them die well. He would sit on the ground like a native, talk with them for hours, interested in everything, applying his best remedies, offering them the presents he had brought, and promising never to abandon them, but to come running when they needed him. He would tell the healthier patients who were caring for the more advanced cases how to act, the medicines to use, and while telling them how to encourage others encouraged them too. More often than not the place was in a mess. He would sweep and clean up, wash clothes, chatting and laughing all the time.

At mealtime, the patients naturally invited him to dine with them. He did. As though it was the thing to do, he dipped out *poi* from the family gourd, and without the slightest revulsion took the portion they held out to him in swollen, bleeding hands. According to Hawaiian custom, a pipe was passed around from mouth to mouth. When his turn came, he smoked it like the rest.

It would not be correct to think that Father Damien could do this because he lacked feeling. In 1880, he wrote:

> I've been with the lepers for almost seven years. During that time I've had a thousand chances to see human miseries under their most terrible aspects right at first hand. Half my patients seem like walking corpses, the worms have already started eating, first on the outside and then inside, until they produce horrible, incurable wounds. To get an idea of the smell, imagine the stench of a coffin just opened.

Father Damien did not let this bother him. One witness said he saw him "bandage the most frightful wounds as though he were handling flowers." He told one patient who was badly infected and asked him to be careful: "Don't get excited, son. Suppose the disease does get my body, God will give me another one on resurrection day. The main thing is to save your soul, isn't it?"

It is not our purpose to criticize the absence of doctors at the Settlement, but simply to state facts. For thirteen years there were none. Things changed in 1878, but not much. No resident doctor was appointed, and appointments followed one another in rapid succession. A doctor would show up for a few days, then disappear for two or three weeks. This easygoing way of fulfilling the hard but noble duties of the medical profession irked Meyer no end. At the same time, he himself fulfilled his duties as head of the administration well removed from the Settlement.

In 1884 Meyer wrote that it was a joke to say there was a doctor at the Settlement. All the Board wanted was to be able to say there was a doctor there. But when the doctor was needed he was not there. The patients could not obtain even the simplest medicines. The more Meyer saw of the system the less he liked it. His final conclusion was that a doctor should come and stay, or stay away.

It seems clear, therefore, that, until the priest got there, the sick were neglected. All they had were some native cure-alls, like *tua-tua*, that were either useless or harmful. Having no bandages, they went about with their wounds exposed to dirt, flies, and vermin. The first touch of a fever — it was frequent with them — killed them, when a few simple remedies might have saved them.

Fortunately, soon after Father Damien came, a man named Williamson, who had caught the disease while taking care of leprosy patients, also arrived. He had been a doctor's assistant at Kahili, and therefore had a good deal of experience. Put in charge of the hospital cases, he and Father Damien worked together. Under his instructions, the priest learned rapidly and soon had acquired considerable skill.

From 1874 to 1878 they were the only doctors at the colony. In 1876 the missionary seems to have been sold on Jayne and Wright pills, for he wrote to a certain Dr. Kibbin:

I take the liberty to inform you that there is a great demand for Jayne's and Wright's pills, to which we are accustomed, and the use of which has benefited us more than any other purgative.

I should be very much obliged to your kindness to send me directly a few dozen boxes of both kinds, to supply those lepers I find in my visits in want of them.

In the meantime I thank you very much for the alcohol, etc., all received in good order.

Meyer himself testifies to Damien's success:

In former years, before even doctors resided at the settlement, a stock of simple medicines was kept on hand constantly, and if any of the lepers got sick, these simple drugs were given out to them either by the hospital steward, the Superintendent or kind Father Damien; and I assert that they got over all their troubles, disorders, or otherwise curable diseases, quite as well as they did after the advent of resident physicians, nor was the death rate higher.

Later Father Damien worked with the doctors, improved his. technique, and got excellent results. He scrupulously prepared the doses, sterilized wounds, bandaged gangrenous members, and amputated them when they rotted. Dr. J. H. Stallard, among others, recalled seeing him amputate a patient's foot at the ankle.

Our improvised doctor was not content with popular remedies, but moved heaven and earth to find better ones. In 1878 he heard of Hoang-Nan pills. It was a Chinese remedy made from a creeping vine discovered by Bishop Gautier. The bark of the vine is covered with a reddish powder and contains a poison that was used as a remedy for leprosy. On August 21, Father Damien wrote to Father Etienne, a Dominican at Trinidad, who could furnish Hoang-Nan pills:

It was with inexpressible joy that I received the box of Hoang-Nan pills and your very encouraging letter. I translated it for several lepers who were filled with joy and confidence. They have gotten together and are taking up a collection to buy a large supply of it. I myself experimented on a good Christian and he is better.

Out of pity for my poor sufferers who call me their Makua (Father) and whose misery is indescribable, in the name of our Lord Jesus Christ who healed lepers, I beg you, Reverend Father, to send me in the most direct way as soon as possible and no matter what the cost, a good supply of this medicine. Be assured that I need very much of it, because the number of lepers is great. All expenses will be paid by our Motherhouse in Paris. . . .

M. Lesserteur, the director of the Foreign Missions of Rue de Bac, wrote of this to the Father General of the Sacred Hearts Fathers: "In view of such an explicit and touching request, I am ready to give him my whole supply."

Fifteen months later, Father Damien reported the results to Father Etienne:

I have not written you sooner, because I wanted to be sure that the effects of this providential remedy are lasting. For six months, we have used it extensively and its reputation is established. It has prolonged the life of some and restored the use of members to others. Two Americans in particular, one of them, the assistant superintendent, has only a white spot on his stomach and his loss of feeling has almost disappeared.

Even [the doctor] . . . is beginning to see its power. In one of the hospital wards he used Hoang-Nan, in another ward an arsenic solution, and Potassium solution in a third. At the end of three months, the results were clearly in favor of Hoang-Nan. To our patients' great joy he let them take it and yesterday he asked me for thirty pounds of my pills.

I hope the Board of Health will adopt them. I believe my supply will last until April. That's when the Board meets. If the Board doesn't act, I'll get some of my friends in Parliament to persuade the Government to buy Hoang-Nan.

His success was talked about in the districts, and his fellow missionaries started sending him orders for his pills. In July, 1880, Father James Beissel wrote him: "I have a lot of lepers here. Please send me your Chinese *laau* [medicine] with instructions on how to use it."

A medical inspector of the U. S. Navy, Dr. G. W. Woods, paid a beautiful tribute to Father Damien. The doctor told the Board that he had visited leprosaria all over the world and nowhere had he seen patients happier or better cared for. This he attributed to Father Damien's devotedness. He also admired the scientific know-how with which the priest treated the patients.

CHILDREN

Of all the sufferers, undoubtedly the most pitiful were the children. They were also the special object of Father Damien's love. Visitors at the Settlement could describe a terrible sight. Father Julliotte, SS.CC., a veteran missionary, says: "I saw one that had only half an eye left. A mass of suppurating, fetid flesh had replaced his nose, mouth and ears which were almost gone." — "Another put his face in his hands to hide his bleeding wounds that made him so horrible." Prof. Stoddard writes:

> I remember how, one day as we were walking along the wards of the hospital at Kalawao, Father Damien turned suddenly to us, and said: "Ah! here is something dreadful I must show you!" We approached what seemed a little bundle of rags, or rubbish, half hidden under a soiled blanket; the curious doctors were about to examine it, when the good Father seized me, and cried, excitedly: "You must not look! You must not look!" I assured him that I was not at all afraid to see even the worst that could be shown me there; for my eyes had become accustomed to horrors, and the most sickening sights no longer affected me. A corner of the blanket was turned slowly toward us — a face in which scarcely a trace of anything human remained. The dark skin was puffed out and blackened; a kind of moss, or mould, gummy and glistening, covered it; the muscles of the mouth, having contracted, laid bare the grinning teeth;

the thickened tongue lay like a fig between them; the eyelids, curled back, exposed the inner surface, and the protruding eyeballs, now shapeless and broken, looked not unlike bursted grapes. It was a leprous child, who within the last few days had assumed that horrible visage.

What could the greathearted Damien do but adopt these little unfortunates, deprived of all affection and so far from those who should have protected them? In him they found both father and mother to love them, to watch over them, to give them the tenderest care. He went to work to assure them a home right in the mission enclosure . . . close to him. Witnesses are unanimous that his two orphanages were closest to his heart. They were his real family. He spent most time with them, and there he received his consolations.

He set up a girls' orphanage and a "Boys' Home." Doubtless, he began by taking care of young girls whom too many vicious people wanted to adopt.

Dr. Mouritz' story of "little Mary" will show how badly Father Damien's orphanages were needed:

I was at the landing, waiting in the lee of the freight house, sheltered from wind and rain, when I was accosted by a diminutive girlish figure, asking if I was Father Damien, as she carried a letter from the Sisters at Kakaako detention station for him. This little girl, not full ten years old, told a pitiful story — she was soaked to the skin with the rain and sea, and shivering with cold, was anxious to get food, shelter and a place to sleep. She was self-possessed, informed me her father had died on the steamer, and was buried at Pukoo, a port of the lee side of Molokai; also on the steamer, too ill to be landed, was her little brother, six years old, who was a leper as well as this little girl herself.

I speedily passed her along to Father Damien and

some kokua woman who fed and warmed the child and
gave her dry clothing. Her brother was landed at day-
light much to the child's delight.

This little girl's name was Mary, and her great dread
and worry was that she would have *no house to shelter
her,* hence the letter to Father Damien from the Sisters
asking him to exercise his good offices in getting this
family settled.

In February, 1878, Father Aubert mentions the first
group of young leper girls. "On approaching St. Philomena's church, I heard singing like that of the Jews weeping on the banks of Babylon over the remembrance of
Jerusalem. It was a group of young leper girls singing in
their native tongue."

In 1880, Father Damien wrote:

I have a small orphanage for young leper girls. An
aged widow, who is not sick, is their cook and mother.
Although their houses are separated from mine, we have
meals in common and share our rations. We each get
seven pounds of beef and twenty-one pounds of *taro*
weekly; with that we think we're pretty well fed. We
have also planted a big field of potatoes as a reserve
when the rations don't get here on time. Some charitable
souls send me bundles of clothes which come to me
through the Mother Superior in Honolulu.

The boys had a school where Father Damien gave them
religious instructions. Under the pretext of impartiality,
the Board members stopped him. He then built — and
most of it with his own hands — a home for the boys like
the one the girls had. Souls came first with him! He was
alarmed at the moral danger to which these children were
exposed — the harmful influence of an education that would
snuff out the life of faith in them.

Organizing the boy's home was a difficult task for the priest. He needed personnel to cook, wash clothes, supervise the boys. Some healthy patients presented themselves. It was a strain on his already overstrained budget. To keep going, he thought up fine financial deals which the administration readily agreed with. And he begged far and wide. He begged from different mission organizations. He even begged at home from door to door, wisely taking some of his orphans along with him. He also grew beans to make a little money.

In 1883, by order of the Board of Health, the superintendent of Kahili Hospital at Honolulu sent him several children under his care, stating that he hated to lose them but there just was no room for them. He hoped Father Damien would find a place for them. They were being put under his immediate supervision.

Despite the poverty of the institution and the disease of its young population, so hideous and misshapen, they all had the family spirit, due to the goodness of the director. There were about 80 of them. Even adults who had no friends asked to be admitted to the orphanage. The place was soon bulging at the seams. But what did space mean? Everybody was so happy. The priest thought they were wonderful.

They learn their catechism very well and attend Mass every morning and the Rosary devotions. Right now, I'm a little bit of a doctor like my heavenly patron, St. Damien; I'm trying to lessen their sufferings and christianize them. Undoubtedly, it is more or less hard to live in the midst of such repulsive people, but they're my joy.

Dr. Mouritz loudly acclaimed Father Damien's two orphanages and said they were "one of the finest works that this priest undertook and carried out."

Let us take out a minute to get some details straight.

On February 2, 1885, Father Damien told his brother Pamphile: "I am in charge of two orphanages; one has about 25 boys, the other 15 girls, *all lepers*. This little world fills my chapel morning and evening and in the day for catechism."

On the other hand, Dr. Mouritz in his book *The Path of the Destroyer* states that in the last week of October, 1885, orders were given to transfer 14 orphans from Molokai to the new Kapiolani Home at Kahili near Honolulu, and that among them were children who were *not lepers*.

The explanation of this seeming contradiction is that Father Damien considered all children born of leper parents as lepers whether they showed any external signs or not.

Be that as it may, this is Dr. Mouritz' explanation:

Thirty years ago [1885] there were many orphans at the leper Settlement in the care of kokua families, but most were cared for by the Catholic mission, under the supervision of Father Damien, at Kalawao, and I claim this was one of the finest works that this priest undertook and carried out.

Father Damien's orphanage was comprised of thirty orphan boys and twelve orphan girls, and more than half these children had a leper father and also a leper mother. Lest I forget to state, fourteen of these orphan girls were removed from the Settlement in the year 1885, to the Kapiolani Home at Kalihi, Honolulu, Oahu, and only one had to be returned some years later as a leper to Molokai.

As we shall see, it was a hard job to take those fourteen orphans away. It resulted in the tragedy of October 29, 1885, which we will take up later. The *kokuas* (aides) did not want to let the orphans go, because they were attached to them and also because the orphans got rations which the *kokuas* shared. And for Father Damien the orphans had become his family. Mouritz tells us: "He strenuously objected to any inroads being made on his orphanage, and suggested that none of the children in his home be removed until all the orphan girls living with *kokuas* and lepers had been deported." All objections were brushed aside. The officials were simply carrying out orders from the Board. Fourteen girls about fourteen years of age were selected wherever they could be found.

In any case, the number of non-leper children at his orphanage was small. On this subject we have the report made by Princess Lilioukalani. Later on we will come back to this report which is so precise and rich in details. Here is what she had to say of his orphanage:

The next subject which engaged the attention of the party was an inspection of the schools under the charge of Rev. Father Damien. The buildings occupied for this purpose are supplied by the Board of Health, one of which is used for a boys' school and the other for girls, being situated in near proximity, and on the opposite sides of the road. Both are within the vicinity of the mission church.

In the girls' school are sixteen pupils in all, ranging in age from nine to seventeen years. . . . Out of these children there were four between nine and eleven years of age who exhibited no external signs of the disease; but one, upon careful inspection by Dr. Arning, was declared to be in the incipient state of disease.

In the boys' school were twenty-six pupils, all of whom were well marked with the disease.

The pupils of each school are separately lodged and fed. They are all either orphans or friendless, and under the immediate care of Father Damien and a native woman named Kuilia, not herself a leper.

In 1880, Father Damien wrote: "Day before yesterday when I returned, I found one of my little girls who asked me to bring her Holy Viaticum. When she finished her thanksgiving, she gave up her soul to God. Yesterday, I myself made her coffin and dug her grave." It seems the administration did not pay for burials. Many died penniless. So they wouldn't have to be buried in a simple blanket, Father Damien made their coffins. He also dug their graves. It is hard to say for how many he did this, but Father Lambert Conrardy's figure of 1300 seems somewhat high.

10   *A Flourishing Parish*

FATHER DAMIEN'S people had souls to save. All the work he did to make living conditions better for them was for this purpose only. He was a Catholic priest sent there to teach them the truths of Christianity, to get them to believe and hope, to merit eternal life by keeping the law of God and the Church. When a man is well he sometimes forgets about eternity, but when a man lives on his deathbed, as the leprosy patients were doing, he thinks of what is beyond the grave. Father Damien found Molokai a huge hospital where he could work for souls to his heart's content.

His work began the minute he got there. The day after his arrival, he wrote to his superiors: "You know how I feel. I want to sacrifice myself for my poor lepers. The harvest seems ripe."

He wanted to snatch those souls, imprisoned in decaying bodies, from the corruption of sin and make them fit for heaven. In 1873, he wrote home to his parents: "My greatest happiness is to serve the Lord in these poor sick children, made outcasts by the rest of men. I'm trying to lead them all along the road to heaven."

Immense moral progress was beginning, thanks to this one man who knew what he wanted to do and had the means to do it. Whether they liked it or not, the seven or eight hundred patients stared death and eternity in the face. They knew that when death put an end to their life of horror, all was not over. It did not help to blaspheme a tyrannical Creator. This they knew. So they were willing to listen to the priest whose very presence was a proof of God's goodness. Each year one of every five died. Without fear of being misunderstood or unwelcome, the priest preached to them of God's just judgment, and especially of Christ our Saviour and of our Blessed Mother, the Mother of Mercy.

His heart was bursting with hope. His victory was sure. His letters are chock-full of a duty well done. No jeremiad, no whining, no disgust at the discovery of moral wounds on top of physical ones. Only conversions, baptisms one after the other. He was preaching, he was exercising his priesthood day and night, everywhere.

Running through his letters, all one sees are communiques of victory. Again in 1873, he wrote:

Good news from my district. Here a priest has something to keep him busy from morning to night. Out of 600 lepers I have a list of 210 Christians and 20 catechumens. In no time my church will be too small. Yesterday, high Mass, magnificent singing, countless confessions and communions. How many dying! Sunday, 10 baptisms. The Feast of the Ascension, 15, and 5 on the death bed . . . I'm on the run all day long and yet manage to see only a third of my patients.

A model Christian settlement was gradually taking shape out of this hellhole.

Does he alone deserve credit for this change? He was there for sixteen years. It is true that other priests helped him some over a period of six years, yet for ten years he was by himself. When everything is carefully weighed, one is led to the conclusion that credit goes to him alone. By hard work, plagued with obstacles and setbacks, he made the Settlement into a model parish. But after his death, it started to go down again.

FELLOW WORKERS

Let us define the limits of Father Damien's jurisdiction at Molokai.

From May, 1873, to February, 1874, he had jurisdiction over the whole island.

From February, 1874, to July, 1880, his jurisdiction was limited to the Settlement. The south part of the island was in charge of Father Andrew Burgermann, SS.CC., who was ill.

From July, 1878, to July, 1880, Father Andrew lived at Kalaupapa, and Father Damien again had to take care of the south part of the island.

In June, 1880, Father Andrew left and for fifteen months Father Damien was again in charge of the whole island.

September 8, 1881, another sick priest, Father Albert Montiton, SS.CC., landed at the settlement. He stayed at Kalaupapa until February 2, 1885.

Then Father Damien was left alone until May, 1888, when Father Conrardy joined him. The latter remained until Father Damien died the following April.

We have closely studied the relations of Father Damien with the Sacred Hearts Fathers who worked with him at Molokai. Since some of the shorter lives of Father Damien have aroused interest — by their silence — we think it would be a good idea to take a look at the records. The lapse of time allows us to do so.

Father Andrew was a Hollander, over forty years of age, who had come to the Sacred Hearts Fathers late in life. After a dozen years of apostolate in the South Pacific, where with his flair for medicine he had great success, he contracted *elephantiasis*. He was sent to Molokai, not to the Settlement, but to the south part of the island to take care of the two hundred Christians scattered among two thousand natives.

They were next-door neighbors — only a day's journey apart — so the priests saw each other once in a while. In 1874 Father Damien even turned over the Settlement to Father Andrew so he could go south and build chapels for his confrere. Father Andrew was not enthusiastic about the builder. He wrote frankly to him: "Don't hurry about the chapel. If the Bishop can't send us a Brother, I prefer to be as I am rather than have a pile of debris. I don't doubt your good will but each to his own trade. If a Brother comes, they will give him all he needs, otherwise we will be left to get along as best we can."

Damien made an agreement with the Provincial:

He is only half satisfied with my plans and that I am doing the building. I hardly have time or the ability to do it well. I insist then that you decide to send two Brothers who could build chapels for him. If you continue your plan to send me, I don't take back my word. Weigh our position here at Kalawao. It's not that I'm afraid to work. On the contrary, I love to work on chapels but still more on the conversion of my poor lepers.

One March night in 1874 Father Andrew slipped while coming down the *palis* and the fall could have been serious. Father Damien welcomed him and took care of him — along with his leprosy patients — so well that soon Father Andrew was on his feet, bragging about Father Damien's care, and stayed on several days.

However, in November of the same year, the Provincial was writing to the Father General: "It is good that Fathers

Damien and Andrew are separated, for they could not get along together." And two months later: "They don't agree at all."

This, of course may well be true, but we must not exaggerate their disagreement. Yet if we are looking for causes of it, we need go no farther than their lively temperaments and quite different characters. Father Damien's first thought was the good of souls. Father Andrew wanted to practice medicine. He was even summoned to appear before the Commissioner of the French government in Honolulu to answer to charges made against him by the Board of Health of illegal practice of medicine. It must be said, also, that he was lacking in the spirit looked for in a religious.

Still Father Andrew was trusted. For months, Father Damien left him in charge of the Settlement. Their relations were good in 1874 and 1875, for their letters contain mutual praise. From a letter of the Father General we learn that in 1876 Father Andrew was coming every two months to hear Father Damien's confession. Damien in turn did the same thing for him.

But an explosion was set off on November 24, 1877, by the death of Bill Ragsdale, the resident superintendent. Father Andrew applied to Meyer and the Board of Health itself for the now vacant job. Would he remain a missionary? Would he lay aside his religious habit? That would depend on the answer from the Bishop, who as yet knew nothing about the proposition. In any case, his mission work would be limited.

Meyer quite candidly informed Father Damien of the situation. Beside himself, Damien lodged an energetic protest: Father Andrew depended on the Bishop and the Bishop alone. He had no right to ask for this appointment without ecclesiastical permission. The Board had no right to accept it without authorization from the Vicar Apostolic.

This would be taking away one of his missionaries. In-dignantly Damien laid down an ultimatum to the Board: "This will not happen or I will leave." Faced with this alternative, the Board understood and bowed to his de-mand. Father Andrew was turned down.

But of all things, the very office Damien had blocked Father Andrew from getting, he himself accepted!* From November, 1877, to February, 1878, he held the office of *luna* [resident superintendent], *ad interim.*

Around the end of February, 1878, he wrote to his Pro-vincial, Father Modeste: "For the last three months I patiently bore the duties of *luna* until Wilder finally got here. I asked him to put Sumner Keolaloa in charge and now I am free." Wilder was a very important person and was to become the president of the Board. In a letter dated November 20, 1877, Father Damien had written to Mr. Rose, a Honolulu merchant: "Our beloved Bill Ragsdale is nearly at the term of his days. Please tell M. Wilder I will grumble to him if he appoints a bad man for this place."

Damien confided to Dr. Mouritz: "I had, and was glad to, resign the office, owing to the fault-finding and con-tinuous complaints made against me."

In reality, there was more diplomacy in Damien's taking the office than one might suppose. Frightened at the pros-pect of Father Andrew's taking a position independently of his Bishop, Father Damien had lodged his strong pro-test with the Board and threatened to cease all collabora-tion if they took a Catholic priest away from his work without the Bishop's permission. Although Father Andrew was acceptable, he had not been formally appointed. Meyer got an order to quash the whole affair, so he tried to pacify both priests at the same time. Father Damien had put himself forward only to keep Father Andrew — against

* See p. 138.

whom he had just complaints — from taking the position.

According to Meyer's records, Father Damien's administration was not too good. He was definitely too exacting. The first month he got this letter from the Board's agent:

Kalae, Dec. 19, 1877

Rev. Father J. Damien
Kalawao
Dear Sir:

Yours of yesterday enclosing weekly report is duly to hand and contents noted.

It matters nothing with regard to the cloth bill which you have found, it is but a little matter, if the other party is dissatisfied, let her be so; do please not tell these people to write to me about every little thing. I believe that they never got anything and now as they get something, they get dissatisfied.

I would caution you to make as little change as possible for the present, and put up with little irregularities for now, or else in case of need you will find that there is nobody to rely upon.

Meyer

Yet, to get back to the mutual good feelings that existed between the two Fathers: At the beginning of 1875, Father Andrew expressed his satisfaction over what Father Damien had done for him. Damien had built a chapel, rectory, and school at Kalauoha in the south. Father Andrew was in admiration. "On returning to my post, I was very surprised to find such a beautiful chapel built in such a short time. I wrote to the Bishop that the chapel of Our Lady of Sorrows is beautiful, really beautiful. There are many parishes in Europe that do not have one like it. The architect has surpassed his masters."

Delightful praise that was returned in kind. Father Damien wrote to the Father General: "Fr. Andrew has been at the Settlement four months. He has done a great deal of good."

Toward the end of the year, Father Andrew wrote again:

In the past two years the untiring Fr. Damien has built or is building six chapels on the island. Three for himself, the rest for me. Since my arrival I have had around 140 baptisms. Fr. Damien has had 300 to 400, so we don't have much to complain about. The Bishop and Father Provincial let us shift for ourselves.

This freedom of action would explain in part Father Damien's initiative that was criticized so severely. The Provincial thought it his duty to keep the Father General up to date: Father Damien was acting just as he wanted to. He had taken over a shipment of materials the Bishop was sending to build a chapel at Pelekuna. He had the whole thing unloaded at Kalaupapa. He then tore down a chapel that was almost new and built another in its place. With the lumber from the old chapel — plus some new expenditures — he then built a small chapel at Pelekunu. The Bishop was galled by this interference with his plans. The Provincial wanted to know what explanation the wrecker and builder could give for his action.

The wrecker and builder did give an explanation in a letter sent to Paris in March, 1876: "The gifts received last year for the leprosarium were used mostly to cover the expenses of the beautiful church I built to replace a small one that was no longer big enough for the second parish of the leprosarium." Quite simply — a larger church for a larger crowd.

Two years later Father Aubert stated that Father Andrew went to a great deal of trouble to take care of his district. He was well thought of, especially because his knowledge of medicine enabled him to supply remedies to the sick, and this won him favor with the Protestants.

When it was time for him to leave, after he had spent several months at the leprosarium while Father Damien was building chapels for him, the people hated to see him go.

The Vice-Provincial, Father Regis, wrote at the end of 1879; "Fr. Damien is pained to see the preference the lepers give to Fr. Andrew." Against this we have the fact that he quite readily turned over the leprosarium to his confrere for several months. But above all, we can't help believing Father Damien knew at that time the facts that would oblige Father Andrew to leave the leprosarium in July, 1880.

The same Father Regis had already informed the Father General at the end of 1878: "Fr. Andrew has told the Bishop of his decision to leave. He does not want to stay at the Mission any longer. It is useless to tell you how he has come to make the step he calls 'my departure from slavery.' I take from his own letter the reason for his apostasy: 'I am a proud man and I say it to my honor!' May God forgive him and keep us from all evil!" However, the priest repented. He went back to the leprosarium, not with Father Damien, but back to Kalaupapa where he exercised his ministry, and especially acted as a medical officer. "In granting as much as we can to the unfortunate character rather than to the bad will of our doctor priest, perhaps we will save him from a bad fall."

"My greatest suffering this year," Father Damien reported to his Provincial,

has been to see my only companion drifting farther and farther away from the Congregation and even the Mission. Last Tuesday he asked me by letter to sell him [Father Andrew] my own house, otherwise he would build another in his own name. I told him the Mission does not *sell* but *gives* its members all they need. To head off a regrettable step I let him understand that if he wished to set himself up independently of the Mission, he would find himself without a church. This advice enraged him. He answered by an abusive letter, telling me his determination to quit the Congregation. He finally accepted a compromise. I want to prevent a break that would be scandalous. But give me your opinion. Should I let him have independent direction of half the leprosarium, the use of money and materials that belong to the Mission? He does not give an account of anything. I do not believe it would be imprudent to keep me advised of any authorizations you grant him, so that I won't say or do anything not in accord with you. . . .

One can understand how much Father Damien must have suffered from his companion in this tense situation that continued for two years (1878-1880).

At the beginning of 1880, Father Regis is formal about Father Andrew's aberrations. He wrote to the Father General:

The scandal he is giving makes it an obligation for us to remove him. The Bishop begs you with tears in his eyes to recall this man. He absolutely cannot be sent to any other part of the Mission and he should not remain at Molokai. We are afraid of only one thing: too severe measures on our part might make him apostatize. That is why we have left him alone until you have the goodness to give him an order to leave the islands. This man knows nothing of the religious life.

By the end of his stay at Kalaupapa, Father Andrew was not speaking to Father Damien. After Damien's death he still had not called a truce and refused to answer questions when material was being gathered for Damien's biography. However, it is true that Father Andrew died with good dispositions.

Months went by before Father Andrew's departure. Father Regis sent this news to the Father General with a disdainful report on Father Damien which cannot be passed over in silence: "Fr. Damien is going to remain alone at Molokai until he gets new orders, in spite of the Rule and especially the need for a guide, for without attacking his virtue and zeal, he is a priest who lacks the mould of Louvain. Besides, he doesn't have a very good head and doesn't know how to get along with people."

To understand Father Regis' severe statements, which were an echo of the Honolulu authorities, it would be necessary to place oneself in the atmosphere of the times, and be thoroughly acquainted with events in Hawaii from 1877 to 1880. One would have to picture to oneself the more polished society in which the Bishop, the Provincial, and their counselors moved. Confined to his own little corner at Molokai, harassed by worries and cares that were more than absorbing, Father Damien looked at things in relation to his own particular sector. This often resulted in viewpoints diametrically opposed to those of the higher-ups. They were quick to label him with narrow-mindedness. As for getting along with people, we have to insist on the rugged simplicity of a real Fleming. Straight talking, frankness that left no doubts, country ways — all these things still stuck to the priest who hadn't been formed in salon society.

But it is certain that his zeal for good dominated all his activity. His procedure, rough and ready though it was, fitted in well with his surroundings. His successful apostolate fully justifies it.

Doubtlessly, Father Damien's letters to Honolulu at this time, expressing weariness and complaints about his companion, ended up by wearying their recipients and making them complain. Does not his constant need and demand for a confessor — a noble scruple he carried to his grave — show that he jumped too quickly into an exceptional situation? But no one is obliged to do the impossible, so they reasoned.

At the Settlement, marriage cases were a good deal harder than at his old district of Kohala because of the forced separation of couples, one being at Molokai, the other somewhere else in the islands. It was hard to check on each case. Even writing to another missionary did not always help. They were too few. It was prudent to write only in doubtful cases.

It was such circumstances that brought the following letter in 1875 from Bishop Maigret to Father Damien:

Is it true that you married the widow of a German blacksmith to a certain Barnaba Waiwaiole of Wailuku? If you have, the marriage is invalid, for this Barnaba has a Catholic wife living. Leprosy doesn't break the marriage bond. Take good note of this. You would do better by getting information from some of our priests before you do these things, when you are in doubt. You have laid yourself open to being deceived, and everybody else too. We can't be too prudent.

We have no answer from the priest or any further information on this case, so it is impossible for us to get an idea of the conduct he followed.

Others of his fellow missionaries, who were "out in the sticks" as he was and whose problems were similar, were more just. Father Gulstan, the future Vicar Apostolic, wrote him: "Since I believe you're even happier now than you used to be, I congratulate you with all my heart." The tough veteran, Father Charles, said: "I beg you pray very much for one who would be happy, if it is God's will, to end my days with you."

Father Damien was alone at the Settlement for fifteen months.

Father Albert Montiton, who was sent to him, was completely different from Father Andrew. He was a Norman from Sourdeval, France, a strong character, a zealous priest and missionary. He had spent twenty-four hard but fruitful years on the Paumotu Islands in the South Pacific. This is what a veteran missionary had to say of him: "You would have to have seen those islands in their savage state, as I did, and as they are now to appreciate the extent of his work. Churches, schools, people as civilized as our own. He was in the midst of diseases and dangers that overcame others." Part of his success was due to his musical talents, especially with the clarinet and harmonium. He knew he was definitely above average in ability.

But he did not escape the scourge of tropical diseases. Elephantiasis got him. It was thought to be leprosy and he was sent to Molokai as Father Damien's assistant. To be more precise, he was told that Damien did not have too good judgment and needed a guide. With his glorious career behind him and his fifteen years seniority over his pupil, he graciously accepted the job. Besides, he had just been received in audience by Pius IX after giving a lecture tour in France.

He was sent to take over part of Father Damien's crushing burden of work. With all his drawbacks, this pioneer missionary was a big help. At Kalaupapa, which he jealously reserved for himself, he performed 65 adult baptisms in 1882. Every morning he gave instructions to those at Mass. Every Friday evening they had the Rosary, Way of the Cross, and Benediction. High Mass every Sunday and Rosary, catechism, and Benediction in the afternoon. He spent his afternoons visiting and instructing the indifferent and sick to be sure they would have a happy death.

He was his own cook and housekeeper. His cow furnished milk for him and the sick. He even made cheese and butter. In addition, the government assured him a weekly supply of meat and rice. With this relative comfort, he could get along without being too much expense to the Mission. "I think I'm fortunate," he admitted. "You couldn't find a better retreat to end your career. Weak as I am, I can still be of some use."

If he had been so for the four years he worked with Father Damien, we would find nothing but praise for him. But unfortunately, Father Damien and Father Albert were two entirely different men who did not get along at all. Again, a good look at the facts will help us to assess the situation fairly.

On his arrival at Honolulu in 1879, Father Albert had made a very bad impression. He was so agitated that he seemed almost possessed. He had had a fall that had brought him much suffering. However, he had the strength, the Vice-Provincial wrote to the General, to write a long letter full of exaggerations, complaints, and accusations, reproaching the Bishop for not keeping promises he had never made. He was described as a troublemaker whose demands and violence offended everybody. What could he do about it? He himself confessed he was incorrigible. "The fox dies in his skin," he always answered. What he needed were other Paumotus.

At first he was given the districts of Waikane and Kailua. There he revealed only galling pessimism. He would have to start from scratch. Everybody was wrong. His district was too large and all he had was one room and a chapel. He always had good excuses for being away. Others could do nothing but bend to his caprice. He even exposed them to the danger of catching his disease. He would make no concessions to others, and had rough treatment ready for those who failed to get in line with his views. In his unlimited violence, he wanted to put his superiors "in the junk yard," and spoke openly of their removal from office. In a word, added the Vice-Provincial, "He is a charlatan who needs a 'Vatican' [the name of his boat at Tahiti] and a violin."

And again: "If you listen to Fr. Albert, no peace is possible. He pretends he has been assigned by Fr. General to keep him informed of everything. He wants to remake everything: laws, customs, men and buildings. With all these goings-on, the church is empty. His quarreling is causing everyone to complain."

That was the man who landed at Molokai on September 8, 1881. A month later, Father Damien wrote to his Bishop: "Fr. Albert and I are of one heart and I hope we continue to be." The Bishop pointed out their merit: "I thank God for your understanding. Both of you are sincerely seeking to do good, although you will often have the chance to merit by giving in to the other's point of view."

The Settlement at Kalaupapa was growing. The increasing number of people attending the church called for enlargements. Father Albert entrusted the work to Father Damien who did not hesitate to retouch his own work. Working straight through from 8 o'clock in the morning to 4:30, along with two helpers, he soon put up the framework of an annex. After this, he rode on horseback every day to Kalawao to make his visits to the patients.

For several weeks he went to take charge of Kalawao. But everything went wrong. For five years, some women, who were like real Sisters of Charity, had been taking care of the children Father Damien had gathered in. Father Albert got into arguments with the women. He chased off any woman who came near the house — unless she came there to sing. "This afternoon he had three of them at the house to sing," Father Damien wrote to the Bishop. —

I don't mind that. But why did he have to poke his nose into the kitchen to see if the cook's wife was there? Either pull in his reins or give him full charge of Kalawao. As you advised me, I have done all I could for him. The treatment with Dr. Miner's lotion has helped him. Everything would have been all right, if he hadn't gotten on his high horse about his rights. Excuse these lines. I'm a little burned up because he just made my man leave who was in charge of all provisions for my 34 lepers and the kitchen.

It seems that Father Albert acted rather hastily by taking things into his own hands during his temporary assignment at Kalawao, even though in conscience he might have felt obliged to do so.

Nevertheless, over the question of the cook, Father Damien gave in. He was too afraid their close union might snap. But the cook, whose wife couldn't enter the kitchen again, might want to take revenge. To keep peace, Father Damien stayed a while longer at Kalaupapa.

The question of jurisdiction was coming up between the two priests. The Bishop felt that he should not settle the question categorically. Father Damien was still responsible for the entire colony. However, in case Father Albert settled permanently at Kalaupapa, Damien would have to put him on an equal footing. Their friendly understanding seemed to be compromised for the moment by the misunderstanding over the cook and his wife, but Damien was ready to let Father Albert have his way rather than cling to his responsibility too much.

This was the reason for Father Damien's letter to the Bishop. They could continue good relations only because he was willing to keep nothing and give in in everything. Yet, he only half approved the creation of two distinct parishes. It was Father Andrew who had thought up this plan that had ended only in increased difficulties, hard words, and jealousy. The catastrophe would have been avoided if they had remained together. . . .

Before coming to Molokai, Father Albert had heard the tales attacking Father Damien's honor, calumnies that he snapped up as an interested party and that affected their first relations. In a letter of December 6, 1881, Father Damien touched on this painful subject: "The petty chicanery of our good Fr. Regis [Vice-Provincial] plus that of my companion gives me something to practice patience on. But I've got a fiery character, if I'm pushed too far."

On December 31, 1881, Father Damien wrote to the Bishop:

> For the honor of my reputation that is being put under suspicion by Fr. Regis and Fr. Albert, I insist that the good Fr. Albert be an eyewitness and not a witness at a distance. On his arrival here, for three straight days he spoke to me as though I had lived evilly with a woman. He said that was what he had heard on Hawaii or at Koolau. This has hurt me deeply, especially coming from my new companion.

To get to the heart of the calumny, we will follow the deposition of Ambrose Hutchinson.

Father Damien was the terror of certain bad characters among the patients who were given heart and soul to wild parties and debauchery. Setting themselves up as his equals they could not believe the priest had any virtue, since they had none themselves. Their hatred led them to peddle scandalous stories about him. Their spicy lies grew in the telling. Gossips picked up these tales like manna from heaven. Stories about a priest's misconduct were something to make people prick up their ears and listen. The lurid tales grew like fungus and were to creep into newspapers and magazines, where the only proof was the editor's word.

Father Damien's maligners had a wonderful time until they were crushed by the mountainous intervention of the avengers of truth. We will come back to this later.

This calumny, which lowered Father Damien's reputation in the eyes of certain persons, began because of three well-known women. They were not leprosy patients, were Catholics, and were interested in working for the Church. They were three Hawaiians: Maria Hoolemakaur, Philomela Kulia, Elikapeka Punana. They had followed their husbands who were patients at Molokai. When Father Damien arrived and for many years afterward, these women helped him, cleaned the house, cooked, did the laundry. Even in the presence of strangers, he called them "mother," *maku ahina*. Their conduct was above suspicion and they aided him greatly in his work. With all that was going on, he would have had a hard job around the house without them.

Despite calumnies these three women went on serving Father Damien, not counting the cost. Philomela Kulia left the Settlement after his death (1889) to return to her relatives and friends at Lahaina (Maui). Elikapeka Punana died at Kalawao, March 29, 1893, and was buried at Makanalua. Maria Hoolemakaui continued to keep house at the Boys' Home which Father Damien has established until she died in the Kalaupapa Hospital, May 15, 1915.

The bitterness suffered by Father Damien's faithful friends, absolutely convinced of his innocence, bothered them a long time and they were slow to forget the attacks of the scandalmongers.

In January, 1882, the Bishop reminded Father Damien that he had to join prudence and patience to his burning zeal. He regretted that his two priests couldn't live together, although both were eager to do good.

In April, new friction was caused by a deathbed mar-

riage; Bishop Koeckemann, for several months now Bishop
Maigret's coadjutor, wrote Father Damien:

Fr. Albert has appealed to me in a marriage case
where you have been divided in opinion and action.
I am obliged to answer despite the repugnance it gives
me because of the pain it must cause you. After Father's
presentation, it is evident that the marriage should not
have taken place: all one could do was to take a chance
on giving absolution in the danger of death. I understand and I praise your zeal for the salvation of a poor
sinner's soul, and I am often tempted to act the same
way out of compassion for poor people. But, when we
have to decide categorically, I must necessarily take the
opposite view. What puts you even more in the wrong
is that your companion had already settled it according
to the rules of theology.

I repeat that I perhaps feel more pain at having to
tell you this than you do in receiving it. It is charity
and misdirected zeal that caused you to do it. I like to
believe that God will not judge you severely because of
your good intention. May this incident not lessen your
zeal for the salvation of souls, but may it teach you to
regulate your zeal from now on by the laws of God
and the Church.

Father Damien was not easily beaten. He answered the
Bishop right away. After thanking him for his good letter,
he added:

The difference of opinion and action between my
companion and me came from him, not me. I have
acted in this case he appealed to you about, as Your
Excellency and the greater part of our Fathers would
have acted. The case falls, at least indirectly, under the
seal of confession. Fr. Albert had no right to question
me. At my evasive answer, he got angry, three days later

at my penitent's funeral. In front of the natives, he said what he supposed I had done was forbidden; and in place of letting me ask your advice, as I intended to do, he rushed off to appeal to you against me.

I suppose he explained it to you from his own viewpoint, more or less correct, just as he solved the sick man's problem, not even wanting to hear his confession, fifteen days after his last visit and two days before my penitent's death. I have acted as I believed best for the sick man's salvation. I based myself on two principles that I have adopted to solve complicated cases: *"In fide unitas, in dubiis libertas, in omnibus caritas"*; *"semper ad edificandum, numquam ad destructionem"* [Unity in faith, liberty in doubt, charity in all things; always build up, never tear down].

According to St. Alphonsus di Liguori's explanation of probabilism, if you have a solid doubt, you can follow a probable opinion. Here it was a question of choosing between two opinions for dealing with a soul that was standing on the threshold of eternity. Three years ago, a priest (Fr. Andrew), finding the same man living with the same woman, believed he could absolve him and give him Extreme Unction. I could even have supposed that their union was then validated, as it is the custom to do each time there hasn't been a Catholic marriage previously.

I would like to take the liberty of asking Your Excellency some questions on the tenor of your Council's decisions.

I. Is it sufficient to learn that a Catholic or mixed marriage has been contracted before one of our Fathers, to refuse to officiate in a second marriage, supposing the first two contracting parties are still living?

II. Is it sufficient to learn that a first marriage, either Catholic, or mixed, or Protestant or infidel, has been celebrated before a non-Catholic minister, to be able to officiate at a second union?

III. May I bless, *tuta conscientia* (with a good conscience), a union legitimate *in foro ecclesiastico* (in the eyes of the Church), when parties are unable to obtain a certificate from the Government? It is to be understood that then I do it *privatim* (privately) and make them understand that they must keep it a secret, and that the contract can have no civil effect, with the assurance from the Government officials that no one will bother me because of it.

It is too bad we do not have the Bishop's answer. As for a copy of the Episcopal Council's decision, we have the substance of it in a letter from Bishop Koeckemann to the Father General:

> However, I have advised our Fathers, confidentially in general and officially every time I have been asked in writing, that we cannot remarry divorced persons, when the marriage (which was dissolved by civil law) was conducted by us, whether the marriage was Catholic or mixed. The same rule should apply when both divorced parties are Catholic and were not married by us, provided there was not an explicit agreement to contract a criminal union under the protection of civil law. As for marriages that are neither Catholic nor mixed, which have been contracted and broken, without us (and this is very frequent here), I leave each missionary at liberty to judge each case according to particular circumstances.

According to the letter, Father Damien's first question was asking for a confirmation of what he thought he understood. The answer to this question was yes. We would even be surprised it was asked at all, if we did not realize the errors and abuses that were prevalent in those first missionary days.

From his second question, Father Damien seems to have been looking for a practical rule: could he consider every

Hawaiian marriage null that had taken place before any non-Catholic minister? The reason for this question was evidently based on the fact that Hawaiian law recognized divorce, and that the contracting parties, when marrying, did not intend to contract an indissoluble union. Undoubtedly, the Bishop had to answer by distinguishing cases, according to the tenor of his letter to the General: only those marriages were null where the law of divorce had been formulated. In Hawaii, these cases came up frequently. Each case had to be examined individually.

As for the third question it seems the answer had to be yes.

How are we to judge Father Damien's conduct in the case which Father Albert presented to the Bishop? According to our data, it was a case of a man who had a concubine and now was on his deathbed. An *impedimentum ligaminis* (an impediment to enter another marriage because a person is bound by a previous marriage) prevented making a valid marriage out of this union; however, the first union, contracted either by the man or his concubine, was not Catholic. Because of lack of details, we cannot fully evaluate the doubt that had arisen in Father Damien's mind over the existence of an impediment. We do not know that the practice of Hawaiian missionaries caused his doubt. He used this doubt to apply a probable opinion. He thought he could marry the dying man. His motive was pure burning zeal.

Fearing with very good reason that he could not make the dying man understand he had to get rid of the concubine, Father Damien fixed up things *in foro interno* (in the realm of conscience), "the way he thought best for the man's salvation." He could not submit the question to the Bishop; the man would be dead any minute. Would it not have been prudent at least to have conferred with Father Albert? Here we have to recall that Father Damien had left the whole matter to Father Albert right up to the last. He himself did nothing in the case until two days before the man's death when Father Albert refused to hear the man's confession, although his last visit had been a couple of weeks before and a zealous priest might suppose a man could change his mind in the meantime. These were circumstances that made Father Damien take over the case. The seal of confession keeps us from knowing exactly what happened. There is no good indication that Father Damien sinned against prudence. If he were wrong, it was in good faith and is a beautiful example of priestly zeal.

Around the end of his stay in the Hawaiian Islands, Father Albert wrote these lines to Father Damien:

> I spent Easter at Kauai . . . there I saw that our famous Henricus Van Guisen [a profligate who had a post at the Kakaako leprosarium and perhaps later at Molokai] was married in 1880 by Fr. Columban to a young lady, eighteen years old, named Karokina Sweetman. What happened to her? It would be interesting to find out.
>
> Maria's daughter, Tiule's wife, who is at Kalawao, has been married in Honolulu. . . .

These extracts show that marriage cases were seriously examined by the two missionaries and that Father Albert had less trust in the natives' good faith than Damien did. He was strict in the application of principles. Still we ought to note that he complained of Father Damien only once.

Father Damien never showed the slightest reluctance at having Father Albert near him to control and guide him. On the contrary, he wept over his departure, for "Fr. Albert has really been a good guide for me; his direction has done me a world of good and I would be happy to have him for my confessor right to the very end."

An interesting insight into Damien's viewpoint is afforded us in the case of the marriage of Mr. Meyer's son; Father Damien wrote the Bishop on September 7, 1882:

> Dr. Mouritz tells me that Mrs. Meyer, a very worthy person, at the desire of her husband before he left for Honolulu, has asked me to come to their home next Wednesday to conduct the marriage of one of their sons to a Honolulu girl. I said I would, supposing the girl is Catholic since I often saw her sister at Mass at Kaluaaha. I have a doubt, however, as she went to Episcopalian schools. Be that as it may, it will not be a religious ceremony properly speaking, so I ask your Excellency to give me permission. I will try to get them to promise to have the children of this union baptized by a Catholic priest and this will be the first step toward introducing Catholicism into a family that is otherwise edifying. I will be unable to get your message before the wedding day. So please don't put me in a bad position.

His desire not to offend the Meyers, to whom he was obligated in many ways, is obvious throughout his letter. But he was not going against the laws of the Church knowingly. First of all, he supposed the girl was a Catholic; then, he could be a witness of her marriage to a Protestant after giving her a dispensation from the impediment of mixed religion. But in case the girl were not a Catholic, Father Damien's role in that marriage would be that of a civil official. The first Hawaiian missionaries believed they could act this way in marrying non-Catholics and unbelievers. But the response of the Holy Office in 1850 was stern.

A license given by the Minister of the Interior on February 23, 1874, conferred on Father Damien the right to conduct marriages on the island of Molokai. There is no reason to believe he used his power in regard to non-Catholics.

The doubt of conscience submitted to the Bishop in the Meyer family marriage case is proof that the priest married only Catholics. How explain the family's request if neither was a Catholic? Perhaps Meyer himself, who had the power of conducting civil marriages (in the Hawaiian annals he is named as the agent for signing instruments on Molokai), did not want to marry his own children. Perhaps a simpler explanation is that the family wanted it to be a religious ceremony and for them Father Damien best personified the Christian religion.

New troubles started brewing in August of the same year, 1882. The position of resident doctor, vacant in 1881, was filled only three years later. In the meantime, Dr. George L. Kakaako was in charge. He alternated between Honolulu and Kalawao, spending two weeks at each place. Father Damien was always there to give out necessary medicines. Dr. Mouritz, until then physician of the districts of Waialua (Oahu), was appointed resident doctor only in May of 1884.

Father Damien's medical practice made Father Albert furious. His irritation brought a prohibition from the religious authorities. The doctor-apostle thought it was a good idea to explain to his Bishop the motives hidden in his priestly heart when he did what he did. Mormonism was encouraging concubinage at Kalawao. There was nothing to stop these unlawful unions. The administration heads favored them and offered their own example. The priest's voice was ridiculed. It was to have his say and to cut these scandalous unions short that he had acted temporarily as medical assistant. He had asked Gibson for official authorization. With this in his hands, he was able to go in and clean out the hospital where the disorder was worst, and then gradually work out. This occupation, he added, did not take up much of his time. It put him in contact with all kinds of patients. While talking to them about their physical wounds, he quickly seized the opportunity to touch on their moral wounds. Nine years' experience had fitted him for the job better than anyone else. Since he limited himself to simple medicines, where was the imprudence and rashness he was being accused of?

In addition, he had asked Gibson for official authorization to be guardian of a large number of orphans. The Bishop knew well his reasons for doing this. He had gathered those children under his protection not without difficulty on account of a jealous administration.

Father Damien must have had a heavy heart to conclude: "Fr. Albert doesn't look at me in a very good light. If my conduct also displeases you, I will most gladly leave Molokai. If you do not soften the unsupportable temperament of my companion, you will soon see me there, even without orders. I can't bring myself to live at war with the priests the Congregation gives me."

The Bishop was in an embarrassing position. He preached appeasement. "It can happen that an action good in itself and undertaken with the best of intention can cause trouble due to circumstances created by false zeal or jealousy. You must be patient with your companion. I am convinced of that. No definitive decisions at a time when everybody is upset. For my part, I don't wish to order or forbid anything."

The Vice-Provincial, Father Regis, was more categoric: "In the present circumstances, this is our advice: Confine yourself to simple remedies and leave doctor's drugs alone, even *laau Kunu*." Father Damien promised to conform to the good advice of religious authority as much as circumstances allowed.

There was calm around the end of the year. The Bishop wrote to the Father General: "There is a good spirit among the missionaries. With the exception of some little clouds between Fathers Albert and Damien, and they were quickly scattered; union and charity are perfect."

There is no trace of tension in a letter in which Father Albert asked his companion to do some shopping for him during his trip to Honolulu at the beginning of 1883. But there is some rumbling in the background:

I wish you the good and firm resolution of preferring more this year the spiritual and temporal good of the Mission to the Board's business. Without going back over a lot of other cases you know quite well, remember that for six months you haven't had time to replace a bad lock on the tabernacle at Kalaupapa, for which you expressly bought the lock on your last trip. Last Sunday after keeping the Christians in suspense, I had to come down from the altar without being able to open the tabernacle. This is edifying!

Another run-in in February. Father Damien could feel he had done his part. He had made several purchases for his confrere. He had given him a free hand at Kalaupapa. But at Honolulu Mr. Cartwright, a benefactor, had given him a load of cloth to distribute to the needy *without distinction*. He asked Father Albert for the names of those in his district who were in need. He was just pulling off in the wagon with the load of cloth when he got his note: "Send what we have received. I will distribute it, however excluding those living in public concubinage; otherwise, keep it all at Kalawao and pass it out as you well please, without my having to bother with it."

Father Damien didn't approve of the exclusion of the truly poor who were leading disorderly lives. He told Father Albert so. The answer came back, formal: "Distribute all your cloth in your own way, I will have nothing to do with it."

A lot of the poor people at Kalaupapa came to Kalawao to get their share of the goods!

At Kalaupapa, the schoolteacher, the wife of a Protestant minister, got in an argument with Father Albert because in his zeal he was teaching the children catechism. Father Damien advised him to take them to church in order to bypass a fight. Father Albert answered he was just jealous. And to accusations of jealousy he added that Father Damien was acting only for his own glory and self-love.

Father Damien put up a defense with the Bishop:

I have always used kid gloves on my companion's touchiness and have fallen in with his way of looking at things as much as I could. I'm letting him justify his prejudices and suspicions of me before God and you. Why attribute to self-love all I have done for the honor and good of the Mission? I have always looked to the Body to which I have the honor of belonging and not to my miserable *self*. . . .

Later on we will take up the question of whether the priest loved and helped his people merely to be loved by them in return, to be praised and thanked for his charity.

In June, 1883, he was again groaning over the hardship of satisfying his neighbor. This time it was a fight over the cemetery. Father Damien had just fixed it up in as proper a way as he could. The entrance gate was not quite ornate enough to please Father Albert. He wanted a grandiose one. The blacksmith's price was too high, so he turned the gate down when it was practically finished. Father Damien refused to allow him to have a new one made. Hence the wrath. He threatened never to put his foot in Kalawao for Sunday services when Father Damien was away. And the Bishop came along with his soothing couplet: "Convinced of your fundamental good dispositions, both those of your confrere and your own, this little storm, I hope, will die down without too much damage."

There were no more storms. At the end of 1883, the Bishop got these lines from Father Damien: "What will give you the greatest pleasure is that we two, your priests, understand each other perfectly well now."

In March, 1884, a new attack of his disease made Father Albert leave suddenly for Honolulu. He went over to Kalawao the day before he left to go to confession. He didn't breathe a word of his trip to Father Damien because he didn't want to cause him any trouble. Father Damien had a bad foot by then. Once in Honolulu, Father Albert had an excuse for his little escapade. It was his visit to Kalawao that had made his sickness worse and he had taken advantage of the unexpected departure of a boat. He added this strange reason: "We are not situated at Molokai to watch over and take care of my type of sickness."

Father Albert's visit to Honolulu was hardly welcome "because of fear of catching his disease, a fear which he alone did not feel." He saw the best doctors in town, Drs. Arning and Fitch. He had a nice place to stay and nothing to occupy him but himself. Here are some of his picturesque detailed recommendations to Father Damien:

> The new radishes are ready to eat, eat them or give them to anyone you want. There's no hurry about the carrots, they can wait till I get back, so can the turnips and cabbage. Give them air and sunshine. Prop up the flowers by the wall with a cord or stick. Have a little bit of cinders put at the base of each of the cabbages to protect them from bugs. . . .

Father Damien had now definitely become his "boy." He told him to whom to entrust catechism and the school children's singing, who was to take their place at Sunday services and the Way of the Cross on Fridays. Would he keep an eye on marauders? Would he bring into the rectory anything that might be stolen from the kitchen? Would he take his young colt and break and train it for the children?

Several letters came from Honolulu to Kalawao, full of small bits of advice for Father Damien. Father Albert urged him to keep a libertine from being accepted as a new *luna* (resident superintendent). Note the fine shades of Father Albert's generosity: "Take for your personal use half of the case of biscuits, and also the ham and onions. No need to tell you to help yourself to all that is in my house and garden, without being too lavish on the natives and others." The implication was that Father Damien was only too inclined to do so.

A month later, Father Albert was bothering his correspondent. The reason? His personal occupations and preoccupations had made him forget or neglect the needs of others and especially of his confrere. Father Damien hadn't sent him a report on a cook he wanted to hire.

Father Leonor Fouesnal, a Breton, who by that time had become the new Provincial, was no easier on Father Albert than he was on Father Damien in his report to the Father General:

> For a month we have had Fr. Albert here, who runs after everybody and whom everybody avoids. He looks like he has been skinned alive. By doctor's orders he has ointment applied from head to foot. Its disagreeable odor does not prevent him from being everywhere, touching everything, getting everything greasy. The Bishop avoids him. Saintly Modeste was obliged to change places in church. Every day he keeps telling me the Mission ought to take care of him.

Bishop Koeckemann's judgment sent to the General was this: Father Albert was well enough to leave Molokai. He didn't know where to place him in the islands. Notwithstanding his talents, his zeal and many virtues, he had never been able to keep peace with his superiors, nor with his brethren, nor with the faithful, nor with strangers. He insisted too much on his own views. What he wanted, he wanted without anybody's interference. Up until now the Bishop had pleased him. For some weeks Father Albert had been trying unsuccessfully to start an argument. He was threatening to leave and go back to the Paumotus. If the General withdrew him, few tears would be shed.

After three years of working in common with Father Damien, Father Albert had no complaints to make to the General. He was wanted back at Tahiti, his desire was to make his retreat there. Not that he didn't like Molokai; on the contrary, he liked it very much. In many ways he couldn't be better off anywhere. But he didn't want to have another post in the Hawaiian Islands. According to the doctors, he had never had leprosy. Since this was the case, he asked to go back to Tahiti. Also he had been with his confrere too much not to know his real character. He had never spoken of Damien to his fellow priests except with great admiration and he had always defended him against backbiters.

For his part, Father Damien esteemed and loved Father Albert. Out of virtue he ended up accommodating himself to Father Albert's fitful humor. He lamented a great deal over Father Albert's departure. He was sick himself and was afraid he would never be able to leave the island again to go to confession. Therefore, on February 25, 1885, he asked the Bishop to keep him:

Bishop, these are my reasons for asking you to keep him here, if it is not already too late:

I) I am crippled probably for life. My terribly bad foot which you saw at Honolulu is far from healed;

although the wound has formed a scab, the inflammation and swelling of the large nerve continues. I drag my leg when I walk. To go and come back from the hospital, which is only a five minute walk, is enough to make me cry all night long.

II) Fr. Albert was getting ready to go over to the other side of the island this week to visit the Christians who have not seen a priest since the 3rd Sunday of Advent. His trip was put off only because of the steamer's delay. He even seemed to get back his old enthusiasm for working seriously there.

III) Though I certainly hope I will be able to take care of the whole Settlement again by getting back my old patience, your Excellency will easily agree that I must definitely give up all efforts to climb the Palis. And neither my foot nor the setup will allow me any longer to go into the other district. Besides, I cannot leave 600 Catholic lepers, many of whom are dying.

IV) If I am really attacked by this terrible disease, we have to admit that death is approaching with slow steps. Without worrying too much about my body, I certainly have to worry about my soul that needs a confessor. Well, Fr. Albert has certainly been a good guide; his direction has done me good and I would be happy to have him as my confessor right up to my deathbed. If you let him leave, Your Excellency, see if you can find another one like him to come to the Settlement to hear my confession, at the same time taking care of Molokai with its five neglected chapels.

Father Damien then told the Bishop: "With great repugnance, I have almost decided to take the steamer next Friday to visit the whole island of Molokai for the last time." Later he scratched this out and wrote in the margin: "It is impossible. The priest [Fr. Albert] will go."

Father Albert left Molokai and was going to use up his energy at Tahiti. He wrote to Father Damien:

I am definitely leaving for San Francisco next Wednesday. The Bishop was a little cold at our first interview, but for some time he has been amiable and gracious toward me.

He gave me a very flattering letter from the New Vicar Apostolic of Tahiti who invites and begs me to return to them.

So please help me thank the Sacred Hearts who have arranged to my heart's desires the things you had misunderstood a little . . .

Please forgive the little annoyances I might have caused you, as I myself gladly forgive you all in your conduct toward me that went against me and caused me pain.

I embrace you with all my heart and urgently recommend myself to your prayers and holy sacrifices . . .

Good-by and till we meet in heaven.

Totus tuus in osculo sancto [All yours with a holy kiss].

The year before, Father Gregory Archambault was found to have leprosy and was sent to Molokai. This was a hard blow for him, but he resigned himself to God's will. Father Damien hoped to find in him a good companion for years to come. Though suffering from leprosy himself, Father Damien did everything in his power for the priest. Father Gregory was able to preach, teach catechism morning and evening, and direct the singing. Because of his condition, Father Damien didn't want to leave him alone too long. Besides leprosy, Father Gregory suffered from severe attacks of asthma. "Many times," he wrote to the Father General, "Fr. Damien has gotten up at night and come over to see if I was still breathing, my asthma was so bad." The climate was almost killing him, so he left Molokai on January 14, 1885. He returned in November, 1887, sent by the Board. By then he was in the last stages of leprosy. All he could do was to hear Father Damien's confession. Three months later he left, and died at Kakaako, November 12, 1888.

Therefore, without underestimating the help given him, we must say unhesitatingly that the religious transformation of the leprosarium was due to Father Damien alone.

RELIGIOUS ACTIVITY

Father Damien, the builder of churches, saw from the very beginning that St. Philomena's at Kalawao had to be enlarged. Out of the 752 patients, half of them were Catholics. "We are getting close to 400 Christians or catechumens, counting non-patients." Merely the odor of the wounds was sufficient reason for expanding: "Often I have had trouble making it through Mass. Molokai has waited long enough for you to come to our aid." Be generous then, Bishop, he said.

Assisted by his patients, he changed Brother Bertrand's chapel by adding a transept and later a bell tower. And we have already seen him at work on the large church at Kalaupapa. The patients there — it was a distance of some three miles — certainly needed one. It was a frame structure, some thirty feet long, sixteen feet wide, twenty-three feet high, and was crowned by a steeple. Later he had to enlarge it too. Father Albert painted it in bright colors that just about put the natives into ecstasy. "You might think it was a beautiful chapel of a religious community," the painter said, quite satisfied with himself. And Prof. Stoddard tells us: "The altar was like a picture, and there was a goodly number of those beautiful, mild-faced, artistically-tinted statues of the saints, such as always remind me of the attractive shop-window in the vicinity of Saint Sulpice in Paris." The painter had the merit of working hours on end with the patients whose feet were being devoured. "Humanly, it's unbearable," he said. They didn't even suspect it.

As we have seen, the south part of the island did not have a chapel. Father Damien provided one in 1874. In four months, he built for Father Andrew four wooden chapels, a rectory, and a school. This was the time Father Andrew took his place at Kalawao.

Father Damien preached for the most part in fluent Hawaiian, taught catechism, repeated the doctrines of the Church in season and out of season, in private and public, everywhere — at church, at the orphanage, in the sufferers' homes, in his yard, on the road. His instructions varied from real sermons to simple conversations. He spoke at High Mass and Benediction, on Sundays and feast days, every morning, at catechism class after Mass, during the day when he visited the hospital. As the case called for, he was ready with an exhortation or rebuke:

When I enter, I begin by offering a remedy that will heal their souls. Those who refuse this spiritual help are not deprived of the material care and helps that I give to all without distinction. Except for a few obstinate heretics, everybody regards me as their father . . .

They are hideous to look at, it's true, but they have souls that were bought at the price of the Saviour's blood. He too in His mercy consoled lepers. If I can't cure them, I do have the means of consoling them. I am confident that many, purified by the sacraments, will one day be worthy of heaven.

In my visit to their homes, there is much good to be done, even if one has to condemn himself to breathing infected air. I have to change my tone of voice from one house to the next. In one place I speak only gentle, consoling words, in another I have to be harsh, to stir the conscience of some sinner; at times I have to thunder and threaten unrepentant sinners with eternal punishment.

Once Father Gregory accompanied him on his visits.

He told how comforting they were, but added that they were nonetheless hard on nature. Several times he came down with a terrible headache. One day when he suffered a great deal, Father Damien told him: "Console yourself. Even after I was here for three years, I still suffered too."

We have his notebook in which he sketched his sermons. He gave comments on Scripture texts adapted to the native mentality, and always added some practical applications. His usual theme was this: "Earth is only a place we are passing through, an exile. Heaven is our real homeland. We lepers, we are sure of going there soon. We will be repaid for all our miseries. No more hideous leprosy, no more sufferings there! We will be changed, be happier and more beautiful, the more patiently we have borne our suffering here below."

At Kohala his prayer leaders had proved so valuable that he wanted some like them at Molokai. He trained many of them so the sick could always have a chance to pray in common:

> On Sunday afternoons we have meetings for the sick, directed by prayer leaders. Four or five houses at Kalawao are filled to overflowing. After Mass, baptisms and dinner, I go over to Kalaupapa where I hold three meetings; one for the natives who are not sick, one for the patients around the port, the third out at the end of the promontory.

In his letters the record of conversions is quite clear. The first month he was there he baptized people by the dozens or half dozens. Every year adult baptisms ran into the hundreds. In 1875, Father Andrew recorded 140 baptisms in two years, and Father Damien had about 300 to 400.

What we have already said about his zeal in comforting the poor sufferers should not be separated from these mass

conversions. Christ made His converts by doing good. The
priest's charity was an argument for his Faith. He came
to Molokai and stayed there as their benefactor. He could
not have had a more powerful introduction to his gospel.
"His voluntary exile," Georges Goyau says,

> among these human derelicts was a proof of the love
> God had for them. His lips didn't have to teach them.
> If they had been mute, his presence among them would
> have been a thundering indication that God, who was
> making him love them even to such extremities, Him-
> self first had an infinite love for them . . . an infinite love
> from which his was derived and where it was rekindled
> every day.

Few able Catholics ever missed Sunday Mass. If they
did, they were sure to receive a visit from their pastor on
Monday, according to Dr. Mouritz. A good number of them
came every day, and took part in the daily recitation of
the Rosary in the chapels. The sufferers had a special devotion to the Way of the Cross and our Sorrowful Mother.
They could often be seen going over the sorrowful road
that led from the Praetorium to Calvary. In May, they
would bring flowers for the Blessed Mother's altar; many
of them wore their rosary around their neck. At least 300
went to Communion every week.

The Sunday fervor on Molokai was astonishing to visitors. High Mass at St. Philomena's was the big event of
the day. The altar was ablaze with lights and flowers. The
choir, a group of children in red cassocks and lace surplices
. . . the music and singing . . . the prayers recited aloud
by all . . . the noble, gentle pastor of his flock, praying to
God for them . . . all of this on an island lost in the Pacific,
offered a spectacle that drew and absorbed the natives and
won the admiration of visitors. At all times, people have
remarked on the simple devotion of Hawaiian Catholics.

The Hawaiians have music in their souls. Edward Clifford spoke of the religious singing he heard:

They sing very nicely. One man had a full sweet baritone, and there was a tiny child who made a great effect with a bawling metallic voice. A refined-looking woman played the harmonium well, with hands that looked as if they must have been disabled. She had been a well-known musician in Honolulu.

I enjoyed the singing of the Latin Christmas hymn "*Adeste fideles*." But the most touching thing was the leper song (composed by a native poet), a kind of dirge in which they bewailed the misery of their lot.

It was the sufferers' *Super flumina Babylonis:*

When, oh when shall it be given to me
To behold my God?
When,
Oh when shall the captivity of my wretched soul
Cease in this strange land where night and day
Weeping,
Weeping alone is my portion;
When, oh when shall I leave this valley of sorrow,
Where the only bread I eat is my continual tears?
When, oh when shall I see my well-beloved Lord?
Prince of the heavens is He,
Guardian of my soul, my Hope, my Savior,
My All . . .

Father Damien wrote about it to his brother Pamphile: "At the High Mass on Sunday, my children sing like consummate musicians. Alas! Tuberculosis and death come to take away from me the best voices of my choir."

Professor Stoddard attended the High Mass and described it:

High Mass at Kalawao — the solemn Mystery offered

almost in the spirit of a *requiem;* for the participants are doomed, and the living are well-nigh dead.

I was directed by Father Damien to a small enclosure at the left of the altar. It was not unlike a witness box; a railing enclosed the single seat, and no leper was ever permitted to open the gate that shut me in.

The neatly robed sanctuary boys were all disfigured — some with pitiful, distorted features; but, fortunately, none of these seem to suffer any pain, or much inconvenience; though fingers and toes are in many cases missing, and the eyelids are thickened and drawn out of shape. The very beautiful sacramental vessels, of richly-wrought gold, were sent to Father Damien by the Superior of St. Roche, in Paris; they were used only at High Mass.

With the greatest sweetness and gravity the celebrant proceeded. The chapel was filled with worshipers, and all of them seemed to be singing, or trying to sing, simple refrains, that sounded strangely enough in the hoarse throats of the singers.

The devotion of the Catholic Hawaiians is remarkable, because the race is much given to childish levity; and I have nowhere else seen such evidences of genuine contrition — certainly not in the meetings presided over by native ministers: the American Protestant missionaries having retired from the field, and left it in the hands of the aborigines.

What a contrast was here; the bright altar, cleanly furnished; the young priest, a picture of health, chanting with clear, ringing voice the *Pater Noster;* at his feet the acolytes, upon whose infant features was already fixed the seal of early death! Beyond the altar-railing corruption ran riot; there was scarcely a form in that whole congregation from which one would not turn with horror, and many of these worshipers seemed actually to have risen from the corruption of the grave.

The solemn boom of the sea-surf was fit accompaniment to that most solemn service; and the long, low sough of the sea-wind was like a sigh of sympathy. The very air was polluted; the fetid odor of the charnel-house pervaded it; and all that chamber of horrors seemed but the portal of the tomb.

This is the Feast of the Master as celebrated at Kala-wao; and to celebrate it thus is Father Damien's blessed privilege. I thought of that verse in St. Luke: "And as He entered into a certain town, there met Him ten men that were lepers, who stood afar off, and lifted up their voice, saying, Jesus Master, have mercy on us!" Verily their prayer is answered; for He hath mercy on them, and blesses them in the person of His servant.

Father Damien had grown accustomed to the odor that bothered Professor Stoddard and other strangers. But as we have seen, he admitted that he had had a hard time getting used to living in that atmosphere.

He again got sick when he took care of patients whose wounds were full of worms. Those worms, he said, seemed like those that eat bodies in the grave. He had given the last Sacraments to a poor man, and on his way back home he swayed like a drunken man, the smell was so powerful. He hoped these acts of mortification would obtain from God the spiritual resurrection of sinners. Sometimes he had trouble giving Extreme Unction because a patient's hands and feet were only one big sore. This was the sign of their approaching death.

It was his daily job to get souls ready to appear before God. In 1880 he declared that since his arrival he had buried from 180 to 200 dead a year. The constant inflow of new patients kept the number up around 700.

Most frightful of all, in the words of an eyewitness, was the anticipated decomposition of the dying. One man no longer had a human form; all that could be seen was a shapeless, mutilated, half-rotten trunk. Even Father Albert, with all his self-sufficiency, said he had to go to the door several times to get air and to stop quivering at the stomach and heart.

According to Father Damien's conviction, oftentimes expressed, his most powerful weapon for conversion was prayer. He believed he had given a Protestant irresistible arguments for being converted. It was wasted effort. Father Damien gave him some more arguments. The man was still stubborn. Next Sunday, Father Damien recommended him to the people's prayers. Monday morning, the man was there to see Father. Like the repentant Jews with St. Peter, he wanted to know "What am I to do?" After making a profession of Faith, he was baptized and received absolution with signs of a sincere conversion.

> It is certainly in the midst of tears [he wrote] that I have sown the good seed among my lepers. From morning to night I am surrounded by terrible physical and moral miseries. However, I try to have a certain gaiety to build up their courage. I present death to them as the end of their troubles and their entrance into heaven, if they trust God. So, many of them approach their last hour with resignation, some of them with joy. In the course of the year, I have seen at least a hundred die with excellent dispositions.

Many times at night his sleep was rudely interrupted. He was wanted on a sick call. Here is one little adventure that happened to him in his long career of sick calls. A woman was dying. The night was dark, the road muddy, and the rain was coming down in buckets. He climbed on his horse and rode off. He was careful to hitch his horse before he went into the house. Quite a few Catholic women were gathered around the dying woman. She had fallen away, but now made a good confession and received Extreme Unction. Those around her fervently prayed aloud. When he went outside, no horse! It had broken the halter and run off. But that was not all. Father's coat was tied to the saddle. It would have kept the rain out. There was no use looking for the horse. Father Damien could not see two feet ahead of him. Through the mud and downpour, he waded back to the rectory. If he had lost his coat, he had helped save a soul.

Without a doubt, leprosy was for some a real grace, helping them to get out of sin and to return to God. Many deaths were very beautiful. Of one he wrote:

I have just buried one of my best Christians, the son of a confessor of the Faith. His death was very edifying. He was sighing for heaven. He kept repeating the words of St. Paul: "I desire to depart and to be with Christ." When I brought him Holy Viaticum, everything about him revealed his faith and love. He rests near the large cross I erected in the middle of the cemetery. Near him lie almost 200 other lepers who died as Catholics in the last year and a half (Dec., 1874).

Almost all of them ended up as Catholics, for the majority of the Protestants asked for the priest when they were dying. He even administered baptism to two Protestant leaders on their deathbeds. "I do everything I can to prepare them all for death. In this work I find my greatest consolation. Most of the patients come here as non-Catholics and die in the bosom of the Church."

11   Moral Cleanup

SOME short accounts of Father Damien's apostolic work
have conveniently left out some of the shades in the picture. Yet, in the interest of truth, they must be mentioned.
Our desires must not be taken for reality. And the fact is
that, even under the healthy influence of the priest, not all
the people become angels, given to prayer and good
morals.

Satan and those he dominated and who represented
him gave Father Damien plenty of trouble. Besides, the
priest had his own personal characteristics to overcome.
Dr. Mouritz gave this as his objective judgment of Father
Damien:

His temperament was mixed, nervo-bilious, the former
element predominating; he was easily excited, easily
peeved, supersensitive, and difficult to get along with at
times. Damien and I clashed and snapped repeatedly.
His years of residence at the Settlement had made him
an autocrat in all matters; he had very fixed views and
brooked no interference with his will. His unyielding
attitude on many affairs outside his proper sphere of
work brought him in conflict with the Board of Health
and the workers connected with the other religious sects
at the Settlement.

Against that opinion, Father Aubert's must be laid. Around the end of 1872, we know that he had approached the Bishop and offered to take over the post at the Settlement. The Bishop told him to stay where he was. Later, Father Aubert wrote: "He did right, for I was not capable of doing all Fr. Damien did . . . he did a great deal of good, perhaps more than any of us could have done. . . ."

Drunkenness, stealing, debauchery accompanied by immoral dances had greatly lessened but not at all disappeared. Drunks found their liquor on the spot. Father Damien told about it in his report of March 11, 1886:

Previous to my arrival here it was acknowledged and spoken of in the public papers as well as in private letters, that the greatest want of the lepers at Kalawao then, was not having a spiritual leader or priest, the consequence of which was that vice, as a general rule, existed instead of virtue, and degradation of the lowest type went ahead as a leader of the community. On the arrival of a new number of lepers, the old ones were soon at work to impress them with the erroneous axiom: *"Aole kanawai ma keia wahi,"* in this place there is no law. Not only in private conversation, but in public meetings, I myself heard this doctrine proclaimed; and for a long time, indeed, I was obliged to fight against its application being made to the Divine law as well as human law. In consequence of this impious theory, the people, mostly all unmarried, or separated on account of the disease, were living promiscuously without distinction of sex, and many an unfortunate woman had to become a prostitute to obtain friends who would take care of her, and the children, when well and strong, were used as servants. When once the disease prostrated them, such women and children were cast out, and had to find some other shelter; sometimes they were laid behind a stone wall and left there to die, and at other times a hired hand would carry them to the hospital.

The so-much-praised *aloha* of the natives was entirely lacking here, at least in this respect.

As already mentioned in other pages, the Hawaiian *hula* was organized after the pagan fashion, under the old deity Laka, who had his numerous altars and sacrifices, and I candidly confess that I had hard work to annihilate Laka's religion and worship, and thereby put a stop to the hula and its bad consequences. Though the people had reached the climax of despair, both of soul and body, may it be said to their honor that I found them less addicted to sorcery and the doings of the *kahuna lapaaus,* or native doctors, than I had found the old natives in Hawaii — circumstances which encouraged me much to stay permanently among them, with the quasi hope of my ultimate success as a Catholic priest.

By a short digression I will speak of another source of immorality, viz.: the evil of intoxication. I first have to explain how they obtained the material. There grows very abundantly along the foot of the mountains a plant which the natives call *ki (Dracaena terminalis),* the root of which, when cooked, fermented, and distilled, gives a highly intoxicating liquid. The process of distilling being very crude and imperfect, produces, naturally enough, a liquor which is totally unfit for drinking. A short time after my arrival the distilling of this horrible liquid was carried on to a great extent. Those natives who fell under its influence would forget all decency, and run about in a nude condition, acting as if they were totally mad. The consequences can be easier imagined than written on paper. The local authorities have endeavored to stop all those horrible proceedings, but for a long time they were unsuccessful. It being discovered that certain members of our police were in league with the evildoers, the *luna nui* (the big boss) and myself went around and both by threats and persuasion, they finally delivered up their implements which were used for distilling; some of the most guilty perpetrators were convicted, but were pardoned under the condition never to do it again.

For a long time, as above stated, under the influence of this pernicious liquor, they would neglect everything except the *hula,* prostitution, and drinking. As they had no spiritual adviser they would hasten along the road to complete ruin. A good many of the sick and prostrated were left dying there to take care of themselves, and several of them died for want of assistance, while those who should have given a helping hand were going around seeking enjoyment of the most pernicious and immoral kind.

Ambrose Hutchinson tells us that Father Damien, with only his strong and unshakable courage, became a policeman to stop public drunkenness and the bestial orgies that followed. Armed with a cane — the gift of a friend — he made daily strolls around Kalawao. He went everywhere he heard the noisy sound of the *uli-uli* a large gourd used as a drum. This instrument was decorated with bright feathers that, fanlike, covered the drummer's fists. He beat cadence for the famous *hula.* This scandalous dance was held in honor of *Laka.*

In the midst of the revelry the alarm was given. Somebody cried: "Father Damien!" As soon as he appeared, the *hula* stopped and the gay dancers scattered in all directions. The priest would enter, seeing only gourds and cups of their liquor. His heavy cane would swing, scattering liquor and broken pieces of gourds all over the ground. He would then come out and shake his cane in the direction of the fleeing natives: "You good-for-nothings!" he shouted after them.

This priest was first and alone in fighting this evil. He had nothing closer to his heart than to make honesty and decency reign among those poor pariahs. The astonishing thing is that Hutchinson says he never heard of any leper attacking Father Damien. But that does not mean they loved him.

Hutchinson lost no love on the administrators sitting in Honolulu and responsible for the leprosarium. They led a life of easy repose in their offices. They arrogated to themselves the right to say that the patients could be left to their own devices since they were in such miserable physical condition anyhow. And the patients took advantage of their license. Too many of them had no respect whatsoever for the moral law, and seemed to have lost all notion of good and evil. They thought only of satisfying their lower instincts and passions. They lived in shameful promiscuity and would let no one put up a bar to their license. Whites as well as natives were scandalizing everyone. Throughout the islands, the Settlement had the reputation of being a hellhole. That is the reason for the violent opposition to being sent to Molokai that was met with every time a suspect was arrested.

From the beginning of his mission at Kalawao in 1873, the libertines lined up in opposition to Damien. Hutchinson affirms that this situation continued until surveillance of public morality was turned over to the resident superintendent in 1884. He himself as an official on the post administered justice as well as he could. But it was a hard job for one man. It was Hercules cleaning out the Augean stables. Yet he took over firmly, patiently, and finally got the desired results. The *luna* was never popular with the inmates, who defied him because they thought he was too young. They flung the worst insults right in his face.

Hutchinson gives an example of what was going on. The assistant superintendent of the Settlement was an American, Clayton Strawn [who later calumniated Father Damien]. Strawn sent Keliaka, an officer with the high-sounding title of *Ilamuku* (marshal), to one of Hutchinson's relatives who was gravely ill.

"Like a hungry bird of prey," Hutchinson tells us, the officer pounced on his helpless prey. This officer seized every movable belonging of the sick man, trunks of clothes, dishes, pots and hogs, etc., and loaded on an oxcart carried them away and taking the horse, saddle, and bridle along with him and against the owner's protests, to which the brute paid no attention, leaving only what the sick man had on his person. A few days after this incident my *Makua Kaue* (kinsman) died. I had the disagreeable task with the help of friends to place the remains of my relative in his coffin with nothing on but a calico print.

This outrageous treatment of the dying man made Hutchinson complain to Dr. Emerson. He told the facts: the man's dying wishes, expressed orally, had been flaunted by the brutal theft of the officer. The doctor gave him the unpleasant job of handing to Strawn the demand for an explanation. Strawn's mistress came out, called him, and Hutchinson handed him the note.

Strawn at once went to see Dr. Emerson, who kept his distance lest he come in too close contact with something touched by the leprosy patients. Strawn admitted that the charges were true. Then he turned to Hutchinson and started cursing him furiously. Hutchinson wasn't going to put up with a thing like that and was ready to fight. Dr. Emerson was afraid serious trouble would break out, so he asked Hutchinson to leave. However, thanks to his vigorous intervention, all the dead man's personal effects were put up at public sale in Honolulu and the proceeds given to the man's daughter.

From then on, this odious treatment of dying patients stopped. They were not robbed of their personal belongings even before they were dead. Everybody was happy about this except some of the employees who were thus deprived of their unlawful gains.

Father Damien found that his remonstrances and intervention were of no use unless he was backed up by the agents of the administration. Without some sanction, his crusade against abuses would have been unsuccessful. Yet for a long time they were indifferent. As a matter of fact, many of the Board's agents took part in the debaucheries.

Where was he going to find convincing arguments to make these ignorant people realize their errors when they were brutalized by vice and hardened in evil? Only royal law could remedy the situation by penal sanctions. But the authorities were content to say: "Let the lepers distract themselves as they want to!"

The missionary could not even get the co-operation of the resident *luna* (Hutchinson's predecessor) and his American assistant. The former had all the power but was old and weak; the natives said he was avaricious and no good. And Strawn, as we have seen, was degenerate. He lived at Kalawao with two leper women, one married, the other single, in a house built for him by the Board. He dominated the whole administration. His word was law since his superiors would say yes or no to anything he ordered or forbade. He judged the priest by himself and helped blacken his character.

But the missionary was not a man to be discouraged. He was about the best policeman they had ever seen. No one dared resist him and he could break up the wildest parties.

Drunkenness led to quarrels and fights. The men and women would go at it, the men using their fists and the ladies using their teeth. Hair was pulled and faces were bit . . . and no one was there to put a stop to it. Except for the priest, Hutchinson knew of only one other man big enough to stop these carryings-on. That man was a giant by the name of Kekelaupio who could easily carry an eight-hundred-pound weight and could handle the biggest roughneck with one hand. He was a descendant of another giant by the same name who had been a companion in arms and faithful friend of King Kamehameha the Conqueror.

Government measures were badly needed to stop the moonshining and heavy drinking! There were neither laws nor sanctions. A new resident superintendent's efforts were useless, especially since his methods, being somewhat unusual, never got the capital's approval. When an influential person would hazard a complaint to the president of the Board about the excesses at the Settlement and the threats made against the better element there, a letter would be sent to the superintendent authorizing him to take what measures he thought necessary and that was the end of it. Nobody said anything further; they had done their duty. It was sheer hypocrisy, calculated to discourage those in charge from keeping order. So the drinking and carousing went on from one end of the leprosarium to the other without anybody being able to stop it.

In April, 1884, Father Albert begged his companion to use his influence with the Board's representative to get a certain Van Diezen out of office as resident superintendent. This rascal was too violent, too meddlesome, and too corrupt to have such a job. Against the Sisters' wish, he had put several natives in jail at Kakaako so he would be freer to have three girls spend the night with him. Out of decency, Meyer could not very well accept the scoundrel. If he became *luna*, there would be war at Kalawao. If the Minister had not intervened, the Sisters would have gone back to America.

Two years earlier Father Damien had written frankly to the president of the Board: "The only complaint I have always had against our inside administration and specially during this period is the disrespect paid to the moral law. How this can be bettered is my daily study. With the grace of God — and the strong arm and good will of the government assisting the Christian influence — I think we could remedy somewhat this rather dishonorable situation of our poor lepers."

Some of the employees at the Settlement did not have leprosy, and Father Damien had no hold on them. He told this to the Board in an earlier report. They had to send *kokuas* for the patients. But they had to distinguish between the married and the unmarried. With few exceptions he maintained that unmarried *kokuas* were not desirable.

On the contrary, he encouraged married couples living together:

> In the fulfillment of my duties as priest, being in daily contact with the distressed people, I have seen and closely observed the bad effect of forcible separation of the married companions. It gives them an oppression of mind which, in many instances, is more unbearable than the pains and agonies of the disease itself. This uneasiness of the mind is, in course of time, partly forgotten by those unfortunates who throw themselves into a reckless and immoral habit of living. Whereas, if married men or women arrive here in company with their lawful mates, they accept at once their fate with resignation, and very soon make themselves at home in their exile. Not only is the contented mind of the leper secured by the company of his wife, but the enjoyment of good nursing and assistance, much needed in this protracted and loathsome disease, and which no other person could be expected to impart.

In his opinion, all the employees should be chosen from the non-leper husbands of patients at the Settlement. Others wouldn't do at all: "My disapproval of seeing unmarried *kokuas* settle here is based on the following reasons:

1. Because, with the exception of a few old people, unmarried *kokuas* are not generally faithful and persevering in assisting those patients in whose favor they were permitted to come here.

2. They are, in general, a source of immorality and a temptation to lead the lepers into bad habits, and through their bad example sometimes create trouble in the place. *

3. Because, having no natural tie here, they, after a long intimacy with the lepers, may leave the place whenever they choose, and although the disease may not yet be visible, it is highly probable that they carry the germs of it to their homes, and thus become a well-fitted medium to spread the disease amongst their numerous friends.

4. They are of very little use here, if of any at all. They will not do anything for the poor sufferers except for payment, with which they go gambling and generally go around from house to house and help to consume the poor lepers' scanty rations; they have no fixed abode, and are too lazy to work for their own support; in some instances they even try to obtain lepers' clothing by some means or other.

For these reasons I venture to recommend to the authorities that they be more strict in the future than they have been in the past.

By 1880 there were more than 200 *kokuas*. To head off any frauds, Damien suggested that some proof of a legal marriage should be shown before they were authorized to come.

But the old abuses were always ready to crop up, for in

* In his general report for the years 1882-1884, to the Board of Health, Dr. G. L. Fitch made this observation of the *kokuas*, or native nurses: "Most of them are there to live off the rations provided by the Government for the sick and as a rule they add to the unparalleled licentiousness of that hideous brothel. (Signed) G. L. Fitch, M.D."

1886 Father Damien wrote a similar protest against the administration's employees.

Every once in a while an outbreak would occur, such as the tragedy at Kalaupapa, October 29, 1885. By government decision the nonleper children of the Settlement were to be sent to the Kapiolani Home at Kalihi, Honolulu. Fourteen girls were picked out. Unfortunately, the steamer arrived at Kalaupapa too late for a day trip. The captain insisted he had orders to be in Honolulu in the morning, so they started moving on board a couple of hours after sunset. Dr. Mouritz tells what happened:

Amongst the little orphan girl deportees of leper parentage was one Abigail, about eleven years of age; she had two foster fathers, Lohiau and Momona, men of middle age and of powerful build, their leprosy not far advanced. These two lepers had made threats against the police several days before the date of the supposed departure of the steamer with the orphan girls; had sharpened, and were seen sharpening, butcher knives. These men openly stated they would resist by force the removal of Abigail.

Several of the girls had said good-bye to their friends, with the usual loud Hawaiian wailing, filling the air. Abigail's little flimsy trunk was being carried by Momona when he was halted by Deputy Sheriff Kanohoahu and police officers Mahiki and Kaumualii. Lepers were not supposed to have contact with the boat's crew (to prevent smuggling of opium or intoxicating liquors), they could come down to the causeway leading to the then primitive wharf, but no further.

The police passed Abigail along to the boat, Momona wished to carry the little girl's trunk, but the officers held him and attempted to take the trunk from his hand. He resisted, and in the struggle the trunk opened and its contents, the girl's clothes, fell into the sea.

Lohiau, carrying a knife in his hand, unperceived in

the darkness, stabbed Kanohoahu twice in the pit of the stomach, and Momona, dropping the trunk, also drew a knife and stabbed Kanohoahu back of the left clavicle, cutting the subclavian artery and piercing the lung. Efforts to wrest the knife from Lohiau ended in his giving a back twist of the weapon, which entered the abdomen of Kaumualii and reached the spleen. Mahiki grappled with Momona, and in the struggle for possession of the knife was stabbed in the right groin, cutting the profunda femoris artery.

Kaumualii died of acute peritonitis in thirty-seven hours; the knives used were rusty, foul and septic.

Kanohoahu died in thirty-six hours from acute septic peritonitis and hemorrhage of the stomach, it was alone possible to staunch the subclavian and lung hemorrhage.

Mahiki recovered in six weeks, his wound was four and a half inches deep and cut a large branch of the deep femoral artery.

On the following Monday, November 2, 1885, the tug "Eleu" came to Kalaupapa with the Board of Health and members of the Honolulu police force. Lohiau and Momona were arrested, deported to Lahaina, tried, convicted, and were sentenced to ten years in prison.

To further add to our cup of misery, the officials of the Board of Health and Father Damien received a scolding; the priest got into hot water, the doctor also, and Deputy Superintendent Hutchinson, because we all had wilfully and stupidly disobeyed the clear (?) instructions of the Board of Health. The priest, Hutchinson, and myself, heard our denunciations before an assembly of lepers at Kalaupapa from the lips of Gibson, the then President of the Board of Health.

It was also decided to censure R. W. Meyer of Kalae, agent of the Board of Health and superintendent of the Leper Settlement. He was severely crucified in the eyes and ears of the lepers, because he had failed to come down into the Settlement and attend to the shipping of the orphan girls.

From time to time efforts were made to rebuild altars to the god *Laka* and to bring back lustful dances. There were numerous Protestants and Mormons at the Settlement. In theory, because of their religion, the Protestants and polygamous Mormons escaped the priest's jurisdiction. Practically speaking, he had enough moral authority and physical vigor to make them stop their disorders.

To preserve the young and abandoned, Father Damien doubled his efforts to give them a refuge. We repeat that was his big work.

Boys and girls who came under the segregation law had to leave their families. On arrival at Molokai, when they were still enjoying relatively good health, they were quickly adopted by patients. These so-called friends soon made slaves of them. It was now their job to clean house, take care of the horse, look for food, gather firewood, cook, and do anything else that was needed. Their lord and master was left free for fun.

These children were to be pitied — especially the girls, who at puberty were forced to submit to shame and immorality. When their bodies were too ravaged by leprosy to be any longer useful they were thrown out. Soon the *luna* and his assistant would be notified, and an ox-drawn cart — the island's sole means of transportation at first — would take them off to the government hospital at Kalawao. There they would drag out their few remaining years of life.

Father Damien witnessed their inhuman treatment. To his great regret, he was powerless to do anything about it. He immediately saw he had to build a home for boys and old men, another for women and young girls without protection. He needed funds. Where would he get them? He turned to his Bishop. The Bishop did not disappoint him in his hope of making things better.

From then on he was in the market for wood which he shipped to Kalaupapa on the *Warwick* and from there to Kalawao it was hauled in oxcarts.

About mid-1879, he built his house not far from the rectory. It had a kitchen and dormitory for a dozen boys. This was the beginning of a first-class institution. As soon as he opened the place, he had eight boys. Others followed . . . and still others. He had to build a much larger dormitory, twenty by forty feet, north of the first one. All this was under the missionary's immediate supervision and direction. It was just the thing the children needed; it was for their welfare and fully served its purpose. The particular interest Father Damien gave to it was the secret of its success.

When his visits to the sick were over, he gladly turned to his children. He would spend two or three hours with those whose health permitted it. He showed them how to pull weeds, and made it a game rather than work. The little farmers set to work enthusiastically. A week had not passed before all the weeds around the place were gone and in their place sweet potatoes, onions, cabbage, banana trees were planted.

Damien knew this wholesome work would keep them from being lazy or getting into trouble. Beside, their good crops brought in money. With this income he was able to hire a man to pound *pai-ai* and mix *poi*. He also could buy flour, sugar, and coffee. Bread was cooked in a nearby oven made out of an old hardened piece of lava — it was a baker's dream! The children had so much *poi*, sweet potatoes, delicious bread, coffee, milk, meat, beans, and salmon that without doubt they were the best fed group in the Settlement. And they never ran short.

Long after Father Damien's death someone maliciously invented the story that he had taken sweet potatoes away from starving children. It was a case of mistaken identity.

It was assistant Strawn, who after having taken over the maintenance of public order when Father Damien had resigned from his job as resident superintendent, punished the incorrigible distillers of *Uala Awuawa* — a strong liquor made of fermented potatoes — by forbidding, not too successfully, the cultivation of potatoes.

The Bishop was more than interested in this great work being done for the children. He gave it his closest attention. He told his missionary in 1882 that the children's material needs were not as great as their spiritual needs, especially those born of unbelieving parents and who had to be protected from corruption.

The priest kept him up to date. Under his charge were ten children born of unbelievers or non-Catholics. He expected more. The catechism was their favorite book. Every evening they learned a chapter by heart. They then recited it the next morning after Mass. The girls had their house a short distance away. He hoped Meyer would stick to his decision to have all the sick girls under fourteen placed in the home. Through his go-between he was getting in touch with the Board in Honolulu. The Board, it was true, was interested only in the children's material well-being. The Bishop and the priest had something better in mind: their spiritual good.

Through Gibson, then its president, the Board decided that only those girls who had no friends could be put in the institution. Later, when everything was perfectly organized, the obvious happiness the children enjoyed there was the best argument for relatives.

In January, 1885, the priest could assure his brother Pamphile of a general improvement of the material and moral conditions at the Settlement. The resident superintendent at the time was a young half-white leprosy patient who was also a very good Catholic. Almost all the employees were Catholics and under the influence of our holy religion. "Little by little we have succeeded in straightening up a lot of disorders. . . . After the recommendations made to the King by the governmental authorities about the good that could be expected from them, His Majesty has asked for Sisters of Charity." We will speak of the work of the Franciscan Sisters later.

12   *The Soul of Molokai*

DR. MOURITZ gives us another picture of the man who
was responsible for the eternal destiny of the 700 or 800
souls at Molokai:

When I went to reside at the Leper Settlement in the
fall of 1884, Damien was then in his forty-fifth year. He
was active and vigorous, of good physique, upright in
his carriage, measured 5 feet and 8 inches in height,
weighed 204 pounds, his chest was 41 inches in circumference, his hands and feet were shapely, although
his fingers were stubbed and calloused from toil.

His features were regular, his face fleshy, round, and
of good dimensions; the color of his eyes brown, his hair
black and abundant; his forehead of average breadth
and height. He had a clear ringing voice, possessed a
powerful baritone, and was a good singer.

The view of his full face gave the onlooker the idea
of force, harshness and sternness, due in part to the
squareness of his chin and lower jaw. His profile was
handsome, was softer and more in harmony with the
entire cast of his features than the view of his full face
presented. Very few of the photographs of Fr. Damien
do justice to him . . . Having a wealth of hair, he

roamed about bareheaded, resulting in his face becoming bronzed by exposure to the wind and the sun's rays.

He wore gold-rimmed glasses, a black cassock bound at the waist by a black belt, and sometimes a stiff black ecclesiastical felt hat with four strings holding its brim. In his right hand he usually carried a big cane and in the other a folded stole.

Thanks to this man of God, simple but full of zeal, the church bells rang on Molokai and the churches filled with worshipers. Religious feasts gave opportunity for wholesome rejoicings. Work, prayer, and relaxation alternated as was fitting. Sufferers were spiritually consoled by his visits and died in his arms when their time came. There was an intense religious life among the better members of the community. Theirs was a religion simple, consoling, elevating, sanctifying. The little church at Molokai radiated its faith, sent up praises to the Lord, and multiplied its works of mercy.

Besides Sundays, on certain other days in the year fervor reached great heights. Father Damien remembered the good he got out of the mission he made at Braine-le-Comte, when he decided on his vocation. He asked his fellow priests to help his people have similar exercises. The mission was a great success.

"Every day, morning and evening, the Christians crowded into the chapels for Holy Mass, instructions, the Way of the Cross, confession, adoration and Rosary. A choir executed religious chants with a perfection you would not have believed possible."

To make it easier for the sick to attend the sermons, the number of meeting places was increased: at Kalaupapa, at the hospital, at St. Philomena's, and in the plain that used to be called "the village of the fools" in memory of the immoral dances that went on there, but which was renamed "Ninive" in memory of the inhabitants' conversion. Some of the Protestants showed no repugnance at coming to hear the word of God. At Kalaupapa, there were even a Calvinist minister with his deacons and a self-styled Mormon bishop with his followers. The missionary said they could make objections. The result was that they lost much of their prejudice; several wanted to become Catholics. There were eleven adult baptisms.

The missionary did not even try to express his feelings at speaking to such an audience. Those who had been there before him had burst out sobbing, and he held back his own tears only with great difficulty.

The last Sunday of the mission, the preacher rode back to Kalaupapa for the closing sermon. A thirty-horse cavalcade escorted him. On arriving he found the chapel so full of Protestants and Mormons that the Catholics had to stay outside. There was just enough room in the sanctuary for him to stand.

These missions were repeated many times during Father Damien's sixteen years at Molokai. It made the good better and brought in some that were not so good.

Two or three times a year the two parishes of the Settlement had great religious celebrations, for example, at Corpus Christi and at Christmas.

In 1874, a year after his arrival, Father Damien organized a Corpus Christi procession which Father Andrew described:

Two repositories draped with the colors of Hawaii had been prepared, one at the end of the peninsula, the other in the hospital enclosure. The canopy and portable altar were about nine feet high and made of bamboo which the men had found in the mountains. For lack of paint, they were decorated with red and white paper in spirals. As someone had just given the priest twenty new drapes for the chapel, he took the old one which the women made into albs, cinctures, oriflammes, and large banners.

At 3 o'clock, the procession started, divided into three groups. The first, with three banners and thirty oriflammes, was made up of the children, the young girls and adults. The second was that of the portable altar which followed the band and the men's and women's choirs. The third was the Blessed Sacrament. Four strong men, clad in green attire, ornamented with a large red cross, carried the canopy. At the four corners, acolytes in cassocks carried flags. In front, choir boys were swinging censers, preceded by little girls in blue and white who were throwing flowers. Another band closed the procession.

Without stopping, the band alternated with the choirs, while the faithful were reciting the Rosary. Everyone able to move was there. Even Protestants followed respectfully or uncovered their heads as the Blessed Sacrament went by.

The priest walked under the canopy, carrying the monstrance. He walked slowly, timing his steps to the cripples who followed along painfully. Tears covered his face. The crowd of lepers sang the *Lauda Sion* with a burst of gripping enthusiasm. On returning, the songs were a little quieter.

The ceremony converted eight Protestants and made about fifteen more start taking instructions.

Father Damien describes another *Corpus Christi* procession in a letter to the Father General, Silvain Bousquet, written August 25, 1886:

Because of our life being so monotonous, I have but little of a journal to communicate. Will limit myself to two subjects: an account of our celebration of the last Corpus Christi day, and mention of a new hope for our physical welfare by the introduction of the Japanese treatment of leprosy in our settlement.

As to the Corpus Christi procession: on last Easter Sunday it was determined that on Corpus Christi day we would celebrate at Kalawao, by a procession. My two choirs of singers at a meeting for consultation held at Kalaupapa decided they would prepare themselves by learning appropriate music for the high Mass and Benediction. With a surprising perseverance, for natives, they practiced each intervening day in their respective school houses, meeting together on certain of these days at either Kalawao or Kalaupapa.

The celebration was fixed for the Sunday in the Octave.

On this beautiful day the majority of my people of both parishes assisted at the first Mass, for communion, they having prepared themselves by good confession. (From Wednesday until Saturday the pastor had been occupied to the limit of his strength in the confessional.) At ten o'clock we had the high Mass.

The church being too small to accommodate all of the faithful the seats were given up to those who came from other portions of the settlement, and the residents of the immediate vicinity of the church remained outside, about the door and windows. The singers not wishing to use the harmonium, placed it outside to make room for the whole choir. In all they numbered about forty, all but three or four being lepers, well exercised under the direction of a blind leper having considerable musical talent, who struck the measure. Their singing would compare favorably with that heard in many Cathedrals.

It was my sermon only that fell short of the general standard. Was too much fatigued to enter fully into the deep subject of the feast. And besides I wished to avoid my habitual fault of preaching too long sermons. Immediately after Mass, without leaving to the pastor time for breakfast, the procession was formed, the cross and the great banner being in advance. Then came the drum, and the musical instruments of tin (may some

charitable soul supply us with some brass instruments).
Then two associations bearing the Hawaiian flag, followed by two lines of Christian women. Then came the
men, and after them the singers, always directed by my
good blind Petro, under a parasol, and guided by another native. Then came the incense bearers before the
canopy. At each corner of the canopy walked a lantern
bearer. Each lantern being carried upon a staff and
beautifully ornamented with flowers. The portable repository well decorated augmented the display.

Arriving at the residence of the superintendent the
repository was placed under the veranda. And then I
exposed the Blessed Sacrament. Favored by the pro-
longation of the chant we had opportunity to rest ourselves upon the grass after our march. The Benediction
given, the procession returned to the church by the
route it came.

After the religious exercises the Christians were all
refreshed by the *agape,* consisting of *poi* and a pig
weighing 300 pounds.

By this you will see that our Blessed Lord grants us
at times consolations with our afflictions.

Christmas was just as beautiful. Christmas, 1882, Father
Damien wrote down his impressions from day to day to
give his brother Pamphile:

Dec. 21 — As I finish Mass, I receive a package of
letters, and among them is yours. A half hour thanksgiving before opening them. What a mortification. This
time I prayed a lot for the family, but with just a little
too much distraction all the same. After that, I begin to
read all the letters without thinking of lighting my little
kerosene stove to make some coffee. Since you were so
kind as to tell me only good news, I was jubilant.

My young people, so anxious to hear the news, hardly
gave me time to breathe. I had to translate and tell
them all that was in your letter — Fr. Leonor's visit, your

sermon notebook of 5782 pages. The old woman who takes care of the children, and the children themselves, were in admiration at Mary's and Pauline's handwriting. Breakfast runs into dinner. After that I pick up my walking stick to visit the sick from one house to the other to prepare them for Christmas. I have the consolation of baptizing an old blind woman who recently arrived and was well disposed. Any delay would have been dangerous. She is in the hospital with serious cases in the company of a good number of Catholics.

Dec. 22 — Today, Friday, after Mass a short instruction in preparation for a good Christmas confession. Afternoon, confessions at the hospital for those who can't come to church. The confessor's nose shares the mortification of his ears. However, with the difference that I could stop up one, if I didn't want to smell the infection too much. Finally, a good number are carefully prepared for a good Communion tomorrow. But how are we going to arrange it?

Dec. 23 — Fast day. A little salt will take the place of the usual good meat in our *poi*. At dawn two good Christian women came to fix up a small repository in the middle of the big hospital room. At 6:30, the priest in surplice and stole goes through the streets carrying the Blessed Sacrament. It is a ten minute walk from the church. Everybody is gathered and on their knees when our Lord arrives. We say the prayers before Communion, then a short instruction. At the moment the priest gives Communion, someone holds a small cloth under the communicant's chin, since many of them are blind and others' lips are in pretty bad condition, so you have to be very careful when giving Communion.

After Communion, an educated Protestant makes his abjuration and receives conditional baptism. While they are saying their prayers of thanksgiving in common, I take Holy Viaticum to a neighboring room and go back to the church as I came.

I find everybody waiting for me for Holy Mass, etc.

After breakfast we have to clean up and decorate the church. Being short of artificial flowers, and other decorations, my young people bring me greenery from the woods which they make into long garlands. To cover the arch and part of the altar takes a half hour. The wooden candlesticks — each with six candles — are only waiting to be lighted at midnight Mass.

Dec. 24 — Sunday morning. Finishing touches on decorating the altar. I'm only half satisfied, since I have only old ornaments to put on it. A mouse in the closet ate big holes in my antependium. The beautiful statue of the Sacred Heart above the altar has only some garlands of leaves.

At 10 o'clock, High Mass as usual. There are some of my catechumens who want to be baptized — right away. Let's go eat a little first and then we'll see. It's about 1 o'clock. During that time, my schoolteacher had given them a few more instructions. Four Chinese and three Hawaiians are found to be prepared well enough to receive the grace of baptism. I had a hard time making my poor Chinese understand the main doctrines of our holy religion. Two old Chinese Christians have helped me, for I don't speak their language. One of them speaks our Hawaiian language fairly well. All four of them have been coming to church faithfully every Sunday for the last six years. Considering their good will and bad health, I believed I could baptize them. The ceremony is over at 2 o'clock. Then into the confessional I go until 9 o'clock in the evening. My confrere, Fr. Albert, arrives with his Christians from Kalaupapa.

CHRISTMAS — 11 o'clock at night the bell rings. Our young people go through the village beating two drums, waking everybody up and shouting "Merry Christmas!" The weather was beautiful. All my Catholics, all dressed up, hurry to church. At a quarter to twelve, the bell rings again. We begin our prayers together, soon my choir (at least twenty) begin their Christmas carols.

Right at midnight, Fr. Albert comes out of the sacristy with his altar boys. The church is well lighted, filled to the doors, perfect order. After the Gospel, the preacher makes a great impression on the hearts of my poor patients. Although he is rather old, Fr. Albert has learned Hawaiian very well. It is about 2 o'clock when all is over. Everybody went home happy and pleased. This is the tenth time we have had Midnight Mass here. The first years we had some disorders, but now the people are more civilized and everything went off well.

At dawn when I said Mass, it didn't do me any good to ring the bell. Everybody was asleep. Necessity obliged me to allow general Communion at the midnight Mass. So there was no great inconvenience. They all come for the High Mass at 10 o'clock, as on Sundays.

To encourage and develop the good dispositions of the better ones, Father Damien formed groups to undertake works of piety and charity. In every parish there are always some who are more fervent than the general run of people. Ordinarily they join associations and confraternities.

At Kalawao there were two religious associations, one for men, another for women; their principal purpose was to visit and aid the sick. The priest hoped they would do much for his people. Their zeal and devotion kept many others on the straight and narrow. So he set up three confraternities: *The Holy Childhood,* made up of youths and children to help the poor and sick; *St. Joseph's,* made up of men to visit the sick in their homes; *Our Lady's,* made up of women to help the sufferers who were particularly neglected. Father Andrew affirmed that they had considerable success in bettering the poor people's lot.

Another association was that of *Perpetual Adoration.* Members took half-hour shifts and kept up a constant stream of adorers of our Lord in the Blessed Sacrament. In 1879, Father Damien wrote to the Father General:

We have established perpetual adoration in the two churches of the leprosarium. It is pretty hard to have regular hours because of the members' sickness. If they cannot come to make their half hour of adoration in the church, I am often edified to see them make their adoration at the appointed time on the bed of pain in their miserable huts. I hope that our brothers and sisters of our beloved Congregation will not mind learning that they have imitators even among the lepers and I especially hope they will not refuse them a place among their ranks in heaven where (I have the fond hope) that a good number of my children have already gone before us. Pray and get others to pray, Very Reverend Father, for your very humble brother in SS.CC. [Sacred Hearts].

Singing and the band heightened the celebration of every feast. In 1875, when Bishop Maigret came for Confirmation, he was amazed at the pomp in his honor. Horsemen were waiting for him at the landing. A Mass of Mozart was sung in church. A cortege of two hundred people with flags conducted him to the boat while the band played on.

The band played at everything . . . even funerals. This was done to affirm their hope in a better world. By the prayers and singing around the body of the deceased, they were told that the soul still lives and that God is good and will reward them. This ceremony calmed their fears and soothed their sorrows. It is a good thing it did, for death was striking the sufferers with redoubled blows. On the average, every other day one of the lepers died.

From 1876 on, the priest could write that practically all the funerals they had were Catholic ones. God had already brought the great majority of the outcasts into the Church and generally the rest asked for baptism before death. So it was that Father Damien founded a "Christian Burial Society."

One of the priests who gave a mission tells us:

I was in church saying my Breviary when a distant and harmonious sound reached my ears. Gradually the procession approached; I could distinguish the big drums, the rattle of smaller ones, and wood and percussion instruments.

Soon the church was full. Fr. Damien gave the absolution and the funeral started to the cemetery.

Some women were holding the funeral pall. Others, in two rows, followed the body. All were dressed in black and wore either a red or white band according to which confraternity they belonged to. The band brought up the rear. The musicians seemed happy to play such excellent music for the good Christian they were burying.

"Poor Juliana," Fr. Damien said to me afterward, "she was so good. She is certainly in heaven, for she suffered her purgatory here on earth!"

I asked him why all the colors. He told me that they had two different burial associations. The Hawaiians loved this pomp and ceremony.

Gone were the days at Molokai when a man had hardly died before he was rolled up in a blanket and carried off to a shallow hole.

The transformation was an accomplished fact. On his second visit to the Settlement in 1884, Professor Stoddard could hardly believe his eyes. In place of a prison and a hellhole; instead of dirty houses where fifteen years before leprosy victims were thrown as outcasts to rot and die together, he saw now two villages of white houses, surrounded by flower gardens and cultivated fields, a hospital, a graveyard, where the dead were buried with religious reverence, and two orphanages filled with happy children. Men and women were out horseback riding. And brightening up and enlivening everything were devoted charity and religion with its calm beliefs and superhuman strength of acceptance; in other words, the lepers were living a social life that was almost normal and harmonious.

When Edward Clifford asked various persons if they missed not being back home, they said:

Oh, no! We're well off here. The government watches over us, the *luna* is good and we like our pastor. He builds our houses himself, he gives us tea, biscuits, sugar and clothes. He takes good care of us and doesn't let us need for anything. We wouldn't want to leave if it meant we would have to leave our *Makua Kamiano* [Fr. Damien].

Clifford admitted: "I had gone to Molokai expecting to find it scarcely less dreadful than hell itself, and the cheerful people, the lovely landscape, and the comparatively painless life were all surprises. These poor people seemed singularly happy."

Father Damien echoed this when he wrote to his old mother: "I am very happy with my lepers and wouldn't want to be separated from them for anything in the world."

13   *Lights and Shadows*

ALONGSIDE Damien's success, the high flights of emotion and enthusiasm and generosity, ran jealousy and bitterness.

Among other things, he was criticized for the relatively large sums of money that came to him from all sides. And all the time, he went on living in a simplicity that was close to absolute privation. But his friends were too numerous and devoted for his enemies to block his work.

When he first arrived at Molokai he was in need of almost everything. This was found out and spontaneously a dozen people in Honolulu, gotten together by chance, gave him $130. Ten out of this first dozen benefactors were Protestants. Theirs was the first of a long line of gifts that never stopped. We must remark that Protestants showed magnificent generosity toward him. They forgot their differences of religion and race to rival Catholics in admiration which redounded to the Church to which he belonged.

Two months after his arrival, he went begging from door to door in Honolulu and came back with enough clothes for three hundred patients. The papers gave good news coverage to what was going on at Molokai and the mounting interest increased people's generosity.

His fellow religious helped him as much as they could. They were already too moved by the pitiful condition of the Settlement not to favor this project of the Mission in a special way. But they had demands to meet on their own mission posts. Nevertheless, the Bishop and the Provincial did all they could, sending him financial help, gifts, and also financial advice. For example, Father Leonor wrote Father Damien: "Do not be offended, if I again preach economy to you. All the Bishop's money is spent and we are wondering how we are going to get along. Not a penny in sight. . . ."

His companion at Kohala, Father Gulstan, had written him: "How can I send you the alms I have received for the lepers? I have over fifty dollars, but I hope to send you much more." From Paris the Procurator-General was forwarding sums of money collected for the leprosy patients. The priest stirred up the fervor of his benefactors: "I still have the big expense of enlarging St. Philomena's. If charity would continue to help me and could furnish me with several donations (from five to eight hundred dollars), the Bishop would let me make something better. As for myself, I don't spare my sweat. But no matter how much the worker does, we need what we need."

His hardest-working promoters were the Sacred Hearts Sisters in Honolulu. They took advantage of being women and Sisters to ask everybody to help him. A steady flow of boxes and bundles came from their convent to Molokai. It was his clearinghouse.

Generous souls in Europe sent their gifts through the *Missions Catholiques* of Lyons and Fribourg. These alms were rather important. "The sum received from M. Arthur de la Villardiere enabled me to alleviate the miseries of my poor lepers. I hope Catholic charity will continue to furnish me with like alms from time to time."

In 1874, a French parish priest added to his offering:

Your example has made my parishioners realize the goodness of the Catholic tree that produces such excellent fruits, that gives birth to such devotedness. I have to tell you of the immense service rendered to the cause of Jesus Christ by a devotedness that seems local, but that is the glory of the entire Church. As to the question of vanity: when a man feels that he is a weak, wounded creature, is it possible? And how could it enter the head of a man alone in the midst of the ulcers and infection of those poor people? . . . We are all fighting for God . . . with pretty unequal courage. . . .

Several years later, another pastor — a Protestant this time — was the source of Father Damien's singular popularity in England. Let's look into the story of the first English money drive for him.

In a London suburb lived Rev. H. B. Chapman, the amiable pastor of St. Luke's Anglican church at Camberwell. After reading an article on Molokai, he spoke about it from the pulpit and invited his parishioners to be generous to Father Damien. That some Catholics, living in the confines of St. Luke's, could add their contributions to those of the Protestants, he got Cardinal Manning, the Archbishop of Westminster, to give his patronage to the idea. When the appeal was publicized, it provoked vehement disapproval from Thomas McClure, honorary secretary of the Working Men's Protestant League, a hidebound outfit. He wrote Chapman:

October 30, 1886

Rev. Sir. — I am desired to express astonishment that you, a clergyman of the Church of England, should endeavour to create sympathy for an idolatrous priest of that abominable system against which you are especially pledged to labour, both as a minister of the gospel and also as a liberty-loving Englishman.

The self-denial and devotion of Father Damien are no more worthy of admiration that that of the devotees of Baal, who cut themselves with knives "till the blood gushed out upon them" (I Kings xviii, 28), or those who cast their bodies beneath the car of Juggernaut. All that Father Damien can achieve as the priest of Antichrist is to make his proselytes "twofold more children of hell than he is himself" (Matt. xxiii, 15).

It is also especially to be condemned that you give to Dr. Manning his full title as representative of the Papacy; and thus, as a minister of Christ, you would assist the minions of Antichrist to obtain a social and illegal status from which England has already suffered terribly, and you are labouring to rivet the chains of terrible idolatry and priestly imposture upon her again.

Instead of making the boundaries clear, distinct, and insurmountable between us and Rome, so that they who would pass from hence to her cannot, you take away the ancient landmarks, remove the gospel warning-lights, and with the feeble glimmering *ignis fatuus* of false charity, you entice people into dreaming that we and the Antichrist are brethren.

I am, Rev. Sir, yours truly,
Thomas McClure, Hon. Sec.

The *London Tablet* published McClure's letter, which it called "fatuous," and added, "Mr. Chapman's reply is very brief, and to the point:"

177, Camden-grove North, October 22nd, 1886

Dear Sir: — Your letter is a very wicked one, though I excuse it on the ground of its utter folly. Go and do thou likewise.

Yours truly,
H. B. Chapman

McClure revealed no inclination to follow the evan-

gelical counsel Chapman had given him. On the contrary,
he strained himself to find arguments and scriptural texts
to show his own lucidity of mind and the pastor's ignorance
of the word of God:

If you understand the teaching contained in the Bible,
you will perceive that leprosy was a prominent mark of
God's displeasure. He visited Miriam with this plague
in anger, though afterwards He displayed His mercy in
healing her. Lepers were to be kept apart, and "several"
houses were erected that they might not mix with men.
They were to pass by on the other side of the streets
and cry "Unclean, unclean!" All these things are doubtless as an idle tale to many. God gives us life to glorify
Him, but in no case is it enjoined by Him that our lives
should be sacrificed, as all men were born for His glory.
Life is given us to preserve to that end.

I certainly decline your counsel, "Go and do thou
likewise," because I believe it to be utterly at a variance
alike with any man's moral or religious obligation though
it is our duty to do good unto all men — a precept but too
much neglected by those who profess most in our day
and generation.

McClure did not cite the Gospel. The same divine voice
had asked one day: "Which of these three, in thy opinion,
proved himself neighbor to him who fell among robbers?"
If the same question had been asked in connection with
the leprosy victims, it would not have put Father Damien
in an embarrassing position, nor the man who quoted our
Lord's words: "Go thou and do likewise."

The English people reacted sharply to McClure's letters
and generously to Rev. Chapman's appeals. A man who
signed his name as "Laicus Anglicanus" (an Anglican layman) wrote to the editor of the *London Tablet*:

Sir, — I am an Anglican, and having been a regular

communicant of the Church of England for more than fifty years, I trust I may have imbibed something of her spirit. I cannot find words sufficiently strong to express the grief and humiliation I feel that any one professing to belong to any sect bearing the name of Christ could have written such a letter as that of Mr. Thomas Mc-Clure to the Rev. H. B. Chapman.

I enclose you the small sum of 10s. for Father Damien's fund, first as an act of reparation for the gross and outrageous manner in which the Rev. Father was attacked in that letter, and, secondly, as an act of thanksgiving to the Almighty for having shown in the person of that eminent servant of God that His power and grace, as exhibited in the life and sufferings of the early Confessors and Martyrs of the Church, is not less now in the nineteenth than in the first six centuries of the Christian era. I think we have tried ill-will, hatred, and all uncharitableness long enough; let us now try what a little Christian charity will do to heal or mitigate our grievances, and I pray that such men as the unhappy writer of that epistle, if there be any more such, would rather learn from St. Paul: *"Charitas patiens est, benigna est, charitas non aemulatur, non agit perperam, non inflatur . . ."** (1 Cor. 13:4).

Rev. Charles E. Taylor, an Anglican churchman, wrote the next day to the *Tablet:*

Sir, — will you allow me to express the disgust and contempt with which I, and I believe all Anglican Churchmen, read the uncharitable effusion that you published in the *Tablet* last Saturday. Many allowances must necessarily be made for a person who considers that brawling in church is a reputable way of forcing himself into notoriety, but one might surely be pardoned for concluding that before such a noble and saintly

* "Charity is patient, is kind; charity does not envy, is not pretentious, is not puffed up . . . ."

heroism as that of Father Damien, every feeling but admiration would be silent. The discovery that this idea was mistaken, brings us to the recognition of this mournful fact, that there exists at least one mind that is incapable of appreciating the exercise of the highest Christian virtues in one of different creed. But the inability of a narrow mind to realize the splendour of such a sacrifice must be but a tribute to its magnitude.

I trust that Mr. Chapman will not be deterred from his work of love by the dread of the inference "that Mr. McClure and Antichrist are brethren."

On November 10, 1886, Rev. Chapman was able to write to the editor that he had gathered a considerable sum for Father Damien:

Sir — I write to inform you that this fund, which now amounts to £650, will be closed on Saturday next, and I beg respectfully to thank you for having materially assisted in the small offering which will thus be sent to this saintly priest. His holy charity is beyond all discussion, which is best described by the word irreverence. Such a life makes one's own appear very easy and selfish, and I consider it an honour to lay the slightest offering at the feet of the man who is brave enough to lead it.

The zeal of St. Luke's rector never diminished. Later we will come back to the interest in Father Damien that Rev. Chapman started in England.

The Americans, who were interested in Hawaii and consequently were up on Hawaiian affairs, imitated the generosity of the English. Their journalists and doctors had visited Molokai. The press of the United States publicized the conditions then existing at the Settlement. Hearts were touched and hands opened.

Dr. Woods, the U. S. Navy medical inspector, came there in July, 1876. We have already mentioned his remarks on the intelligent care the missionary was giving; it may have left much to be desired, but it was the best Father Damien could do. On Wood's arrival at Molokai, he was met by "at least a hundred men and women on horseback, and three times as many on foot." Bill Ragsdale came forward and introduced himself; he then

presented me to Father Damien as the true "Father" of the Settlement and his "right-hand coadjutor." The priest was at this time — July, 1876 — in the prime of life, being about thirty-three [actually he was 36] years of age, and the perfection of youthful health and vigour. His face was smooth and rather thin, but not emaciated; his features irradiated by an earnest expression intensified by a fixed gaze of calm dark eyes. The chin slightly projected, with a deep sulcus below thick widely parted lips, and the head, poised upon rather a long neck, was covered with black curly hair carelessly brushed or unbrushed. He wore a *soutane* which had seen much wear and not been too well cared for, and carried in his hand a broad brimmed straw hat of native manufacture.

Father Damien showed Woods the Settlement and told him: "This is my work in this world. Sooner or later I shall become a leper, but may it not be until I have exhausted my capabilities for good to these my unfortunate afflicted children. I have endeavored to help them morally, materially, and as a healer of physical wounds."

About this same time, Dr. Rolando Kueln, a resident of Nicaragua, came for a visit. When he attended a convention of the American Medical Association in New Orleans in 1903, he told reporters: "The whole world was interested in Father Damien's mission to Molokai, and especially the clergy of the Church of England, and *en masse* they wrote him, enquiring if he wanted anything — not a pittance — but anything. His reply was: 'Yes, send me enough cloth to make every leper on the island a new suit of clothes.' " Father Damien thought only of his people. The doctor added: "I have seen the time when he did not have enough to buy postage."

Kueln treasured a letter from Father Damien as the most valuable earthly possession he had. He would not let it out of his sight for a minute. "I don't suppose there are many others extant," he said. It was written on October 3, 1888:

Dear Sir, — Your kind letter to hand. I read it with interest, calling to mind our previous cordial meeting at Lahaina and here. I am glad to hear that you are happy, and that Almighty God's blessing seems to accompany you. Let us always be faithful to Him, and serve Him the best we can, recognizing ourselves to be great sinners. Let His holy grace enter into our hearts, and by and by no human respect or motif will prevent us from practising our holy faith as the Lord desires and commands it. Being both loyal to our King, Kalakau, whose name is now very seldom mentioned here at the settlement, let us be more and more loyal to our Divine Lord.

You are well and healthy. I am getting old and weak. I know that my days are numbered, and do not expect to be in this miserable world for a long while. I feel my disease has gone down to my lungs, and very soon I hope all will be right — when the body is under the green coverlet.

Our new Priest, L. Conrardy, is with me. J. Dutton continues good work nursing our sick boys, numbering now eighty-eight. We are over 900 lepers all told, and though we are sick, peace and happiness seems to reign at Molokai.

Give my respect to all who take so much interest in the care of the lepers, and may God's blessing be with you all.

> Yours truly in Christ,
> J. Damien, Catholic Priest

After his second visit to the Settlement, Prof. Stoddard narrated in the *Indiana:*

Other lepers gathered about us as we entered the churchyard; the chapel steps were crowded with them — for a stranger is seldom seen at Kalawao — and as their number increased, it seemed as if each newcomer was more horrible than the last until corruption could not go farther and flesh suffer no deeper dishonor this side of the grave.

The chapel door stood ajar; in a moment it was thrown open, and a young priest paused upon the threshold to give us welcome. His cassock was worn and faded; his hair tumbled like a schoolboy's, his hands stained and hardened by toil; but the glow of health was in his face, the buoyancy of youth in his manner; while his ringing laugh, his ready sympathy, and his inspiring magnetism told of one who in any sphere might do a noble work, and who in that which he has chosen is doing the noblest of all works.

This was Father Damien, the self-exiled priest, the one clean man in the midst of his flock of lepers.

These articles and others like them won countless benefactors for Father Damien in America. Checks and bales of goods came from all parts of the country. A Boston pastor sent him a magnificent harmonium. Archbishop Gross of Portland, Oregon, set up a center for gifts and called himself "the agent of the lepers." Portland bankers lent him money at no interest. We must mention too the "widow's mite" of an Irish working girl in Massachusetts who sent him all her scanty savings.

A Protestant on his return from Oceania wrote in a Berlin paper in 1883: "A Catholic priest has been established at that lepers' hell. He is the only one to have penetrated and stayed there, to give these poor desperate souls the consolations of eternal life. Voyagers of all nations, salute when you pass the cliffs of Molokai!"

The concert of praise in the world press was not unanimous. It exasperated some of the more bigoted Protestants at Honolulu. This praise seemed to them to be biting criticism of their ministers who were not represented at the leprosarium. Some of the Hawaiian papers betrayed their spite and jealousy, alleging prudence and elementary precaution in defense of their pastors. To forestall unfavorable opinion, others invented ministers at Molokai, "voluntarily obscure because they never thought their activity needed panegyrics."

Father Cornelius Limbourg, who succeeded Father Regis as Vice-Provincial, made a formal and flat contradiction of this claim: "I affirm that a white Protestant minister never has resided at the leprosarium. There have been some native Protestant ministers who were lepers or Kokuas accompanying their wives."

Father Aubert said:

I have seen Protestant ministers there and talked to them. All of them, if not lepers, were at least there with their leper wives. The first were forced to be there. And in the second group, you have to admire their attachment to their wives. But I have never seen or heard it said that they had done anything that amounted to much for the other lepers in general. The extremely sharp eyes of Protestant reporters have seen nothing.

We must hasten to add, however, that these attacks did not represent the feeling of the whole Protestant community. One Protestant paper ran an article entitled "Charity." The writer began by remarking that after St. Paul's discourse on charity, there was little left to be said. Then he added that he should point out a deed that spoke louder than ten thousand discourses — the charity of Father Damien. Freely, without any hope of reward in this life, the priest had gone to Molokai among the leprosy victims. Though the publishers and readers might not agree with the ideas in Father Damien's head, they could do nothing but admire the love in his heart. None of them would dare do what he was doing. While they sat safe and snug in Honolulu, they should remember the poor priest on Molokai. The article ended with a plea for help — through Bishop Maigret send Father Damien a book, a little wine, anything he could use, and some money out of love of holy charity.

Other attacks, which at first sight seemed better founded, hurt Father Damien but never discouraged him. But the Catholic Mission headquarters did lend an ear to them. That is the truth of the matter, a truth that must be told and explained. Father Damien's superiors lived in the eddy of crosscurrents where inevitably Hawaiian politics entered. The superiors were moved by the noise of these recriminations. Concern about money dominated and absorbed all others that somehow got connected with it. Why all the money drives in America and England? Why so much money in the hands of one priest? How could the patients, whose needs the State was supplying, still need so much money? Why did Father Damien pose as the sole benefactor, concentrating in his own hands the supplies, the administration, the entire responsibility of the Settlement? Why was the money, regardless of its source, not turned over to the Board of Health? Why did the priest not tell what he did with the money? Could not the Catholic Mission have turned the money to its own use?

Offhand there seems to be some point to these questions. In theory, the Hawaiian government promised to take care of the patients at Molokai, and it was nettled that anyone would accuse it of not scrupulously using public funds in their behalf. After all, Father Damien had a limited role, generously sustained anyway by the Board's massive administration.

The Missionary's thought and action in this business also deserves examination. At the beginning, with no purpose in mind but to provide for his poor charges' most pressing needs he had gone around begging alms. He got them. Indeed, the day came when money flowed in too abundantly. His superiors were troubled about the spirit and vow of poverty of their religious.

The donations were addressed to the priest personally, but were destined for his people. He acted merely as a middleman, a distributor who judiciously and impartially gave out the supplies without making any distinction of race or religion. The Hawaiian legislature voted a staggering budget for the leprosarium. But generous as it might be, the State was in no position to fulfill all the patients' desires, nor even all their needs. All one needs to do is read a number of the letters from the Board's representatives, especially those of 1883. The government was in the greatest financial difficulties. The Board of Health was short of money. Everyone had to learn to economize. Some of the employees at the Settlement had to wait for their pay. It was impossible to carry on an indispensable job of blasting rocks out of the harbor without money.*

By force of circumstances, Father Damien found himself the distributor of generous offerings — but not without stirring up jealousy, and in the first place, among government members themselves. Through the banks, they knew

* See Father Damien's letter to the Minister of Interior, p. 161.

how much money was coming from England. Why leave all the money in his hands?

Naturally, no one attacked him directly. They were not ignorant of his energetic ability to put up a fight. They would have been paid off with a vehement and definitive protest, such for example, as the customs office got when it wanted $100 from the Catholic Mission as duty on church ornaments offered by American Catholics. At once Father Damien wrote to the president of the Board:

I beg to inform you that I feel somewhat surprised at the custom house officers claiming from the Catholic mission the round sum of one hundred dollars for church furniture sent to my address by some charitable persons from the U. States.

Being requested to give the estimate value of contents, in 7 boxes, as usually I do, receiving anything for the lepers from other countries, I simply stated that I was sure the church furniture did not exceed 1000 dollars, but supposed it cost several hundred dollars less — no bills or accounts having been sent to me — it being a donation in favor of the churches of the lepers. On this guessing statement of mine they make out a 10% bill — for the full thousand — and send the same to C.M. (the Catholic Mission) In justice C. M. has nothing to do with it and it will be very painful to the donors to be informed that their sympathizing charity toward the Kalawao lepers has been a charge rather than a benefit.

[*Written in the margin*] Before applying to the American consul, in this confidential note, rather than to apply to a consul or custom house office — I prefer to send you this confidential communication.

Now as a friend of mine and a member of the B. H. — I humbly beg your Excellency to use your influence with the Cleghorns and to see if that sum can not be returned to C.M. and thus avoid an unpleasant comment on the government. The treaty too comes in favor of a free passage as also the source where it comes from and the object and people for whom it is intended.

But someone must have dropped a hint to the missionary Fathers, especially the Provincial. Since Father Damien had so much money for the patients, wouldn't it be right to turn it over to the government or Board of Health for custody and distribution? It would be used for general improvements and the really poor.

Father Damien, however, knew quite well what he could expect from official generosity. Around him he could see its employees on the job. He was far from being satisfied. For him there could be no delays.

The powers in high places went on with their secret maneuvers. Father Provincial even succeeded in convincing himself that all that money in the hands of a religious was against the spirit of poverty. With this in mind, he agreed wholeheartedly with the Board's secretary who wrote him that Father Damien's incomprehensible conduct was unfortunate. After the whole world had raised him to the clouds, now everyone was criticizing him. And though everybody knew that he (the Provincial) and the Bishop did not approve of Damien's conduct, the secretary was afraid this blame would come back on the Mission.

We may well pause here to reflect on this matter. We will come back to these unjustified recriminations when they become stronger at the end of Father Damien's life.

First of all, we must note that he had nothing to do with the first news published about him and his work. Moreover, he was annoyed about it and made those responsible wait a long time before he wrote them again.

In 1876, he explained to his mother and brothers why he had delayed answering their letter. He had been opposed to having his previous letter printed in the *Annales,* official magazine of the Congregation of the Sacred Hearts. "Once and for all, let me tell you that I do not like that at all. I want to remain unknown to the world. And see, on account of these letters, people in different places are talking about me . . . even in America."

He was more resigned later when he saw how the publicity was benefiting his people. It was no longer a question of his modesty but the comfort of his adopted children. Were not his supplies coming in for the express purpose of helping out the needy? They enabled the Settlement to hold out when the steamer with weekly provisions was late. Along with the officially established methods of aiding the patients, he found a hundred different ways of putting these gifts to good use. It was the intention of the donors that he distribute their gifts himself. By his heroic life, which forced the authorities to take some interest in his pitiful charges, he had won their confidence. One patient even raised his voice in protest and demanded publication of his letter in a newspaper that was extolling the financial help given by the Board of Health. He pointed out that it was the clear will of the contributors that Father Damien dispose of the money as he saw fit; that was clear from such letters as those of Rev. Chapman. How did the Board in Honolulu know who was in need and who was not? What the government did with its $100,000 he did not know; but he did know that he, like the rest, got only $6 per year — certainly not enough. Besides that, they didn't even get money, but had to take poor grade clothes at exorbitant prices from the Kalawao store.

The government was needlessly offended over private charity. Certainly no government has, or ever had, a monopoly on assisting the poor. This idea is ridiculous to say the least. The missionaries, and Father Damien first of all, highly praised the Hawaiian government's efforts to aid their unfortunate fellow countrymen. They also realized what the King and his ministers could not deny — that a great deal still remained to be done at Molokai. The best proof of this is in the considerable improvements they made later.

As for the exaggerations found in some fantastic articles giving Father Damien an exclusive role he never had, but which he actually shared with the official agents, they were not and cannot in any way be substantiated by his letters. At no time did he write anything beyond the real facts. Some have mistakenly blamed him for articles written without his knowledge, and which he would have condemned in his own strong way, if he had known of them.

Unfounded attacks that the Catholic Mission was making money under the pitiful cover of leprosy victims in need were not even worth considering. What can one say to a certain class of egoist too coldhearted and narrow-minded to understand the generous enthusiasm and great heart of Father Damien? There will always be people who are cynical and evil-minded enough to misrepresent the most exalted virtues.

Despite these facts, the political situation in the Hawaiian Kingdom had its repercussions on the Settlement; and it shaped the thought and actions of the administrators on the higher levels. The religious authorities, for their part, had the daily job of putting up with the touchiness of the administration. And the missionaries scattered throughout the entire territory had to be considered no less than the Settlement and its priest.

A word on the political situation. The government of King Kalakaua had as its principle "Hawaii for Hawaiians." Often it ran into opposition from the foreign element in Honolulu, which in greater part was Protestant. At the same time, the Bishop's dissatisfaction naturally grew because of his difficult position during this period of political uncertainty.

To counterbalance the influence of Protestant foreigners,

the King favored Catholics. Public opinion had no trouble in identifying Catholics with the government party. Unfortunately, the position of the King and his cabinet grew critical because of waste, corruption, and scandals. They were overthrown by a revolution on June 30, 1887.

The position of the Catholic Mission was, of course, delicate. It was then that the superiors learned of large sums being sent to Molokai without any mention being made either of the government or the Mission. They waited for reactions. Father Damien, the hero of Molokai, would be the cause of the unpleasantness.

The situation got even darker. Father Damien reported a contingent of Anglican Sisters headed for Molokai. New rumblings. . . . The King and Gibson, his minister, could no longer support Catholics. . . . They did not at that moment dare entrust the establishment to Catholic Sisters. . . . This would only exasperate their opponents who were already furious over the King's extravagance and caprice. . . . Father Damien was the cause of all these troubles.

Fortunately, the storm blew over when the old regime fell (June 30, 1887). During the whole affair, Father Damien's renown was of incalculable help to him. It brought in the material assistance he knew how to use better than anyone else. It protected him against the outcries and maneuverings of his enemies. World-wide admiration prevented him from being sacrificed to misunderstanding and jealousy. To have dared remove Father Damien from his people would have brought down the criticism of decent persons the world over.

In the pile of documents from this period we have been unable to find one in which mention is made by any superior of wanting to remove him from his post. Even from those who rose up against him, we do not find any trace of a plan or suggestion to have him replaced. The contraction of leprosy made his stay there final.

In the last resort he was dependent on the Father General, Sylvain Bousquet. At no time, even when stupid reports were sent in, did the General doubt him. He never had any idea of recalling him. He simply understood Father Damien's heroic charity. Bishop Maigret, his bishop until 1881, and Father Modeste, his provincial until 1878, also defended him.

Besides the admiration and respect of Meyer and several other personages, and numerous doctors whom we have already cited or will cite, we can also point to that of His Majesty, King Kalakaua, who met him at different times both in Honolulu and on Molokai. Then, we have Gibson and several members of the royal family, especially Princesses Liliuokalani and Kapiolani.

KNIGHT OF THE ROYAL ORDER OF KALAKAUA

To counter the maneuvers of the opposition and to get the friendship and support of foreign courts, the King took a trip around the world. His sister, Princess Liliuokalani, who acted as regent, visited the patients on Molokai and decorated their pastor. The story of her trip has too much local color and touches Father Damien too closely to omit it in his biography.

On September 15, 1881, the Queen (she had this title in the King's absence) took passage on the steamer *Lehua*. Clothed in a black robe with a train, and lying nonchalantly on a mat, she was accompanied on the trip by Princess Likelike, her sister, Kapena, the prime minister, ladies in waiting, and army officers. A child of the royal blood waved a fan above her head. The members of her retinue and others kept a respectful distance. When she wanted to speak to anyone she made a sign to him. He would approach and kneel. The Queen would talk to him in her own kind way about his health, his family, about anything. She was a goodhearted person. People knew her and loved her.

The steamer dropped anchor at Kalaupapa. Flower-decked boats took the passengers ashore where an improvised wharf was festooned with more flowers. Almost 800 leprosy patients were waiting for her. Nearby a large tent, like a native hut, had been erected; a flower-strewn road led the way to it. The Queen passed under triumphal arches, escorted by seventy patients dressed in uniforms they had picked up; they vaguely looked like soldiers.

Amid the ovations, she took her place on the platform with her escort. A choir of young leprosy sufferers, dressed in white with red or blue sashes, came forward to sing a long native melody. Some of them were still quite beautiful with their large eyes and black hair. Some of the timid ones hid their hands, others kept handkerchiefs over their mouths, while others let only their profile be seen in an effort to disguise the wounds that disfigured them.

The Queen saw more than she heard. She saw faces swollen until the people's eyes were half shut, black scabs and running sores, mutilated members, gangrenous hands and feet. Some of the sufferers hid their wounds under bloodstained bandages; others let their wounds show as though they no longer thought of them. The Queen recognized several persons in the crowd. She burst into tears. Her retinue imitated her. And the singing ended in sobs. She attempted to speak but her tears choked her and her words stuck in her throat. Kapena, the prime minister, took her place to deliver a speech that touched everybody's heart. The Hawaiians never get tired of hearing orators — who are so plentiful among them — and who get off long periodic sentences heavily loaded with metaphors.

Under the guidance of Mr. Meyer and Father Damien, the royal escort went through the Settlement. The Queen wanted to see everything — housing, hospital, orphanages, churches, rectory, stores. Her woman's heart understood what Father Damien had done and this helped renew their friendship.

However, the sadness that had overcome her on the platform never left her the whole day. She left with a broken heart.

Pitiful scenes took place that evening at the pier. Parents, husbands, and wives who had accompanied the Queen, tore themselves away from children and dear ones they had seen again for a day . . . in such conditions! A young mother locked her little ten-year-old boy in her arms, head bandaged. They had to separate them by force and carry her on board ship. For a long time, she stood in the back of the ship where they had thrust her, looking toward a point on shore where her little child perched on a rock and kept throwing her kisses.

In their reports, the newspapers praised the affection of the royal family for 800 of its poor subjects who were suffering at Molokai with no hope and yet with no complaint. But they also exalted the merits of Father Damien: "This young priest," wrote the *Commercial Advertiser,* "is the glory and boast of Hawaii. He resuscitates the saintly heroism of the bloody arenas of the ages of old; nay, he does even more. Would it not be great favor to be thrown a prey to a wild beast rather than be condemned to live in the poisonous atmosphere of a leper settlement?"

Since Father Damien was "the glory of Hawaii," it was only fitting that he be decorated. The Regent Liliuokalani provided for this without delay. The occasion presented itself when Bishop Maigret's coadjutor, Bishop Koeckemann, recently appointed Bishop, wished to offer his homage to the Princess Regent; the audience took on a special splendor.

Her Highness entrusted to him a document and decoration as well as a letter for Father Damien. No doubt, the good Queen was never happier than when she signed the following document:

Kalakaua
King of the Hawaiian Islands

To all who shall see these Presents, Greetings: Know ye That We have Appointed and Commissioned, and by these presents We appoint and Commission
Reverend Father Damien De Veuster
to be
Knight Commander
of the Royal Order of Kalakaua, to exercise and enjoy all the Rights, Pre-eminences and Privileges to the same Right appertaining, and to wear the Insignia as by Decree created.

In Testimony Whereof, We have caused these Letters to be made Patent and the Seal of Our Kingdom to be hereunto affixed.

Given under Our Hand, at Our Palace, in Honolulu, this twentieth day of September, in the Year of Our Lord, One Thousand Eight Hundred and Eighty One.

Liliuokalani, Regent
By the King,
The Chancellor of the Royal Order of Kalakaua
No. O. Dominis

The letter informing the priest of his nomination as a Knight Commander read:

Reverend Sir.
It is my desire to express to you my great appreciation of your heroic and self denying labors, among the most unfortunate of the subjects of this Realm, and in some public manner to testify to the fidelity and patient, loving care with which you labor for the physical and spiritual good of those who are necessarily shut off from the tender ministrations of relatives and friends. —

I am aware that your labors and sacrifices are dictated solely by a desire to benefit your unfortunate fellow men and that you look for your reward and inspiration to the divine Father and Ruler of us all — nevertheless, in furtherance of my desire I ask you, Reverend Father, to accept the Order of Knight Commander of the Royal Order of Kalakaua in testimony of my sincere appreciation of your efforts in alleviating the distresses and mitigating in many ways the sorrows of the unfortunate lepers of Kalawao, as I had occasion to observe during my recent visit to that place.

> I am your Friend,
> Liliuokalani, Regent

The interest the priest took in these human honors was only in proportion to the advantages he could get out of them for his people. So far as he himself was concerned, he was indifferent. For several days, indeed, the incident did furnish him with material for jokes. After enumerating all his absorbing duties to his brother Pamphile he went on: "Add to this that Sir Knight will have to be in the confessional from two to nine o'clock!" In a letter to his Bishop, he added this postscript: "Too much fanfare in the papers about the pastor of Kalawao. It is making some gentlemen here jealous. Your blessing on your unworthy son."

Father Damien had to answer Queen Liliuokalani according to protocol. He wrote out two carefully prepared responses. "Having received your kind letter," he told her,

requesting me to accept the honor and mark of distinction Your Royal Highness wishes to bestow on me as an acknowledgment for my humble services to the lepers, I am very willing although unworthy and submit myself to your kind request, by accepting from your Royal hands the honorable title of the order of Knight Commander of the Royal Order of Kalakaua, this being a

permanent and public testimony of the existing union
and good understanding between the Royal family and
the Catholic Church.

He ended his message with due regard to protocol —
but surely not as serious as he sounds: "In regard to my
mission at Kalawao, I give your Royal Highness and the
honorable Board of Health — my pledge as a Knight Commander of the Royal Order of Kalakaua to do my utmost
for the spiritual and temporal welfare of the unfortunate
lepers."

It was the French consul who presented this answer to
the Queen. He had written about it to the Bishop:

> I am grateful to the Princess for furnishing me with
> this opportunity of asking you to offer Fr. Damien my
> own sincerest congratulations.
> The Consul of France who appreciates, as does the
> Hawaiian Government, what this worthy ecclesiastic has
> done, in a pure spirit of sacrifice, for the alleviation of
> suffering humanity, is particularly pleased by this mark
> of distinction accorded to one of the members of the
> Catholic Mission, and although the new Commander is
> not of French nationality, he is happy to congratulate
> him officially on an honor that sheds glory on the entire
> Mission.
> I would be obliged to Your Excellency if you would
> obtain for me the response Fr. Damien will address to
> Princess Liliuokalani, in order that I may personally
> present it to Her Royal Highness.

His decoration still had to be publicly presented and the
event celebrated with appropriate ceremonies.

The new Bishop was deputed by the Queen to bring
the jeweled insignia to him. He began his pastoral visit
of the vicariate at Molokai. He himself tells us of the voyage and what happened:

We landed at Kaunakakai, at the southern part of the island, at two o'clock in the morning; we saw Fr. Damien waiting for us in the moonlight. He led us to the old country house of King Kamehameha V, where we rested a while. At daybreak we mounted on horses and after a two hour ride through arid country we came to Mr. Meyer's house, where he and his family welcomed us and gave us breakfast.

About ten thirty we again mounted and in an hour we arrived at the summit of the towering mountain that overlooks the leprosarium. The time had arrived to risk our lives and descend the famous Palis. We handed over the horses and mules to Mr. Meyer's servant, then, loaded with our luggage, we started down about noon. This dangerous exercise lasted an hour and a quarter. We had to grab onto trees and rocks, slide on our backs, avoid the abysses where a few weeks ago a whole herd of cattle had gone over. The stench of their rotting carcasses still reached me. Seeing that I couldn't carry my baggage, Fr. Damien, strong as a Turk, took it for me.

. . . We were welcomed at the foot of the mountain by a band and a troop of seventy horsemen, all carrying banners. For over a mile they conducted us to Kalawao to the accompaniment of music.

The Bishop gave a long description of the civil and religious ceremonies that marked the memorable day; the garlands of flowers, the cavalcades, the joyful shouts of the mixed crowd of Catholics and Protestants, Liliuokalani's letter, the document, the jeweled insignia of the Order of Kalakaua that sparkled on the priest's breast. This celebration took place under a four-sided triumphal arch surrounded by hundreds of Father Damien's people.

The newspapers again loudly celebrated the glory of the priest at Molokai and praised the Queen for rising above partisan prejudices of a petty clique to reward merit without regard to any particular religious belief.

Ambrose Hutchinson noted that the day he received the decoration, the Bishop made Father Damien wear it on his breast until evening. It was the one and only time he exhibited it in public. Afterward, on the King's anniversary and on national holidays he wore a simple colored ribbon on his lapel as a sign of his loyalty to the Hawaiian government and to please his people who liked such things so much.

Father Albert Montiton gives us as a proof of Father Damien's popularity at the Settlement in telling about "the haste which all the lepers regardless of sect or party showed in signing the letter of thanks to the Queen." All the patients were enthusiastic about the decoration which they considered a personal honor to each one of them. In his modesty, Father Damien did not tell them otherwise.

He explained to Edward Clifford he didn't like to wear his brilliant decoration. It didn't go well with his ragged and dirty old cassock. The Regent's original letter to Father Damien, written on parchment and bearing the royal coat of arms, is in the museum at Tremeloo. As for Father Damien's Cross of the Order of Kalakaua, all efforts to find it have ended in failure.

Four years later, on July 21, 1884, Queen Kapiolani visited the Settlement. This voyage was to bring greater attention to the situation because of the more detailed study that was made of the patients' real needs and of improvements that could be made right away, and also because of the decisions officially taken to bring these improvements about. We will go into details later on these projects and their fulfillment. Nothing was more important to the priest than real zeal in his people's cause.

To say that Damien was indifferent to these royal messages, loaded with compliments addressed to him, would be an exaggeration. But what we can say with certainty is that the messages on which he put the highest value were those dealing with the material welfare of the leprosarium. We have five letters Queen Kapiolani wrote him. Here is an excerpt:

I received your letters. Regarding the kerosene stove, we were unable to see Mr. Gibson (the Prime Minister) who is too occupied for the moment. As for making clothing, it is better for us to proceed slowly. I haven't seen the Sisters to ask them to help us. I think that the clothing for the men, women and children will be sent next Wednesday. For the shipment of blankets to the lepers it would be better for you to come here some day. Then we could discuss this question in detail. Because of your great devotion to our people, folks here give me whatever I ask for your lepers. How are the plants going that I sent you? How is the Doctor? Please be kind enough to give me some news.

Once more my kindest regards,
Kapiolani

Thus we see his great devotion to the sufferers of Hawaii took in everything. Although he was a missionary — or rather because he was a missionary — nothing that affected them was indifferent to him. He wanted them to have plenty to eat, to be decently dressed, and to suffer less and less. This was his great preoccupation. But all this was to make them more receptive to spiritual things . . . to make them believe in God, to hope in Him, to serve Him out of love. He was soon to have plenty of chances to practice these virtues himself.

"Those animosities and that lowness of spirit which are the marks of a narrow and uncultured intellect," to quote the *Hawaiian Gazette*, were to start in again on him. Once more persecutions began.

And to top it all, leprosy put its deathly finger on him.

14 *A Priestly Heart*

IT IS foolhardy to try to penetrate God's secret dealings with a soul. Though it be only a human judgment, we can form an opinion based on the impressive collection of carefully considered affirmations, of actions and reactions produced under such circumstances that it is hard to believe there is room for error. Let's explore the master ideas that brought Father Damien to the heights of heroism.

The busy missionary kept a personal notebook that was worn and dirty from use the last twenty years of his life. Across those small pages he jotted down, helter-skelter, his sermon notes, outlines in dogma, scripture, apologetics, and personal notes: meditations, retreat resolutions, even examinations of conscience. No doubt about it, this was the most intimate expression of his soul. In these pages we find his soul laid bare.

In the present chapter we are going to try to bring to light the guiding thoughts and dominating motives of his life. As sources we will use his notebook, his other writings, his own actions, and the testimony of those who lived with him. We think this delay in telling our story will be worth while, if we can penetrate deeper into a soul like his.

One can enter a leprosarium for many reasons. Molokai

had a reputation of being a graveyard, a place in anarchy, a Sodom calling down fire and brimstone from heaven. There was no doctor, no police, no comfort, and above all no hope. A supernatural ideal sent Father Damien there: "Voluntary death to all that flatters nature is the principle of a higher life" — to the eyes of faith.

Would he remain on these heights for long? Experience proved that he fed his soul on these thoughts of faith and gave them to others. Ambrose Hutchinson declared:

> Father Damien was a man of deep faith. He believed in the goodness and the love of Almighty God. He preached faith and hope with all the ardor of his soul in order to uplift the people out of the depravity into which they had fallen and to turn them into good and sincere followers of Jesus Christ . . . His daily labor among them without expectation of any worldly reward was a severe test of this faith and it could never have been upheld if the grace of God had not helped him in a special manner.

For himself, Father Damien felt the need of studying the Word of God and needed a good explanation of Sacred Scripture. He asked for the works of Cornelius a Lapide, a well-known Catholic theologian. For his people, he told the Board in his report that one of the most powerful means "to introduce moral habits among the lepers" has been "a solid religious instruction." The gospel, the fundamental teachings of the Church, the theological summaries in his notebook furnished him the answers he needed to the questions that came up. Let us not require more erudition from him.

The following note sent to Tremeloo in 1875 is a good summary of his other letters:

> I find my greatest happiness in serving the Lord in

these poor suffering children who have been rejected. I am trying to lead them all along the way to heaven. Dear parents, dear brethren, and friends, follow that same path so we may meet above. Riches, even life itself, are nothing if we do not save our soul. Pray very much for me.

When sorrows were great in Belgium, he suffered, he sympathized, he consoled. But then: "God wills that we learn not to attach our hearts to things here below. Let us remember that earth is an exile and happy are they who die in the Lord." At times, he envied his Christians to whom he administered the last Sacraments and then accompanied to the grave. At the death of Pauline, his favorite sister, he said: "If only we could join her in heaven. While waiting, let's send as many souls as possible there. They will be our immortal crown."

Never did the least intellectual difficulty harass or torment him. The great truths of the last things, of the divine judgment and eternal sanctions always come up in his letters and talks. He was Catholic — which means universal — so he did not toy with the crushing chains of materialism nor all the pseudo doctrines of the mind. Even less was he bothered by racial controversies. He gave the same care to Hawaiians, Chinese, Portuguese, and anybody else.

His spirit of faith made him see the guiding hand of divine Providence in the course of events, its special intervention in favor of those who are trying to do good:

Here I have been serving infected people for ten years without having contracted the disease. The newspapers cited my example this week as a proof that people shouldn't get too excited at seeing lepers in our small villages. There is no danger in living close to them, they say. They see only the exterior, without understanding that God takes care of those who in His name devote themselves to the unfortunate. As for myself, from the time I arrived I have entrusted the business of my health to our Lord, our Blessed Mother, and St. Joseph. That is what they have done up to now. In the face of the too real dangers that surround me I repeat: "Lord, I have placed all my hope in You. I will never be confounded."

His confidence in God's help remained unshakable. It increased his energy a hundredfold, since he was convinced that God owed it to Himself to bless his work. He rejected all professional remunerations for himself. You will recall that the government offered him the job of resident administrator at a good salary. "If you offered me a hundred thousand dollars, I wouldn't stay here five minutes for that money," was his answer. Not that the good Fleming did not know how to carry on business affairs. He certainly knew how to go into action when the rights of a third party were involved. But he was working as a priest, therefore he was disinterested by his state of life; he was working as a religious, therefore poor by profession. He used to say: "Let us all try, each in his own state in life, to lay up treasures we can carry into the other world."

His father died. His theme did not vary a bit. He repeated to his mother: "The tears you shed have weakened you. Why all these tears? Isn't he better off in heaven than on earth? Let us all work for heaven. Let us all turn our desires toward it. Let us work courageously to prepare an eternal home for ourselves."

He was a deeply religious man. His day began with prayer, kneeling before a crucifix or prostrate before the tabernacle. There he got the courage for the hard task of "beginning again each day." Father Albert said: "He practically never left his Rosary. He took it to bed with him and said it day and night . . . anytime he got a free moment."

Here is what he wrote on January 31, 1880:

> The cemetery, church and presbytery form one enclosure; thus at night time I am the sole keeper of this garden of the dead, where my spiritual children lie at rest. My greatest pleasure is to go there to say my beads, and meditate on that unending happiness which so many of them are already enjoying. There, too, my thoughts dwell on the sufferings of purgatory. I confess to you, my dear brother, the cemetery and the hut of the dying are my best meditation books, as well as for the benefit of my own soul as in view of preparing my instructions.

By 1885, he had seen more than 1800 die! For how many of them, thanks to him, leprosy had been the way to eternal life! His ministry was not in vain. New courage came into his soul.

He practiced the first and greatest of the Commandments: love of God and neighbor.

The best, the most solid and most compelling proof of his deep and all-embracing love for God was the very passion that attached him to his charges. "The sight of what souls have cost Jesus Christ," his notebook reads, "ought to inspire us with the greatest zeal for the salvation of the whole world. We should give ourselves to all, without exception, without reserve. The measure of our zeal should be that of Jesus Christ."

In 1876, he wrote to his nephew, Jean de Veuster, and to L. Peeters, minor seminarians at Turnhout, Belgium, who were aspiring to become missionaries: "Let us often meditate on what our Lord has done for the salvation of souls, and we will know what we have to do to draw hundreds from the road of vice and perdition."

He summed up his method of the apostolate in his report to the Board:

> Kindness to all, charity to the needy, a sympathizing hand to the sufferers and the dying, in conjunction with a solid religious instruction to my listeners, have been my constant means to introduce moral habits among the lepers.

As for his charity, we have already seen how thoughtful, active, hard working it was, how attentive to all needs, how anticipating. His good-humored charm cheered his people when they had the blues. His attentive care calmed their fears. Through his priestly ministrations he communicated to souls the mysterious resources of divine power.

He completely forgot himself. Wilmington, a patient at Molokai, said: "Father Damien impressed me as one always willing to do good, never thinking of his own welfare but always preoccupied about others." And one of the Sisters at Father Damien's orphanage, Sister Leopoldina, in whom the patients confided, tells us:

> His charity to the lepers was unlimited. He would give all he had to the needy even if he himself had to suffer thereby, neither did he expect thanks for his help. He forgot himself for his neighbor, and he did not mind if he himself should suffer, if he himself was poor, or if he himself should contract the disease. His only desire was to love and help the poor lepers.

If he reserved his special love for his faithful, that is not to say that he bartered his charity for conversions or meted out justice along sectarian lines. He took care of God's creatures, endowed with immortality and dignity, and not just those who happened to belong to the right party. His heart expanded to embrace unbelievers and non-Catholics with sincere affection and anxiety over their conversion.

He was never intolerant of anyone. Clifford, a Protestant, affirms; "Fr. Damien always showed a true and wholesome charity while he dealt with views which he considered erroneous." He tried to be a friend of everyone, the government people as well as the patients. He knew only one patient who got in an argument with him: a Protestant minister who was ravaged more by jealousy than leprosy. This man published some anonymous articles in magazines against Father Damien. Everybody knew where they came from, and there was no need to refute him. He even made his coreligionists detest him. His church was almost empty on Sunday. The priest completely forgave him for all he had done and was still doing against the spiritual good of many.

The servant of God went beyond that ordinary measure where human prudence and moderation would have seemed more reasonable. The heart has reasons the mind does not know of. His Bishop stated:

> The government doctors come to the leprosarium only as visitors, and the few that reside there, with fat salaries, rarely stay beyond a year, broken up by numerous absences. I do not blame them for taking all their precautions in their dealings with lepers. But what right have they to blame the devoted priest for not taking the same precautions? He considered them useless, since from the first day of his arrival, he generously consented to fall a victim to that disease.

There was no lack of complaints against him. Later we will take them up in detail. One thing for which he definitely was blamed was undertaking too much for his miserable people. One person said: "He has such a good heart that he seems to have identified himself with the

Settlement to the point of demanding that everything and everybody work to its advantage." And another commented: "He is a very zealous missionary, devoted to his people to excess. I say to excess, for he does not know how to *sapere ad sobrietatem* [to be wise with moderation]. He is esteemed and loved just the same, because his good will is well known."

The virtue of fortitude consists in remaining steadfast in trials, and facing even death rather than fail in one's duty. His energy and fortitude were outstanding throughout all the years he stayed at the leprosarium.

Our prudence — which might be a little cowardly — could easily tag his "extravagance," his boldness and defiance of death as rash. His detractors had a field day over his foolishness, his stubbornness, and hardheadedness. Father Aubert, his confrere, believed it was his duty to justify Father Damien:

> Fr. Damien, hardheaded? . . . He was firm and bold in his decisions, yes. He had to be resolute and tenacious to stay at Kalawao for life in spite of troubles from the Puritans [sic] in power, with the conviction that he would never escape the disease. It takes courage and steadfastness to keep going in a situation that is so hard on nature. It takes heroic self denial to count yourself happy to die a leper.

Father Damien's successors at the Settlement, who benefited by the improvements made for the people, loudly praised the various facets of his unbelievable strength of soul. One of them, Father Wendelin Moellers, SS.CC., admired him not so much for having exposed himself to the disease nor for having lived in the midst of walking corpses, as for having lived *alone* in the midst of a people who were more than ungrateful, more than licentious.

Later on, priests and Sisters could see and encourage one another. Damien was alone. He felt keenly the need of going to confession, yet for long months he had to endure this privation that was so hard on him.

Was Father Damien a proud man? Father Julliotte said: "We are discussing a man who was perfectly balanced and who simply took on an obligation. As for pride, we know quite well that it quickly disappears in a leprosarium. You are too far away from the noise of the world for it to reach you. The sad monotony of the days in our vast hospital is certainly the most perfect sedative."

He enjoyed a vigorous, robust, powerful nature. By instinct, his impetuous character easily made him stubborn and excited in the face of an obstacle. But his virtue would then reveal itself in the form of patience, gentleness and, at times, of prompt regret after impulsive and regrettable outbursts of weakness that were hardly voluntary.

When some of his contemporaries were questioned about his touchiness, the answer in substance was this: "Without doubt, when you gave him trouble. But he quickly came back to apologize, which he evidently was not obliged to do." Wilmington says when he came to the Settlement he brought with him a young boy who had promised to live at Father Damien's orphanage. The Superintendent let Wilmington have a house and the boy decided to stay with him. Father Damien came by Wilmington's house for a visit and asked if the boy wanted to live at his orphanage. The boy refused because he said he had heard that an epidemic was raging there. Father Damien abruptly got up and left. He went about twenty steps, turned around, and came back to apologize to Wilmington for his sudden burst of anger.

His personal notebook takes up this weakness on which he had to focus his attention to avoid being taken by surprise. This was the usual battlefield of his soul where he showed no quarter to the least slip. It was a fight that kept him humble and brought him sanctifying victories.

We do not have to insist on his practice of mortification. His position among his diseased patients kept the importance of this virtue before his eyes. We read in his notebook:

> Mortification of the body satisfies for sins. It keeps the body in check and suppresses its uprisings. Following the example of Jesus Christ, all the Saints have practiced it both in body and soul. We should suffer all physical and moral trials and pains without murmuring. We can become good Christians and religious only by practicing it. To do good to souls I must lead a hard and mortified life not getting discouraged over anything. There are sinners that can be converted only by doing penance for them.

Meditating on these considerations helped him to acquire that mastery over himself which, while moderating his fiery temperament, enabled him to overcome any softness and repugnance of his nature.

He treated his people with surprising ease. Wilmington says:

> Father Damien was careless about leprosy. His house was always full of leper boys who also ate with him. He invited me once to his house and gave me to drink out of his own drinking cup. I told him he should not do so, he might contract the disease. With undressed sores on their arms he handled the leper boys and when reproved for his carelessness, he used to say that this body rots quickly anyhow and that the soul alone counted. . . . He forgot himself in order to help others.

Later when the concert of admiration arose and its

echoes sounded at the doors of the Kalawao rectory, Father Damien remained humble. He had too great an esteem of humility to fall into self-admiration or give himself over to the intoxication of glory.

Human nature, it is true, is only too much borne in that direction. When the smoke of incense swirled around him, he reread in his notebook:

May all the honor, all the praise that they can give to me, return to God whose servant I am. In this sense, let them do it. However, let me watch over my vile self. Jesus Christ and His Church are all, and I must be effaced. Humility, sustained by confidence and obedience, works wonders and preserves us from discouragement in times of contradiction.

Let us desire contempt and rejoice when we get it. Let us never be touched by the praises of men.

He felt the need of repeating the verse of the Psalm which he wrote very clearly in his notebook: *"Non nobis, Domine, non nobis, sed nomini tuo da gloriam"* (Not to us, O Lord, not to us; but to Thy name give glory). And he added: "I am only a useless servant; never seek human praise, it is theft, an injustice. If anyone praises me, answer right away: 'Praise God, not me.'"

In all sincerity he wrote to the Father General: "I consider my little stock of virtues the principal cause for many of the unconverted being so obstinate. We need men who can work miracles here, if not scholars at least saints prepared to sacrifice themselves everyday for the salvation of souls." To the mother house of the Sacred Hearts Fathers: "God keep me from giving into vanity because of some good He deigns to do through my ministry. They say a great deal about me in the papers and churches. May all the glory return to the Author and Perfector of all good. As for myself, I want to remain unknown at the leprosarium of Kalawao. I am very happy among my numerous sick children."

It is worth considering for a moment the happiness he talks about despite the reasons for sadness and bitterness that surrounded him. Father Damien had a joyous nature. By temperament he was an optimist. "Then, let's look at the pleasant side of things at the Settlement!" Reasons for desolation were unlimited. The disillusion, the heartbreak of that prison at Kalawao! Was there any room for joy? Father Damien had a tremendous amount of joy.

He was convinced that he was in the place God willed him to be. He had confidence that God would give him success. Daily he saw proof of His merciful intervention in the transformation of souls and at times in the relief of bodily sufferings. One after the other, his flock began to pray, to sing a hymn of peaceful resignation to God. What more was needed to make the pastor's heart swell with joy?

"I am happy and content," was the constant refrain of his letters. God consoled His faithful servant. "When you know how to embrace the cross, it becomes sweet," St. Teresa of Ávila had said. Sister Leopoldina tells us he was always joyful, never sought any human satisfaction but placed all his hope in heaven.

His radiant joy drove away the sufferers' sadness. He admitted to Father General: "It is with tears that I sow the good seed. From morning to night I am in the midst of moral and physical miseries that break my heart. However, I always try to appear happy in order to keep up my poor lepers' courage."

Professor Stoddard on his return to the United States after his first visit to Molokai wrote Father Damien: "You seemed to me to be happy, much happier than those who live in the world. You have the right to be, for no one has ever accomplished a work so noble under such adverse conditions." Before the Students' Medical Society, Dr. Hubbard made a similar statement: "If there is nothing like accepted good for bringing peace and joy into the heart, what man has more right to be completely happy? And to what extent must the promise of the harvest cause him to quickly forget the sweat and pain it cost him!"

Religious of the Sacred Hearts

The call to the religious life is an invitation to submit oneself to the strictest rules in a spirit of faith. On entering one of the great spiritual families that are the glory of the Catholic Church, a religious cannot withdraw from that family without breaking laws that are now binding on him. He cannot even sanctify himself in any other way than by fulfilling his new obligations: the religious vows, the rules of his order. Despite their isolation and the instability that goes with their ministry, religious missionaries are not dispensed from these obligations. They give proof of great virtue, if in spite of difficulties they remain faithful to their obligations.

Father Damien did not try to get out of them. On the contrary, he drew up a rule of life that would help him keep them:

Father Damien's Rule of Life
Sept. 3, 1879

5 A.M.   Rise and go to the church as soon as possible. Morning prayers, Adoration and Meditation

6:30   Mass and instruction. Thanksgiving until quarter to eight.

7:45   Take care of various matters for the good of the faithful.

8:00   Breakfast followed by a short recreation and domestic affairs.

9:00	Small hours (on the porch).
9:30	Spiritual reading followed by study and correspondence until noon.
12:00	Dinner. After dinner visit the sick and the Christians in general in such a way that each week I may know all that goes on in each house in my district.
	If I can return by 5 o'clock, say vespers and occupy myself with domestic affairs.
6:00	Supper
	When twilight sets in, Rosary, Breviary, Night prayers.
9-10	Retire

The Sacred Hearts of Jesus and Mary are particularly honored in the Congregation to which Father Damien belonged. He had an especially tender devotion to our Lord Jesus Christ who saved us by His suffering and example and to our Blessed Mother through whom are dispensed the treasures of divine mercy.

At the beginning of his retreat notes (1881) he wrote: "The sacrifice the religious makes of his whole being is an act most pleasing to God and most glorious for the soul. I am in a state where fidelity to God is an absolute necessity for me. God alone suffices for me." And again: "My religious vocation is a special favor from God. God will require a detailed account of my correspondence to this grace. In this state, I have special means of sanctification and perseverance. Therefore, nothing contrary to any virtue will go unnoticed and the least infraction will impose a very severe penance on me here below or a worse punishment hereafter."

The sacrifice of a religious consists in the practice of poverty, chastity, and obedience, according to the spirit and tenor of the Rule of the religious order to which he belongs:

As a religious I must be poor in spirit, in desire, in deed. To imitate Jesus Christ's poverty more closely, I will ask for only what is strictly necessary and useful, never for what is pleasant or superfluous. I will never complain if at times I am denied what I ask for. I will think twice before buying things that are more or less necessary for me. I will keep a strict account and I will never use any trickery to get what I desire from my Superiors. I will simply ask and never order. As for the little bit obtained through the work or help of the Christians I will take only what is necessary and give the rest to the poor.

He kept his resolutions. His people's needs absorbed all the alms he received. The money which the Superior sent him in small quantities — for he also was poor — only too quickly found its use:

Not having a cent of income, and having to pay for many things . . . It is very natural that the purse should be empty at the beginning of the year. Please send me, if you will, something to take care of necessities. I have even borrowed part of the lepers' money I was keeping on deposit. Part of it will be repaid perhaps . . . or perhaps not.

So as not to act as an owner, he scrupulously forwarded his accounts to his superiors. We have some of his annual reports. For example, the 1878 report took in some articles that ran to a total of a little over $300. No doubt everything was included, as —

1 axe handle	.25
1 broom	.50
1 hook	.50
1 knife	.50
tobacco	2.00

Nor could he be accused of getting rich during his term as temporary superintendent; instead of getting the $3,333 offered him he was content with a monthly salary of $41. He reported to his Superior what had been done with these dollars: "I have not put them in my purse. They went to the chapel and the poor."

He wrote the Father General:

It is taken for granted that we do everything gratuitously. The Lord can well repay us, as He did His apostles. Or rather, He has already done it. If Our Lord were to say to me "When I send you forth without purse or wallet, did you lack anything?" I would certainly have to answer Him: Nothing, Lord!

In fact, leaving everything I had at Kohala for my successor, I came to Molokai without bringing anything with me. I do not possess one cent of income and yet I lack nothing. I even have something to give out as alms all the time. How do you explain this mystery? It is the secret of Him who promised a hundredfold to those who have left all things for His sake.

His heroic charity, his mortification, his very life so opposed to the inclinations of nature inclines us to think that he did not intend to give the least freedom to lower tendencies. That bitter struggle he carried on against the immoral element at the place and his joy in overcoming them strengthens our conviction. Undoubtedly, without grace a man cannot suppress all the assaults of the flesh. But what man merited grace more? His existence was a continual mortification; his work to clean up morals was a perpetual bridle on unlawful pleasures; his desire was to be a witness of evangelical purity and to stand as a barrier against immoral infiltration.

Nevertheless, as the *Imitation* says: "No one is so perfect or so holy but he is sometimes tempted; men cannot be altogether free from temptation. . . . There is no state so holy, no place so secret, that temptations and trials will not come." Damien certainly was not immune. He could not have preserved his virtue without fighting, without discipline, without watchfulness and prayer. "Purity of thought is necessary. Ask for this grace," he prescribed for himself in his retreat resolutions:

> In all circumstances watch over your exterior when alone and with others. Watch over your senses. Above all be especially reserved with women. Every stain that tarnishes purity wounds charity. Purity is indispensable for the functions of the sacred ministry; it makes it honored and fruitful. Avoid every dangerous object and occasion.

He practiced this virtue like the saints. This was the unanimous conviction of all those who saw him and observed him with their own eyes . . . fellow missionaries, patients, visitors. This conviction even had to be backed up by most solemn oaths to meet head on the odious calumny which we will talk about later. We will try to give a conscientious summary of all the documents accumulated on this painful subject.

Father Damien's submission to his superiors' orders and desires was prompt and complete. We remember how troubled his conscience was when he came to the Settlement until he had obtained the written authorization of his Provincial. It was useless for Father Aubert to tell him that as he had been brought there by the Bishop he had nothing to worry about. To his way of looking at things — which some will find to be quite narrow — the will of God could be made known to him only by the mouth of his religious superiors.

In the course of his apostolate at Molokai, a certain independence of character caused some orders to cost him a

great deal. Yet he never seems to have had the slightest
bad will in opposing them. One day he received a formal
order from the Bishop forbidding him to receive some visitors whose stay was somewhat disturbing. They were Mormons who had come to exploit the defenseless charity of
the Catholic missionary. Father Damien wrote them this
letter:

Kalawao Feb. 1, 1880

Gentlemen:
    Please have the kindness to inform your headman at
Laie that I have received from my bishop a positive
prohibition to receive as I am used to do any of your
people who in the future may visit the leper Settlement.
    This my bishop's order pains my heart very much.
Please excuse me — I want to obey orders.

And another letter to his Provincial ended:

    I again ask you to give me such authorization to use
when it is absolutely necessary. If you give me this permission, I will no longer be exposed to the scruples of
conscience which are only too well founded when I find
myself absolutely obliged to act and yet do not have
permission to do so.

Very obediently yours,
Fr. J. Damien,
Missionary priest of SS.CC.

In 1885 his brother Pamphile had at least something of
a desire to join him in the Hawaiian Islands. With what
clarity Father Damien wrote to him at the end of August,
1886! It was, he said, God who willed that obedience
place Pamphile in his native country. Pamphile's mission
was to work for the salvation of their family and fellow
countrymen, just as his was to be with the leprosy victims.
It was best for both of them to leave the decision to ec-

clesiastical and religious authorities. In no way whatsoever
was it up to him to have the consolation of his brother
working with him, the brother to whom, after God, he
was indebted for being on the missions. He added: "You
understand me without my further explanation."

We will come back to Father Damien's spirit of obedience when his superiors themselves suspect his intentions
and think it their duty to judge his apparent aberrations
severely.

Father Damien had deeply impressed the stamp of the
Congregation on his soul. He had an exalted idea of what
it meant to have a vocation to the Congregation of the
Sacred Hearts. It was a vocation of complete love and
lowliness; a vocation that gave the soul over to the Sacred
Hearts of Jesus and Mary; a vocation of imitating the
Savior in the four states of His mortal life. He was proud
and attached to his Congregation.

For the Father General he showed a childlike veneration. He never hesitated to lay his heart bare before him.
He kept a deep respect for all the priests he had known
in Europe. News of a death among them brought him real
sorrow. It was a relief for him to pour out his soul to his
brother Pamphile who represented for him both his family
and his Congregation.

In the majority of his letters he mentioned the Sacred
Hearts of Jesus and Mary. In the four sermons written in
his own hand and dealing precisely with the Sacred Heart
we read this affirmation: "It is this Divine Heart that gives
strength to the missionary who has left all things . . . He
knows that he has brought, across the seas, this Friend in
his heart."

In the life of the Church one of the principal obligations
of the Sacred Hearts religious is perpetual reparative adoration. The tabernacle is the center of the religious' life. The

documents that tell of Father Damien as an adorer and
an apostle of adoration are very beautiful: "Without the
Blessed Sacrament, a position like mine would be unbearable. But having Our Lord near me, I am always happy
and have the drive to work for the good of my dear lepers."
And in his notebook we read: "The Eucharist is the bread
of the strong that we need to continue with distasteful jobs
as a remedy against disgust in a ministry that is hard and
often discouraging."

Later when sufferings were all but crushing him, he
declared: "Without the constant presence of our Divine
Master in my poor chapel, I just could not go on living
my life here with the lepers at Molokai." There we have
touched on the secret of his heroic life. He had written all
this to Rev. Chapman, his English benefactor. The Anglican minister answered him that his life taught him
more than all the commentaries and that the Blessed Sacrament now meant much more to him.

If he lived, so to speak, by the Blessed Sacrament, he
had his people live the same way. When Father Aubert
entered the chapel at Kalawao he saw an edifying sight:

Adorers were kneeling before the Blessed Sacrament.
This I was told was no extraordinary ceremony but a
daily practice. Every day the good Christians at Molokai
came there to seek relief from their sufferings. They did
more; they offered themselves as victims in reparation
for the outrages committed against the Sacred Hearts
by sinners.

The Christian life must be lived in imitation of the life
of Christ. A Sacred Hearts religious must accentuate that
resemblance. Father Damien's personal notebook often in-
sists on the dispositions of tending to that perfection with
which our divine Model always did everything to please
His heavenly Father: "I do always the things that are pleas-

ing to Him." He was determined to measure all his activity alongside that of Christ, as did the great Apostle St. Paul.

He imitated the Christ Child by his astounding simplicity. As a matter of fact, this was a particular characteristic of his. Some took him for a common man with rough, common ways. Didn't he do all kinds of jobs that belonged to farmers and laborers? But the more observant were quick to see his kind heart, his way of anticipating others, his pleasant and easy ways. Edward Clifford wrote: "All who knew him personally must have been struck with the absence of what is called 'goodliness' in so good a man. He was completely without airs, and was just a hard-working, simple-minded, unselfconscious man, who thought little about himself, but continually about his business."

One of his confreres had this eulogy for his simplicity: "He is a little too childlike . . . but he is without guile."

Mother Judith, SS.CC., says:

Simplicity was certainly one of his distinctive characteristics. Like all upright souls, who forget themselves and seek only God, he unswervingly did everything he could for the good of his lepers. He went along, indifferent to the rich or poor. He conducted himself with the King and his ministers just as he did with an ordinary simple native. He talked to everybody without any ceremonies. To Reverend Mother Marie Joseph, who had sent him help, he gave the name "chere maman," but seeing that this embarrassed her, he stopped.

And he honored the Christ Child in a wonderful way by his unceasing care of his orphans. They, of course, were his special project. His greatest tenderness went to these little fellows. He had all the weakness of a "daddy" for them. Father Albert said: "He was their daddy. He had the ordinary weakness for his adopted children who responded, you may be sure. He gave them too much free-

dom by letting them have objects or instruments which, it
seems to me, he should have kept exclusively for himself.
But then that was asking too much of him."

He betrays himself in a letter to his brother in 1883:

After Mass I sat down to read your letters without
thinking to warm my coffee. As you were telling me good
news, I was jubilant. My orphans who are so eager to
know everything hardly gave me time to breathe. I had
to translate it all to them, the contents of your letter in
great detail: Fr. Leonor's visit, your notebook with 5782
pages of sermons . . . our good old mother and her little
children. They admired the beautiful writing of Maria
and Pauline. In a word, breakfast ran into lunch. After
which, I left, walking-stick in hand, to visit the sick.

Father Damien imitated the divine Workman of Naza-
reth. Like Him, he handled the saw and plane, and did
ordinary manual labor. He led the hidden life in the gray
solitude of the leprosarium, far from the world and all the
fuss made over him.

Like Him, he preached the Gospel. Following in His
footsteps, he taught, healed the wounds of sin, and freed
his flock from the brambles of heresy to lead them into the
true fold.

There remained one more stage — to be conformed to
the crucified life of the Savior. He was not a man to back
down in the face of such a terrible ordeal.

PART III

Calvary

15　　*The Lion Is Wounded*

WHEN Father Damien's leprosy was discovered, Dr. Mouritz was the resident doctor at Molokai. In him we have the best witness one could ask for.

In his vast mission district on the island of Hawaii, the young missionary had come in contact with several leprosy victims. At the time, the question was brought up whether Father Damien had contracted the disease at Kohala. Dr. Mouritz was asked and he concluded that nothing could prove he did.

The inroads of leprosy are slow, hard to trace. It is certain that from the time he began entering the sufferers' huts and giving them the Sacraments on Hawaii, he felt a kind of tingling or burning sensation on his feet and legs. During his first years at Molokai the same phenomena reappeared more noticeably and more often. Without doubt, the germs of the disease had already attacked him as he himself affirmed before his death in a report made at the request of Dr. Morrow, a leprosy specialist of New York.

It is quite possible that this was a period of incubation, Dr. Mouritz says, since this period lasts a minimum of ten years in white or non-Hawaiian lepers. In 1874 Damien again felt a dull pain in his feet. They burned so much that the priest, restless and feverish, could not sleep until he had soaked them in cold water or left them uncovered during the night. In 1876 one arm and his back were covered with dry spots that disappeared after treatment with corrosive sublimate. In the following years they became yellowish, grew fainter when the priest drank sarsaparilla, and reappeared when he stopped.

Mouritz writes:

The true duration of his disease was between ten and eleven years, for during the summer of the year 1878, whilst acting as assistant superintendent of the Settlement, true prodromal symptoms of leprosy manifested themselves, to wit, chills, osteal pains, slight swelling and tenderness of the joints, slight irregular fever, tingling numbness of the extremities, supersensitive and painful sensation in patches along the extensor surface of the upper and lower extremities; all of which signs, even in the absence of skin lesions, clearly indicated primary infection of Damien's system with leprosy. After about five years of intimate contact with lepers (from the year 1873 to 1878), he suffered the before-mentioned symptoms.

In June, 1878, his superiors knew he had leprosy. "The leprosarium is confided to the care of Father Damien, himself a leper," Father Modeste wrote to the Father General.

Toward the end of the year, the sensations and spots had disappeared to such an extent that he thought he had been completely cured. He wrote to the Father General in January, 1879: "My health is very good and all symptoms have disappeared." Doubtless there was a relapse, for Father Regis, the Vice-Provincial, had to reassure the Father General fifteen months later: "Good news, Fr. Damien is not a leper. His sickness, according to the word of a reputable doctor, was only a skin eruption. It has disappeared entirely."

In reality the disease had only abated. In the autumn of 1881, he again felt violent pains in his left foot. The following year, they spread through his whole leg. He was to suffer frightfully from the sciatic nerve until June, 1885. Meantime, the left foot was becoming insensible.

In the absence of other signs, Mouritz says these pains in his left foot were thought to be rheumatic.

In December, 1884, something happened to Father Damien that removed all doubt. He soaked his feet in boiling water but did not know that it was so hot, and he felt no pain. Only when he took his feet out, did he notice large blisters. He consulted Dr. Arning, a leprosy specialist, and the honor goes to him for having diagnosed Father Damien's case six months before the development of any apparent signs. He discovered the symptoms in a deposit of leprosy in the structures connected to the peroneal nerve in the knee.

The story goes that the doctor hesitated to give his diagnosis, but the priest urged him to do so.

Finally, the doctor said, "What you think is true; you too have leprosy."

"I'm not surprised," Father Damien answered. "I've been sure of it for a long time."

In a special report made to Gibson on January 1, 1886, Dr. Mouritz wrote:

In May, 1885, there were no striking changes in his face, except the forehead, when examined by Dr. Arning and me. In August, 1885, a small leprous tubercule manifested itself on the lobe of the right ear, and from that date to the present, diminution and loss of eyebrows, infiltration of the integument over the forehead and cheeks is slowly, but certainly going on, so that the case of Father Damien is a confirmed, tubercular one, the symptoms and signs now present placing it in that class. The Father is careless; has eaten repeatedly with lepers; and, also, has a leper cook.

Doctor Mouritz did not admit the theory of infection through sexual relations. He maintained the falseness of this widespread idea. Of course, as he adds "this unproven and untenable assumption has caused the greatest anguish of mind to many unfortunate lepers."

"I have reason to believe," he continues,

that the unfortunate Damien was spared the torment and distress of even suspecting that his infection with leprosy would be attributed to immorality. Be this as it may, when it first became known publicly that Father Damien had leprosy, some such accusation of his acquiring the disease by immoral acts must have leaked out. The matter was abruptly brought to my notice in the early part of the year 1885 by a certain prominent physician who visited the Leper Settlement at that time.

On or about May 7, 1885, this certain physician stated to me whilst we were eating breakfast: "Dr. Mouritz, Fr. Damien will come to the dispensary at Kalawao at 10 o'clock; I want you to be there; we can see how his leprosy is progressing. I also wish to examine him specially for evidence of other diseases. We will make a thorough examination." I agreed.

In due course and at the appointed time Father Damien arrived, serene and undisturbed. When asked to disrobe, he consented readily; we found sufficient proof that he was undoubtedly a leper, but nothing more.

We searched his mouth, throat, and cervical glands, and also carefully scrutinized his entire person and found absolutely NO TRACE of any other disease. This event happened nearly thirty years ago, but the details are fresh in my memory; strange to say the "victim" of our examination did not display any resentment, and did not seem to realize the important bearing the discovery of any incriminating evidence might have on his future.

Father Damien possibly realized that the syphilis-leprosy theory which was then hypnotizing a certain portion of the popular mind, might be invoked in connection with his acquiring leprosy; but, he also well knew that syphilis can be contracted innocently and accidentally, and that, in such a case, the question of morality should not enter into the matter.

The contact of Damien with leprosy was always careless and reckless during the few years I was connected with the Settlement. I never hesitated to scold him and lecture him, because it set a bad example to other non-lepers.

These last words express the conviction which Mouritz often expressed and backed up: Father Damien contracted leprosy by his lack of precaution and hygiene. It was not the practitioner's business to look for an excuse in the priest's idea of what his duty to souls was, namely — the need of becoming all things to all men, to go to all, to attract all. Yet, he could not help admitting this: "If Father Damien was uncleanly, it was often from necessity, not choice, for how can a man wash his hands before eating where there is no water to wash with?" Mouritz even found good grounds to excuse the priest because of the primitive conditions at the leprosarium, especially in the first years. With almost nothing to give to the lepers, Father Damien had to become as Mouritz calls him "a jack-of-all-trades." Leprosy was very virulent at the time and most of the patients had arrived in an advanced stage.

Now a leper himself, Father Damien rejoiced over the bond that brought him even closer to his people:

I am forbidden to go to Honolulu, because I have

contracted leprosy. The marks were discovered on my left cheek and ear. My eyebrows are beginning to fall out. Soon, I will be disfigured entirely. Having no doubts about the true nature of my disease, I am calm, resigned and very happy in the midst of my people. God certainly knows what is best for my sanctification and I gladly repeat: "Thy will be done!"

On October 14, 1885, Father Leonor, who succeeded Father Modeste as Provincial, wrote to the Father General: "In his last letter, poor Father Damien told me: 'There is no more doubt about me, *I am a leper*. Blessed be the Good God! Do not feel too sorry for me. I am perfectly resigned to my lot. I ask only one favor of you; send someone to this tomb to be my confessor.'"

By Father Albert's departure he had really been walled up in a tomb for no one had yet replaced him. As for the knowledge that he was condemned to death in the near future, that hardly bothered him. He even tried to console others about his affliction.

He wrote to the Father General:

As I wrote you about ten years ago that I then had suspicions of the first germs of leprosy being in my system, the natural consequence of a long stay with these lepers, be not surprised or too much pained to know that one of your spiritual children is decorated, not only with the Royal Cross of King Kalakaua, but also with the cross more heavy, and considered less honorable, of leprosy, with which our Divine Savior has permitted me to be stigmatized. My robust constitution has thus far resisted well for thirteen years of service here, but now it begins to be undermined by little and little in proportion as the *bacilli leprae* invade the system.

I am, though, still up, and with some management continue my active life as heretofore. In fact my work has been doubled by the departure of our much regretted

Father Albert. Instead of one leprous village and one church under charge, I have now double service morning and evening on Sundays and Festivals.

During the week besides the visits to the sick at their houses, the care given to about forty orphans leaves me but little free time.

The priest made this astonishing declaration to his English friend Edward Clifford: "I would not be cured if the price of my cure was that I must leave the island and give up my work."

The sensational news of his leprosy flashed like lightning across two continents. His friends were stunned; they now redoubled their affection and generosity to him. His enemies, on the contrary, were displeased for to them his glory was a torment. At any rate, they said his leprosy was the inevitable result of his own imprudence and lack of hygiene.

They were not entirely wrong. Father Damien had certainly committed a grave imprudence by going to live at Molokai. A still more serious imprudence of his was that of not using effective safeguards, of not hesitating to come in contact with the sores of the lepers when he was trying to help them.

At the beginning he certainly kept the lepers out of his rectory. He took much better care of himself. He tried to get the lepers to go along with him — a hard, if not hopeless, job. He had to be careful not to hurt anyone's feelings by too much circumspection. These dear children of his might very quickly close their hearts to him.

The story Father Cornelius tells might give us some insight into the situation. At his village of Heeia, there was a leper woman in the family that prepared his daily ration of *poi*. One day he asked the boy who brought his bowl of *poi* if the woman ever stuck her fingers in the calabash of *poi*. The boy replied in a matter-of-fact way that they all used the same bowl! This shows that you had to tell some things to these people very strongly, and even then you could never be sure that it would do any good.

Father Damien soon got used to leprosy and lepers. His first precautions disappeared under the powerful drive of his compassion. Let the terrible scourge fall on him too ... by the grace of God! So far as he was concerned, he tossed all caution overboard, for it stood in the way of his complete dedication. He set to work with the one great virtue of boundless charity.

But we should note well how solicitous he was that others be careful. Even Dr. Mouritz who was so critical of his lack of prudence gives us an example. When the doctor began to reside at Kalawao, he experienced difficulty in getting his laundry done satisfactorily. One day he engaged a new laundress. Hardly had she pulled up her sleeves for work, when Father Damien was at the doctor's door to beg him not to employ the woman because, although she herself had so far not developed leprosy, her three husbands had all died of the disease and she was suspected of being a carrier.

On March 17, 1886, Father Damien had the opportunity of expressing officially his ideas on the spread of leprosy. The following is taken from his report:

> During my long residence at Kalawao, numerous physicians and friends have requested my opinion as to the danger of contracting the malady and the manner through which it is spread. Without any pretence of being a competent judge of a matter in which experts disagree, I might be permitted to express my opinion based upon a long and and interested experience. Leprosy is contracted by inoculation and respiration.
>
> 1. By Inoculation. I adopt the ideas of a well-known doctor who, a dozen years ago warned me often that I

was exposed to contract the disease in this way. This can be done through vaccination; or, better, through the contact of the virus with the blood; in wearing garments used by a leper or sleeping upon the same mat; in smoking the same pipe or working with utensils which have been used by them.

2. By Respiration. Leprosy can be contracted by breathing, for a considerable time, the vitiated air in their houses, or in the places where they congregate. Those who live with them and are in daily contact, are greatly exposed. . . .

Experience has demonstrated that inoculation by mosquitoes can be one of the most certain methods of contracting the disease.

Father Damien knew what he was doing when he made himself a Hawaiian to the Hawaiians; in awaiting the time when he would become a leper to the lepers, in order to gain them for Christ. Dr. G. W. Woods, who visited and admired him, stated: "The fact that he exposed himself continually to the attacks of a malady from which he had the conviction that he would ultimately die; even the care which he took to avoid precautions which, he felt, might have placed a barrier between himself and the patients at the lazaret, had they noted his repugnance or his fears; all of this united to make of him a leper and a victim of leprosy."

Father Damien also told Clifford that he had always expected to become a leper sooner or later, though exactly how he caught it he did not know.

How could he miss it, when all day long he took care of them, heard their confessions, gave them the sacraments, lived and worked with them? He breathed the same air, touched their wounds, handled their tools and they handled his. The priest-carpenter often cut his hands while sawing or planing or hammering.

One old-timer who knew him well relates: "He had the habit of smoking and from time to time he would set his pipe down on the workbench. The lepers working with him or the children surrounding him would use this chance to take a few puffs." We cannot imagine Father Damien forbidding them and explaining that he might catch their disease. Dr. Mouritz is very definite: "I have never seen any other priest, doctor, or other contact, assume the same careless and indifferent attitude toward infection with leprosy as Father Damien did, save and except Dr. Fitch."

Dr. Mouritz adds about the latter: "Dr. Fitch was one of the most reckless and careless physicians in his contact with leprosy; he seemed to take delight in putting to proof his non-contagious view of the disease."

But no matter what its origin, the missionary now had leprosy. It quickly spread over his still robust and vigorous body.

During the course of 1885 in the little village of Tremeloo in Belgium, his mother, the most interested person in the world, knew nothing of what had happened.

Worn out by age and work and separations, sickness was now added to the good old woman's burden. Fathers Damien and Pamphile knew that the tragic news would be fatal to their mother. They tried to keep her in ignorance of it.

Father Damien told his brother the news in guarded terms. Pamphile had been suffering; so Father Damien wrote to him thus:

> I was very sorry to hear of your illness. You say it seems to have degenerated into consumption. May God prevent it from being so! As for myself, I cannot hide from you for long that I am threatened by a yet more terrible disease. Leprosy, as you know, is contagious. In reality I am still as robust as I always was. But for three years my left foot has lost all feeling. I have in

my body a poison that threatens to spread throughout. Let's not go shouting this out, and let's pray for each other.

All that he told his mother was that he had a little "inflammation." His letter was in French. He begged pardon for not writing in Flemish. Not that he had forgotten his beautiful mother tongue but the words did not come so easily to him. The year before he had had a hard time writing and rewriting a Flemish letter to his mother.

He also asked pardon for the infrequency of his letters. The older he got, the more his duties as a priest and the cares of the lepers took up his time. "Thanks be to God," he added prudently,

my health is passable. I am just about the same, except that my beard which is about a finger in length is beginning to get gray.

I live always with seven or eight hundred lepers. I have filled a cemetery with the dead; and soon, for lack of space, we are going to have to dig up the first part and put the coffins one on top of the other.

Ah! if you knew the beautiful music we have in my church! Come to hear it; come and spend your old age with me! You could help me cook. We have everything . . . good coffee and eggs, and kerosene with which to cook.

Last night, a terrible storm shook my house. I could not sleep and wanted to write you. The wind tore off half the roof and I had to put it back on today.

For a couple of months I have been suffering a little. We were coming back to the leprosarium in a little boat that could not land because the ocean was too rough. The captain landed me on a rock not far from the dock. I had to swim ashore. I got wet and since then have had a bad cold.

I had another accident. I wanted to wash my feet, so I was imprudent enough to soak them in almost boiling water, and the skin came off. It looked quite bad. . . .

It's all right now, the inflammation has disappeared, soon I'll be healed. In the meantime, I'm having a hard time saying Mass; I have to sit down to preach; and since I can no longer walk, I ride around in a wagon. So, in the midst of our patients, I myself am playing the part of a sick man.

And you, my dearest mother, how are you? Do you still have good legs? It seems that Leonce has fixed up a real nice room on the second floor for Pamphile when he comes to visit you. Perhaps he also thought of Joseph. . . . A doctor advised me to breathe some of my native air. Up to now neither our Bishop nor I have found this advisable. What would become of my poor sufferers? No! Since I can always do a little good, I will remain at my post until death. We won't see each other here, but in heaven.

Mrs. de Veuster died soon after hearing that her son had contracted leprosy. She was 83 and had been a widow for thirteen years. Her health had been declining steadily, although her mind remained clear and sharp. The family had been hiding the news from her, but some tongue that was miles too long came to tell her that her son was a leper. For a long time she cried and then said: "Well, I will go with him to heaven."

She did not read any more, but she did finally succeed in finding out what the papers were saying. One of them even went so far as to say that "the flesh of the leper priest at Molokai was falling off in hunks."

The priest whom she thought was decomposing amid unspeakable sufferings was her little boy, so brave, so good, her own beloved son, for whom she had a special predilection. She kept all his letters to her in a drawer as though they were a treasure. She imagined him all alone, tortured, far from help, not a word of tenderness. The shock broke her old heart.

From then on, she kept murmuring prayers, and repeating the ejaculations that were suggested to her. On April 6, 1886, about four in the afternoon, turning her eyes for the last time toward the image of the Blessed Mother and the picture of her Joseph, she bowed her head in that direction and died calmly and peacefully.

Brother Joseph Dutton was present when Damien received the sad news. "Pray for my good old mother!" he said to Dutton, who later tells us that the Father's sorrow was restrained on this occasion.

Father Damien had no doubt that his mother had gone straight to heaven for she had fulfilled all her duties very faithfully. And he knew she was calling him to meet her there.

16   *Final Labors*

QUEEN KAPIOLANI, the wife of Kalakaua, visited the Settlement in July, 1884. On this visit she was escorted by Dr. Arning and accompanied by Princess Liliuokalani, who, as regent, had herself made the same journey three years before. The report which the Princess made of this last visit is excellent and full of interest for us.

They landed at Kalaupapa on Monday, July 21, 1884. The party was welcomed by Ambrose Hutchinson, then assistant superintendent, and Fathers Damien and Albert. The meeting took place in a building in which the patients had been gathered. Through their spokesman, they expressed to the visitors their good wishes, their complaints, and their needs. Hutchinson was the first to draw attention to the necessity of separating children born of lepers in order to preserve them from contagion. Taking a little girl about ten years old in his arms, he said: "Here is one of them, and there are here between fifty and sixty just such cases as this, and of various ages. These should be kept aloof from the diseased and properly cared for in a separate asylum, and not be allowed to remain where there are so many chances of them becoming patients through contagion." As a result, the following year the Kapiolani

Home was established at Kalihi (Honolulu) for the children of lepers.

That evening the party went to Kalawao on horseback. Quarters were provided in a new house recently built for the special accommodation of visiting physicians. Father Damien was one of the guests at the supper. Next morning they began inspecting the leprosarium. The report includes the doctors' remarks on established cases of leprosy.

They then went on to the store house. Princess Liliuokalani reports: "Upon a close observation of the stores, all the articles provided seemed good, with the exception of the sugar, bread and salmon; this last mentioned article was so mouldy and soft as to be *unfit for use;* the sugar was dark and dirty, of about No. 3 or No. 4 quality; and the bread was tolerably good for medium bread though inferior to that supplied to the Oahu jail." Then followed a visit to the slaughterhouse and to the orphanage.

Up until now the water had been obtained from Waileia Valley but the Board recognized that this was inadequate. The royal party went to look over the ground and plans for bringing water from Waikolu Valley. On the way, the affectionate and goodhearted Queen was deeply moved at what she saw in the huts of the lepers. She delivered a talk in the afternoon at Kalawao. In the evening they sailed from Kalaupapa.

In her report the Princess made proposals and suggestions that were well worth considering. She was down to earth in her ideas on the food, shipping of *poi,* on the *kokuas,* and on the water supply. She proposed the establishment of a place for non-leper children of leper parents and finally expressed the desire of having Sisters for the hospital at the leprosarium.

In January, 1886, the Board of Health, desirous of giving medical science all possible information on leprosy as it was in the islands, asked Father Damien to submit a report drawn from his long experience. This work was hard for him. "I am sick and weighed down with cares," he had written to Father General's secretary: "I am ruining my sight by writing absolutely necessary letters and saying my breviary at night." However, he did the best he could. He put into it "all his little talent for the honor of the Mission."

The report is a fifty-page document, written in English, and comprising eight chapters covering the following points: (1) the advantages of sound nourishment; (2) the necessity of good drinking water; (3) the lepers must be well housed; (4) they must have warm, clean garments; (5) the utility of physical exercise; (6) that it is right and proper that spouses be permitted to live together at the lazaret; (7) of the good effects of morality and the evil effects of debauchery; and (8) of the judicious use of medicaments.

An appendix was also added treating of the propagation of leprosy. The author notes that nine-tenths of the lepers presented symptoms of syphilis before they contracted leprosy. "As to the others," he said, "I affirm that they became lepers without ever having been syphilitic. Their ailment is due to contagion contracted through inhalation or by inoculation."

The report is marked by prudence, reason, justice, and goodness, and is written in a style suited to the material it contains. The author states the truth without extenuation or exaggeration. He exhibits proof of good judgment in taking care to prove his statements, in proceeding in order, and in proposing only feasible improvements. In order that the lepers might not be entirely exiled from humanity, he declared himself ready and willing to give his life, counting his efforts in their behalf so far, as nothing.

The suggestions in the report inspired the Board. The greater number of improvements carried on within the next few years followed the lines mapped out by the hand of the priest. After Molokai had attracted the attention of the entire world, after Father Damien had really "put it on the map," the Hawaiian government became more and more inclined to perform its full duty toward its leper citizens. The leper-missionary ended his mission by obtaining practically all that he had asked.

As his leprosy spread the priest knew that he had entered upon the twilight of his life. He used his last years to consolidate and assure the continuation of his work. Far from lessening his drive, his sickness seemed only to increase it. Time was running out and before he died he wanted to finish the job he had begun for his lepers.

Now that he could hardly walk, he rode on horseback or in a wagon. "I am a little disfigured," he wrote, "but leprosy has not yet attacked my hands." He still did manual labor as he used to. As a matter of fact, he had become the real director of the leprosarium. From the time Gibson was president, or from June, 1887, when Mr. Trousseau took over, the Board of Health had followed his guidance which was marked by good, practical sense and true charity, the kind of guidance that knew how to combine the physical to the moral, and human feelings to religious ones.

The visits of Princess Liliuokalani in 1881, and of Queen Kapiolani and the princess in 1884 were inspired by humanitarian motives of goodness and compassion. But, in them can also be discerned some political notions. In the years from 1880 to 1890, competition between the political parties in the Hawaiian Islands was intense. It would not be entirely unrewarding to study this history thoroughly in order to be able to speak authoritatively. What motives, therefore, were behind the benevolence of King Kalakaua and his government toward the Catholic

Church? Why was Father Damien so well received by the Premier at Honolulu? Why was this and that affair referred to the priest at the Settlement for solution during those years?

This can all be explained, in part, by the political situation. The government of Kalakaua was opposed to the intrusions of foreigners upon the Hawaiian scene. For this reason it was opposed and thwarted, when possible, by the foreign element resident in Honolulu. Determined to restore the former system of personal power, the King became an authoritarian. At one time he took into his confidence an adventurer named Moreno, whom he made chief of his cabinet. There was a general outcry and protest from England, from France, from the United States, and, above all, from the Hawaiians. Occupied with money matters in order to provide the enormous sums spent on his personal pleasures, the King practiced favoritism on a wide scale. The system of general elections gave rise to widespread corruption. It was discovered, in 1886, that he had accepted $75,000 from a Chinese named Aki, for a monopoly on the sale of opium; and then he had sold the same so-called monopoly to another Chinese for $80,000. The government borrowed $600,000 from Spreckles, the American sugar king. All of these scandals and many others brought on the revolution of 1887.

The man closest to the King was Gibson, who directed his political career from 1878 to 1887, in the capacity of prime minister, for the greater part of the time, though there were periods when he filled all the ministries. At the close of the regime, his only colleagues were three natives. The rule of Gibson, as the "power behind the throne," was overthrown by the revolution of June 30, 1887. Arrested on July 1, 1887, he was exiled to San Francisco where he died January 1, 1888.

Gibson's motto was "Hawaii for Hawaiians"; therefore

he favored everything that savored of the ancient Hawaii, even to the resuscitation of pagan feasts and the exploiting of the witch doctors, called *kahuna*.

Dr. Mouritz, placed in charge of the lazaret during the Gibson regime, lost his position when the latter fell from power. It is not accurate to state that he was favored by Gibson, because the latter had no love for physicians and always spoke slightingly of them. Concerning them, he wrote:

> The sooner medical men get down to some sensible base and conclusions on leprosy, the better it will be for all mankind. The average thinking layman in Hawaii Nei can draw conclusions on the subject of leprosy as good, if not better, than many members of the medical profession. The layman is not wedded to any pet theory, does not try to look wise when he talks on this subject of leprosy. Is it not a fact that doctors pretend to know a great deal more than they do know?
>
> Their so-called dogmas, theories, and nescience change with the wind; their views are bewildering, prone alas, at times to be blindly self-assertive, dogmatic, and tyrannical; pledged to individual schools of thought, and sometimes their attitude to each others' theories and arguments assumes the fierce form of dog-eat-dog! This may be overdrawn, but if you reflect, gentlemen, you must admit its truth.

And this is the same man who had written his clairvoyant article on Father Damien when he first arrived at Molokai: "If a noble Christian priest, preacher, or sister should be inspired to go and sacrifice a life to console these poor wretches, that would be a royal soul to shine forever on a throne reared by human love." He repeated this almost verbatim in his "Report on Leprosy" in 1886: "In order to cure the Hawaiian race of its ills it requires the spirit of divine love, not the stern, scientific methods of

London, Berlin, Paris, New York, and elsewhere." This conviction had given Gibson an attachment to the Catholic priest even before he knew him. He upheld him, and more than once kept him from being "taken over the coals."

Whatever one may say about him, Gibson did possess great ability, excellent qualities, and noble sentiments. His friendship with Father Damien was all to his credit.

Through Superintendent Meyer, the Board listened to the priest's suggestions, and furnished him money and supplies. Bishop Koeckemann, however, dared not place too much stock in the government's extreme solicitude, which was not so disinterested as first appeared. "Our situation in regard to the Board," he wrote, "is not at all clear. These gentlemen want to use us, but they only half like us." Be that as it may, they did consent to large expenditures for various undertakings that were of general interest and indispensable for the Catholic missionary.

In March, 1886, Father Damien congratulated the Board on the better housing conditions, but added some requests:

> I estimate the number of houses at present, both large and small, somewhat over three hundred nearly all whitewashed, and so far, clean and neat, although a number of them are not yet provided with good windows. These houses, of course cannot have the proper ventilation they need, and naturally create an unpleasant and unhealthy smell; I therefore humbly pray that the Board will be kind enough to take steps and see that this still-existing evil be soon remedied.

To replace half dilapidated buildings in 1887 the Board furnished him the material to erect two large dormitories for his orphans. "They are," he said, "the biggest and most proper in the whole leprosarium." Each one would house

a hundred children. He soon erected dining halls of the
same proportions. The priest directed the construction and
installation with his old-time drive if not with the same
vigor. Father Gregory Archambault told him, "I see you
are working always on the new dormitory as though you
were twenty-five."

The lepers at Kalawao no longer lacked drinking water,
thanks to the reservoir and the main that Father Damien
had put in a long time ago. But those at Kalaupapa were
not so fortunate. They were forced to make the long trip
to Kalawao for their supply. In 1886 the priest discovered
two sources that could supply the whole leprosarium. One
was at Paihamau, the other at Waikolu. He made plans,
suggestions, requests. On May 6, 1887, the Board advanced credit for $35,000 and Mr. Meyer said the instal-
lation could begin:

> The water is to be brought from Waikolu and there
> will be no scarcity of water; the pipes will go up shortly,
> and I have written Ambroise to break in some four or six
> pair of oxen to cart pipes in their places.

The priest got the strongest of his people to work, and a
year later the job was finished.

About that same time a new treatment was introduced
in the Kakaako Hospital near Honolulu. It was a discovery
of a Japanese doctor, Dr. Goto. The remedy seemed to be
producing an almost complete cure. It promised to be more
effective than *Hoang-Nan* pills, which relieved without
curing. Father Damien studied it carefully.

"It consists," he wrote, "in taking two hot baths each
day in a certain solution; taking a gram of certain pills at
each meal, and an ounce of a certain kind of medicine an
hour later." A great number of lepers seemingly had been

cured in Japan. After six months of treatment, Father Damien saw remarkable improvement in some more advanced cases. A ray of hope!

King Kalakaua, who had visited the hospital at Kakaako, and the doctors wanted to introduce the treatment at Molokai. The committee furnished him with a bathtub and a hot-water heater. Along with fifty of his children Father Damien tried the experiment for several weeks and they were all greatly helped. His appetite returned, he could sleep, and his pains ceased. He had strength enough to visit the leprosarium either on foot or on horseback.

Anxious to bring this new remedy to all his lepers, he drew up plans for a building that would hold about a hundred patients. He laid the project before the Board. It called for quarters for the steam boilers; fifteen bathtubs; two bathrooms, 33 by 9 feet; a dining room, 60 by 18 feet; a kitchen, 21 by 15 feet; and six dormitories, each 39 by 18 feet. Another large bathroom was to be placed at the disposition of lepers living in their own homes. The entire establishment was to be enclosed within grounds of 400 by 320 feet, to the east of the rectory.

Gibson wrote him on August 10, 1886, that he would be happy to carry out his project and that a large shipment of medicine had just arrived. But four months later, he informed Father that the Board had vetoed the project on account of the expense, for the moment, and added: "If you can find a way to utilize the already existing buildings, we are ready to help you." It goes without saying that the priest did use the existing buildings. He installed a bathroom where he and a hundred other lepers followed out Dr. Goto's remedy.

In the middle of 1887, a Frenchman, M. Trousseau, succeeded Gibson as president of the Board and the priest could tell him of his complete satisfaction with the Japanese remedy. He and a hundred other lepers had experienced great relief. They were impatiently waiting for the new shipment of medicine that had come in.

The priest's dream from the very first had been to replace Brother Bertrand's chapel at Kalawao with a more imposing edifice. In 1886, everything worked together to help him realize this. A storm blew down the steeple of St. Philomena's. Moreover, he had just received two huge tabernacles from America that demanded suitable surroundings; one of these was for Kalawao, and the other for Kalaupapa. He wrote to his American benefactor, Father Daniel E. Hudson, C.S.C.* of the University of Notre Dame, Indiana:

> After having built a good, solid support which is itself three feet square and of which any good mason would be proud, we have finally placed in position the tabernacle of Kalawao. We had some difficulty in lifting the interior tabernacle on account of the heavy weight of the metal part (2000). The woodwork fits perfectly well over the interior safe; and the canopy, though a little too high for our low church, comes right under the ceiling. Truly, the tabernacle looks superb; and if I succeed in making the altar which I have already begun in accordance with my plan, we will have a really decent and beautiful place to consecrate and to preserve the Blessed Sacrament.
>
> Our people admire greatly and appreciate keenly the noble design and the delicate workmanship of your American artisans. Since the altar and tabernacle will take up a great deal of space, and as my faithful here are always on the increase, I am obliged to enlarge my church considerably. Fortunately, although my hands are quite sore, they are not yet crippled.

* Founder and editor of the *Ave Maria* magazine, and a power in contemporary American letters.

American Catholics furnished the tabernacle; English Catholics and Protestants built the church with their checks.

The priest did not care to ask Rev. Chapman to interest his coreligionists in a work that was specifically Catholic. All he asked of him was to get in touch with Cardinal Manning. His Eminence blessed the undertaking and the money drive; but Catholics combined their gifts with those of Protestants and soon Chapman had the necessary funds. The pastor of St. Luke's reassured the priest about the intentions of Protestants:

> 177 Camden Grove North,
> Peckham, S.E.
> Dec. 3, 1888

Dear Father,

I herewith send you a draft on Bishop and Co. of Honolulu for a thousand pounds, which has been subscribed by many who are grateful to God for the example of your heroic self-devotion. Personally, I have done nothing in the matter, except receive the funds and I require no thanks whatever. The honor is with those who are thus allowed to testify to you their respectful love. This money is for your own disposal, *entirely as you think fit,* and is devoted to the erection of a Chapel for your Catholic lepers at Molokai.

Since plenty of stone was available the church would be built with stone; it would have a pointed arch, a square tower surmounted by a balustrade, and a sheet-metal roof. He had only one worker who was a professional mason; of course he was a leper, as were the men who quarried the stones, hauled them, mixed the mortar, and did the carpentry work.

They had bad luck when they were unloading the sheet

metal from England. The canoe overturned and it all sank
to the bottom of the sea. Father Damien had to replace
his metal roof with what he could get. Father Cornelius,
the Vice-Provincial, surprised him in the midst of his work:

To my utter amazement, I saw him on his new church
which he was roofing, giving orders to masons, workers
and carpenters. And yet he has the appearance of a real
leper, his face puffed, his ears swollen, his eyes blood-
shot, and his voice hoarse. But that doesn't discourage
him. He is happy. He works as though he were not sick
at all, and he'll stop only when he drops.

This was his last construction job. With the exception of
the steeple, he completed it just a short time before his
death. (The priceless relic was restored after World
War II by the Hawaiian government and declared a public monument. A caretaker was appointed for its upkeep.)

Father Albert's sudden departure in March, 1885, did
not cut down on Damien's priestly work. He redoubled his
efforts the moment he knew he had leprosy. Up until the
end of 1887 he took care of two churches, and then again
from March to December, 1888.

The following letter shows quite graphically how he
spent Christmas in 1886:

Christmas Eve — I take my therapeutic bath at five
in the morning; at six I leave for Kalaupapa. I say Mass,
preach, then hear confessions until 11:30, still fasting.

I come back to Kalawao, eat, then go into the confessional and stay there until seven.

I say my breviary. I drink a cup of coffee and go back
to the church at nine where the children and young
people are waiting for the general examination in the
catechism; that lasts until 11:30.

At midnight, High Mass begins and I preach for over a half hour.

Four o'clock in the morning, I return to Kalaupapa to sing a second Mass and preach another sermon. After this I give solemn Baptism to several catechumens.

At nine o'clock, I say the third Mass at Kalawao; but this time I'm worn out and one of my good catechists preaches the sermon.

After this I think about getting Christmas dinner.

The total number of baptisms administered at the leprosarium from 1873 to 1889 rose to 1089, of which 939 were to adults and 150 to children. Some of the Protestant and Mormon lepers, who had at first refused his spiritual ministrations, came around when they saw he was a leper himself. There were always some reprobates. The priest begged the administration to repress their excesses. He watched over all of them.

He continued to give the first place to all the works of charity and piety he had introduced. We find these words written in his own hand: "This is the fifteenth year that we have had Nocturnal Adoration, *lepers that we all are.*" Perhaps he was talking about Nocturnal Adoration from Holy Thursday to Good Friday. They are still doing it!

What were the stages of Father Damien's leprosy? Dr. Mouritz gives us the story. We have seen that by 1885 he was disfigured. In March, 1886, Dr. Mouritz asked the Bishop to let Father Damien come to Honolulu to take Dr. Goto's treatment that was supposed to work wonders. He was admitted at the hospital for leprosy suspects at Kakaako. But, says Dr. Mouritz,

. . . within two weeks Father returned to the Leper Settlement, stating that he felt homesick for Kalawao, since he had to remain idle in Kakaako; but meanwhile he had learned all about the carrying out of Dr. Goto's treatment, and he would establish his own bathhouse at Kalawao, and another for the boys and the girls at his home. He did nothing, however, until almost the end of the year 1886. In the meantime, every mail brought him alleged cures for leprosy from all over the world; to what extent he used the multitude of medicines sent him, I do not know. If he did use them it made no difference in the progress of his leprosy, which rapidly advanced, and with remarkable severity. At the beginning of the year 1887, the skin of the abdomen, chest, and back, both extensor and flexor surfaces of the arms and legs showed tubercles, masses of infiltration, deep maculation in varying degrees of extent and severity. The mucous membrane of the nose, palate, roof of the mouth, pharynx, and larynx became involved; the skin of his cheeks, nose, lips, forehead, and chin became excessively swollen, deep copper-colored macules and deep infiltration alternately prevailing; his body became emaciated.

Early in the year 1887, Father Damien was able to get the much-talked-of Goto bathing and medicines established at Kalawao. He proceeded immediately to demonstrate his belief in the treatment by excessive use of both medicines and bathing, using hot water at a temperature of 108°, and remaining in the same for hours; drinking a tea of the nature of a semi-bitter tonic, Aesculus Turbinate, is part of the treatment; also, a handful of herbs is used in the bath, supposed to dissolve in the water and liberate medicinal properties; together with all this, a teaspoonful of pills weighing about two grams each is taken daily. After a few weeks of vigorous use of this Goto treatment, it had the effect that I have already stated, giving Father Damien a semi-asphyxiated appearance; symptoms of aphonia and dyspnosa showed up; he tottered in his walk; his clothes appeared like bags hung on his figure; and, the lobes of both ears became enormously enlarged, reaching to his collar. Bronchial catarrh, and oedema of the feet completed the train of grave symptoms; yet, in the face of this evidence of the unsuitability of the Goto treatment for his case, he claimed it was doing him good, and that he felt better than he had for the past two years. He lost at least thirty-five pounds in bodily weight at this time. About the month of June 1887, many of the lepers began to drop off the Goto treatment; this also influenced Father Damien, and he changed the hot bath part of the treatment to one bath every other day; but the mischief had been done; his system refused to respond and he grew weaker.

In September 1887, it became apparent that Father Damien had given up all hope of getting any relief or stay of his leprosy, and his weakness became apparent to himself; the slightest exertion brought on difficulty of breathing; his temper, which previously had been alternately cheerful and irritable, became preternaturally calm, and permanent gloom settled down upon him.

His face, although dreadful and distressingly disfigured by masses of leproma and general leprous infiltration, showed unmistakable signs of grief and anguish. This despair and anguish, a condition of mind quite common amongst the victims of leprosy, came upon the suffering priest at recurrent intervals in two forms:

First — "Melancholia Attonita," where he remained motionless and silent, with his eyes fixed into space.

Second — "Melancholia Religiosa," strange to say, occasionally troubled him — *the delusion of his being unworthy of heaven.* This was most remarkable, for if there was any man in the universe who would seem to have had every prospect of future happiness and salvation, that man was Damien.

Brother Joseph Dutton, who was an eyewitness of Damien's last days, says that:

When he felt that his end was approaching, and since

he had yet quite a number of pieces of unfinished work on hand, about the new church, etc., he strained every nerve and muscle to get them completed. I am sure that these extra exertions hastened considerably his end; and I feel that all who noted his great efforts during those last weeks will join me in confirming this belief.

Dr. Mouritz agrees with Dutton:

The question has often been asked and variously answered, "Why was not another priest sent to help and to relieve Damien of his work?" The answer is "Even if a priest had been sent to his assistance, Damien would not have relinquished his work; he preferred to struggle on to the end and to die in the harness!"

He stuck to his work and even appeared to me to work harder as his strength gradually became sapped by the disease. I departed from the Leper Settlement in the month of January, 1888, and even then Damien's death was plainly in sight. His stomach had become gravely involved; he suffered constant gnawing pain, continuous sensation of hunger, nausea, heartburn, vomiting, syncopal attacks and great depression. Added to his other troubles, the leper is affected with a voracious appetite, which causes him to overtax his stomach; this condition is due in part to fibroid changes in the walls of the stomach, atrophy of the circular muscular fibers of the pylorus, together with dilation; the stomach bolts and rapidly ejects its contents, almost as soon as the food enters, hence the leper feels constant gnawing pains and hunger.

Finally, Dr. Mouritz noted: "Still Father Damien lived some fifteen months after I left the Settlement. He had resided in Hawaii a few weeks over twenty-five years. He passed away about 8 a.m. on April 15, 1889; this was the Monday before Easter — he had prayed earnestly for death at this season, hoping to greet his Master on Easter Morn."

17   *English and American Friends*

THE sensational news of Father Damien's leprosy increased the affection of his friends and brought him new collaborators. Among the friends who brought him most comfort were two English Protestants, Rev. Chapman and Edward Clifford; two American laymen, Dutton and Sinnett; and, finally, a Belgian missionary, Father Conrardy, who imitated his heroism.

THE REVEREND CHAPMAN

The noble sentiments expressed in the letters of St. Luke's rector, Rev. Chapman, whom we have met before, are edifying because of the fine quality of the charity that made him help the leper priest.

> 177 Camden Grove North
> Peckham, S. E.
> June 4th, 1886

Rev. Father in Christ:

I write to you in all humility to offer you my deep and respectful sympathy — though I would not dare to say my pity — as you hang on the cross of an awful pain with which the Lord has honored you. It will be a source of real comfort to you to know that your bravery has fired some of us to follow your example so far as God gives us grace and as it pleases Him to call us to the sweet life of sacrifice. You have taught me more by the story of your life than all the commentaries I have ever read; and the Blessed Sacrament is more to me since I have read of a voluntary leper than it ever was before.

If money can in any way relieve the necessities of those under your care, I will, on the receipt of a letter from you, do all in my power to collect 500 pounds and forward it as you shall direct. I am only a clergyman in the Church of England, but your example is more calculated to make converts to your Communion than any sermon I have ever listened to. It was reserved for Pere Lacordaire, by his writings, to alter the tenor of my life; and, now, God has used you to confirm the law of sacrifice, in one of His most feeble sons. Kneeling at your feet, I would ask for your prayers which, next to my mother's, I shall prefer to all others. Those who descend to the lowest ascend to the highest; and I doubt not that in Molokai you understand the festival better than at St. Peter's, Rome. I ask God daily that it may be not long before He gives you your crown; and though I shall never be near enough to see you wear it, I shall rejoice in your coronation while I remain in the outer courts. This letter is a small tribute of love to a man who has taught me the meaning of true heroism. May God bless and keep you in the hollow of His Hand.

I remain in simple reverence,

> Yours affectionately in the Crucified,
> (signed) H. B. Chapman
> Vicar of St. Luke's
> Peckham, London, S. E.

On Saturday, October 23, 1886, the London *Times* published Father Damien's answer:

THE APOSTLE OF THE LEPERS AT MOLOKAI

Through the courtesy of the Rev. H. B. Chapman, Vicar of St. Luke's, Camberwell, who has yielded to our urgent request, we are able to publish the following touching letter from Father Damien:

Kalawao, Molokai,
Sandwich Isles,
August 26th, 1886

Reverend Sir:

Your highly appreciated letter of June 4th is to hand. Thanks to Our Divine Savior for having fired up in you, by the example of a humble priest fulfilling simply the duties of his vocation, that noble spirit of the sweet life of self-sacrifice. As you say in your letter, the Blessed Sacrament is indeed the stimulus for us all, for me as it should be for you,* to forsake all worldly ambitions. Without the constant presence of Our Divine Master upon the altar in my poor chapels, I never could have persevered casting my lot with the lepers of Molokai; the foreseen consequence of which begins now to appear on my skin, and is felt throughout the body. The Holy Communion being the daily bread of a priest, I feel myself happy, well pleased, and resigned in the rather exceptional circumstance in which it has pleased Divine Providence to put me.

Your statement regarding your connections with the Church of England leads me to say a few words of what a middle aged, well educated man [Joseph Dutton] has done, who until a few years ago belonged to the Episco-

---

* At the time this letter was written (1886), validity of Anglican Orders had not yet been finally determined. This was done on September 13, 1896, by Pope Leo XIII, in the Encyclical Letter, *Apostolicae curae.* Consequently, Father Damien might possibly have been giving the benefit of the doubt to the belief of Anglicans in the validity of Anglican Orders. This is the most we can say.

palian Church in America. He became not only a convert to the Catholic faith, but shortly after his abjuration he made a long retreat in a Trappist Convent, and following the Divine inspiration of self-sacrifice, came a few weeks ago to this far-distant and poor country, resolved to spend his remaining days at Molokai, asking the authorities that he might be permitted to come and work here with me without salary for the relief of the distressed lepers. He now resides here with the leper priest, and as a true sympathizing brother, helps me caring for the sick. He too, though not a priest, finds his comfort in the Blessed Sacrament. Without doubt you will admire with me the almighty power of God's grace in favor of my new companion, and please allow me to pray daily for you and your brethren that we may all have one faith, belong all to the same *one, true,* Apostolic Church, and become all one in Christ Jesus, and thus obtain the same eternal crown in Heaven.

In regard to your intended collection in favor of the unfortunate lepers under my care, I would say that any amount, however small, will be gladly received for the relief of over 600 poor, unfortunate lepers. Be it understood that, for me personally, having made the vow of poverty, my wants are few. A draft from the Bank of England, on Bishop and Co., bankers in Honolulu will be the simplest and the safest way for remittance.

May the eternal blessing of God be with you, your family, and those who may contribute in any way to the relief of my poor, sick people.

> Yours affectionately in Our Lord,
> (signed) J. Damien De Veuster
> Catholic Priest for the Lepers

P.S.   To give you some idea of our place, I send you by same mail a small pamphlet, *The Lepers of Molokai.* May it be of interest to you and your friends. —

> J. Damien

Three months later, Rev. Chapman sent him a new gift of 975 pounds sterling with these delicately expressed lines:

I thank you for your fine letter of August 26th; more than all, for the prayers which you promise for those amongst whom I live, and after that, those for myself. You will find enclosed a small sum ($4,875.00) which Christians have charged me to send you and which they will thank you for accepting. The best way, they think, to do you a favor and to bring a smile to your lips, is to aid you to help your lepers. They leave you absolutely free to use this sum as you see fit. Your entire life is a guarantee of the good use to which you will put it.

You have the happiness of being loved and appreciated by your Cardinal Archbishop (Manning) towards whom I myself owe a great debt of gratitude. I beg you to salute respectfully, for me, your companion, Dutton. I thank God for him, and for the life he has chosen; well aware through knowledge of my own heart, how rare is such heroism.

May this little flower of love which England sends you, spread about you its perfume. May it prove to you the affection of those who address you and who hope to meet you in heaven.

> Your friend who loves you,
> (signed) H. B. Chapman

The worthy Anglican decided to widen the circle of his request. Not content to write to the Catholic *Tablet*, he addressed a letter to the editor of the London *Times*. It was published together with another letter from Miss Agnes Lambert.

> 177 Camden Grove North;
> Peckham, S. E. October 16th

Sir:

An account of Father Damien's work, and the heroic

penalty which he has paid, appeared not long ago in most of the papers. The case is as simple as it is sad. This manly priest, himself under a vow of poverty, lives in the Island of Molokai, which is confined to lepers, among whom he has irretrievably cast his lot. He has himself fallen a prey to the disease, and in a cheerful letter which he has lately written to me says that he would most gladly receive any contributions for his poor people. I have received the willing sympathy of his Eminence the Cardinal Archbishop in the publication of his appeal, and shall be happy to undertake all acknowledgments and transmissions. The case speaks for itself though I could have wished it had a worthier channel of expression.

I am, Sir,

Your obedient servant,
(signed) H. B. Chapman

Milford House
Elms-road, Chaphan Common, S.W.
October 18, 1886
Sir,

This morning my attention was drawn to a sentence in the last number of a weekly review, declaring the subject of the lepers to be so repulsive "That nobody can possibly want to know any more about them." Immediately afterwards, someone else drew my attention to the paragraph in the *Times* containing the appeal of the Rev. H. B. Chapman, Vicar of St. Luke's, Camberwell, for the poor leper flock of the heroic Father Damien in the Island of Molokai. In spite of the opinion expressed by your contemporary of the hundreds of thousands — in our Indian Empire alone there are 135,000 — of human beings afflicted at this moment with the most terrible disease that can disfigure and destroy mankind; will you let me, in the hope of assisting Mr. Chapman's generous efforts, supplement his letter by reminding your readers that the increase of leprosy in the Sandwich

Islands has been so great in recent years that the Government of that little kingdom has been obliged to enforce segregation of the affected, and has set apart the Island of Molokai for the purpose. One heroic priest after another has cut himself off from his kindred and all that makes life glad, in order to devote himself to their service. In 1873, Father Damien, a young Belgian priest just ordained, volunteered his service for the settlement then numbering 800 lepers, of whom between 400 and 500 were Catholics; and who, dying at the rate of from eight to twelve per week, had for long been without the aids and comforts of religion. For thirteen years, besides ministering to their spiritual wants, Father Damien has been "doctor, nurse, and even in some cases undertaker and grave-digger" — in fact, all things — for his stricken flock. But at last he has himself fallen a victim to the terrible disease. In a letter to Mr. C. W. Stoddard, Father Damien tells his story as no one else could tell it; "since March last my confrere, Father Albert, has left Molokai and this archipelago, and has returned to Tahiti and the Poumoutous. I am now the only priest on Molokai, and am supposed to be myself afflicted with this terrible disease. . . . Impossible for me to go any more to Honolulu on account of the leprosy breaking out on me. . . . Having no doubt myself of the true character of my disease, I feel calm, resigned, and happier among my people. Almighty God knows what is best for my own sanctification, and with that conviction I say daily a good *fiat voluntas tua*. Please pray for your afflicted friend, and recommend me and my unhappy people to all servants of the Lord."

I think that few can refuse Mr. Chapman's appeal after this. And let it be remembered that small things as well as substantial aid can comfort and brighten the dreary existence of these unhappy people. Blankets, and even chromolithographs, illustrations from *Harper's Weekly*, the *Graphic*, and such like have already been welcomed by them and would be welcomed again. So that the least

among us can help to give some little solace to the sad
lives of the doomed exiles of Molokai.

I am, Sir,

Your obedient servant,
(signed) Agnes Lambert

These letters brought on a flood of donations. The sum
Rev. Chapman was able to send to Father Damien was
estimated at 2,625 pounds sterling, approximately $13,125.

The priest also received boxes of books and illustrated
material for his lepers' amusement and instruction. These
were splendid offerings, but not the only proof of the admiration for the priest in England. Chapman wanted to do
even more, as is very evident from the following letter:

I would have liked to give you my services; but it
seems to be God's Will that I remain here with the poor
among whom I live. In spite of the fact that I am too
poor myself to help them, I lack the courage to leave
them. Were it not for this, I would come to you, to care
for you until you leave for Heaven.

Once more, may the Savior console you in your martyrdom, by the thought that having been raised on the
Cross yourself, by this means you will attract many
others to it. I know that for you, I do not belong to the
Church. Yet nothing can prevent me from kneeling at
your feet, a humble disciple before an eminent servant
of God.

Allow me to call myself your friend.

Your friend who loves you,
(signed) H. B. Chapman

Father Damien wrote him his warmest thanks, and
added:

As we are now in the cold season, I am sending today
to our Honolulu importers an order for goods to supply

a great many lepers, five to six hundred, with suitable cloth and other necessaries; it is my intention to keep in reserve the balance of the fund for future wants.

With the arrival of these goods the scent of the flower of English love will be greatly appreciated and long remembered by a great many poor, destitute sufferers whose cold and benumbed limbs will feel again the comfort of warm cloth.

Edward Clifford

Edward Clifford was a cultured, well-to-do Englishman. As he was an artist, he spent his spare time painting. But like Rev. Chapman, he was very enthusiastic about moral beauty, as the following quotation from his writings shows:

One Sunday morning, in the spring of 1887, I read an account of Father Damien in the magazine of the Soho Girls' Club, and I made up my mind almost immediately that I would go and see him, and find if there were any way of helping him. The thought of doing so naturally gave me great delight, even though it seemed to me then that visiting Molokai would be the nearest thing to descending into hell.

Clifford arrived at the leprosarium on December 17, 1888; stayed there a couple of weeks and then spent a month in Honolulu writing his book *Father Damien*, which appeared shortly afterward.

He could not land at Kalaupapa because the sea was too rough, the spray rising fifty feet into the air. They went on to Kalawao and put off in a boat for a rocky point about a mile and a half from the town. From there Clifford could see some twenty lepers on the beach, and Father Damien in the midst of them, wearing a large straw hat. When the sea became calm for a while, they made for shore. Of this meeting, Clifford wrote:

Father Damien caught me by the hand, and a hearty welcome shone from his kindly face as he helped me up the rock. He immediately called me by my name, "Edward," and said it was "like everything else, a Providence" that he had met me at that irregular landing place, for he had expected the ship to stop at Kalaupapa, and Father Conrardy had gone there.

At first, the three hundred whitewashed huts spread out at the foot of the black *palis* seemed a beautiful sight. But soon sadness came over Clifford. He was in the valley of death. At the sight of the white cottages wherein leprosy was devouring its victims like worms in a grave, he thought of the whited sepulchers in the Gospel. As the visitor saw more, he never ceased to marvel at the tangible, the prodigious, the almost magical results which had crowned the efforts of the Catholic priest.

Clifford had landed with a load of gifts and money:

First came an engraving of Mr. Shields' "Good Shepherd" from Lady Mount Temple; then a set of large pictures of the Stations of the Cross from the Hon. Maude Stanley; then a magic-lantern with Scriptural slides; then a number of colored prints; and, finally a grind-organ which could play about forty tunes by simply having its handle turned and this was given by Lady Caroline Charteris. Before he had been at the settlement half an hour, Father Damien was showing his boys how to use it; and I rarely went through Kalawao afterwards without hearing the grind-organ active.

There were beautiful silver presents from Lady Grosvenor and Lady Airlie, and several gifts of money. And, most valuable of all, there was a water-color painting of the *Vision of St. Francis* by Mr. Burne Jones and sent by the painter. Clifford told Father, "It's worth $500.00," and he could hardly believe his ears.

I gave him on Christmas Day a copy of Faber's hymns which had been sent him by Lady Grosvenor's three children. He read over the childishly written words on the title-page, "Blessed are the merciful, for they shall obtain mercy," and said very sweetly that he should read and value the book.

From India the goodhearted Clifford had brought a whole case of gurjan oil that was supposed to work wonders. The oil was brown and sticky, but when mixed with limewater it formed a kind of ointment used by the lepers of the Andaman Islands (off the coast of Burma). Not wanting to offend anyone, the priest took the treatment and said he felt better. His lungs were attacked and he had lost his voice. However, he forced himself to sing a song, which, he said, had been impossible for several months. As for the lepers at Molokai, the energetic rubbing of this mixture was too hard on them, so they had little interest in it.

The priest consented to sit for the artist. They did this on a little balcony upstairs. Shaded by honeysuckle in bloom, it opened on to the two rooms of the priest's living quarters: a bedroom and his workroom or study with its shelves of books and its huge map of the world. Clifford says, "Some of my happiest times at Molokai were spent in this little balcony, sketching him and listening to what he said."

In this manner did Clifford describe the man who had sat in front of him for his sketches:

A thick-set, strongly-built man, with black curly hair and short beard, turning gray. His countenance must have been handsome, with a full, well-curved mouth and

a short, straight nose; but he is now a good deal disfigured by leprosy, though not so badly as to make it
anything but a pleasure to look at his bright, sensible
face. His forehead is swollen and ridged, the eyebrows
are gone, the nose is somewhat sunk, and the ears are
greatly enlarged. His hands and face look uneven with a
sort of incipient boils, and his body also shows many
signs of the disease.

He had to sleep with his mouth open.

When the work was finished, Clifford got his reactions:
"He looked mournfully at my work, 'What an ugly face!'
he said; 'I did not know the disease had made such progress.' Looking-glasses are not in great request at Molokai!"
When Clifford suggested sending Pamphile a photograph
of the picture, Father Damien said, "No! Don't do it. It
would hurt him too much to see me this way."

While Clifford was sketching, Father Damien said his
breviary, told him the story of his life, and spoke about his
work. "I need scarcely say that he gives himself no airs of
martyr, saint or hero. A humbler man I never saw. One
day I asked him if he would like to send a message to
Cardinal Manning. He said that it was not for such as he
to send a message to so great a dignitary; but, after a
moment's hesitation he added, 'I send my humble respects
and thanks.'"

Father Damien asked many questions about Rev. Chapman and those who had sent him gifts; made Clifford give
their names; and was astonished that being Protestants they
were so friendly to him. The Englishman sang hymns for
him; the ones he liked best were "Brief Life Is Here Our
Portion" and "Safe Home in Port." Watching closely while
he sang, Clifford noticed that "at such times the expression
of his face was particularly sweet and tender." Father
Damien once remarked, "English is now my native tongue."
Clifford was relieved on one point in their talks: "I was

glad to find in conversation with him that it was no part of his belief that Protestants must be eternally lost."

He insisted vigorously that I satisfy myself that his accounts were in perfect order and that the donations made him were divided equally between Catholic and Protestant. With him, the lepers were at home. They always surrounded him. They came up to see how my painting was getting along, or they remained on the balcony to grind out music on Lady Charteris' mechanical organ.

Clifford's stay at Molokai was short, but it was long enough for him to be convinced of Father Damien's energy in carrying out his work. His final judgment of the priest in his book *Father Damien* was to this effect — by his efforts to get food and clothing and materials through the Board, by his intense labor and his splendid example, he had come close to building up an ideal leprosarium, one that far surpassed what any nation had done.

When saying good-by to his dear friend whom he would not see again, the priest gave him a little card of flowers from Jerusalem and wrote on it, "To Edward Clifford, from his leper friend, Joseph Damien de Veuster." He then asked for Clifford's Bible and wrote: "I was sick, and ye visited me."

While the ship weighed anchor and pulled out, Clifford stood on deck waving a last good-by to Damien who, surrounded by his lepers, was standing on the rocks waving back "till we slowly passed from their sight."

About this time, other letters and messages and generous offers of help came to Father Damien.

The Baroness Marie de Kinckowstrom sent him, from Sweden, these touching words:

There are hearts here in the remote parts of Sweden who love and admire you. . . . We, also, in the Far North, have our lepers. Your devotion has gone so far as to enter their ranks . . . their number is on the increase now also. It is with sorrowful interest that we read the details in a Swedish newspaper . . . I take the liberty to recommend to your prayers, the kingdoms of Sweden and Norway, the Lord will lead them back to the Catholic Faith.

Among his American friends, other than Brother Joseph Dutton and Brother James Sinnett, must be listed, first of all, Archbishop William Gross, of Portland, Oregon, who liked to call himself "agent for the lepers." In January, 1888, Father Damien wrote to the Archbishop and described his condition. For three years the malady had been spreading over his body. Despite this, though, he was still able to discharge his duties. Entire helplessness would not result until the internal organs become infected. He no longer hoped for deliverance from approaching death. "Our holy Faith," he added, "is the one that is most respected at the lazaret and the Divine Master has there His chosen friends."

Father Hudson sent him two tabernacles. Professor Stoddard published a book, *The Lepers of Molokai*, in 1885.

To Miss Elizabeth Harper, of Brooklyn, New York, Father Damien wrote a letter, acknowledging receipt of two packages of "very interesting pictures," and adding: "Your moneyorder of $25.00 . . . in conjunction with Mrs. Commins' contribution will be sufficient to buy a pair of good, winter trousers for each one of my three dozen boys."

Another pious lady sent him these lines: "You have left all for God and the service of the unfortunate. You must enjoy the happiness that none can take from you, a foretaste of the Great Recompense." But, this time, Father

Damien was obliged to ask Brother Dutton to act as his secretary. "Tell her," he said, smiling, "that it is true. I do possess that joy."

BROTHER JOSEPH DUTTON

Ira Barnes Dutton was 43 years old when he landed at Kalaupapa on July 29, 1886. Father Damien was there at the dock to meet him, for as far as we know he was expecting his arrival. Here is the way Dutton described the meeting years later:

> Forty years ago this morning, I landed at Kalaupapa. Father Damien was there waiting, with his buggy — low, wide and rattling — and a steady, old horse. I introduced myself as coming with King Kalaupapa's permission. (It was before the islands became a territory of the U.S.) We climbed into the buggy and were off to Kalawao. The autos that whiz everywhere nowadays were unknown then. Father Damien's old buggy would be a curio now. . . .
>
> He was now a leper in the advanced stage; he died nearly three years later. I was happy as we drove over that morning. The Father talked eagerly, telling how he had wanted Brothers here; but, the mission had none to spare yet. So, he called me "Brother," as I had come to stay, and gave me at once the full care of two churches. He was full of plans that morning, talking of what he wished for the lepers, the dreams he always had.

Dutton had lunch the same day with Dr. Mouritz. Later, the Doctor described him thus:

> Brother Dutton took lunch with me, and I scanned him carefully. . . . It was a hot, dusty trip; yet, Dutton showed no fatigue, nor travel-stained clothes. He wore a blue denim suit, which fitted his tall, well-knit, slim, muscular figure. He stood about five feet seven inches

tall; had dark brown hair and grayish blue eyes; a low voice, placid features, and a pleasant smile. He was reserved and thoughtful, had nothing to say about his past life or the reason for his seeking seclusion and work at Molokai, and turning his back forever on the world.

It was learned later that he was born on April 27, 1843, at Stowe, Vermont. Four years later the family moved to Janesville, Wisconsin, where Ira was reared an Episcopalian. His mother, a devout, religious woman, later followed her son into the Catholic Church.

When the Civil War broke out Dutton volunteered as a member of the City Zouave Corps which enrolled as a body as Company B of the 13th Wisconsin Volunteer Infantry. He served in Kansas, Kentucky, Tennessee, Alabama, Louisiana, and Texas. In 1865 he was promoted to the rank of First Lieutenant and was mustered out of service in Madison, Wisconsin, in 1866. The same year, in Mt. Vernon, Ohio, he married a girl who proved to be faithless; and, after a lapse of fourteen years, during which period she was living with another man in New York, but running up bills in his name, he divorced her.

Then followed years of heavy drinking. These he called his "wild years." One day, however, he received the grace to quit drinking, took the pledge, and never touched a drop again. In 1883, he received a greater grace; and was received into the Catholic Church on April 27 by Father J. A. Kelly, O.P., and was given the name of Joseph. In 1884, he was confirmed by Bishop McCloskey at Gethsemani, Kentucky. He remained with the Trappists for two years as an oblate, without taking vows. Concluding that this was not his vocation, he left the monastery and went to St. Louis, Missouri, where he met a Redemptorist Father, a former provincial, about to go to a conference of the Order in New Orleans, Louisiana. He invited Dutton to go along. It was at the Redemptorist house in New

Orleans that he first learned of Father Damien. Here is
how Dutton tells it:

> It was there in the convent, in the reading-room, that
> I saw for the first time a mention of Father Damien — a
> brief item in an old-time Catholic paper about Molokai
> and the Father. I had never heard of him.
> Why this suddenly impressed me with the certainty
> that I had found my real vocation I have never tried to
> elucidate; but, have acted as there was need only to go
> ahead, leaving the whys and wherefores to any who like
> such problems. I learned later of Charles Warren Stod-
> dard, professor at Notre Dame University, and that he
> had been to Molokai; at once, then, I decided to go and
> see him about (1) how to get to Molokai, and (2) once
> there, if I could be sure of finding plenty of work. I
> went; I saw him; and, as expected, I was satisfied as to
> both questions; so, I set off at once.

Professor Stoddard's booklet about Father Damien's work
undoubtedly influenced Dutton in making this decision. In
any case, Stoddard encouraged him and told him how to
get to Hawaii. While at Notre Dame he also saw Father
Hudson, who, as we have seen, was one of Father Damien's
benefactors.

Dutton at once settled his affairs; said good-by to his
aged mother; and after a visit to Memphis, Tennessee, set
out for California.

"I started from Memphis for San Francisco. Though I
had ample means, I traveled on an immigrant ticket; and,
from San Francisco, on a sailing vessel, the cheapest way,
for I had the desire of making a pilgrimage of this journey."

Dutton arrived in Honolulu, July 22, 1886, attired in a
neat, blue demin suit, his habitual attire for the remainder
of his life. His first visit was to Bishop Koeckemann. He
showed him the letters that he had brought from Notre
Dame, and said that he wanted to go to Molokai and to

work there without pay. The Bishop was delighted with his offer, but could not give the necessary permission without consulting the Board of Health. Gibson, the Board's president, himself a Vermonter, received him cordially, sent out his clerk, Mr. Hendry, also from Vermont, to buy whatever Dutton needed, and offered to pay him a salary. Dutton refused: "I wanted to give myself entirely free, and so was gladly accepted."

"The steamer was not making the passage to Molokai that week," Dutton relates, "but Mr. Gibson arranged to have it come and call for my passage; however, I had already bought a ticket ahead of him. The steamer left me at Kalaupapa on July 29, 1886, nearly three years before Father Damien died. And I have never left the grounds of the leper settlement; in fact, I have not been away from the Baldwin Home* for years."

Indeed, Dutton never left the leper colony until 1930, when he was taken to St. Francis Hospital in Honolulu. Actually, he never left Kalawao from 1893 until 1930, when he went to Kalaupapa, a distance of two miles, for an eye operation!

During the intervening years, he lived a life of extraordinary fervor, marked by unswerving devotion to duty. Father Damien blessed Divine Providence for having sent him a companion, a man filled with contrition for the "wild years" of his life. Dutton had resolved to get along agreeably with others, to ask no favors, to create peace among those about him, and to help them in every way. At first he lived with Father Damien, but later built a cottage for himself nearby. A thousand needs immediately presented themselves — ulcers to dress, aid to the priest in his carpentering and building, finishing the tasks which his chief commenced but left undone in order to start some-

* See p. 443.

thing else equally important to him. "Brother Joseph," Father Damien would say, "you are going to finish these." And he would add laughingly: "I am the carpenter; and Brother Joseph the joiner."

Dutton rose at half past four and retired late, often at one in the morning. The care of the orphanages fell, little by little, to Brother Joseph. The relations between the missionary and his helper are described in the writings of the latter:

The good understanding between us was positive and actual. There were times when one did not care to be too much with Father Damien; that should be said. But there was love between us. This is not to say that our tastes and personal habits were the same; it would not be correct to say that. Everyone has some repugnances; and, in taking up this new life, I found, as I expected, many things naturally repugnant, very different. I was firm in one resolve — to get along with everyone and everything. . . . If my intimate association with him was longer than it had been for others, it was partly because I admitted my own faults, and partly because I always saw him place in me the most entire confidence and have in his heart a deep love, no matter what his exterior appearance might be. Also, I used to be quite open with him in speaking of all these things; he, likewise with me; and, this seems to have given us confidence in each other.

Father Damien gave Brother Joseph his warmest friendship, and made him witness to his will along with a fellow priest.

There seemed to be nothing that Brother Joseph could not do; nothing that he refused to do. He accepted the most repulsive tasks, imitating Father Damien, but always acting under a physician's orders. He cared for the sick in their homes with a rare patience, and was credited with possessing more skill than the doctors. Frank and yet discreet, good-natured in conversation, he made friends with all with whom he came in contact. "He has a divine character," said Dr. Mouritz; "nothing ever causes him to lose his temper." Father Damien deserves praise for having attracted this good son of St. Francis to Molokai, where he served the lepers faithfully for forty-five years.

In January, 1889, from some jewelry whose possession Dutton had reserved, he had a large crucifix made which he offered to Pope Leo XIII. The Pope charged Dr. Denis J. O'Connell* to thank him. "I talked a long time with the Holy Father," the latter wrote after his audience. "His Holiness asked me to tell Father Damien and yourself that he sends you his apostolic benediction."

The contrast between these brothers in heroism must be stressed. The Fleming, from peasant stock, had a hasty temper; was stubborn, obstinate, impatient, and careless in his appearance. The former Army officer was extremely neat in appearance; he spoke in low, modulated tones, never once departing from a well-bred, courteous manner. However, they understood each other perfectly. From the prolix and frank pen of Dutton, we read these words:

> The Father loves me deeply and I return his affection. It is not because our temperaments and tastes are similar, but that, upon the threshold of my new life, I resolved to accommodate myself to everything. After twenty years at Molokai, no one can accuse me of ever having infringed seriously upon this resolution. This does not result from any virtue on my part, but is a grace given me by God in granting me faith.

---

* Rector of the American College in Rome. Later rector of Catholic University of America, and Bishop of Richmond, Va.

Father Damien tried to induce his new helper to enter the priesthood. Brother Joseph was obliged to speak of his former life, of his unfortunate marriage, in order to convince the Father that it was an impossibility.

As long as Father Damien lived, Dutton pronounced an annual vow, "to serve the Catholic Mission in the asylum of Molokai," an engagement which placed him under the jurisdiction of the Bishop of Honolulu. Following Father Damien's death, he continued his work under the direction of the Board of Health. As an eyewitness, he remained always one of the stoutest defenders of Father Damien whose memory he zealously shielded and protected.

As director of the Baldwin Home, Brother Joseph spent his life in handling its current affairs, supervising its physical setup and disciplinary problems. He also provided proper recreational facilities for the young, leprous boys who were cared for in the Home, and to that end sought help from his friends.

"Life here has been good," such was his own estimate of nearly half a century spent among lepers. From 1893 to 1928 he did not set foot beyond the enclosed grounds of the Home. In 1908, President Theodore Roosevelt ordered the U. S. Atlantic Fleet, then on a cruise around the world, to defile off the island of Molokai to salute the lone former Army officer in a gesture of good will for his devotion to the lepers; and, to grant this very request which Brother Dutton had made so that the patients might see them and be more proud of their country. Dutton personally thanked Rear Admiral Sperry. In return, the latter and ten Fleet captains wrote him personal letters. President Roosevelt sent him his autographed photograph. In 1917, when the United States entered World War I, as a veteran soldier, he offered his services to go to the front. He was then 76 years of age. An ardent patriot, he collected $9,000 as a contribution to the war effort.

In 1925, the United States Battle Fleet sailed in review before Kalawao while Dutton stood at attention next to the flag. These were memorable occasions for the lepers who gathered on shore to watch as each vessel dipped its colors in passing the black rocks upon which stood an old man with no claim to honor other than that of service to his fellow men.

This event received great publicity and an avalanche of correspondence flowed in to the island. After Brother Joseph's death a notebook of 128 pages was discovered which contained nearly 4000 addresses of correspondents in all parts of the world. Dutton had tried to answer the never ending stream of letters, "but in spite of his industry, he acknowledged before his death that he was some 400 letters in arrears in his correspondence." To facilitate matters, he had form letters printed which he sent to a thousand correspondents.

Among his treasured souvenirs were a long, unsolicited letter from President Harding, sent in 1923, which praised his work and that of Father Damien; and a letter of praise from President Coolidge, sent to him in 1928.

To good friends he sent little gifts at Christmas and Easter — enameled Madonnas, curious shellwork, Hawaiian canes, photos, sometimes of himself or his mother. "It is my life," he explained; "as soon as I find something that gives me pleasure, I want to share it with my friends. Doubtless, through that trait, I have added to the embarrassment of many, in burdening them with things which afford them little or no pleasure." An honest man!

Dutton received some honors. A school in his native land, at Beloit, Wisconsin, was named after him. In 1929, the New York radio apprised him that the Holy Father sent him his blessing; the Hawaiian Parliament voted him a testimonial.

"The Brother of all the World" is Dutton's title and expresses what he had desired to become. He succeeded through his generosity. He made his will in favor of the lepers. He died after having distributed all that he possessed. In the last twenty years of his life he became a member of numerous societies, reading their reports and publications with interest. At the Baldwin Boys' Home his magazines were passed among the youth, but only after having been severely censored; and he well knew how to use the scissors. At one time, from his island home, he carried on a campaign against indecent illustrations.

As noted previously Brother Dutton was outstanding for his ardent patriotism. As a veteran of the Civil War he was a member of the Grand Army of the Republic. Each year, the members of this organization, at their annual encampment, would vote to send Brother Dutton a silk flag. Dutton had a tall flagpole erected near his cottage and with military regularity would hoist the flag at dawn and lower it at sundown. Even when sick, he would leave his bed to carry out this loving duty. In fact, when he was 85, he was still running up the flag, a task he would never delegate to others. Brother Jules, SS.CC., a mission Brother, with him at the time, and now the cook at the Sacred Hearts seminary in Washington, D. C., relates that Dutton left his room against the doctor's orders, to lower the flag at sunset. Feeling tired, he sat down on the steps of his cottage. A leper boy saw him there and ran to tell the Brother. Immediately Brother Jules hastened to his side. As he started to lift him, Dutton protested, urging him first to lower the flag. Brother Jules, however, was more concerned over Dutton and disregarded the old veteran's request. In a few minutes he had him in bed; and this was the beginning of the end.

In good health until the age of 85, Dutton at last fell ill. He was prevailed upon to go to a Honolulu hospital for an operation for cataract, and treatment for a more severe ailment. The Hawaiian Legislature voted him a monthly pension of $300 but the sick man received but one check — he died on March 26, 1931, after having received the last Sacraments, and was interred with all the solemnities of the Church, beside Damien's grave at Molokai.

Dutton's correspondence has its droll aspects. One finds there the hand of the bureaucrat and one has the impression that the ideas of the good man always revolve around certain fixed points. When one hears him repeat: "It has been so many years since I have set foot outside the grounds of the Baldwin Home," one gets the idea that he is repeating them for the record. Was the modesty of the lay worker apparent or real? Some authors have gone to the extreme in eulogizing him, in an effort to refute reports that Dutton merely traded upon the fame of Father Damien in an attempt to take up the mantle fallen from the latter's shoulders.

No extremes are needed. The plain truth is enough. Joseph Dutton was sincerely humble, devout, loyal, friendly, skilled in many diverse lines, an ideal collaborator for Father Damien, and a perfect administrator after his death. His amiable simplicity was spontaneous, never forced; and his disposition was always equable.

BROTHER JAMES SINNETT

James Sinnett got himself engaged by the Board of Health as a nurse. He had previously gained some experience as a nurse in Mercy Hospital, Chicago. Living in St. Louis, Missouri, the Board forwarded his passage money to Honolulu. An Irishman, he had traveled widely and had met with various adventures more or less disedifying, before he applied for work as a nurse at Molokai. So it was that he too, in order to expiate the disorders of his past life, sought to place himself at the disposition of the leper

priest. He passed eight months with him, the last of Father
Damien's life.

Installed at Molokai, Sinnett gave every evidence of possessing an exemplary character and an admirable devotion
to the work he had undertaken. Father Damien, in order
to place him in a position of equality with his other helper,
gave him the name of "Brother James," as he called Dutton,
"Brother Joseph." It was Brother James who nursed the
Father during the final phase of his illness and closed his
eyes in death.

Brother James was given the post of auxiliary to Brother
Joseph in the administration of the boys' orphanage. When
Robert Louis Stevenson visited this establishment some
months after its founder's death, he found that conditions
as to cleanliness, fresh air, and light were not so good as in
the preventoriums and sanatoriums in England. "The sad
state of the Boys' Home," he wrote,

> resulted from the lack of control by Father Damien,
> from negligent ways, and his mistaken notions of hy-
> giene. It was the Chinese quarter, the "Chinatown."
> Someone would ask him, "Is your Chinatown getting on
> all right?" and he would laugh heartily. He laughed good
> naturedly, but he continued in his mistaken ideas with
> placid obstinacy. I was able to ascertain this truth, he
> worked with the means at hand and gave the most press-
> ing needs his first attention. It would all be done better
> later.

Brother Joseph and Brother James were overwhelmed
with work. Even by pooling their pedagogical and man-
agerial knowledge and ability, they did not succeed to
perfection. "It is a little better already, don't you think so?"
Brother Joseph asked of Stevenson. "Soon the Sisters will
take it over. You will see that they will put things in order."

Brother James acted as secretary to the Father when his

eyes began to tire of writing. Edward Clifford was still in
Honolulu when James sent him news of his sick friend:

> I tell the Father sometimes that he looks younger
> when he takes your Gurjin Oil. He thanks you with
> affection, and wants you to know that he is better. Our
> children do not forget you either — you who gave them
> such fine means of entertainment (the grind-organ and
> the magic-lantern) and who brought from the ends of
> the earth a remedy to cure them. The Father charges
> you to transmit to Rev. Chapman his affection and his
> great gratitude.

With his own hand Father Damien added: "I agree
with all that Brother James has written. Au revoir! May
God bless you!"

Another letter was dispatched from Sinnett to Clifford
on February 21, with this postscript: "All my affection and
all my good wishes to our good friend, Edward. I hope to
arrive soon at the summit of my Golgotha. Eternally yours.
J. Damien."

Clifford was dismayed to learn that his Gurjin Oil had
failed to cure his friend and he wrote to Brother James:
"Read in the book of Father Faber that I brought, the
chapter on 'The Will of God and Christian Perfection.'"
By return mail the Father, in his turn, exhorted Clifford
"to walk in the narrow way so we shall soon arrive . . . to
the House of the Eternal Father. A good voyage, my dear
friend, until we meet in heaven. *totus tuus!* [All yours!]
J. Damien."

Clifford received a precious last letter from Sinnett containing the details of Father Damien's last hours. It closed
with these lines:

> I tell you with a sad heart that the steamer which
> carries this letter also bears me away. I leave with deep

regret the dear lepers whom I have learned to love. Following the decease of our dear leper-priest there has been a complete change in the order of things here. It is no longer an institution where children learn virtue. They have no longer the salutary fear of Father Damien. Drunkards have recommenced drinking; the distillers, to distill; and, disorders have reappeared among the young people. Hardly a week had passed when seven of them were given a sentence of fifteen days at hard labor. At the moment in which I write you, three armed men have barricaded themselves in their house and refuse to submit to a three months sentence for illegal distillation. The new broom does not sweep clean.*

Some days after the departure of Brother James, an insurrection broke out. Lepers attempted to kill the assistant steward as well as Father Conrardy. It was necessary to send "fifteen police well-armed" to put down the troublemakers. Sinnett had not waited to witness such disorder before leaving the island. His great and good friend was no longer there to sustain and inspire him.

What became of him? We do not know, except that he is reported to have visited St. Louis in 1895 for the funeral of his sister.

---

* Mr. Meyer bears witness to the truth of Brother James's statement in his report to the Board of Health, of April 1, 1892. He says: ". . . Law and order have not been very exemplary during the last two years. Although no more serious riots have occurred since the serious one of August, 1890, there has been, nevertheless, a great laxity of order. . . ."

18   *Father Lambert Conrardy*

MAY 17, 1888, was an unforgettable day in Father Damien's life. That was the day he saw Father Conrardy land at Molokai to help him in his cruel, priestly isolation. He had come from the United States — from Oregon. His Archbishop, William Gross, the "agent of the lepers," had this to say of him:

> I have tramped all over Oregon with Father Conrardy and he is a noble, heroic man. . . . He is about forty years old and by reason of his outdoor life and the hardships he has endured in the rough, Western life is admirably fitted for the work at Molokai. Though he knows and realizes perfectly that ultimately he must succumb to the disease, his voluntary going is real heroism [June 2, 1889; *The Church News* — Washington, D. C.].

A leper now for three years, and suffering from the crucifying miseries of his disease, Father Damien asked himself if he was going to die without spiritual assistance, without the help of a priest. Now, heaven was sending him a friend, a fellow countryman, a brother after his own heroic heart who would never leave him.

Not belonging to the religious congregation of which

357

Father Damien was a member, this priest was to suffer
misunderstanding and opposition, more or less justified,
from the authorities and the missionaries whom Father
Damien loved and venerated. On this score, his companion's presence was to bring the leper priest new and
painful sufferings, especially since his superiors used it,
with so little justification, as an argument to prove the
latter's own stubbornness and pride.

Who was Father Lambert Conrardy? He was a Belgian
Walloon, born at Liége, July 12, 1841. After studying
under the Jesuits, he was ordained priest June 15, 1866,
and worked for a while in his native diocese. During the
epidemic of 1869 he was a pastor at Stavelot. He cared
for the sick poor, giving them everything he had, even
his bed.

There is no doubt, however, that he was an original
character and not too much of a conformist. In his parish
he decided to have Vespers chanted in French because,
as he explained, the people got bored listening to the Latin
singing without understanding a word of it. This unusual
priest required an unusual apostolate, and particularly so
since he was undoubtedly a priest of astounding faith,
charity, and bravery. Martyrdom seemed his only road to
heaven and since martyrdom did not appear probable in
Belgium, he went traveling about the world in search of
dangerous undertakings.

In 1871, he made one effort after the other at the Foreign Mission Seminary to be sent to China. At first he was
accepted for Hindustan, where he stayed only two or three
years. By 1874 he was working with the Indians in the
Rocky Mountains in the United States. There, at least, he
could chant Vespers to his own liking, give free rein to his
initiative, and run all the risks he wanted to. He remained
in his Oregon parish for fifteen years.

The parish was so vast that it took him three months to cover it. He went on foot, on horseback, in rain and in snow, without a gun, without even a knife to defend himself. The Indians knew he was not afraid of being scalped. One day, a chief stopped him and announced that he was going to be hanged, since he was not afraid of scalping. Father Conrardy pulled out his watch: "Take it," he said, "since you want to hang me, I'm giving you a present." Dumfounded, the chief asked time to think it over and went off to consult the old men of the tribe. They advised respect for this mysterious being who was willing to give up his watch for the pleasure of being hanged. After several such adventures and some cures he worked, he was called the "Condemned Man" and all of them respected him.

Privations spurred his ingenuity, and never affected his good humor. For instance, not having all the usual liturgical furnishings, he used potatoes for candlesticks. During Mass he stuck the candles in the potatoes, and after Mass, was hungry enough to eat the improvised candlesticks.

In 1877, Father Conrardy had learned of Molokai's existence through a letter in the *Annals of the Propagation of the Faith* wherein Father Damien complained that he couldn't do the job by himself. Conrardy wished to join him then but was still needed by his Indians. On November 4, 1887, he wrote to Damien: "I always regret not having become your companion at the time I wrote you my first letter, in 1877, I believe."

At that time, it was customary for all personnel in any single mission to belong to the same religious order or congregation, so that all might be under the same rule and superiors. One can see evidence of this rule being followed in Oregon from the following letter of Father Conrardy: "I've been here among the Indians for thirteen years. Do you want me, my dear fellow countryman? I can still work

at least twenty years. My bishop has just confided this
mission to the Jesuits. If I don't come to Molokai, I must
join the Jesuits, in order to stay here."

He preferred to stay independent and work as a free
lance rather than join the Society of Jesus. Sincerely and
above everything else he wanted to devote himself to the
lepers. That was his vocation as events proved. Archbishop
Gross, the "agent of the lepers," kept in close contact with
Father Damien, and far from opposing Father Conrardy's
departure for Molokai, actually encouraged it.

At the beginning of 1888, Father Conrardy again was
saying how badly he wanted to come:

I have only one regret that will remain with me, —
that of not having left Oregon for the leprosarium years
ago. . . . You will see how a man from Liége can work.
You tell me to lay aside all human considerations; this
I do, dear Father, but don't you think that as a secular
priest at the start, I have the right to ask to be permitted
to minister to the lepers, of course, under his Lordship,
Bishop Hermann's direction, and yours too. I think that
it would be best for me to go to the Islands at once
rather than to spend one to two years in the Novitiate;
not that I won't like the Novitiate, but because the wants
of others require my active ministry.

And a few days later:

I made my sacrifice. I give myself up, with the intention of serving the poor lepers. It is also my intention
of going to the lepers as a secular Priest, hoping in the
course of time, that I may be allowed to join your society.
After a few years of life in the Island at your side, I
will be better fit to become a member of your Congregation, that of the Sacred Hearts of Jesus and Mary.

But the Bishop of Honolulu laid down his conditions. Father Damien was asking that Father Conrardy be accepted as he was; the Bishop let him know:

> I understand that he wants to go directly to Molokai and make his novitiate there, which is not possible. If he wants to stop at the leprosarium on his way to the novitiate, I find no difficulty. But if he wants to stay with you immediately, it would be embarrassing for me to accept him, outsider as he is, to the Congregation, in spite of his undoubtedly fine qualities.

Damien thought it well to refresh the Bishop's memory:

> In your letter of December, 1887, to him, you told him that you could easily obtain permission from the Prefect of Propaganda for him to work here as a secular priest. Later it would be decided whether it were better for him to enter the Congregation. The last lines of your letter have brought me consternation. You oblige me to write to him in that sense (of going to a novitiate in Europe). I need him right away. To tell you the final result: that would spoil everything. He will go to Mexico or somewhere else. And thus neither I nor Your Excellency nor the Congregation will ever see him again. That is why I humbly beg you to let him come as soon as he can. Once here, he could bind himself under your authority by temporary vows, as Dutton, while waiting to be admitted to the Congregation. The circumstances I am in are exceptional; why can he not come to my aid through ways that are a little exceptional?

February 13, 1888, the Bishop clearly agrees:

> Father Conrardy's letter to you and your letter to me, have made me decide to give in to your ardent desire. I have already written to Father Conrardy in the same sense, but I have added a P.S. in which I promise him

authorization to go straight to Molokai without first going through the novitiate. It is because of your health that I consent to deprive him of the advantages of religious profession. We will see later what can be done for his good.

In the two months that followed this decision, the Bishop had to suffer from the opposition of the missionaries surrounding him. The tone of the following lines, which he wrote to Father General on April 26, shows that he was not only sorry for having given in, but that he held Father Damien responsible for this decision which could alienate the missionaries and lower esteem for the Mission:

Father Conrardy wanted to become a Sacred Hearts Religious. I referred him to our novitiates. But Father Damien held the opposite opinion. He *ordered him* (?) to come to Molokai immediately. This puts me in a very embarrassing position. If I oppose his views, he will denounce me to the four winds as an enemy to the lepers' welfare. He can see only the leprosarium and himself. Everything else has to fit into his ideas. In his letters he tells the truth by suppressing truths. Often he certainly presents it under a false light. The Government, the doctor, the Congregation are blamed directly or indirectly for overshadowing our hero. An Hawaiian paper has just printed part of an article from the California paper in which Father Damien asks Father Conrardy to come so there will be some one to take care of his lepers after he is gone. As if none of our own were willing to take his place. Many of our priests are ready to go the minute they are given the sign. Father Albert would still be with him, if he were a little more accommodating to his confreres. Mr. Dutton has suffered martyrdom in spite of his heroic virtue. I have had to give him a quasi-independent position with Father Damien. With this new priest there will be perfect accord at the beginning.

How long will it last? Long enough to fill the world
with the glory of the Belgians to the prejudice of the
Congregation and the Mission. Several of the Fathers
have already expressed their opposition to this affair.

The Bishop's harsh judgment of Father Damien did not
prevent him from writing Damien these simple words a
few days later: "I have just written to Father General
about Father Conrardy, to know what to do — if he is to
stay permanently with us. Recommend this to God. Very
affectionately yours."

The Bishop's evil genius, Father Leonor, Provincial —
whom we will take up soon and not without reason — sent
the following lines to Father Damien on May 28:

I was far from expecting what has happened. Yesterday a flood of letters came in to Bishop from all sides
asking him if they had ever refused to go to Molokai.
Some of them too remind him of their requests to go.
Why say in the newspapers then that you and the lepers
are going to die without the Sacraments because no one
will come to help you? I know the Bishop has spoken to
you on this subject, against which he no longer has any
defense. Conrardy's case, as a priest, is different from
Dutton's, a layman, and falls under the prohibition the
Bishop received from the Prefect of Propaganda, and
that for good reasons.

However, it was too late to do anything about the matter.
Father Conrardy was with Father Damien. He had arrived
in Honolulu on Saturday, May 12, left for Molokai on
Tuesday, May 15, and landed May 17.

Who was at fault in this affair? It is certain that Father
Conrardy was much too expansive and loved to recount
his adventures. While passing through Honolulu he showed

a reporter Father Damien's letter asking him to come. The next day the Protestant paper, *Hawaiian Gazette,* ran a story:

> Father Conrardy, a Belgian priest, has arrived from San Francisco to join Father Damien at the leprosarium of Molokai. All Christians, Catholic and Protestant, must respect and admire the zeal and abnegation of this minister of Jesus Christ, who in this way, voluntarily sacrifices himself for love of poor suffering humanity, as before him, Father Damien has done.

From this the public might conclude that he would not have had to come so far had the Sacred Hearts Fathers in the islands been a little more charitable or a little less prudent. It was a public insult to the Mission. In the minds of the Fathers, and then of the Bishop, Father Damien was the guilty one. This was one of the numerous misunderstandings that clouded his last years.

At the beginning of June the Bishop again referred the matter to Father General. Here is his version of the facts. The American and Hawaiian papers picture Father Conrardy as Father Damien's successor, surmising that no one on the Mission is willing to take his place. They are "two martyrs and heroes." In a circular letter, he (the Bishop) has just made it clear, in a formal way, what the missionaries' dispositions on this matter are . . . all have volunteered. On the other hand, this new hero has made a very poor impression on all the Fathers and Brothers who have seen and heard him. He doesn't think Father Conrardy is bad, but he's lightheaded and holds liberal views about independence. He's full of himself. He takes great care of his body. By himself he drank a whole bottle of wine at a meal . . . without water. In three days he saw more people in Honolulu than the Bishop saw in a year. He's a troublemaker, and to get rid of him the Bishop sent him off to the leprosarium. Father Conrardy had written that he already felt at home there. Since Father Damien is on the verge of becoming helpless, the Bishop was going to send Father Wendelin who is an excellent priest and religious. And the Bishop added to his letter of June 3:

> I have just received a letter from Father Damien that is hardly respectful. He wants what he wants. Conrardy is his man.
> I am not going to get in any discussion with him; but I will tell him that I am the one who has the power of spiritual administration of the leprosarium, according to my conscience and the Rule of Propaganda. I will avoid as much as possible the newspapers in rectifying the falsehoods.

However, the Bishop thought he should make a public statement about the good dispositions of the missionaries.

This "hardly respectful" letter of May 31, 1888, has been lost. But from the Bishop's letter of June 10 we learn that it dealt with: (1) the contradictions in the Bishop's letters; (2) the fact that Father Conrardy had been invited to come as soon as he could (letter of February 1); and (3) the fact that the Bishop wanted to send him back now at all costs.

On June 3 the Bishop also wrote to Father Damien:

> My letter to Conrardy was written after reflection. It would give me pleasure to explain some of the grave reasons that governed my decision, if I believed you well disposed to receive them. But your letter of May 31 seems so inappropriate in content and tone that I content myself with telling you that I am not only within my right but even have the obligation to look after the spiritual administration of the leprosarium according to the Rule . . . even at the risk of going against those I esteem and would like to please as much as possible.

Father Wendelin's orders to go to Molokai upset Father Damien. Eight days later the Bishop reassured him. It was not a question of removing him as pastor of the leprosarium, but of replacing him when he could no longer discharge the duties of a priest, which would be soon. Then the Bishop tried to justify his apparent contradictions, by saying that they existed more in the priest's interpretations than in reality.

The preceding letters of the Vicar Apostolic were answers to letters from Father Conrardy, and were influenced by persons and circumstances. Certainly the Bishop wanted to have a good missionary for the Mission. But, since he was responsible to the Congregation of the Sacred Hearts and to the Congregation of the Propagation of the Faith in Rome, as Bishop, he had to protect his own freedom of action and leave Father Conrardy his. At first he had taken an optimistic view of the case; hence his first favorable decision and his intention of doing all he could for Father Conrardy in the circumstances — particularly so, since on February 24 Father Conrardy had assured him that he wanted to become a Sacred Hearts religious, and would submit to the Bishop in everything. The Bishop had then invited him to come right away, as Father Conrardy himself was resolved on coming as soon as he could. Considering the excellent dispositions of the petitioner, the Bishop was running no compromising risk.

The Bishop did not withdraw his decision of having him enter the novitiate — a thing, he said, that would be excellent for his sanctification. But he did not wish to rush things; Father Conrardy could stay at Molokai for a few weeks while they waited for an answer from the mother house in Paris.

Meanwhile the Provincial, Father Leonor, continued to make things hard for Father Damien:

Considering the delicate circumstances and the exceptional position you have put yourself in, along with your compatriot, in relation to the Bishop and the entire Mission (I have written proof of it), I have resolved to have nothing more to do with you, until new instructions come.

In this delicate affair that, inconsiderately, you have gotten into with your compatriot, you have shocked and even unjustly insulted all your confreres in religion and on the Mission. And that, without making you leave Kalawao, can become a terrible headache for you. Therefore, be prudent; and, before writing to your Superiors, meditate on humility. Remember that a haughty manner can bring you myrrh from the very ones who before have been so lavish with their gold and incense. Be more resigned. Remember what I told you: "When it becomes impossible for you to administer the Sacraments, you will have someone to take care of you, and to live at Kalawao."

The Provincial let himself go when writing to the Father General about Damien. When reading these texts which seem so harsh to us, we must keep in mind that in those days, there was greater regard for seniority and years of service among the missionaries. Hence superiors were inclined to be a little harder on junior missionaries than on the veterans. After informing the major Superior of the small zeal of certain missionaries for their Christians, he added:

But the worst of all is Father Damien who has been elevated so high in the clouds by his heroism, that now no one can make him come down. As for myself, I limit myself to keeping his accounts and fulfilling his orders for supplies in silence. The Bishop corresponds with him and his new promising hero and for an answer he has to take a beating and even insults, that make us fear that after so much devotion, so many labors and sacrifices, the flattery and praises are going to take away all his merit. The Bishop will do all he can to get rid of Conrardy by sending him to the novitiate. But I do not believe that he will go. He is too avid for the glory that has brought Father Damien the title of a hero, a title which is out for himself.

Let us note, first of all, in Damien's favor that the authorities did not treat him with the same regard that they reserved for the others. For example, of the missionaries spoken of in Father Leonor's letter to the Father General, and who were guilty of rather serious neglect in their ministry, the Bishop had said nothing save the following remark and this he said to Father Leonor only: "Let's try to hide this shameful thing and *above all do not reprimand them, for that would irritate them too much.*" Yet, this same prelate did not hesitate to reprimand the poor leper priest and to let Father Leonor vent his wrath on him. Why this difference? If, at least to their subjective selves, Father Damien was becoming irritated, if he was writing spleenful letters, if he was so unmanageable, may we not infer that the Bishop and Father Leonor no longer weighed their words when writing to him? And again, why this difference? Precisely because they were convinced that he was a man who could "take it"; that, after reflection, he would accept, with respectful submission, any remarks that they made.

The Bishop and Father Leonor reproached Father Conrardy for publishing Father Damien's letters in the papers. But it must be remembered that they had not been written with publication in mind. For example, his letter of July 17, which was printed, carried this notice: "Without waiting for the author's permission, we are using it in its entirety." On July 2, the Bishop wrote to Paris:

I don't ask anything better, to quote your own words, than "to keep up admiration for this generous missionary." The best way to get that result is to say little about it. If I reported things the way I see them, the hero would appear drab rather than glorious, as the papers paint him.

Father Damien is unjust to the rest of the missionaries, by posing as the only hero. [*There's nothing to this; for, when and how did he ever pose, i.e., affect a pretentious attitude?*] While he is neither the only one nor the first to ask to stay with the lepers. [*Doubtless. But one thing is sure, he was the first and only one at that time who stayed there fifteen years and gave himself without counting the cost, leprosy included.*] Equally has he been unjust to his Superiors whom he blames at least indirectly for doing nothing for the poor lepers. [*There is not a single document that offers any proof that he ever said or wrote one word against them, or affirmed that they were doing nothing.*] And yet, they furnished the chapels and other necessary objects until outside help was forthcoming in abundance. [*He never denied it; indeed he was happy to acknowledge it in very clear terms.*] It isn't pleasant to see one's self blamed before the entire world to protect the glory of one individual. [*This blame, which because of his extreme touchiness the Bishop imagined, simply didn't exist. As for his "glory" — it redounded to them also.*] And I believe that the Christian law is pretty well observed by silence in such a case. [*The glory of Christian virtue redounds to Christ who gives the grace to practice it. It is the law of Christianity not to appropriate this glory to one's self.*]

As in most events, there are two sides to the *Conrardy Case;* and both sides deserve to be examined. We shall look at it, therefore, both from the viewpoint of Father Damien and Father Conrardy, and from that of the Bishop and the Father Provincial. Here are the two points of view as presented to the General Chapter of the Congregation of the Sacred Hearts.

SUMMARY OF FATHER DAMIEN'S POINT OF VIEW
SUBMITTED ON JULY 26

Because of the progress of the disease, he expressed his relief at having a priest and fellow countryman at Molokai who had offered his services several times in the past dozen years. Bishop Koeckemann wrote to Father Conrardy on February 8: "Come here as soon as possible; you will go at once to Molokai to see things with your own eyes." In a postscript, on February 11, he wrote to Father Conrardy: "I invite you to come as soon as possible to assist Father Damien." March 10, the Bishop had once more urged him to come. Father Damien, as always, the practical man, enclosed the original copies of these letters. He went on to describe his companion. Father Conrardy was 47; he had spent 14 years on the Indian missions. He seemed cut out for a missionary life.

Moreover, he gave unmistakable signs of having a special vocation for working among the lepers:

> He has been living with me here for more than two months, though I am a leper, like a very good confrere and companion. He renders me many services in our great leprosarium. He helps me watch over and direct the eighty orphans who live with me. Being a practical man, he has already begun to speak Hawaiian. He acts as though he were one of us, bound by vows, and living isolated and completely happy among these unfortunates.

He took the liberty to speak to Father General and through him to the General Chapter, in order to find out the best way of keeping this good priest; and, to obtain for him the favor of being accepted, in some way, *into the Congregation without being obliged, however, to go through the novitiate*.

The following points were to be considered:

1. He had left the diocese of Oregon, where the Archbishop had a high opinion of him, in the hope of being received under these conditions.

2. For years he had been used to living isolated and far from civilization, among the Indians. He felt repugnance at the idea of being forced to conform to the routine of a regular novitiate.

3. Father Damien greatly needed his services, which were more and more necessary, both for the leprosarium in general and for the orphans in particular; he had to learn the Hawaiian language and get used to a climate that was very different from the one he had just left. It might be that Father Damien would live long enough to see him capable of taking his place. Finally, if Father Conrardy had to leave Molokai, he could take his (Father Damien's) place only when he returned. So, he would no longer have the same opportunity of forming himself (actually with Father Damien) for this painful sort of life.

In a postscript, Father Conrardy wrote:

> I ratify the reasons Father Damien has advanced to exempt me from a regular novitiate, Bishop Hermann having promised me, and Father Damien having assured me that I will be taken into the Congregation as an Oblate. [*To be an oblate is to be affiliated with the Congregation, but without vows.*]
>
> If I am forced to leave the leprosarium, I will prefer to return to my old mission, rather than go to Europe to spend a year and a half and more. That is why I beg you to affiliate me with the Congregation in some way, and to allow me to make my novitiate among the lepers.

SUMMARY OF BISHOP KOECKEMANN'S VIEWPOINT, SUBMITTED TO THE FATHER GENERAL ON JULY 29

The case of Father Conrardy has been clarified and modified since his arrival. His presence, his way of speaking and acting, do not justify the good opinion that his letters made one form of his heroic virtues. The Bishop would wait for the answer to his last letter from the interested party before informing him of Father General's agreement to receive him as an *oblate*. If the Bishop had not yet sent an answer directly to Father Damien that was according to his desires, it was because he intended to insist *absolutely* that Father Conrardy make a regular noviciate, before being admitted to the Mission on a definite basis. Moreover, the Bishop had advised him formally of this in an answer to two high and mighty letters coming from Molokai. Considering the course of events, Father Conrardy's admission depended not only on the answer from Father General, but also on the judgment which the Bishop, in his own right, reserved to himself.

When the Father General admits an oblate-priest to a house in France, there is reciprocity. On the one hand there are advantages, and on the other, duties of practical obedience. Now, with Father Damien at Molokai, Father Conrardy would have a great many advantages without any real and serious submission. Independent as far as money was concerned — which came to them from the outside in large sums — they could do what they wanted until they fell to quarreling between themselves or got mixed up with the government or the patients, or until some scandal arose. Then the Bishop, the Mission, and the Congregation would be blamed. The stranger, of course, could simply leave.

Strange priests had always caused trouble. They began with perfect submission. Then they wanted to act in their own way, and gradually wanted to run everything.

Going over the beautiful letters from Father Conrardy, the Bishop had really believed he would make an exception to the Rule for him. But the newspaper articles inspired by him, and a quarter-hour interview, had been enough to dissipate that illusion. The Bishop was speaking in his own name, as the one responsible. But his impression was shared by all the members of the Mission who had seen him. The Mother Superior of the Sacred Hearts Sisters had roundly expressed her repugnance at having him as a confessor for her Sisters. Father Damien was no suitable director to form Father Conrardy in the religious life, because he himself seemed to have joined an Order apart, above all religious and ecclesiastical authorities who did not approve and further his views. If these two heroes stayed together long, he was afraid that they would end up disgracing the Mission, either by their direct complaints, or by their eulogies of themselves as though they were the only ones devoted to the work, or by false reports that sooner or later would provoke contradictions.

Protestants, jealous of the Catholic religion, were inclined to praise one member in particular and ignore the rest. Finally, and for all these reasons, in spite of the shortage of missionaries in Hawaii, for the good of the Congregation and the Mission, the Bishop preferred to face the difficulties *without an outsider* than to have "a fifth wheel on the wagon."

There wasn't a serious reason that prevented Father Conrardy from going to the novitiate. When the Sisters came to Molokai his presence would be more of an embarrassment than a service. Did he feel too weak to go through the ordeal of a novitiate? Or did he think he was so perfect that he didn't need one? In this dilemma the Bishop had no confidence in heroic virtues, which would be solid only if based on humility and ruled by obedience. [*After the space of sixty years, the heroic life of Father Conrardy still remains very beautiful and very pure . . . in his own original way. The prelate's attitude seems to us to have been dictated by the chagrin of his missionaries. This chagrin, apparently, was provoked by the praise that this stranger received in the local press.*]

FATHER LEONOR TO THE GENERAL CHAPTER

When the Provincial wrote the Fathers of the General Chapter, he went at it a little too strong. They knew Father Damien's position. But it was impossible for them to judge the sick Father Damien by the well Father Damien. The incense his heroism had brought him had intoxicated him; and the "gold" he had received and was still receiving had blinded him. "Judge," he wrote with his pen dripping bitterness, "what a drunken man can do who has never touched a drop. . . . So it is excessively difficult, not to say impossible, to direct him. He seems to think he is practically independent."

A month later Bishop Koeckemann wrote to Paris:

On the subject of Father Damien, I am sorry to have painted him to you in a somewhat obscure light. The purpose of my remarks was to answer your request to set his work among the lepers in greater relief. I have explained the reasons for our reserve on this subject, and I take back nothing of the facts I laid before you. Father Damien does not have the family spirit; he greatly prefers his Belgian compatriot, who is not a member of the Congregation, to his confreres in religion. [*This affirmation we can simply deny. During his life Father Damien gave proofs by the hundreds of his profound attachment to his Congregation, to its superiors and members. The last cry of his heart, just when he was dying, is an undeniable proof of it.*] He has so identified himself with the leprosarium that he seems to demand that the whole Mission be subordinated to the good of the leprosarium. When he is crossed he does not hesitate to blame ecclesiastical, religious, and political authorities through letters published in the papers, which contain errors and omissions that wrong the rest of the Mission. [*Once again, all this publicity had neither his consent nor approval, at least explicitly. They were published without his knowledge.*]

[*The following quotation, which is but a continuation of the above, shows that the Bishop now goes back on his affirmations and seems to acquit Father Damien.*] But to be just in his regard, I must add that he himself does not perceive this evil, and believes that he is doing right; for he has an excellent heart and a head that is just a trifle hard but at the same time weak in judgment. His best friends find that he is often imprudent, lacking tact. He makes enemies. His admirers write things contradicting the truth to increase his praises. He does not correct these errors; he lets them pass, I think, for the glory of God and the edification of his neighbor. [*How could the priest revise, correct, or stop publications of his letters in England, the United States, or even at Honolulu?*] I hope that he will not die soon. [*His death occurred hardly six months after the Bishop wrote these lines.*] After his death you could publicly and widely acclaim his praises; but, while he is living, my advice to you is to keep a certain reserve.

I have communicated Father General's final word to Conrardy. The latter has answered, no doubt in agreement with Father Damien, asking for time to decide and to present his arguments for not leaving the leprosarium. He said his position is much better than the novitiate, much more perfect. I am in no hurry to answer him, for fear of making him write something regrettable in the papers.

Since he has been at Molokai, he has conducted himself irreproachably, without troubling the Mission in any way. By his excessively amiable ways, he has won the lepers' affection. They would make dangerous comments if I forcibly withdrew him. So I wait patiently for him to leave on his own accord.

In October the Bishop, in another letter to Paris, revealed that he was still troubled, a consequence of the bad feelings caused by his successive decisions about Father Conrardy, and especially their results. He ended:

Authority has the strict right to judge his case. I have not answered his last letter. I am leaving him at Molokai just as he is; without any commitments on one side or the other. I don't like that too much. But I am not morally free in his case. For he has so gained the affection and admiration of the lepers by his winning ways that the majority of them would curse me, if I sent him away unwillingly. Besides, he is really doing good. And he is not superfluous even with presence of a third priest who is going to Molokai.

Conrardy has taken on all the priestly services at the Settlement for several weeks, while Father Damien has become helpless on account of the progress of his disease. He is doing all that has to be done to contract leprosy.

On November 20, Father Leonor spoke in the same way to Father General. As proof that they were concerting together and encouraging one another against the outsider: "The Bishop has appointed Conrardy Father Damien's curate. He is a very imprudent man, as Father Damien is, in his dealings with the lepers and can't miss catching the disease himself."

At the beginning of December, the judicious Father Cornelius Limbourg, SS.CC., acting as an official delegate of the Father General, submitted his report. We give excerpts from it:

. . . I am trying to be as conscientious as possible. I have seen Father Conrardy at work. He is active, zealous, like Father Albert. He wants to do good, and really, what else could one look for at Molokai, in that leper prison? He lives poorly. He has a jovial character, which is certainly necessary. He is impetuous but he knows how to listen to advice. He has been very pleasant to me, like a confrere, and even listened to me and respected me as though I were his superior. He is 47 and I am 40. That is why I think he will be able to render great service at Molokai.

At this date, the Bishop seemed to have gone back on his mistrust. He avowed to the Father General that Father Conrardy's way of acting at Molokai had corrected his first unfavorable impressions. He had learned the Hawaiian language and made himself popular with the lepers by his amiability. . . . Father Wendelin, who had lived with him for a month, was very well satisfied with him and strongly wanted to keep him. Finally, the Bishop asked the Father General for a letter of admission for him into the Congregation as an *oblate*. However, he was never admitted.

In all truth, Father Conrardy was a consoling angel, "the friend and true brother to Father Damien," as Sister Vincentia McCormack described him. One day she surprised him and found him in tears at the head of the dying leper priest's bed.

He lived and ate at the Kalawao rectory. He wrote:

> Will I escape the contagion? Humanly speaking, I believe, it is impossible. Our cooks are lepers; lepers make our bread. . . . At table I sit next to Father Damien. At first, the sight of his wounds took away my appetite. I suffered from constant headaches. Now I'm used to it all. . . . Finally, I can only say: "God protect me!" and ask my friends to pray for me; so that I may persevere in my undertaking.

Father Damien tried to think up ways to spoil him: "Often he would bring me an orange or some candy. Forgetting that he himself, covered with sores, is a leper from head to foot, he would say: 'Take it; no lepers have touched it.' "

Father Conrardy makes these beautiful statements about his friend: "What a man . . . that Father Damien! What activity! What forgetfulness of self and what goodness! I have sworn never to leave him." He kept his word.*

After Damien's death, Conrardy lived six years at Molokai. Deep down the Bishop harbored some resentment against him. Shortly before Father Damien's death, the prelate wrote to the Father General:

> Fathers Damien and Conrardy are writing everywhere in such a way as to ignore the ecclesiastical and religious superiors of the Mission, whom they blame at least indirectly. [*A patent exaggeration.*] The last issues of the *Annales Catholiques* again published a letter from Conrardy which rather displeased me because of certain falsehoods and omissions of the truth. It's all for Damien and him [Conrardy]. I do not dare to say anything against it in public in order to avoid scandal. [*That would betray a sentiment he wouldn't want to admit.*] To keep from detaching the leprosarium from the Mission the presence of another member of the Congregation is morally necessary.

Apropos of the prospect of separating the leprosarium from the Mission, which the Vicar Apostolic foresaw, Dr. Mouritz has furnished some enlightenment:

> One subject, it appeared to me, Damien was always pleased to discuss. He was imbued with certain lofty ideas and believed in the possibility of their future realization — the Leper Settlement to be a special diocese,

---

* Father Conrardy wrote to Father Imoda, S.J., at St. Ignatius College in San Francisco, these precious details about Father Damien: "Father Damien's ears are badly swollen and his face, neck, and hands are covered with boils and swellings; one knee is particularly affected, but, in spite of all that, he is very active, always working at something. Besides providing for the whole household, about one hundred strong. . . . The Father's hands are much better since the eruption disappeared on the outside."

Damien to be vicar-apostolic, with special powers direct
from the Pope, and the work of the whole Settlement to
be carried on under strict ecclesiastical lines, like a monastery. R. W. Meyer took delight in teasing Damien on
the possibilities of this scheme panning out, and would
often say, "Father, how soon shall we see you with
shaven poll and tonsure, assuming this will mark your
new order?" Damien would laugh heartily and refuse to
be drawn out.

Dr. Mouritz' recollection could have something to them.
Father Damien, loaded down with accumulated mistrust
and opposition from his religious superiors, could have en-
visioned a possible liberation in conscience, with the conviction that he was doing God's will. He was considering it.

In 1898 the Americans, who had annexed the Hawaiian
Islands, took charge of the lepers and from then on they
would lack nothing. Not getting too much encouragement,
Father Conrardy had left three years previously for China
in search of more neglected lepers.

In the vicinity of Canton, he discovered them — pitiful,
left to themselves. No one bothered with them, except to
burn them, often while they were still alive. Father Conrardy adopted them. He wanted to gather them all on a
little island. He had no money. He had to become a doctor
in order to be approved by the Chinese officials.

From 1899 to 1900 we find him — now 55 — following
the medical courses at Portland, Oregon. With his doctor's
diploma in his hands, he went to Europe, to England to
give countless sermons and talks, to beg from door to door,
to publish appeals in papers and magazines. Bad luck often
overtook him; sometimes he fell sick; once he was arrested
as a swindler. But his courage was unconquerable. Father
Conrardy said that if God would give him ten years in
China, he would be a happy man. He prayed to have the

most horrible place in the world and thought he would soon have it.

After begging in Canada and the United States, he finally arrived in China, May, 1908, provided with some 150,-000 francs.

The island of Shek Lung, opposite Canton, seemed best suited to his purpose. He bought some 20 acres, built barracks, and gathered the lepers there. Surrounded by a thousand dangers, he lived alone with his seventy patients. But his ingenuity and devotion were such that soon he had obtained excellent results. The day was coming when the Chinese government would support his work. Father Conrardy could die, but the future of the Shek Lung leprosarium was assured. It then had seven hundred patients, five nursing Sisters, two priests — it was a second Molokai. Later the patients would say: "The sun never shone on two men like Doctor Conrardy. We owe him ten times more than we do our own fathers."

Like Father Damien, his teacher, Father Conrardy knelt at their feet to wash and bandage their wounds, mix his tears with theirs to console them: "Courage, my good friend, soon you will be as beautiful as an angel and happy forever!" On leaving them, he embraced them and even pushed his heroic charity to the point of respectfully kissing their open sores.

Before he became a bishop, a certain Father Deswazieres was Father Conrardy's fellow worker. He used to beg Father Conrardy to be more prudent. "Catch leprosy!" Father Conrardy replied, "that would be the most beautiful decoration for me! But I'm not worthy of it." He died of pneumonia, August 2, 1914. They buried him, as he had wished, rolled up in a mat, between two lepers.

19   *The Storm Breaks*

THE ravages and suffering of his leprosy ought to have
been enough to test Father Damien's virtue. But during
the last three years of his life, he went through an agony
far more cruel. We have no right to suppress this phase of
his story. History and truth are inseparable. All the more
so because these facts, painful though they be, do demonstrate his greatness.

The opposition he ran into came entirely from Honolulu:
the government, the Board of Health, certain Protestant
clergymen, and, above all and by repercussion, his own
superiors, who felt that they had been compromised and
put in a bad light by his successes. The world press was
not interested in the Hawaiian Islands except for what concerned the leprosarium and its Catholic priest. . . . He
monopolized everything to the detriment of those around
and above him who were carrying on the work as well
as he. . . .

Wasn't money piling up in his hands to the point of
making people believe that the government allotted the
lepers a laughably low budget, or one that was misspent?
. . . Was the Catholic priest's plea for help going to inspire
Protestant Sisters in England and bring them to Molokai?
In such fashion questioned the opposition.

According to Canon Law the position of a diocesan priest and that of a religious priest are quite different. Differences between the former and his superiors may often be straightened out in the priest's own way. This is not the case with a religious priest. His vow of obedience obliges him to renounce his own will and to obey his superiors as God Himself, within the limits determined by the Rule and as long as the command is not opposed to the moral law. Moreover, in conscience, as a priest, he owes obedience and respect to his bishop. When those in authority fail in understanding and kindness to their subordinates, when they refuse to trust them, one can easily imagine how it can cause torture of soul.

Matters were moving along smoothly so long as Father Damien had Bishop Maigret as his ecclesiastical superior and Father Modeste as his provincial. Their dealings with him were characterized by kindness and obvious sympathy. And they gave him credit without any hesitation. If at times they reprimanded him, it was because he wanted to go too fast. Chapels do not spring up like mushrooms.

When these two were replaced, however, things went bad for him. In 1878, Father Regis was appointed vice-provincial to Father Modeste; and in 1883 the latter was succeeded by Father Leonor. As for Bishop Maigret, in 1881, he received as his coadjutor Bishop Koeckemann, a German, who very soon succeeded him.

Bishop Koeckemann and Father Leonor owed their positions solely to an exemplary past during which they had proved their qualities. They certainly had not intrigued to get where they were. They accepted their responsibilities with courage and great virtue. Their mode of life and the principal details of their apostolate are in the archives of the Sacred Hearts mother house. It would be outrageous for the author to tarnish their real worth.

But we have the duty of making known our candid opinion in their regard insofar as they enter into this story.

Both of them, with all their souls, sought only to do good, and to maintain the respect of justice and truth. Both had a real passion for the cause of Holy Mother Church and the Congregation of the Sacred Hearts. Their entire activity in the Hawaiian Islands had no other objective. They gave themselves completely without limiting their zeal, without compromising with error, without flattering those in power, without minimizing in the least the attack of their adversaries, without fearing to oppose their subordinates who would provoke that attack either voluntarily or unwittingly. In this light, all their writings and their attitudes could be explained and justified, if, like all humans, they had not possessed a mixture of good qualities and faults.

According to all appearances, Father Damien's mistake was that of considering only the interest of his lepers, of being too stubborn in his actions and words. The superiors had to consider the general interests of the whole Mission. It seems they lacked the comprehension and balance to soften or resolve the inevitable conflicts that came up. Since the situation was quite unpredictable in this period of political instability and of change in regime, and since the deposed King and his government had relied on the Catholic minority, the leaders of the Roman Catholic Church had to be very careful in their dealings with the new regime, composed of stanch Protestants. Given the situation, is it not possible that these superiors displayed a certain lack of balanced judgment, a tendency to exaggerate the misdeeds of the so-called culprit, even a sort of blindness in not absolving the poor accused priest who was being devoured steadily by leprosy? Were they the kind of leaders — touchy, if not autocratic — who feel that they are slighted by the success of a subordinate?

The thing they never understood or appreciated was not

so much the priest's devotion and real virtue, as his exceptional character that was above the common run, even of missionaries. They themselves had been pioneers and trail blazers for a much longer period than Father Damien. No one had ever proclaimed *their* exploits. If Father Damien had become a celebrity, he had only done his duty — as they saw it — just as they had done. All this noise and excitement over him seemed uncalled for. It could come only from his more or less unreasonable way of acting, his imprudent proposals, his lack of balance.

One would think that the superiors, in their reports to the Father General, would not judge their inferiors except after mature reflection and a careful weighing of the pros and cons. Yet, in 1879, Father Regis, the Vice-Provincial, gave a rather unfavorable report on Damien in his letters to Paris: "He is a man almost without judgment." And the following year: "He needs a guardian, he is a defective priest, he has no head, he doesn't know how to get along with people."

Certainly, like any mortal, Father Damien could make mistakes, but his humility opened his eyes to see them and his good sense rectified them. We have had occasions to prove that already. As for putting the leprosarium of Molokai under a guardian, what would have been gained? It would have been no more talked about than the rest of the leprosaria in the world. "A defective priest!" May God grant more of them to His Church! How many objections against the Church would fall! How much souls would gain in virtue!

As for his inability to "get along," we note that Professor Stoddard, Edward Clifford, and other distinguished visitors were won by his gentleness and amiability, and became his faithful friends.

Father Leonor was not any more favorable to the priest: "He is an imperious man, capricious, proud. He passes

himself off as a consoler, a nurse, etc. . . . of the lepers . . .
and he is nothing of the kind." And in 1888: "The worst
of all the missionaries is Father Damien who has been
lifted so high in the clouds by his heroism, and now no one
can make him come down."

The Bishop could scarcely control his expressions any
longer: "Our famous hero of Molokai," he wrote in 1887,
"has received so many compliments that he seems in danger
of losing his head."

Apart from these characterizations, however, the documents available show no trace of vanity in him. He would
pass off a compliment with a great burst of Flemish laugh-
ter. Witnesses all agree on his humility. Is it necessary to
repeat his displeasure when he saw that his name began to
appear in the papers after the publication of a letter he
wrote? He reprimanded those he thought responsible. "I
have not answered you sooner," he wrote to his own, "because I didn't like the publication of my last letter in the
Annales. See, they're talking about me now even in America. Once and for all, let me tell you I don't like this one
bit. I want to remain unknown to the world."

He was the last one to organize a publicity campaign.
He knew nothing of publicity agents that today can make
men great. If he finally did submit to fame, he did it for
the very same reason for which he became a beggar, a
gravedigger, and a leper — for the good of his patients.
Seeing that the press could serve them by speaking of him,
he let it speak, just as he would have silenced it, had
silence been more useful.

But along with this and to his heavy cost, the press
stirred up bitter hostilities against him.

We have already noted that the English and American
journals organized a very profitable money drive for him.
When Honolulu learned this, there was an explosion in the

opposition press and a storm in governmental circles. The Hawaiian Islands, that soon were to be annexed to the United States, were the victim of virulent political squabbles from 1880 to 1889. The opposition wrote:

These sums which are being sought for and received by Father Damien are either necessary or they are not necessary. If these donations are needed it is because the governmental Board appointed to provide for the lazaret, fails to do its duty, or else, shields the profiteers who rob in order to enrich themselves at the expense of the lepers.

If the donations are not necessary, then they are of a fraudulent nature. Is it to fill the coffers of the Catholic Mission that these appeals are permitted to be made to American and English charity? It is the government's duty to put a stop to these irregularities by charging the Board of Health to receive and expend all of these gifts to the lepers.

Under either dilemma the government is at fault and Hawaiian honor is compromised.

Journalists waxed eloquent on this national and philanthropic theme. The embarrassment of the government can be easily imagined. It declared that it allotted $100,000 per year for the leprosarium and justified its honest use the best it could. But no answers from those in power could ever satisfy their opponents who were maneuvering to succeed them. Attack followed attack and both camps blamed the Mission. One side put its honesty in doubt, the other blamed it for causing this disturbance.

The superiors were frightened. Seeing the specter of a revolution rising, they feared for the very existence of the Mission. Father Leonor wrote to the Father General: "We strongly fear a change in government that will put the enemies of the missionaries in power. I think blood will be shed." The Bishop let Father Damien know: "The government may change. We have to be ready for anything."

On June 30 the revolution broke out. The crown and even the life of the King were threatened. Gibson, the prime minister, was jailed. "Happily for him and for us," the Bishop said, "they could find nothing compromising on him." The revolutionists forced the King to sign a new constitution that deprived him of practically all his powers.

In the days that followed, the Bishop gave a report to Paris:

> The revolution had been well prepared. The papers rose up against the government, especially against the King and his Prime Minister, Gibson. Their complaints were not without foundation; however, we had no reason to join the revolutionists, because the guilty ones had treated us well and we had nothing to hope for from the opposition who lose no love on the Catholic Church. Through error or malice this opposition was trying to identify us with politics with which we had nothing to do. We still thought the revolution lacked organization and that it would all boil down to words. Things were more serious. . . .

For the first time, on July 17, His Majesty left his palace and ostensibly went to the Catholic Cathedral of Our Lady Queen of Peace to ask prayers for peace in his realm. His adversaries interpreted this in a bad light, just as they did the prelate's allocution, though he kept aloof from politics. "In general," concluded the Bishop's letter, "the change cannot favor the Catholic Mission because the new men in government are ardent Puritans. For the moment, not feeling well established enough yet, they are benevolent toward us."

Things finally straightened themselves out. But, the superiors had lacked presence of mind. They could have found reasons for defending their Father Damien. Instead, they had made it hard for him. Let us go over five of their most virulent censures.

I

Father Leonor to the Father General: "Through false-hoods written by Father Damien to England, he has received considerable amounts of money and others are coming to him from America (total 28,621 gold francs) without counting the gifts and provisions of all sorts.

"The worst thing is that according to a letter from our only friend in the Government, Mr. Gibson, the Prime Minister, a doctor and some Sisters of St. John (Episcopalian) are forming a group in London to come to help Father Damien."

And, the Bishop to Father General: "In his impatience, he has written to the four winds, exaggerating the material misery of the lepers, insinuating (if he has not said it openly) criticism of the Mission, the Government, and even of the Sisters. To him (and that comes indirectly from his way of presenting things) the Journals are attributing in good part what is due to the King and his Prime Minister, etc. . . . They are justly offended."

The reference here is to letters that resulted in gifts and personal help from England before February 6, 1887. They were addressed to Rev. Chapman. Before that date, Father Damien had written to him twice (August 26, 1886: in answer to a letter of June 4; and on January 20, 1887, in answer to a letter of December 1). Therefore we have here all the correspondence between Father Damien and Rev. Chapman.

The letter of August 26 speaks of the Blessed Sacrament and Brother Dutton. He adds: "Any amount, however small, will be gladly received for the relief of over 600 poor, unfortunate lepers." He enclosed a copy of Stoddard's book *The Lepers of Molokai* to give him some idea of the leprosarium.

The letter of January 20 thanks him for the gifts that have already found their destination: warm clothes for the winter.

Where are the falsehoods Father Damien was accused of?

In order to avoid such incidents in the future, Father Leonor ordered Father Damien to send him all his letters unsealed so that he could censor them.*

If we look through the correspondence, we will see quite clearly that Father Damien had sent his letters to his superiors, both ecclesiastical and religious, and not only those letters that were sent abroad but even those addressed to the Board. Also, he submitted to them his *Report on the Lepers of Molokai*, dated August 10, 1886.

Nevertheless, at the beginning of April, 1887, Father Leonor wrote to the Father General that: "Father resigned himself to it . . . although with much difficulty."

Is this "although with much difficulty" Father Leonor's interpretation of the fact that his religious had answered him obediently; that he would send all his letters to his superiors; and that, therefore, he would have no changes to make in his way of doing things?

The following extract from the report of Father Cornelius, the official delegate, to the Superior-General, Sylvain Bousquet, confirms our supposition: "For some time Father Damien has been sending his letters to Father Leonor, unsealed. But several times Father Leonor sent them on

---

* The Rule of the Congregation requires all religious to submit letters to the superior unsealed. Exceptions to this rule are letters to the Holy See, to the Superior-General, to the Father Provincial, and to those who take their place.

without reading them. Lately, the latter reproached Father Damien for writing to a Protestant minister in England. The letter had been published. Father Damien answered: 'I sent it to you unsealed; so we are both in the wrong.'"

II

Father Leonor to the Father General: "*This fine Father passes himself off as the consoler, provider, nurse, undertaker, gravedigger, etc. . . . of the lepers, and he is nothing of the kind.*" *The Bishop wrote to Father Damien:* "*According to what I see in the newspaper the world is under the impression that you are at the head of your lepers, their procurator, their doctor, their nurse, their gravedigger, etc. . . . as if the Government was there for nothing.*"

The following quotation is taken almost verbatim from Stoddard's book: "He was indeed Jack-of-all-trades: physician of the soul and of the body, magistrate, schoolteacher, carpenter, joiner, painter, gardener, housekeeper, cook, and even, in some cases, undertaker and gravedigger." Professor Stoddard had spent several days at the leprosarium and talked to the lepers. He was able to see both the work of the priest and the priest at work. Who would dare call into doubt, after reading what we have already said above, that the priest was the soul of the leprosarium?

From the report of Ambrose Hutchinson — who became steward of the lazaret on January 4, 1879 — we see the priest acting as police officer to the drunks and the immoral crowd; handling the square and hammer; a good samaritan who gave his lepers all the help in his power; and a faithful angel and consoler of the sick and dying.

This was nothing in the eyes of Father Leonor and the Bishop. And yet it was a public fact! When he received the decoration in 1881, the *Commercial Advertiser*, a Honolulu paper, wrote that:

> Damien, the soldier of Christ, has lived for many years among the exiles of Molokai; constantly in the midst of the sick, and separated from the rest of mankind as if he were a pest-laden person whom the healthy dare not approach. He has dedicated himself to their service; he bandages their ulcers, brings them to place confidence in the Divine Master and to hope for a better life. And, at death, he prepares their bodies before taking them to their last resting place.

Why had not the superiors protested when, on April 30, 1886, in presenting his report to the legislative assembly, the president of the Board of Health dared to say of Father Damien that he had had "thirteen years of intimate contact with a malady so repulsive that it can be considered the most complete corruption of the human body to be found this side of the grave! Breathing the same fetid air, cleansing frightful ulcers, watching beside the dying and handling half-decayed cadavers."

Whom are we going to believe? Stoddard, Hutchinson, the *Commercial Advertiser,* the president of the Board of Health, all of whom affirm that Father Damien was the providence and consoling angel of Molokai; or, Father Leonor and the Bishop, for whom he was nothing of the kind?

III

Father Damien is the sole object of praise in the press, that takes no account of what the government and the Mission are doing.

Here are some texts. The Bishop to Father Damien:

January 2, 1887: "I regret that the admiration for this work of charity is erroneous. I have a kind of passion to render justice to everybody, even our enemies and the enemies of good. . . . I see with displeasure that the newspapers who admire you, exaggerate by putting things in a false light, without taking into account what the government and others are doing. The Mission has its part too. It seems to me that adhering to the strict truth, you could be praised enough wihout injuring others, at least indirectly."

The Bishop to Father Damien, January 24, 1887: "Now, allow me to add prosaic reflections to all this poetry, in regard to the Lepers of Molokai. I wish in no way to diminish the glory of your heroism that has justly won you the admiration of the world. On my own part, I have often contributed to it. But this business has its prosaic side too. When it is a question of large sums of money. According to what I see in the newspapers the world is under the impression that you are at the head of your lepers, their procurator, their doctor, their nurse, etc. . . . it is possible that some jealous enemy is anxious to prove to the world that you (and to blame us) have gotten the money under false pretenses.

"As for the Catholic Mission with its ecclesiastical and religious superiors, it has to be effaced or to be blamed indirectly, and at times even directly, in order to set off the hero in a more brilliant light. I cannot see how the glory of God and the honor of religion gain by it. *Suum cuique dare justitia est* (Justice demands that each one be given his due). In strict truth, you have enough glory. Don't go punching holes in the sack that contains your incontestable merits."

What the Bishop and Father Leonor do not seem to have seen was the big difference between what Father Damien was doing for the lepers and what the government and the Mission were doing. Certainly there is small proportion between appropriating a large budget, distributing it to the needy, doing good with other people's money *and* sacrificing one's self, immolating one's self for the lepers. The world is in the habit of admiring not the government for distributing millions to hospitals but, rather, the Sisters who spend their lives working there.

It was precisely this devotedness of the heroic priest that was being exalted. We cite Stoddard:

> Such indeed he has been for more than a decade; but within a twelvemonth — from the time when together we sat with the dead and dying, when I saw with my own eyes the evidences of his wholesome and holy influence, and heard with my own ears of the works of mercy to which he consecrated his life, heard it from the lips of those whose hearts were overflowing with gratitude — in one brief year he had been seized, treacherously, I might almost say, and his fate is sealed in common with that of his ill-starred flock. . . . Reverend and beloved Father! In my heart you live forever; nothing can touch you further, and when you are laid to rest, I believe that you will have achieved a record of modest heroism almost without parallel in these times.

As for the newspapers, Father Damien was not the editor. Always, and particularly when he talked to any journalist, he was very careful to do justice to the efforts of the Board and public officials. If the press did not talk about the Mission, that was not his fault.

He was trying to be a worthy member of the Sacred Hearts Congregation and the Hawaiian Mission. Didn't the praises of which he was the object redound to the credit of his Congregation? Was it up to him, a missionary in Hawaii, to chant the praises of the Hawaiian Mission?

In reading the censures of the prelate, one is justified in asking whether perhaps, unconsciously, a little jealousy had not crept in. Why complain that the Mission, of which he is the head, should be effaced for putting a hero in the limelight?

We may get a small clue to this when we read from Father Leonor's own pen:

> The Vicar Apostolic is truly suffering from the disease of jealousy. I myself am the object of it. Public esteem for anyone other than himself is his torment. He terms it injustice, evil intentions, or a mark of disdain for himself as chief of the Mission. Some Honolulu gentlemen wanted to present me with a horse and buggy. He told me to refuse this gift and to make them understand that such gifts should be given to him, the Bishop, and not to me.

IV

The gift of 975 pounds sterling, sent from England, was the cause of friction with his superiors. With regret they saw alms and offerings pouring into Molokai.

The Bishop to Father Damien, January 27, 1887:

"On the subject of the 975 pounds sterling, I don't want to use this money in any way, except the reimbursement of $40.00 and the new account S. G. Wilder and Company, of which the Mission in general has more need than the leprosarium. But I do not insist. It is up to you to make arrangements with your religious superior in order to safeguard your vow of poverty."

We are surprised that the Bishop disowns his missionary when he should have known that Father Damien was receiving gifts all along. The correspondence proves this beyond a doubt. Besides, the report Father Damien submitted to the Board through the Bishop mentions:

Each year the Board issues an order for six dollars to

enable them to buy at the said store what they are in
need of, especially in the line of clothing . . .

Besides the allowance by the Board of Health, Christian charity has given us a helping hand in the matter of
clothing, and assisted us to our great satisfaction. In previous years it was nothing unusual to receive from time
to time a cart-load of clothing for distribution to the
needy . . . Thanks for the aid in the past. May the future
prove that untiring perseverance of charity continues to
assist the Board of Health in supplying the unfortunates
of Molokai with all their necessities; especially with
warm clothing, because, may I here remark, that the
yearly allowance of six dollars to provide clothes and
other indispensable articles is quite insufficient for those
who have no private means, and no friends or relatives
to give them a helping hand . . .

Queen Kapiolani herself did not believe she was offend-
ing anyone by sending gifts to the Settlement. Up until
January 24, 1887, there was no cry of scandal or disapproval. On the contrary, Father Leonor had written on
January 10 of the same year: "Through the newspapers
we learn that collections are being taken up for you. We
are very happy about it."

Then why the sudden discontent when the money
arrived?

The Bishop to the Father General, February, 1887:
"When he announced this large sum in a triumphant tone,
I thought it my duty to make some prosaic observations."
We are acquainted with these reflections as contained in
the third censure. Two weeks earlier the prelate had told
him:

At present you have more than 24,000 gold francs at
your disposal. I see nothing wrong in your providing for
the needs of the excellent Mr. Dutton, without his asking or even receiving anything from the government. Let

his refusal be made in an unoffending way. The government can change from one day to the next and we have to expect anything, even serious obstacles, in the practice of charity. Remember the hospitals of Paris.

Not knowing the best thing to do with that check, Father Damien asked the Bishop's advice:

The donors wrote me that they leave at my own disposal the use of the check for my lepers. As I am not sure what is best to do I will send it to Your Excellency, or directly to the bank, if you will authorize me to leave part of the money in my name. I will pay several bills for my lepers directly from this deposit. As this is not a contribution from Catholics, but in large part from Protestants, I think that that would avoid all suspicion of the Catholic Mission.

Thanks to some jealous Protestants who were enraged at Rev. Chapman, this suspicion had already cropped up in England.

The Bishop would not touch the question, but referred the priest to his religious superior, the Father Provincial, with some "prosaic observations" which Father Leonor called: "a somewhat rude answer." (Father Leonor to the Father General, February 8.)

What was the priest's answer to the Bishop? We have only part of his rough draft. He answered something like this: "It is strange! Your Excellency tells me that I have justly won the sympathy of the world. That is expressed by the gifts (975 pounds sterling). My Superiors have only blame for me. From strangers, gold and incense; from my Superiors, myrrh."

It would be difficult to say which of the two first used the expression: gold, incense, and myrrh.

Since his ecclesiastical Superior was giving no solution

tc his difficulty, it was up to the religious Superior to do so, without harshness. But here is what Father Leonor wrote to Father Damien, February 14:

First of all, I want nothing to do with your gold. *[Later, April 4th, he will no longer show this contempt for the gold.]* It will be at your disposal; keep your check book; however, to avoid all difficulties and perhaps annoyance for those who will remain when God will judge it proper to call you from this world, I command you to make a will immediately in the name of the Monseigneur, as legatee, willing him all the funds which might be held in your name in the bank.

April 10, 1889, the Bishop wrote: "Perhaps Father Damien is dead already. He leaves around 3,700 pounds sterling in the bank in my name."

At the end, money came in so fast, Father Damien didn't have time to spend it.

Once again, where is Father Damien's fault?

V

Father Damien was the occasion, if not the cause, of Protestant Sisters threatening to settle at Molokai. On December 1, 1886, Rev. Chapman wrote to Father Damien: "As for myself, I can only humbly join with them (Cardinal Manning and Joseph Dutton) in the same sentiments and no effort will be lacking on my part to make the Island of Molokai more happy than it has ever been. . . ."

In his letter of January 28, 1887, to his Bishop, Father Damien told him his suspicion which Dutton shared: "Is Chapman in contact with the famous Bishop Willis and our Doctor Mouritz to introduce Anglican Sisters here?"

The Bishop had reasons to believe that such an expedition was likely.

1. *The Advertiser, a Honolulu paper, had announced help in the form of personnel. December, 1886, the Bishop wrote to Father Damien: "Today the Advertiser copied an article from Boston announcing help of which I have no knowledge: Two priests and two sisters of charity and much money."*

2. *Mr. Gibson, the Prime Minister, had more definite information: "The worst thing is that according to a letter from our only friend in the Government, Mr. Gibson, the Prime Minister, a doctor and some Sisters of St. John (Episcopalian) are forming a group in London to come to help Father Damien"* (Father Leonor to the Father General, February 8, 1887).

This project was never realized. Even had it existed, there is no evidence that Father Damien was concerned in the plan. It was purely the invention of the Hawaiian authorities who had asked for some years that Catholic Sisters be sent to Molokai, but without result. Thus began an inquiry into the origin of these baseless accusations.

The Bishop to Father Damien, February 5, 1887:

> I thank you for your interesting letter of January 28; although it was not very flattering, it was frank. If you had used the same frankness a long time ago, we would have been able to have a clearer understanding. I now understand the insinuations of blame of the Mission that appeared in your letters and those of your friends that were printed in the papers. . . . You are right in crying "wolf." You were able to give the first warning.

Let us note well that Father Damien had only a suspicion.

Father Leonor to the Father General, April, 1887:

> It is he [Father Damien] who through his imprudent and even untrue letters forces these poor Sisters [Fran-

ciscan Sisters] to this sacrifice. But they have come here
for the lepers, at least in part, and they will not allow
Episcopalian Sisters to come from England to supplant
them.

Even if the Protestant Sisters had got there first, Reverend Chapman and his friends would have been responsible. Father Damien had nothing to do with it.

The leper priest's manner of acting with his accusers
was that of a man of very great virtue. As long as he
thought he could disarm them, he used moderate words, in
his own defense. In none of the writings of this period that
we possess did he let himself contradict them haughtily or
with a grave lack of the respect due to authority. When he
saw that disagreement irritated them and that it was all
useless, he remained silent. In him there was no trace of
rancor. He continued to love his superiors and to cor-
respond with them as if nothing had happened, not un-
worthily nor stiffly, but in all simplicity and obedience. He
did not intrigue to attain his ends. He confided his sufferings to no one, neither laymen nor confreres, nor to his
brother Pamphile, nor to his major superiors to whom he
had the right of appeal.

Hence comes our difficulty of not suspecting his profound sufferings, of understanding them so little, of not
grasping their keenness in an open and sensitive nature like
his, for we fail to find any expression of them from his pen.
In spite of possible disillusionments with individuals, he
maintained to the very end the undying loyalty he had
vowed to the Sacred Hearts, and which he expressed so
beautifully at the moment of death.

20   *Gethsemani*

WE WILL try to discover the state of mind of Bishop
Koeckemann in regard to his subordinate at the leprosarium
by analyzing his important letter to Father Damien of February 5, 1887.

The prelate praised the priest's frankness. He described
complaints against the Mission which had appeared in the
press. Without going into any discussion about the remark
whereby the priest attributes to him the refusal to send the
Franciscan Sisters to Molokai, he explained that the Sisters
were not numerous enough for such an undertaking there.
The Sisters had not been called to the Hawaiian Islands
for the exclusive service of the lepers, but to care for the
sick, i.e., the curable sick. Following their installation at
the hospital for leper suspects at Kakaako near Honolulu,
he had witnessed their entry into the General Hospital at
Wailuku. . . . The government had handled this matter, he
said, without referring it to the Bishop, "as perhaps they
should have done." The Bishop was left out of the picture.
Mother Marianne had not gone, as she had said, to the
leprosarium, and the Bishop was keeping silent. The Sisters
had come to do something. But just exactly what, he did
not know. He had no objections if some of them went to

Molokai. But it was not clear when that would be feasible. Arrangements would have to be made, involving large expenses. The Sisters had been very successful at Kakaako by the regularity of their work and the separation of the sexes. But how could that be done at Molokai?

At this point in his letter, the Vicar Apostolic went to the heart of the difference between himself and Damien. *The priest was concentrating exclusively on the lepers; while the Bishop had to think of the whole Mission. The priest saw the end, the Bishop had to look out for the means to attain that end. The Prelate was powerless to create things that depended on the will of others. Experience had taught them both how much they could count on other people's word, who were themselves dependent on circumstances beyond their control. They mustn't forget that they were in enemy country. People could compliment them, and yet try to destroy the work of the Catholic Church. Perhaps Chapman had this in the back of his head. Father Damien was quite right in crying "wolf." He should have been the first to do so. The Bishop would talk to Gibson and Mother Marianne. Alas! All influential persons were enemies of the Catholic religion, their compliments notwithstanding. They were jubilant in setting the Bishop against his clergy. The subordinate would get all their sympathies. This was not Father Damien's intention. But the devil was smarter than they, and knew his business. If he couldn't block a work, he would try to spoil it. He was taking his revenge by sowing seeds of discord between superiors and subjects who would form into two camps.*

After so much gold and incense, the Bishop wrote, myrrh was not to the taste of Father Damien. Finally, he protested that he had never ceased to admire his heroism and publish it on every occasion. If he had counted too much on his humility, he was sorry. The Bishop then made an act of humility himself by admitting that he thought that he himself was always honored more than his personal merits deserved. But, for the glory of God, the good order and welfare of souls, it was not desirable that the Bishop be pointed out as one opposed to good. This hurt him deeply. . . . He was speaking clearly and frankly, without any bitterness. He freely forgave Father Damien, all the more so, since the latter saw nothing wrong in what he was doing.

In answer to this baring of the Bishop's soul, we must admit that we can find nothing in Father Damien's attitude or writing which resembles an open criticism. He did express his surprise and furnished explanations for his behavior. He made statements but with nothing resentful about them. For example, his answer to the Bishop's remark of December 6, 1886: "I am sorry that admiration for this work of charity makes some stray from the truth. . . . Thanks for your good letter and the stone in my garden" (Father Damien to the Bishop, December 9, 1886).

Father Leonor's letter to the Father General on February 9, 1887, of which we have seen excerpts, definitely went beyond all bounds. It seems there was much more than just a difference of temperament between superior and subject. After speaking of "falsehoods he has written" which resulted in considerable sums of money (28,621.20 gold francs), and the formation of a Protestant group who were coming from London to help Father Damien, the Provincial added:

He makes people believe that the lepers are in need of everything and that his superiors are opposed to his recourse to a certain treatment. We have seen it published in a paper. Now, all this uproar from a head swollen by praises is against the Government that is taking great care of the lepers, clothes them, and feeds them much better than they would have been at home.

This good Father passes himself off as the lepers' consoler, providence, nurse, undertaker, gravedigger, and *he is nothing of the kind*. He deserves high praise for the sacrifice he has made of his existence, his liberty, his life, but unfortunately those praises have reached him; he has gobbled them up, and become drunk with them, and now he is becoming dangerous. Hardly had he gotten the bank book in his hands when without saying a word to anyone, he presented each leper with new clothes. [*Documents show, on the contrary, that he spoke of it to Dutton, to the Bishop, to Mr. Meyer, and to Father Leonor himself.*] A prime insult to the Government that had just finished distributing clothes. Then, after a somewhat rude reprimand from the Bishop, he answered rather bitterly: "after receiving incense and gold from everybody, I did not expect that it would be my Superior from whom I would receive myrrh." And the Bishop answered him: "But you didn't want that myrrh, and have spit in my face." Upon receiving this letter, however, he sent me his bank book that I might handle the deposit at the bank, putting it in my name if I deemed it proper. I left it in his name. Let him straighten it out himself. It is too delicate a matter to deal with a man as imperious, capricious and proud as he has become as a result of all the praise he has received.

Two days after this letter was sent, Father Damien received these words from the Procurator-General of the Congregation of the Sacred Hearts in Paris. They are so different, so much more balanced and just: "If some well-known Religious Order had a Molokai, the news would not be slow in reaching the public and the alms would be encouraged equally. I think you understand me and that that is what you wish to realize for Molokai."

On February 14, 1887, Father Leonor wrote to Father Damien. After explaining the arrangements in regard to the money, he ordered him to make out his will naming the Bishop as his heir. He comes back to the alleged accusation, implicit perhaps, against the government of leaving the lepers groveling in want. This was, of course, false.

At last, the priest would have the Franciscan Sisters at Molokai. Father Leonor advised him to leave to Mr. Heselden [of the Board of Health] the task of deciding where their establishment should be located, and all the other details which would be decided as the latter might see fit. After all that the Bishop had made clear to him, this, too, was a bit of myrrh. Then the Superior, conscious of his spiritual role, invites his inferior to imitate our Lord, gladly receiving the gold, gently breathing the incense that had been so lavishly given him, but also accepting the myrrh without complaint. "This is what I believe it my duty to tell you with all the affection of my heart and begging you to receive it without believing that I want to cause you any pain."

Father Leonor went to both extremes. Too firm, and too soft . . . if only he had been able to attain the happy medium! On February 28, 1887, still in a bitter tone, he wrote:

> Allow me, without frightening you to take up the article of the Rule on writing letters and sending them to both ecclesiastical and religious superiors. [*Here he quotes in detail the article of the Rule of the Congregation of the Sacred Hearts.*] I suppose you didn't intend to have the letters printed in England, and nevertheless they have been. Have them pass through the hands of your Superiors. That will save you ten or twenty cents on each letter and you will have the assurance and consolation of having fulfilled an obligation of obedience, and of humility . . . (of which you have not made a vow).
>
> Being your Superior, whether I like it or not, I am also obliged, *whether I like it or not*, to say things that

your temperament can hardly bear. But, in conscience, I cannot overlook those things without saying something for they are facts that have made an impression on everybody. If you want to shake off the yoke and think and say that I am not worthy, nor capable of directing you, that will be a big relief to me. . . . Please take all this as I give it to you, without bitterness or harshness, without the least thought of causing you any pain, but only for the great good of both of us.

For more than four years Father Leonor's mind had been prejudiced against Father Damien. At the end of 1883 the Provincial had denounced to the Father General the leper priest's blind zeal that kept him from correcting his excesses, his indiscreet and exaggerated words and writings. The question then was on marriages.

Let us repeat that a competent theologian has studied conscientiously the priest's file on marriage cases. He was able to form his own judgment. He concluded that though the priest may have acted a little too hastily in some cases, the evidence definitely does not indicate that his zeal was *blind*.

On November 22, Father Damien unburdened himself:

You ask me to answer your letter again, in which you express little confidence in me; in which you ask me to keep quiet and not say a word; in which you reproach me as believing that I am greater in dignity and merit than you.

I tell you again that I did not raise a hue and cry about the coming of the Sisters to the Settlement. I said nothing; I wrote nothing in this sense; I believed even that there was no longer a question about this project. If the Superior comes to visit the leprosarium with one of her Sisters, accompanied by your Reverence, I will clean my house and all three of you will be comfortably lodged. That day, if my presence displeases you, and

you let me know in time, I can go away. I never believed I would fall so low in my Superiors' eyes.

Those who observed him at that time were at a loss to
explain his attacks of sadness. By nature so gay and expansive, he became melancholic. Dr. Mouritz believed he
was a victim of "melancholia religiosa" that is, of scruples
— "the delusion of his being unworthy of heaven."

God's representatives were all in agreement in con-
demning him. Had he been deceived? Had he been on the
wrong road? Had he been lulling himself with delusions
while following the bent of his temperament, with cease-
less activity and unbalanced generosity? Had his poor judg-
ment, his pride, his stubbornness in seeing nothing outside
of his leprosarium, led him to realize a work that was con-
trary to God's will? He was going to die soon, and would
he be condemned at God's Tribunal as he had been at that
of his superiors?

Such scruples in the soul of a lonely man, eaten alive
with leprosy, must have provoked interior tortures that one
can hardly imagine.

At times he found that the leprosy that was devouring
him was going too slow, he was so crushed by fatigue and
discouragement. You can guess this from certain admis-
sions: "I won't be much longer in this miserable world. I
hope green grass will soon be growing over my body, and
then everything will be for the better."

If only he had had a priest to hear his confession!

Since his confession in the boat while Father Modeste,
then his Provincial, stood on board the steamer, in 1873,
Father Damien, who had a delicate conscience, had to
suffer the agony of having his confessions months apart.

His suffering was doubled in February, 1885, when
Father Albert left the Settlement. It was to go on until a

year before his death. He wrote of it to his old companion: "If I cried when you left, it was because I regretted and could foresee the solitude in which I would have to spend the rest of my days."

At first he asked that a confrere be designated to replace Father Albert, as article 392 of the Sacred Hearts Rule prescribes.

We will say in Father Leonor's favor that at first he too regretted that he could not send him a confessor. Long discussions followed, ending in nothing. The Superior hoped to arrange the matter, if Father Damien could not go to Lahaina, on the neighboring island on Maui. This would have been the best solution. The Fathers who could visit Molokai regularly, he wrote, suffered from seasickness, as he himself did. He noted that the situation of the priest on Molokai was in every way exceptional; and that he could only pray that the difficulties would straighten themselves out.

On December 30, 1885, Father Damien complained of this to the Bishop:

> I murmur a little against the somewhat tyrannical way the good Father Leonor intends to incarcerate me here. As long as my health permits and the Government does not oppose it, why do not my Superiors allow me to move about, when there is need of it? Damien is hardheaded. You know my situation better than anyone else. I still hesitate to lay it before the Superior General.

At the beginning of February, 1886, Father Leonor was categorically maintaining his interdiction:

> Again there is a rumor that you are coming to Honolulu. It is *my duty*, very dear Father, to let you know again the decision taken by the Provincial Council and

not by me. Be patient. But, in case you do come, there are two places you can go: to the Mission or to Kakaako [hospital for suspected cases]. At the mission you will be relegated to a room which you are not to leave until your departure. Otherwise you will run the risk of putting the Mission in quarantine; for strangers, knowing that we have a leper, will be afraid of us who are not lepers. If you go to Kakaako, you will go to the lepers' chapel without saying Mass there; for neither Father Clement nor I will consent to celebrate Mass with the same chalice and the same vestments you have used, and the Sisters will refuse to receive Holy Communion from your hands.

To these harsh words, the Provincial, instead of softening his expressions, and of interpreting the decisions of the Council, of which he was the most influential member, added these even harsher words: "Your intentions prove to us that you possess neither delicacy nor charity toward your neighbor and that you think only of yourself. They reveal too much egoism and I would like to believe that these sentiments are neither in your heart nor in your head."

Four months later, in a letter to his Bishop, Father Damien was perfectly right in characterizing this order from his Provincial as "an imperious refusal expressed in the tone of a police officer rather than a religious superior." The isolated man confessed, with his habitual frankness, that that was the greatest suffering he had ever endured in his life. But in virtue of his vow of obedience, he had responded with an act of perfect submission.

They left him entirely alone and forbade his leaving the island. At least they could visit him! "I am a leper, blessed be God!" he wrote to Father Leonor. "But please, and it's the only thing I beg of you, let some one descend into my tomb once a month to hear my confession!" Even that was meted out sparingly to him!

The good Father Colomban comes every two or three months [from Honolulu] and leaves immediately. . . . I don't know where this is leading to. I am resigning myself. . . . It is at the foot of the altar that I make my confession and that I seek relief from my interior sufferings. It is before the Tabernacle and the statue of the Blessed Mother that I sometimes give voice to my feelings.

One is tempted to incriminate his superiors. This is always a delicate matter and is usually an unreasonable course to pursue. They can, in the case of a disputed question, see deeper and farther and in a different way. Father Leonor, influenced by the Bishop and the Fathers in Honolulu as well as by his relations with the members of the government and public opinion, judged that the priest's detention at Molokai — painful though it might be for the victim — was normal; and even that he had to stay as an edifying example to his children, who were themselves retained there by law.

Be that as it may, rather than risk an unfounded judgment, since the accused can no longer defend himself, it is more worth while to repeat here what the spirit of faith suggests in a like case. God, who did not spare His own Son, does not spare His good friends. The saints have endured great sufferings here on earth; and among them, as we know, have been the trials from superiors. Father Damien had to submit to this wise, mysterious law. Humbly, he bore the cross.

Despite all this the day finally came when he escaped from his prison, and went to Honolulu. Later he was to lament that this expedition might possibly have been an act of disobedience to his superiors, but how much has been written on the subject in an effort to prove that on his part, properly speaking, there was no disobedience!

No one was more submissive than he; no one interpreted his vow of obedience more strictly. His perseverance in remaining confined to the leprosarium only strengthened his conviction that he was there through obedience. In his *spiritual notebook,* he laid down this rigid rule for himself: "Be exact in the least orders and prescriptions. Death to all the caprices of self-will! Like a corpse, let the Superiors do with us what they judge best."

In 1878 he had asked the Provincial, Father Modeste, in cases in which he had to act without being able to refer them to superiors, to be allowed to act as he thought best. "In this way, I will no longer be exposed to scruples of conscience."

Now, at the beginning of 1886, Father Damien strongly wanted to go to Honolulu. Two motives urged him. He wanted to learn the Japanese treatment, recently introduced at Kakaako, for himself and his fellow sufferers at Molokai; and above all, he wanted to go to confession. It had been three months since he had seen Father Colomban.

Even before he asked permission to carry out his plan, Father Leonor had let him know that he was opposed to it. We have taken up that prohibition already, and also the priest's will to submit to it. "In virtue of my vow of obedience, I have answered with an act of submission." At this date, June 16, he was quite determined not to make the trip.

And yet, several persons advised him to go: Dr. Mouritz, who had even suggested it to the Bishop, Mr. Meyer, and Father Colomban.

On July 2 his resolution is still the same. On the feast of the Sacred Heart, he wrote to Bishop Koeckemann: "Mr. Meyer advised me to make a short visit to Honolulu in order to consult Goto. In virtue of my vow of obedience I cannot follow his advice. I wait for Your Excellency to obtain the revocation of the severe order that Father Provincial believed it his duty to give me. My sacristan will give you the news here."

This sacristan was able to play his role in this affair *viva voce*.

On July 7, 1886, Father Damien apparently changed his mind suddenly and sailed on Saturday, the tenth.

How explain this sudden reversal? Had he received permission between July 2 and 7? In view of his firm will not to disobey, he must either have received permission or had very strong reasons for presuming it.

The prohibition seems to have been lifted. There are circumstances and letters that support this hypothesis.

The good superintendent, Mr. Meyer, went to see the prime minister, Gibson, and the redoubtable Father Leonor. He interceded for his friend to whom he wrote on July 8:

I received your letter of yesterday in which you express your determination to go to Honolulu, and in which you ask my advice as to the manner of going.

While I have the greatest sympathy for you and firmly believe that, under present circumstances, a visit to Honolulu to find out what can be done for you, is truly a duty which you owe to yourself; while I admit all of this, yet I cannot tell you just how you could best make the trip. . . . If you come early I shall be there and we can talk together.

. . . Father Leonor seemed undecided but when I said to him that the Minister was far from being intransigent and that the trip was necessary, he seemed to share my idea. When we meet I shall be able to talk with you better than I can write.

After his visit to Honolulu, there is no trace of tension between Father Damien and the Bishop if we can judge from the latter's letters of July 21 and 25.

In the Bishop's correspondence with the Father General (July 28 and 29; August 25; September 29; November 13, and December 15), we find not one word about any dis-

obedience; nor even in the correspondence of Father
Leonor to Father General (September 15; October 10,
and November 20; probably to the secretary of Father
General). We should note, however, that after the letter
of July 3, we have only three letters for the year 1886.
The lapse of time between the date of Father Damien's
trip and the letter of September 15 is long enough for us
to wonder if we have all the letters. It is evident that
Father Leonor did not write much during the last half of
1886.

We can conclude that this is what happened. The Bishop,
urged by Father Damien to obtain the revocation of his
Superior's order, thought it his duty to intervene with the
Provincial, asking him to withdraw his prohibition. Not
daring to oppose the Bishop's wish, Father Leonor gave in:
"All right, but if he comes, he will bear the responsibility
for what happens!" Learning this and not having seen a
confrere for three months, Father Damien decided to take
his now famous voyage.

Some have made a case of the Bishop's supposed response to Father Damien. It is not to be found in the
archives; its existence is likely, even probable. This supposition is borne out by a statement contained in a letter
written by Father Damien on August 25, 1886, to the
Father General, Sylvain Bousquet:

> By obedience to our Vice-Provincial, my visit to Hono-
> lulu for that purpose to consult Dr. Goto was deferred
> until last month when I was permitted to make a short
> visit . . .

It was, then, with a clear conscience that Father Damien
departed for Honolulu. Dr. Mouritz, writing thirty years
after this event, gives the following description of this
incident in his book, *The Path of the Destroyer:*

About the month of March, 1886, I wrote to Bishop Hermann, head of the Catholic Mission, on the desirability of Father Damien proceeding to Honolulu and taking the Goto treatment of hot baths and other medicines, which was then in vogue, very popular with the lepers, and said to cure the disease. . . . In due course Bishop Hermann answered my letter, wrote to Father Damien to come to Honolulu, all arrangements being made for his sojourn at Kakaako hospital. Father Damien went to Honolulu, but within two weeks returned to the Leper Settlement, stating he felt homesick for Kalawao, and that he had to remain idle in Kakaako.

Actually Father Damien stayed only from July 10 to 16. He returned to Molokai with the deputies and ministers (Father Wendelin, July 31, 1886). The latter did not make the trip on the *Molokai* which was the leper transport ship but on the *Lifelike,* which sailed on the sixteenth.

A couple of weeks after this interlude, the Bishop wrote of it to Father Pamphile:

Father Damien is not so unfortunate as you think. Father Colomban goes to see him every two months. Besides, your brother can communicate with Honolulu and Maui, every week. He has been here recently to consult the Japanese doctor, whose treatment he is going to follow at Molokai. His sickness has not disfigured him excessively. He is very cheerful and did not turn down the honor of receiving at the same time, on the day of his departure, a visit from the King, his Prime Minister, and the Bishop. The Queen sent her compliments through the King who had forbidden her to visit him in person.

That was the last time Father Damien had left his island; the last time he saw his Bishop. He spent five days at the hospital in Kakaako, taking Goto's treatment there.

He edified the Franciscan Sisters in charge of the hospital, spending all his spare time with the lepers. Sister Crescentia was appointed to take care of Father Damien. Here is what she relates:

Father Damien came to Honolulu in 1885 and in 1886. During his second visit he had to stay in Kakaako Branch Hospital because he had contracted leprosy and had been ordered by the Doctor at Molokai to try the remedies in use at the Kakaako Hospital. Rev. Mother Marianne charged me with attending to his wants. I was extremely happy and honored to have been chosen for this work.

Father Damien always said his Mass in a respectful and pious manner. His presence inspired devotion because he was known to have sacrificed his life for the lepers. He avoided human praise and did nothing for vainglory. He always spoke to the patients at Kakaako about spiritual matters and it was seldom that he consoled them with the hope of regaining bodily health.

His charity was of course his outstanding virtue and surely it was founded upon love of God. He would never have stayed so long at his difficult post at Molokai if his charity had lacked that solid foundation. Father took care of the bodies of the lepers in order to gain their souls. In his generosity he gave away to the poor until he himself was hungry and he preferred to suffer himself rather than see others suffer. During his short stay in Honolulu he talked only about his poor lepers, how much he loved them, how he desired to help them and to ease their sufferings; how happy he felt that Almighty God had granted his desire and had sent Sisters to care for his unfortunate children. During his visit to Honolulu, he edified us greatly by his cheerful patience and by the willingness with which he took all the medicines prescribed for him.

He saw again his great benefactress, Mother Judith,

superior of the Sacred Hearts Sisters. To this old friend and "businesswoman" of the lepers, he confided the immense sufferings going on in the depths of his soul. At one moment he asked her if he should accept the offer made him of staying and dying at Kakaako "his heart was so heavy." Mother showed him the linen and delicacies she had prepared for his children. That was enough to strengthen him again. He took his packages and left joyfully for Molokai.

Six months later, on December 30, he speaks again of his voyage in his yearly report to Father Janvier, secretary to the General:

Here is a little word that is rather painful for me and which perhaps will be also for the good heart of our dearly beloved Very Rev. Father General. Last July, not having seen a confrere for about three months, I escaped, almost contrary to obedience, and went to Honolulu where I had the consolation of going to confession to the Bishop. That same week, I returned here, and since that time I have seen the good Father Colomban only once, at the beginning of October. Here we are at the end of the year and I don't know when my confessor will come.

This good Father has too much work at Maui to come to Molokai often where there are nevertheless so many chapels without priests. Not being free to go outside of our establishment, I find it impossible to go to see any of my confreres. I can only wait patiently for the arrival of a priest. Pray then and get others to pray for me. May God deign to confirm me in grace as He did the Apostles.

It is the privation of the companionship of my confreres from our dear Congregation that is more painful to bear than the leprosy. Please keep this secret between us and the Father General. Come to some agreement to settle my case. I ask nothing better, be it understood, than to remain and die at Kalawao; leper or not, let me *perficere cursum usque in finem* [finish my course to the end]. *I am content and happy over everything else and can complain of no one.* While waiting for a confessor, I confess from time to time before the Blessed Sacrament. My two parishes are going along fine; I binate almost every Sunday.

That this very tardy confession of his *quasi-disobedience* was only a scruple is obvious. It was the effect of that *melancholia religiosa,* diagnosed by Dr. Mouritz. Alone with his thoughts, Father Damien must have mulled over and over in his mind the hard and categorical orders from his superiors, without any possible solution, until the situation became an obsession. Was it through pride and egoism? And the permission itself, so unclear — "If he comes, he will be responsible for what happens"; was it really a permission? Instead of acting firmly, indifferent to all trips, had he given in too much to his desire to go to Honolulu? In place of obeying, had he followed his own will?

A troubled, restless soul needs a spiritual guide. An intelligent guide would have reassured him very quickly that his intention of going to Honolulu was pure. He went to receive the Sacrament of Penance which was instituted by our Lord to forgive sins and to give peace to agonizing hearts. Like all other Christians, he had the right of recourse to it. It follows that to experience such scruples often supposes great perfection.

21 · *Stevenson's Letter*

THE reaction and general admiration, provoked in England by the heroic life — and soon by the death — of Father Damien in the midst of his lepers, was to have a counter-reaction that was extremely painful. To the Rev. Gage, a Methodist minister, this powerful attraction for a Catholic priest seemed a danger to his coreligionists. He wrote to his friend in Honolulu, the Rev. Hyde, asking him for "authentic" reports on the hero, with which he would be able to combat this exaggerated enthusiasm.

Pastor Hyde was, in Dr. Mouritz's words, "scholarly, polished, and refined; he came from New England and belonged to the best class of Americans." He taught philosophy to the young clergy of the Hawaiian Islands and lived in a Honolulu mansion. But he was a fanatical enemy of the *Catholic missionaries*.

According to Mouritz, Rev. Hyde visited Kalawao on September 2, 1885. He came for the dedication of the Protestant church at Kalaupapa. Mouritz goes on to say:

> . . . he made a careful examination, investigating fully the schools and homes which Father Damien had founded for the orphan and friendless children. The doctor marveled greatly at the vast amount of work

417

undertaken by Father Damien, and the promising results obtained with such a paucity of material. Dr. Hyde emphasized the benefits that would accrue in having more commodious and up-to-date buildings in every respect, for girls and single women, for boys and single men; nursing was also debated and the conclusion was reached that paid, trained, foreign nurses were out of the question; Sisters and Brothers of Catholic organizations being alone available and promising success.

Dr. Mouritz points out that the Rev. Hyde had "the *ear* and confidence of wealthy men connected with the then Fort Street Church . . . both, Mr. Charles R. Bishop and Mr. Henry P. Baldwin." It was he, again according to Mouritz, who finally persuaded them to found the two homes at Kalawao that bear their names.

The reply from the Rev. Hyde, addressed to the Rev. Gage follows:

Honolulu, August 2, 1889

Rev. H. B. Gage
Dear Brother:

In answer to your inquiries about Father Damien, I can only reply that we who knew the man are surprised at the extravagant newspaper laudations, as if he were a most saintly philanthropist. The simple truth is, he was a coarse, dirty man, headstrong and bigoted. He was not sent to Molokai, but went there without orders; did not stay at the leper settlement (before he became one himself) but circulated freely over the whole island (less than half the island is devoted to the lepers), and he came to Honolulu. He had no hand in the reforms and improvements inaugurated, which were the work of our Board of Health, as occasion required and means provided. He was not a pure man in his relations with women, and leprosy of which he died should be attributed to his vices and carelessness. Others have done much for the lepers: our own ministers, the government physicians, and so forth, but never with the Catholic idea of meriting eternal life.

Yours, etc.
C. M. Hyde

By putting together in this letter some crude statements picked up in his anti-Catholic surroundings, or even thought up by himself, one can see that the Rev. Hyde was trying to lessen the role played by the priest and even to besmirch the memory of this heroic apostle. The Rev. Gage had not asked for this letter to bury it. He had it published in the *English Churchman,* from which it was widely reproduced in other publications. At first it produced the effects the ministers had expected.

To correct these errors, the Sacred Hearts Fathers worked out long and incontrovertible refutations, some of which were published. Bishop Koeckemann himself had to take up his pen at the demand, among others, of the Archbishop of Boston: "The extract from the *Boston Congregationalist,*" said the Bishop,

is an infamous falsehood, and what is more, an atrocious calumny. It is the more injurious in that it is partly founded upon facts, which, through malicious misinterpretation and sectarian jealousy, are presented under a prejudicial light. The good works done by others do not, in the least, diminish the real merit of Father Damien. He consecrated his life to the welfare of the most unfortunate of human beings; he must justly be regarded as an extraordinarily heroic man. His visits to Honolulu did not amount to more than a total of six months during sixteen years. He was looked upon as the strongest moral authority and the most dependable and zealous resident on the Island, acting always as the confidential agent of the Board in full accord with Mr. Meyer. Physicians generally visited the Island; a small number receiving good salaries, rarely lived there longer than one year. He considered precautions as useless because, from his entrance, he had consented to fall victim to the malady. Building chapels, erecting houses, making coffins, digging graves, cultivating the earth — could he be expected to observe the refinement of manner or to wear immaculate garments?

But I am amazed that anyone would attack his morals after his death, especially since, while living, I have never heard the purity of his life suspected. In the candor of his simplicity, he never deemed it necessary to take unusual precautions against evil interpretations of the rectitude of his life. It would seem that his accuser belongs to that class of people to whom prejudice systematically denies the merit of voluntary celibacy and who, therefore, do not believe in the chastity of priests in general. "All men take not this word, but they to whom it is given."

It is extremely painful to learn that prejudice and sectarian jealousy can lead to such an extreme.

Then, suddenly, the Sacred Hearts Fathers stopped defending their confrere. An absolutely independent witness spoke up. The great English writer, Robert Louis Stevenson, answered Hyde. At that time, Stevenson was living at Tahiti. He spent long months at Honolulu, stayed eight days at Molokai, made a searching inquiry, then wrote an open letter for the world to read. It follows:

Sydney, February 25, 1890

Sir,

It may probably occur to you that we have met, and visited, and conversed; on my side, with interest. You may remember that you have done me several courtesies, for which I was prepared to be grateful. . . . But there are duties which come before gratitude, and offences which justly divide friends, far more, acquain-

tances. Your letter to the Reverend H. B. Gage is a
document which, in my sight, if you had filled me with
bread when I was starving, if you had sat up to nurse
my father when he lay a-dying, would yet absolve me
from the bonds of gratitude. You know enough, doubtless, of the process of canonization to be aware that, a
hundred years after the death of Damien, there will
appear a man charged with the painful office of the
Devil's Advocate. After that noble brother of mine, and
of all frail clay, shall have lain a century at rest, one
shall accuse, one defend him. The circumstance is unusual that the devil's advocate should be a volunteer,
should be a member of a sect immediately rival, and
should make haste to take upon himself his ugly office
ere the bones are cold; unusual, and of a taste which I
shall leave my readers free to qualify; unusual, and to
me inspiring. If I have at all learned the trade of using
words to convey truth and to arouse emotion, you have
at last furnished me with a subject. For it is in the interest of all mankind and the cause of public decency
in every quarter of the world, not only that Damien
should be righted, but that you and your letter should be
displayed at length, in their true colors, to the public
eye.

To do this properly, I must begin by quoting you at
large: I shall then proceed to criticize your utterance
from several points of view, divine and human, in the
course of which I shall attempt to draw again and with
more specification the character of the dead saint whom
it has pleased you to vilify; so much being done, I shall
say farewell to you forever.

After citing the letter of Rev. Hyde to Rev. H. B. Gage,
Stevenson continues:

To deal fitly with a letter so extraordinary, I must
draw at the outset on my privilege of private knowledge
of the signatory and his sect. It may offend others;

scarcely you, who have been so busy to collect, so bold
to publish, gossip on your rivals. And this is perhaps the
moment when I may best explain to you the character of
what you are to read: I conceive you as a man quite
beyond the reticences of civility; with what measure you
mete, with that shall it be measured you again; with you,
at last, I rejoice to feel the button off the foil and to
plunge home. And if in aught that I shall say I should
offend others, your colleagues, whom I respect and remember with affection, I can but offer them my regret;
I am not free, I am inspired by the consideration of interests far more large; and such pain as can be inflicted
by anything from me must be indeed trifling when compared with the pain with which they read your letter.
It is not the hangman, but the criminal, that brings dishonor on the house.

You belong, sir, to a sect — I believe my sect, and that
in which my ancestors belonged — which has enjoyed,
and partly failed to utilize, an exceptional advantage
in the islands of Hawaii. The first missionaries came;
they found the land already self-purged of its old and
bloody faith; they were embraced, almost on their
arrival, with enthusiasm; what troubles they supported
came far more from whites than from Hawaiians; and
to these last they stood (in a rough figure) in the shoes
of God. This is not the place to enter into the degree or
causes of their failure, such as it is. One element alone
is pertinent, and must here be plainly dealt with. In the
course of their evangelical calling, they — or too many of
them — grew rich. It may be news to you that the houses
of missionaries are a cause of mocking on the streets of
Honolulu. It will at least be news to you, that when I
returned your civil visit, the driver of my cab commented on the size, the taste, and the comfort of your
home. It would have been news certainly to myself, had
any one told me that afternoon that I should live to
drag such matter into print. But you see, sir, how you
degrade better men to your own level; and it is needful

that those who are to judge betwixt you and me, betwixt Damien and the devil's advocate, should understand your letter to have been penned in a house which could raise, and that very justly, the envy and the comments of the passers-by. I think (to employ a phrase of yours which I admire) it "should be attributed" to you that you have never visited the scene of Damien's life and death. If you had, and had recalled it, and looked about your pleasant rooms, even your pen perhaps would have been stayed.

Your sect (and remember, as far as any sect avows me, it is mine) has not done ill in a worldly sense in the Hawaiian Kingdom. When calamity befell their innocent parishioners, when leprosy descended and took root in the Eight Islands, a *quid pro quo* was to be looked for. To that prosperous mission, and to you, as one of its adornments, God had sent at last an opportunity. I know I am touching here upon a nerve acutely sensitive. I know that others of your colleagues look back on the inertia of your Church, and the intrusive and decisive heroism of Damien, with something almost to be called remorse. I am sure it is so with yourself; I am persuaded your letter was inspired by a certain envy, not essentially ignoble, and the one human trait to be espied in that performance. You were thinking of the lost chance, the past day; of that which should have been conceived and was not; of the service due and not rendered. *Time was*, said the voice in your ear, in your pleasant room, as you sat raging and writing; and if the words written were base beyond parallel, the rage, I am happy to repeat — it is the only compliment I shall pay you — the rage was almost virtuous. But, sir, when we have failed, and another has succeeded; when we have stood by, and another has stepped in; when we sit and grow bulky in our charming mansions, and a plain, uncouth peasant steps into the battle, under the eyes of God, and succors the afflicted, and consoles the dying, and is himself afflicted in his turn, and dies upon the field of honor —

the battle cannot be retrieved as your unhappy irritation has suggested. It is a lost battle, and lost for ever. One thing remained to you in your defeat — some rags of common honor; and these you have made haste to cast away.

Common honor; not the honor of having done anything right, but the honor of not having done aught conspicuously foul; the honor of the inert; that was what remained to you. We are not all expected to be Damiens; a man may conceive his duty more narrowly, he may love his comforts better; and none will cast a stone at him for that. But will a gentleman of your reverend profession allow me an example from the fields of gallantry? When two gentlemen compete for the favor of a lady, and the one succeeds and the other is rejected, and (as will sometimes happen) matter damaging to the successful rival's credit reaches the ear of the defeated, it is held by plain men of no pretensions that his mouth is, in the circumstance, almost necessarily closed. Your Church and Damien's were in Hawaii upon a rivalry to do well; to help, to edify, to set divine examples. You having (in one huge instance) failed, and Damien succeeded, I marvel it should not have occurred to you that you were doomed to silence; that when you had been outstripped in that high rivalry, and sat inglorious in the midst of your well-being, in your pleasant room — and Damien, crowned with glories and horrors, toiled and rotted in that pigstye of his under the cliffs of Kalawao — you, the elect who would not, were the last man on earth to collect and propagate gossip on the volunteer who would and did.

I think I see you — for I try to see you in the flesh as I write these sentences — I think I see you leap at the word pigstye, a hyperbolical expression at the best. "He had no hand in the reforms," he was "a coarse, dirty man"; these were your own words; and you may think it possible that I am come to support you with fresh evidence. In a sense, it is even so. Damien has been too much depicted with a conventional halo and conventional features; so drawn by men who perhaps had not the eye to remark or the pen to express the individual; or who perhaps were only blinded and silenced by generous admiration, such as I partly envy for myself — such as you, if your soul were enlightened, would envy on your bended knees. It is the least defect of such a method of portraiture that it makes the path easy for the devil's advocate, and leaves for the misuse of the slanderer a considerable field of truth. For the truth that is suppressed by friends is the readiest weapon of the enemy. The world, in your despite, may perhaps owe you something, if your letter be the means of substituting once for all credible likeness for a wax abstraction. For, if that world at all remember you, on the day when Damien of Molokai shall be named Saint, it will be in virtue of one work; your letter to the Reverend H. B. Gage.

You may ask on what authority I speak. It was my inclement destiny to become acquainted, not with Damien, but with Dr. Hyde. When I visited the lazaretto Damien was already in his resting grave. But such information as I have, I gathered on the spot in conversation with those who knew him well and long; some indeed who revered his memory; but others who had sparred and wrangled with him, who beheld him with no halo, who perhaps regarded him with small respect, and through whose unprepared and scarcely partial communications the plain, human features of the man shone on me convincingly. These gave me what knowledge I possess; and I learnt it in that scene where it could be most completely and sensitively understood — Kalawao, which you have never visited, about which you have never so much as endeavored to inform yourself; for, brief as your letter is, you have found the means to stumble into that confession. "*Less than one-half* of the island," you say, "is devoted to the lepers." Molokai — "*Molokai Ahina*," the "grey," lofty, and most desolate island — along all its northern side plunges a front of precipice into a sea of unusual profundity. This range of cliff is, from east to west, the true end and frontier of the island. Only in one spot there projects into the ocean a certain triangular and rugged down, grassy, stony, windy, and rising in the midst into a hill with a dead crater; the whole bearing to the cliff that overhangs it somewhat the same relation as a bracket to a wall. With this hint you will now be able to pick out the leper station on a map; you will be able to judge how much of Molokai is thus cut off between the surf and precipice, whether less than a half, or less than a quarter, or a fifth, or a tenth — or say, a twentieth; and the next time you burst into print you will be in a position to share with us the issue of your calculations.

I imagine you to be one of those persons who talk with cheerfulness of that place which oxen and wainropes could not drag you to behold. You, who do not even know its situation on the map, probably denounce sensational descriptions, stretching your limbs the while in your pleasant parlor on Beretania Street. When I was pulled ashore there one early morning, there sat with me in the boat two sisters, bidding farewell (in humble imitation of Damien) to the lights and joys of human life. One of these wept silently; I could not withhold myself from joining her. Had you been there, it is my belief that nature would have triumphed even in you; and as the boat drew but a little nearer, and you beheld the stairs crowded with abominable deformations of our common manhood, and saw yourself landing in the midst of such a population as only now and then surrounds us in the horror of a nightmare — what a haggard eye you would have rolled over your reluctant shoulder towards the house on Beretania Street! Had you gone on; had you found every fourth face a blot upon the landscape; had you visited the hospital and seen the butt ends of human beings lying there almost unrecognizable, but still breathing, still thinking, still remembering;

you would have understood that life in the lazaretto is
an ordeal from which the nerves of a man's spirit shrink,
even as his eye quails under the brightness of the sun;
you would have felt it was (even today) a pitiful place
to visit and a hell to dwell in. It is not the fear of possible infection. That seems a little thing when compared
with the pain, the pity, and the disgust of the visitor's
surroundings, and the atmosphere of affliction, disease,
and physical disgrace in which he breathes. I do not
think I am a man more than usually timid; but I never
recall the days and nights I spent upon that island promontory (eight days and seven nights), without heartfelt
thankfulness that I am somewhere else. I find in my
diary that I speak of my stay as a "grinding experience"
—I have once jotted in the margin, *"harrowing* is the
word"; and when *Molokai* bore me at last towards the
outer world, I kept repeating to myself, with a new conception of their pregnancy, those simple words of the
song —

"'Tis the most distressful country that ever yet was
seen." And observe, that which I saw and suffered from
was a settlement purged, bettered, beautified; the new
village built, the hospital and the Bishop-Home excel-
lently arranged; the sisters, the doctor, and the missionaries, all indefatigable in their noble tasks. It was a
different place when Damien came there, and made his
great renunciation, and slept that first night under a tree
amidst his rotting brethren; alone with pestilence; and
looking forward (with what courage, with what pitiful
sinkings of dread, God only knows) to a life time of
dressing sores and stumps.

You will say, perhaps, I am too sensitive, that sights as
painful abound in cancer hospitals and are confronted
daily by doctors and nurses. I have long learned to admire and envy the doctors and the nurses. But there is
no cancer hospital so large and populous as Kalawao
and Kalaupapa; and in such a matter every fresh case,
like every inch of length in the pipe of an organ, deep-

ens the note of the impression; for what daunts the on-looker is that monstrous sum of human suffering by which he stands surrounded. Lastly, no doctor or nurse is called upon to enter once for all the doors of that gehenna; they do not say farewell, they need not abandon hope, on its sad threshold; they but go for a time to their high calling, and can look forward as they go to relief, to recreation, and to rest. But Damien shut to with his own hand the doors of his own sepulchre.

I shall now extract three passages from my diary at Kalawao.

"A. Damien is dead and already somewhat ungratefully remembered in the field of his labors and sufferings. 'He was a good man, but very officious,' says one. Another tells me he had fallen (as other priests so easily do) into something of the ways and habits of thought of a Kanaka; but he had the wit to recognize the fact, and the good sense to laugh at (over) it: A plain man it seems he was. I cannot find he was a popular one."

"B. After Ragsdale's death (Ragsdale was a famous *Luna,* or overseer, of the unruly settlement) there followed a brief term of office by Father Damien which served only to publish the weakness of that noble man. He was rough in his ways, but he had no control. Authority was relaxed; Damien's life was threatened, and he was soon eager to resign."

"C. Of Damien I begin to have an idea. He seems to have been a man of the peasant class, certainly of the peasant type: shrewd; ignorant and bigoted, yet with an open mind, and capable of receiving and digesting a reproof if it were bluntly administered; superbly generous in the least thing as well as in the greatest, and as ready to give his last shirt (although not without human grumbling) as he had been to sacrifice his life; essentially indiscreet and officious, which made him a troublesome colleague; domineering in all his ways, which made him incurably unpopular with the Kanakas, but yet destitute of real authority, so that his boys laughed at him and he must carry out his wishes by the means of bribes. He learned to have a mania for doctoring; and set up the Kanakas against the remedies of his regular rivals; perhaps (if anything matter at all in the treatment of such a disease) the worst thing that he did, and certainly the easiest. The best and worst of the man appear very plainly in his dealings with Mr. Chapman's money; he had originally laid it out (intended to lay it out) entirely for the benefit of Catholics, and even so not wisely; but after a long, plain talk, he admitted his error fully and revised the list. The sad state of the boys' home is in part the result of his lack of control; in part, of his own slovenly ways and false ideas of hygiene. Brother officials used to call it 'Damien's Chinatown.' 'Well,' they would say, 'your Chinatown keeps growing.' And he would laugh with perfect good-nature, and adhere to his errors with perfect obstinacy. So much I have gathered of truth about this plain, noble human brother and father of ours; his imperfections are traits of his face, by which we know him for our fellow; his martyrdom and his example nothing can lessen or annul; and only a person here on the spot can properly appreciate their greatness."

I have set down these private passages, as you perceive, without correction; thanks to you, the public has them in their bluntness. They are almost a list of the man's faults, for it is rather these that I was seeking: with his virtues, with the heroic profile of his life, I and the world were already sufficiently acquainted. I was besides a little suspicious of Catholic testimony; in no ill sense, but merely because Damien's admirers and disciples were the least likely to be critical. I know you will be more suspicious still; and the facts set down above were one and all collected from the lips of Protestants who had opposed the father in his life. Yet I am strangely deceived, or they build up the image of a man, with all his weaknesses, essentially heroic, and alive with rugged honesty, generosity, and mirth.

Take it for what it is, rough private jottings of the worst sides of Damien's character, collected from the lips of those who had labored with and (in your own phrase) "knew the man" — though I question whether Damien would have said that he knew you. Take it, and observe with wonder how well you were served by your gossips, how ill by your intelligence and sympathy; in how many points of fact we are at one, and how widely our appreciations vary. There is something wrong here; either with you or me. It is possible, for instance, that you, who seem to have so many ears in Kalawao, had heard of the affair of Mr. Chapman's money, and were singly struck by Damien's intended wrong-doing. I was struck with that also, and set it fairly down; but I was struck much more by the fact that he had the honesty of mind to be convinced. I may here tell you that it was a long business; that one of his colleagues sat with him late into the night, multiplying arguments and accusations; that the father listened as usual with "perfect good nature and perfect obstinacy"; but at the last, when he was persuaded — "Yes," said he, "I am very much obliged to you; you have done me a service; it would have been a theft." There are many (not Catholics merely) who require their heroes and saints to be infallible; to these the story will be painful; not to the true lovers, patrons, and servants of mankind.

And I take it, this is a type of our division; that you are one of those who have an eye for faults and failures; that you take a pleasure to find and publish them; and that, having found them, you make haste to forget the overvailing virtues and the real success which had alone introduced them to your knowledge. It is a dangerous frame of mind. That you may understand how dangerous, and into what a situation it has already brought you, we will (if you please) go hand-in-hand through the different phrases of your letter, and candidly examine each from the point of view of its truth, its appositeness, and its charity.

Damien was *coarse*.

It is very possible. You make us sorry for the lepers who had only a coarse old peasant for their friend and father. But you, who were so refined, why were you not there, to cheer them with the lights of culture? Or may I remind you that we have some reason to doubt if John the Baptist were genteel; and in the case of Peter, on whose career you doubtless dwell approvingly in the pulpit, no doubt at all he was a "coarse, headstrong" fisherman! Yet even in our Protestant Bibles Peter is called Saint.

Damien was *dirty*.

He was. Think of the poor lepers annoyed with this dirty comrade! But the clean Dr. Hyde was at his food in a fine house.

Damien was *headstrong*.

I believe you are right again; and I thank God for his strong head and heart.

Damien was *bigoted*.

I am not fond of bigots myself, because they are not fond of me. But what is meant by bigotry, that we should regard it as a blemish in a priest? Damien believed his own religion with the simplicity of a peasant or a child; as I would I could suppose that you do. For this, I wonder at him some way off; and had that been his only character, should have avoided him in life. But the point of interest in Damien, which has caused him to be so much talked about and made him at last the subject of your pen and mine, was that, in him, his bigotry, his intense and narrow faith, wrought potently for good, and strengthened him to be one of the world's heroes and exemplars.

Damien *was not sent to Molokai, but went there without orders*.

Is this a misreading? or do you really mean the words for a blame? I have heard Christ, in the pulpits of our Church, held up for imitation on the ground that His sacrifice was voluntary. Does Dr. Hyde think otherwise?

Damien *did not stay at the settlement, etc.*

It is true he was allowed many indulgences. Am I to understand that you blame the father for profiting by these, or the officers for granting them? In either case, it is a mighty Spartan standard to issue from the house on Beretania Street; and I am convinced you will find yourself with few supporters.

Damien *had no hand in the reforms, etc.*

I think even you will admit that I have already been frank in my description of the man I am defending; but before I take you up upon this head, I will be franker still, and tell you that perhaps nowhere in the world can a man taste a more pleasurable sense of contrast than when he passes from Damien's "Chinatown" at Kalawao to the beautiful Bishop-Home at Kalaupapa. At this point, in my desire to make all fair for you, I will break my rule and adduce Catholic testimony. Here is a passage from my diary about my visit to the Chinatown, from which you will see how it is (even now) regarded by its own officials: "We went round all the dormitories, refectories, etc. — dark and dingy enough, with a superficial cleanliness, which he (Mr. Dutton, the lay Brother) did not seek to defend. 'It is almost decent,' said he; 'the sisters will make that all right when we get them here.'" And yet I gathered it was already better since Damien was dead, and far better than when he was there alone and had his own (not always excellent) way. I have now come far enough to meet you on a common ground of fact; and I tell you that, to a mind not prejudiced by jealousy, all the reforms of the lazaretto, and even those which he most vigorously opposed, are properly the work of Damien. They are the evidence of his success; they are what his heroism provoked from the reluctant and the careless. Many were before him in the field; Mr. Meyer, for instance, of whose faithful work we hear too little; there have been many since; and some had more worldly wisdom, though none had more devotion, than our saint. Before his day, even you will confess, they had effected little. It was his part, by one striking act of martyrdom, to direct all men's eyes on that distressful country. At a blow, and with the price of his life, he made the place illustrious and public. And that, if you will consider largely, was the one reform needful; pregnant of all that should succeed. It brought money; it brought (best individual addition of them all) the sisters; it brought supervision, for public opinion and public interest landed with the man at Kalawao. If ever any man brought reforms, and died to bring them, it was he. There is not a clean cup or towel in the Bishop-Home, but dirty Damien washed it.

Damien *was not a pure man in his relations with women, etc.*

How do you know that? Is this the nature of the conversation in that house on Beretania Street which the cabman envied, driving past? — racy details of the misconduct of the poor peasant priest, toiling under the cliffs of Molokai?

Many have visited the station before me; they seem not to have heard the rumor. When I was there I heard many shocking tales, for my informants were men speaking with the plainness of the laity; and I heard plenty of complaints of Damien. Why was this never mentioned? and how came it to you in the retirement of your clerical parlor?

But I must not even seem to deceive you. This scandal, when I read it in your letter, was not new to me. I had heard it once before; and I must tell you how. There came to Samoa a man from Honolulu; he, in a public-house on the beach, volunteered the statement that Damien had "contracted the disease from having connection with the female lepers"; and I find a joy in telling you how the report was welcomed in a public-house. A man sprang to his feet; I am not at liberty to give his name, but from what I heard I doubt if you would care to have him to dinner in Beretania Street. "You miserable little ——" (here is a word I dare not print, it would so shock your ears). "You miserable little ——," he cried, "if the story were a thousand times true, can't you see you are a million times a lower —— for daring to repeat it?" I wish it could be told of you that when the report reached you in your house, perhaps after family worship, you had found in your soul enough holy anger to receive it with the same expressions: ay, even with that one which I dare not print; it would not need to have been blotted away, like Uncle Toby's oath, by the tears of the recording angel; it would have been counted to you for your brightest righteousness. But you have deliberately chosen the part of the man from Honolulu, and you have played it with improvements of your own. The man from Honolulu — miserable, leering creature — communicated the tale to a rude knot of beach-combing drinkers in a public-house, where (I will so far agree with your temperance opinions) man is not always at his noblest; and the man from Honolulu had himself been drinking — drinking, we may charitably fancy, to excess. It was to your "Dear Brother, the Reverend H. B. Gage," that you chose to communicate the sickening story; and the blue ribbon which adorns your portly bosom forbids me to allow you the extenuating plea that you were drunk when it was done. Your "dear brother" — a brother indeed — made haste to deliver up your letter (as a means of grace, perhaps) to the religious papers; where, after many months, I found and read and wondered at it; and whence I have now reproduced it for the wonder of others. And you and your dear brother have, by this cycle of operations, built up a contrast very edifying to examine in detail. The man whom you would not care to have to dinner, on the one side; on the other, the Reverend Dr. Hyde and the Reverend H. B. Gage: the Apia barroom, the Honolulu manse.

But I fear you scarce appreciate how you appear to your fellowmen; and to bring it home to you, I will suppose your story to be true. I will suppose — and God forgive me for supposing it — that Damien faltered and stumbled in his narrow path of duty; I will suppose that, in the horror of his isolation, perhaps in the fever of incipient disease, he, who was doing so much more than he had sworn, failed in the letter of his priestly oath — he, who was so much a better man than either you or me, who did what we have never dreamed of daring — he too tasted of our common frailty. "O, Iago, the pity of it!" The least tender should be moved to tears; the most incredulous to prayer. And all that you could do was to pen your letter to the Reverend H. B. Gage!

Is it growing at all clear to you what a picture you have drawn of your own heart? I will try yet once again to make it clearer. You had a father; suppose this tale were about him, and some informant brought it to you, proof in hand: I am not making too high an estimate of your emotional nature when I suppose you would regret the circumstance? that you would feel the tale of frailty the more keenly since it shamed the author of your days? and that the last thing you would do would be to publish it in the religious press? Well, the man who tried to do what Damien did, is my father, and the father of the man in the Apia bar, and the father of all who love goodness; and he was your father too, if God had given you grace to see it.

Even after this masterly refutation, this unbiased testimony, the virtue of the saintly religious was attacked in the Protestant press in Honolulu.

On June 7, 1890, the Bishop addressed the editor of the *Advertiser* in regard to an article signed by *"Fair Play"* and directed at Stevenson himself:

For myself [wrote the Bishop] one point alone holds my attention. It is my strict duty to examine it since it attacks the moral character of Father Damien. "Fair Play" seems to assent to the odious and bold assertion of Hyde. Upon the publication of the latter's letter, the

Catholic Mission did not take up the matter; it awaited the expression of public opinion. Prior to the appearance of this letter, I had never heard anything said which in the slightest degree could besmirch the chastity of Father Damien, although I had secret but most searching inquiry made. I learned from certain sources worthy of credence, that the outrageous rumors which were circulated had no other foundation than certain charitable acts performed by the Father with the utmost candor of spirit. Here, public opinion gives no credence to these absurd rumors, even though there are always people on the lookout to stock-up on stories of scandalous behavior, for reasons best known to themselves.

The same edition of the paper carried an article from the *Liverpool Courier* containing a letter written by Rev. Hyde to Mr. Breta in confirmation of his first assertion, and adding that the Catholic Mission in no way had denied the truth of his statement. Bishop Koeckemann therefore added: "As head of the Catholic Mission here, a longer silence on my part would seem to credit this attack. I ask you to insert the following statement: 'I declare in the most peremptory and formal manner that there is absolutely no truth in the statements of Rev. Hyde against the moral purity of the late Father Damien.'"

Father Aubert developed and proved this short statement through three critical studies. They proved the innocence of Father Damien and the perfidy of his accuser. "The Doctor [Hyde]," he concluded, "is a 'natural man' incapable of understanding the things of God," and he called upon Mrs. Hyde to prove his statement.

Dr. Mouritz, who did not write his book, *The Path of the Destroyer,* until 1915, and did so then with the sole object of scientific exactitude, disposes of the calumnies against Father Damien thus:

Several writers who have given to the world what

purports to be a history of the life of Father Damien
have commented on the fact that hostile opinions were
held about the priest in the village of Kalawao, the
scene of his earthly labors. This is nothing remarkable;
quite a minority of the residents were opposed to the
ways and the work of the priest. The opposition and
non-appreciation of the man came in the main from
two sources:

A. The non-members of the Catholic Church; this
opposition was not personal, it was in fact only friendly
rivalry.

B. The dissolute and debauched Hawaiians and a
few foreigners. This opposition to Damien was personal,
and highly slanderous.

(a) Father Damien was a most zealous, untiring
worker on behalf of the Catholic Mission, and everything pertaining to the welfare of his flock, and his
policy, fulfilled in every sense . . .

(b) . . . Damien fought the makers of distilled
liquors, the drunkards, card players, gamblers — in
short, the debauched and dissolute element. Quite
naturally, they fought back, aided and abetted by
some of the foreign lepers; but they signally failed to
defeat Damien. They spread around stories abusing
him and accusing him of lax relations with certain
women, but their statements were too absurd, scandalous, and malicious to carry any conviction of their
truth.

When the unfortunate priest fell a victim to leprosy,
the element hostile to him in the Settlement pointed to
the fact as corroborative of the truth of the charges they
had made, but they overlooked one particularly significant condition, which was this: *The very women whom
Damien's name was connected with were some of the
cleanest in the leper reservation; they were Kokuas or
helpers; non-lepers — I know from personal observation
they were not affected with leprosy at the time of their
death.*

During the time I was connected with the Leper Settlement, I had free access to Father Damien's rooms at all hours, both day and night — on the priest's premises there were no locked doors nor screened windows.

Dr. Mouritz surely knew of the Stevenson-Hyde affair, but he never mentioned it. However, in his book, Hyde was not omitted; he was given two pages and a fine portrait.

As late as the year 1905, Father Damien's moral character was again questioned in an article in the May 20 issue of the *Boston Transcript*, which was reprinted in the *Honolulu Advertiser*. The Father Provincial asked the accusers for facts. The Mr. E. C. Bond, a Protestant minister's son, living at Kohala, wrote in the *Advertiser:*

It is disgusting to see revived at this late day, an old story that profitably should have been laid to rest forever with the bones of the two reverend gentlemen with whom it was concerned. . . . As I understand the incident thus revived, *it was merely a case of mistaken identity*, very easily accounted for. Father Damien's predecessor in this district did create a scandal by alleged immorality, which presumably was the cause of his removal shortly afterward.

In the August 20 issue of the *Advertiser*, the same Mr. Bond wrote that his previous statement should be corrected to read "Father Damien's successor" instead of "Father Damien's predecessor." Then he added: "As an aside it may interest you to know that I myself labored for a time under the impression that Father Damien was the man who raised a scandal by immoralities in this district. . . . Perhaps the guilty man's name was Fabien."

Fr. Reginald Yzendoorn, in his *History of the Catholic Mission in Hawaii*, writes: "This statement of Mr. Bond was correct. Early in 1880, Father Fabien, who, after

Father Damien's departure in 1873, had been in charge of the district of Kohala, was accused of immorality, but the courts of Waimea refused to try the case."

Again, Mr. Bond wrote further on September 17: "When he [Dr. Hyde] wrote to me to know what was wrong with his statement concerning Father Damien, which had been disputed, my answer was that he got the wrong man."

Later, someone thought it a good idea to circulate the tale that Robert Louis Stevenson had lived to regret his letter in defense of Father Damien.

In 1911, the editor of the *Ave Maria* (published at Notre Dame, Indiana) wrote:

> Feeling sure that some day "in his resting grave" the defender of Father Damien would need to be defended himself, we took care several years ago to secure from Mrs. Stevenson a statement regarding the *"Open Letter to the Rev. Dr. Hyde."* In answer to our inquiry as to the truth of the assertion, so often repeated, that her husband regretted the letter, and that before his death his opinion of Father Damien had undergone a change, Mrs. Stevenson entered an indignantly emphatic denial.

Mrs. Stevenson's words were:

> As to the *"Open Letter to Dr. Hyde,"* nothing can make me believe that Louis ever regretted the subject-matter of that piece of writing. To me, up to his last hour, he spoke always in the same strain. His admiration for the work and character of "that saint, that martyr," as he invariably called Father Damien, remained unchanged; and, any mention of the cowardly attack on the dead man's memory brought a flush of anger into his face and a fire to his eye that were unmistakable. . . .

As the editor of the *Ave Maria* has said before, we repeat again with emphasis: "This testimony, we think, should forever settle the matter."

22   *Death and World Renown*

BEFORE he died, Father Damien had the happiness of seeing religious Sisters established at the Settlement. From the time of his arrival he had been asking for them. In 1873, he wrote: "If I had a dozen hospital Sisters here, what good services they could render me."

At that time, people were of the opinion that it was inhuman to expose women to the disease. For a long time even the most virtuous souls did not find it too easy to go and live with the lepers. We can even say that, in great part, it was Father Damien's example that accustomed them to this kind of heroism.

However, the King, the Queen, the Premier, the Board of Health, the doctors, all agreed in desiring the help of the Sisters to care for the sick on the islands. On January 8, 1883, Doctor Fitch wrote the Bishop:

> Since I am constantly in contact with lepers, I have learned to recognize their needs. I am not Catholic but I know perfectly well, through experience, the merit of those devoted Christian women, the Sisters of Charity. They take care to see that food is well prepared, that children are well cared for; and above all, they cause the love of virtue and the practice of chastity to reign.

I have discussed this matter with many eminent members of Protestant churches and all look upon it as an excellent work for which they foresee great success.

In addition, he worked extremely hard to obtain the necessary resources for their establishment.

Appeals were made to forty-nine religious congregations. Twenty-two did not answer; twenty-five said that the undertaking would be impossible; two sent replies that opened up negotiations. Father Leonor made several voyages that were finally successful. The Franciscan Sisters of Syracuse, New York, were the first to accept. On November 9, 1883, seven of their number sailed for Honolulu.

At the convent of the Sacred Hearts Sisters on Fort Street, King Kalakaua and Queen Kapiolani, accompanied by Gibson, the prime minister, visited them and showed them much consideration. Four of the Sisters were assigned to the Kakaako hospital, and three to the hospital at Wailuku (Maui). So, none went to Molokai.

Up until 1888 Father Damien asked for them in vain. The Bishop could not see his way clear to consent to their immediate installation there. We know how he exhorted his leper priest to be patient. But special circumstances suddenly made the Bishop grant Father Damien his wish.

With the government's approval, Mr. B. C. Bishop, a Protestant banker in Honolulu, decided to found a home for leper girls at Kalaupapa. He wished this institution to be supervised by Sisters and insisted that Bishop Koeckemann be asked first of all to obtain them.

At this time, there was a rumor that some Episcopalian Sisters were anxious to take up this heroic work. In fact, they were ready to start traveling. With this prospect facing him, the Bishop lost no time in getting the superior at Kakaako to send Sisters to Molokai at once.

Mother Marianne, Sister Leopoldina, and Sister Vincentia landed at the Settlement on November 14, 1888, to take possession of the Bishop Home. Father Damien left his room where he had been confined by fever for the past six weeks, and rode over to welcome them. A few days later, Father Wendelin, the newly appointed pastor of Kalaupapa, joined him.

Mother Marianne was a woman of superior intelligence with an extraordinary heart. With her companions, she surrounded the fast declining old fighter with kindness and affectionate veneration. She believed it was her duty to resign as provincial in the United States in view of all the good she could do in the Hawaiian Islands, where she had led her Sisters. Since 1883 she had been superior at the Kakaako Hospital; in 1886 she was awarded the decoration of the Order of Kapiolani from the King. For thirty years she stayed at her heroic post as superior of the Bishop Home until her death in August, 1918.

God was definitely blessing His servant at the end of his career. He gave Damien the greatest consolation there is for a man of action about ready to fall — that of seeing that he has not suffered and labored in vain; that others are going to take up where he has left off. Father Conrardy would take his place at Kalawao. One of his confreres was at the post at Kalaupapa. And like angels from heaven, the daughters of St. Francis were coming to adopt, as he did, and in his own mind, better than he, his leper children:

> He conducted us [Mother Marianne related] to the orphanage of the leprous girls at Kalawao. "My children," he told them, "I shall die soon but you will not be abandoned. The Sisters whom you see have come to care for you. You will return with them to Kalaupapa." There was general regret. All the girls wept. Finally they accompanied the Sisters. There were two whom it was impossible to tear away from him. Clinging to his feet they cried, "Father, we want to stay here until your

death." It was necessary to leave them and it was not until after his death that we went to search for them. This time they came willingly to Bishop Home, where they passed away shortly afterward.

He took us also to visit the boys' orphanage and he showed us how to make their garments. At a later visit, he asked us, suddenly, "Will you take care of my boys when I am gone?" Three times he repeated the question. We promised him . . . and we have kept our promise.

Following Father Damien's death, Mr. Henry P. Baldwin, another Protestant in Honolulu, did for the boys what Mr. Bishop had done for the girls. The Baldwin Home was thus founded, and now all the leper children could benefit from the material help and irreplaceable care of the Sisters.

At last, in the evening of his hard day's work, Father Damien could rest, could go to sleep, could die reassured. "My day is done," he told them, "I can die now. You will continue to carry on the work even better than I could do." The Sisters' methods were more perfect than his; their medical technique more exact. They would guard against contagion. All this was new to him; he had never bothered about it; but he did not wish to cross his new co-workers. He forced himself to remember that he was a leper; and when he forgot, he tried to make up for it at once.

In this regard, Sister Leopoldina related of him:

Rev. Father Damien had always wanted to build a separate chapel for the Sisters in the Bishop Home but did not have sufficient funds at hand. We had thus transformed one room of our residence into an oratory where the Blessed Sacrament was reserved. Being a leper, Father Damien never entered that room. One day I was drying some beautiful birdwings for the inmates of the Home. To pin them on the line to dry, I had to go into the garden behind our residence. Our Rev. Mother had the gardener dig the ground behind the wall of the chapel-room intending to plant flowers there. When I came into the garden, there was Rev. Father Damien kneeling piously on the heap of dirt adoring the Blessed Sacrament. The sight moved me to tears. Father noticed my weeping; and in his humility and charity, he asked me if he had perhaps hurt my feelings — which fact moved me still more.

And again:

Rev. Father Damien invited us to go and see his new church as he had it nearly finished. Our Rev. Mother sent Sister Vincentia and me but forbade us to partake of any food offered to us. Father Damien had ordered a nonleper woman to prepare some refreshments for us and invited us to table. We informed him about our Superior's order, but Father insisted, perhaps in order not to disappoint the nonleper cook. After some hesitation, we complied with his request judging that our Superior would not urge her command had she known that a nonleper had prepared the refreshments. The next day Rev. Father Damien came to Kalaupapa, and for the only time entered our parlor and there he knelt before Mother Marianne and asked pardon for his conduct.

On February 21, 1889, Father Damien wrote to Edward Clifford: "I try to make slowly my way of the Cross, and hope to be soon on top of my Golgotha." The gurjun oil given him by his English friend had moderated his terrible pains a little. "I desire very much to see the Bishop once again but God is calling me."

For some time now the Bishop had been a little more gentle in his dealings with his priest. To Damien's New Year greetings, he answered with a meerschaum pipe and an affectionate letter: "I also wish you all the spiritual and material happiness compatible with the will of God for many years to come, and a great reward in eternity. The devil will still try to hinder the good by sowing weeds, but let us hope that the Lord will help us in our weakness and will lead us all to a good end."

Concerning this letter, Father Englebert, one of Father Damien's biographers, observes shrewdly that blaming the devil for the previous misunderstandings was one way for the Bishop to vindicate Father Damien; and, to a certain extent, to ask his forgiveness.

Father Leonor, still quite sure of himself, was not inclined to be mollified. He continued to load down his inferior with moral lessons and reproaches that were no longer in season. "Don't be so absolute in your ideas!" he wrote to him on January 28. And on March 18: "Again you have dipped your pen in acid" simply because the priest, with good cause, was in a hurry to obtain the large crucifix from Wailuku. About a week later the Provincial returned to the subject: "Don't be so impatient. Sometimes, even often, it is impossible; and you never count on that . . . 'it's necessary,' 'I need it,' 'send it at once.' And when we have to write to France for what you want, do you think I will get it sooner by throwing myself into the water? Calm yourself, then, and do *as the others do*."

About the middle of February, the Bishop had the priest get his accounts in order, as he was growing steadily worse. In principle, the Bishop had been letting him have a wide latitude to dispose of the money according to the wishes of the donors. However, when it was a question of objects pertaining to religious cult, he had the missionary submit all ideas and plans for his approval.

He had allowed Father Damien to enlarge St. Philomena's Church and had unreserved praise for the renovations and improvements. However, he said he was offended to learn how it was written up in American and European journals. He complained to the Father General that Father Damien and his companion, Father Conrardy, ignored ecclesiastical and religious superiors too much in their writings. So he had had Father Wendelin join them "to keep the leprosarium from being detached from the Mission."

Around the end of February, Damien took a turn for the worse. On February 21, Brother James Sinnett wrote Clifford, telling him these facts: the priest was coughing a great deal, his diarrhea was very violent; painful eruptions were breaking out all over his hands; he had even quit using the gurjun oil; his case now seemed hopeless and all human remedies were of no use; the light caused him severe pains during the day; at night he could not sleep; and, "Nevertheless he is as energetic as ever in bettering the condition of the lepers."

In obedience to his superiors, he had already drawn up his last will and testament:

Last Will and Testament

I, J. Damien de Veuster, Catholic priest, a leper of the leper Asylum of Molokai, being of sound mind and memory, do make, publish and declare this my last Will and Testament, namely:

I give and bequeath all of my estate, real, personal, and mixed, which I possess in the Hawaiian Islands at the moment of my death, to the Right Reverend Hermann Koeckemann, Bishop of Alba, and Vicar Apostolic of the Hawaiian Islands, and to his Successors in Office.

I hereby nominate and appoint Rev. Father Clement to be my executor.

In witness whereof I have hereunto set my hand and seal this eighteenth day of November, in the year of Our Lord, one thousand eight hundred and eighty-seven.

J. Damien de Veuster (Seal)

The above document, written on one sheet of paper, was at the date thereof signed, sealed, published, and declared by the said J. Damien de Veuster, to be his last

Will and Testament in presence of us, who at his request and in his presence and in the presence of each other, have subscribed our names as witnesses thereto.

> Father James Beissel (Seal)
> Catholic priest
> Joseph Dutton   (Seal)

Codicil added to my will this day, February 28, 1889.

I hereby associate the Rev. Father Wendelin, now resident priest at Kalaupapa, with Rev. Father Clement, as executors to my Will.

> J. Damien de Veuster

Hawaiian Islands, Honolulu:

I certify that the foregoing is a full and true copy of the original Will of J. Damien de Veuster, on file in the Clerks' Office of the Supreme Court, and that said Will was admitted to probate by said Court, on the 13th day of January, 1890. J. H. Reest, Deputy Clerk.

Thus did Father Damien liquidate his scanty possessions. He had turned over his old horse, which was Mission property, to his companion. "Today," he wrote to the Provincial, "I sold my bay horse with saddle, bridle, etc. to Father Conrardy for twenty-five piastres." By the above will he had left all the pounds sterling and dollars that he had to the Provincial with the understanding that he was to dispose of them according to the donors' wishes. That done, he told Father Wendelin: "How happy I am to give up everything, to die poor, and to have more for myself."

He was forced to go to bed. He lay upstairs on a pallet spread out on the floor. The man who had received so many alms and distributed so many gifts, had given away everything. He had no sheets, no change of linen. Rolled up in a miserable blanket, he shook with fever. They found a bed for him and then had a hard time making him take it.

Brother James never left him. Often, Father Conrardy and Brother Dutton were at his bedside. Too, Mother Marianne came often from Kalaupapa to visit him. As for the lepers, they were always in his room. "Impossible to chase them out," said Brother James.

From England, Rev. Chapman and Edward Clifford sent him messages of affection. The latter wrote: "You are happy to think that Our Lord has chosen you as the instrument of benediction for bodies and souls of so many hundreds of your beloved sick folk. You have given your life for them. May you experience the Holy Presence and the mercy of the Master. . . ." The priest charged Brother James, his secretary, to write them that he was thinking of them affectionately and praying for them.

Dr. Morrow, the leprosy specialist of New York, had asked him to describe the progress of his disease. About a month, then, before he was to appear before God, March 10, 1889, Father Damien dictated a report to Dutton that would satisfy the specialist's scientific curiosity. We believe it worth while to reproduce those observations here *in extenso.* Especially so, as nothing allows us to believe that the holy priest knew, while he was alive, that three months after his death his virtue would be attacked publicly. Nor does anything allow us to doubt that he would have accepted that suffering, as he had accepted the others, without bitterness toward anyone, without revolting, without any thought of revenge:

Kalawao, Molokai

Rev. Father J. Damien De Veuster, Catholic priest, native of Belgium, Belgian parents, 49 years of age. All of the members of family very strong and healthy; no taint of scrofula or syphilis. No relatives on these islands. Served as priest on the island of Hawaii from 1864 till

1873. Occasionally, heard confessions of lepers, and
ministered to them in their cabins sometimes; but had
no constant or very particular contact with them until
he came here, to the Leper Settlement, in 1873. Since
that time, until now, his contact and association have
been almost constant. In 1873, was strong and healthy,
with remarkable robust constitution. Has never had any
sexual intercourse whatsoever.

Is quite sure that when near to lepers, as at confession
or in their cabins — before coming to the leper settlement — he felt on such occasions a peculiar sensation in
the face; a sort of itching or burning and that he felt
the same here, at the settlement, during the first two
or three years; also, he felt it on the legs. He is confident
that the germs were in his system, certainly within the
first three years of his residence here; can trace it back
positively to 1876. Small, dry spots appeared at that
time, particularly on arms, and some on back. On these
spots perspiration did not appear, as elsewhere. Upon
treatment with corrosive sublimate lotion the spots would
disappear, but return again. Finally in 1877 and in 1878,
these spots assumed yellowish color and became larger.
In 1877 he took sarsaparilla as blood purifier, when the
spots, still yellow, became more defined; they would
remain until lotion was applied.

This describes the first marks; but, even still earlier,
there was a suspicious foreboding of what was to come;
his feet had a peculiar sensation; they were hot and
feverish and made him restless; he could not sleep without first giving them a cold water soak; nor without doing this, could he keep them covered at night. This was
in 1874 and 1875. Still, he continued to enjoy strength
and health.

In 1881 he was vaccinated, at the time of the smallpox epidemic in Honolulu. The operation was performed
by one deputized by the Board of Health, who said that
the vaccine matter came from America. In some degree
the operation was successful. During a few days he had

some fever, and there was inflammation at the point of vaccination, on a space about the size of a silver dollar, some matter flowing therefrom. (In connection with this, it is well to state that the natives, and some others, have a firm belief that leprosy was greatly spread throughout the islands by means of vaccination material and methods, at this time, and perhaps at other times.)

In the autumn of 1881, he began to be badly troubled with severe pains in the feet, especially in the left one; and in 1882, sciatic nerve trouble came on, clearly defined all along the left leg.

At the close of 1882, or early in 1883, entire insensibility of one side of the left foot took place, and so remains until this day — the outside portion of the foot — and Father Damien is able to draw a line marking the division of the sensible part from the insensible portion of his foot. This is the only part of his body that has been so attacked. The pain of the sciatic nerve, and of the inside portion of his foot, was intense, and almost constant, accompanied by the formation of nodes in the left groin. All these pains disappeared, at once, about June 1885.

Then the right ear became swollen, with tubercular enlargements, making the whole thing an immense affair. At the same time began the disfigurement of his person in a general and marked manner. The eyebrows began to fall out, the other ear became enlarged, and tubercular swellings took possession of the face, hands, etc. The knuckles and knees are in hard enlarged knobs, becoming suppurating ulcers. Many sores on hands and wrists, and some about the neck; the eyes are weak and at times very much inflamed. His nose was greatly obstructed, causing much distress during the past two years; the obstruction appears as catarrh. The bridge of the nose is much sunken. The foot that was partly insensible, was, for a time, exceedingly weak. Now, since the disease has spread over the body, it becomes strong again.

Damien was acquainted with the theory of the affinity of leprosy for syphilis because he had combated this theory in his report of March, 1886, to the Board of Health. It was, therefore, with full reflection and intention, that, in the presence of his friend, Brother Joseph, he took the heavens to witness to his virtue. We add that, at the time, Dutton did not read any of these implications into Father Damien's declaration.

On June 9, 1890, Brother Joseph wrote to the Bishop: "I took these notes from his own dictation, keeping as closely as possible to his exact words. I read the Report back to him before he signed it. This declaration in the text, 'I have never had sexual intercourse with anyone whatever,' he made spontaneously and wished that I word it exactly as he had given it."

When Brother Joseph had finished his work of drawing up the report, Father Damien read it over carefully, then, at the bottom of the last page, in order to testify to the exactitude of the text, wrote with his own hand —

"Correct: J. Damien De Veuster
    March 10, 1889.   Catholic Priest"

Moreover, Father Damien had expressed a desire that an autopsy should be performed after his death. Was that again in the hope that this examination would prove his innocence beyond a doubt?

New ulcers appeared at the joints of his fingers and these forced him to stop saying Mass. This was a very painful privation; he had been happy that his disease had respected his hands.

On March 19, feast of St. Joseph, he received a letter from Mother Judith, his old friend in Honolulu, wishing him a happy feast day, and congratulating him on the twenty-fifth anniversary of his coming to the Hawaiian Islands.

To Dr. Godwyn Swift, the physician of the leprosarium to whom we are indebted for several photographs taken at that time, Father Damien had a note written: "Dear Sir, If possible, please, come to see me; I feel some pain in the lower abdomen. Grant this favor to your very weak friend. J. Damien."

As long as his sight was a little clear, he persisted in saying his breviary daily even though the light caused him intense pain. Sinnett wrote to Clifford:

Father Damien wrote to his Bishop entreating not to be dispensed from the obligation of the breviary, which he continued to recite until his final prostration. . . . Every night, a little after he heard the clock strike eleven, he would remind me it was time to commence the prayers preparatory for Holy Communion; these he followed with the fervor of the saint that he was. At eleven forty-five I would awaken Father Conrardy who slept on the first floor; we proceeded to the Church for the Blessed Sacrament. Returning, I walked before him with a lighted lantern until we reached Father Damien's bedside. Then he received his Lord with the fervor of a seraph.

The disease, which was invading the windpipe, progressed to such an extent that it kept him from sleeping more than an hour or two at night. His voice was lost in raucous whispers.

The sturdy oak was broken. This forty-nine-year-old man, cut down in the prime of life, lay prostrate. After fighting and defending himself valiantly, the champion of the helpless had fallen himself. Leprosy, the conqueror, was at his throat, in his lungs, in his stomach, and in his intestines. After ravaging his body outwardly, it was now destroying him from within.

All the witnesses declared that the patience and resignation of the dying man never changed. His eyes, under the hideous swelling, were gradually going out. He could hardly see Burne-Jones's picture of St. Francis of Assisi hanging over his bed. Stigmatized in a more ignominious way than the Poverello, his soul seemed to take on a mysterious light. All the worries of his conscience disappeared. Without a doubt, deep in his soul he felt joyous gratitude to God, for he had nothing more than this to say to the Rev. Chapman and his brother, Pamphile:

> I am gently going to my grave. It is the will of God, and I thank Him very much for letting me die of the same disease and in the same way as my lepers. I am very satisfied and very happy.

His last sufferings did not turn his thoughts away from his flock. The last lines he traced out were to call the doctor to the bedside of a leper: "Dear Sir, Jobo Puhomamia has been spitting blood since yesterday morning. Please spare a moment to go and see him. He lives in the second house after that of James Lewis. Grant this favor to your friend. J. Damien." To this he added the postscript: "in the same house is the dying woman of whom I spoke to you last night."

Fathers Wendelin and Conrardy attended to his needs. Father Wendelin recounted:

> I heard his general confession on March 30, then I confessed to him. Together we renewed the vows of our Congregation. He was radiant with happiness. He said to me: "Don't you represent our Congregation for me? Then don't fail to tell Father General, when you

write to him, *how happy I am to die a child of the Congregation of the Sacred Hearts.*"

The next morning, Sunday, March 31, he received Holy Viaticum. During the day, he manifested his joy that death was approaching: "Look," he said, showing me his hands, "all my wounds are closing up, the crust is becoming black. It's the end. You know that well. Look at my eyes. I have seen too many lepers die to be deceived. The Lord is calling me to celebrate Easter with Him."

He received Extreme Unction on April 2 from Father Conrardy. "How good God is," he said during the day, "to have made me live long enough to see at this moment two priests at my side and the Franciscan Sisters at the Settlement! I can sing *Nunc Dimittis,** the work for the lepers is in good hands; and I, I am no longer necessary; I am going to heaven."

"When you are there," they asked him, "you won't forget those whom you are leaving orphans, will you?"

"Oh, no! If I have any power with God, I will intercede for all the inhabitants of the leprosarium," he answered.

His confrere, Father Wendelin, begged him to leave his cloak to him, as Elias had done to Eliseus, so that he might have his great heart.

Father Damien did not believe that he was any Elias. . . . "What would you do with it? You couldn't wear it. It's all full of leprosy."

"I asked him for his blessing," said Father Wendelin, "which he gave me with tears in his eyes. He also blessed the courageous Franciscan Sisters for whose coming he had prayed so long."

Some days passed and he seemed to be a little better.

---

* *Nunc Dimittis* — "Now, thou dost dismiss Thy servant, O Lord . . ." (Luke 2:29).

The lepers, coming to say good-by, found him sitting in a chair, wrapped up in blankets. The laughing nonchalance of the Hawaiians, darkened by their forthcoming loss, had given way to a kind of aching despair. He, who had once been so lively, sat there calm and gentle; he thanked them affectionately for their visits, saying he would see them in heaven. They were struck by the joy in his eyes.

"Saturday, April 13," Father Wendelin wrote, "He was worse and lost consciousness at times. He went to Holy Communion a little after midnight for the last time."

During these last moments of lucidity, he showed his great attachment for his Congregation. He insisted that his confrère say the Community prayers with him. "How sweet it is to die a child of the Sacred Hearts!" he exclaimed.

As Father Wendelin had to go to Kalaupapa for Sunday services, they said good-by to each other. When Father Wendelin returned during the day, he found Father Damien delirious.

The following day, April 15, Father Conrardy sent a note to Father Wendelin stating that Father Damien was dying. Father Wendelin left for Kalawao, but on the way he met a messenger who told him that the priest had died. Gently, "with a smile," he had died in the arms of Brother James, "like a child going to sleep."

Father Damien went to God at the beginning of Holy Week, a few days before Easter, just as he had predicted.

They clothed him in his cassock. Soon all the marks of leprosy disappeared from his face and the wounds on his hands dried up. Around eleven o'clock they carried him to the church where his remains, surrounded by lepers weeping and praying, lay in state until the next morning. In the afternoon the Franciscan Sisters lined his coffin with white silk and covered the outside with a black cloth on which was sewn a white cross. He was buried in his priestly vestments.

The funeral was held on the following day. Except for the immense sorrow of those attending, the funeral was just like the ones Father Damien had conducted during the past sixteen years, several times a week. After Holy Mass, the procession, preceded by the cross, started for the cemetery. In the front ranks of the procession were the musicians of the band and the members of the different confraternities; these were followed by the Sisters with the women and children from the Bishop Home. Then came the coffin carried by eight lepers. The coffin was followed by the two priests with their acolytes, and Brothers James and Dutton with their orphan boys and the remainder of the men of the island.

Damien's wish was fulfilled. He wanted to rest under the shade of the tree where he spent his first nights on the island. They buried him at the foot of the large pandanus tree. And there for forty-six years, he rested among those whom he had loved so well and so much.

Over his grave, the Mission erected a large, black marble cross with the following inscription in English:

V.C.J.S.*

Sacred to the Memory
of the Revd Father
DAMIEN DE VEUSTER
Died a Martyr to the Charity
for the afflicted Lepers
April 15, 1889
R.I.P.

* *Vivat Cor Jesu Sacratissimum!* Live forever the Most Sacred Heart of Jesus! — The motto of the Congregation of the Sacred Hearts of Jesus and Mary.

At the solemn funeral Mass celebrated in the Honolulu Cathedral fifteen days later, the Bishop acceded to the general expectation and delivered a funeral oration that, even on his lips, turned into a panegyric. We will reproduce it *in extenso*:

We are assembled here to honor the memory of a man whose fame has spread over the whole globe.

There is perhaps not a city, small or large, in the civilized world where the name of Father Damien is not known and blessed by all sympathetic hearts. Every good man has a right to our respect, but there are degrees in the merits of good men.

A good Christian is justly honored by his fellow Christians; a generous benefactor is entitled to the gratitude of those who have received his benefits; a zealous propagator of the Gospel of Christ who works honestly for the salvation of souls, and who practices himself the works of charity he preaches to others, will always earn the admiration of fair-minded people.

Father Damien unites all these claims to our admiration in an eminent degree, and even many others in addition. But he has two more glorious titles which raise him above the rest of good men — he is a hero and a martyr of Christian charity.

History points out to us many heroes of different kinds. The most celebrated are perhaps those brave men who risked their lives on the battlefield for the defense of their country, with the firm resolution to conquer or to die in the attempt.

Father Damien seems to me to have been a hero more glorious than he who falls on the battlefield, sword in hand. At about the age of thirty-four, in the full strength of youth and in perfect health, he offered to share the fate of those unfortunate ones, separated from their families and friends. He asked, as a favor, the permission to live at the lazaret, in order to console and to comfort, physically and morally, the suffering portion of humanity assembled there through inevitable necessity.

His hierarchical superiors, with joy and admiration for his singular merit, accorded him their consent for his voluntary immolation. He not only exposed himself to the loathsome disease, but he faced the danger with a supernatural Christian indifference, perhaps with more hope than fear to fall a victim of his charity.

Without doing harm to anyone, he has, like Christ, conquered by means of his death. For many years he suffered all the symptoms of leprosy. During these last two years, it had become evident that the disgusting sickness had taken hold of his body. Nevertheless, he still continued his arduous work as long as the least ability remained, until God called him to his reward, a real martyr of his devotion to the Work of Christian Charity. . . .

It was not that the priest of the lepers was unknown while alive, but after his death, the press, regardless of party or opinion, surpassed the funeral panegyric of his own Bishop. Never, perhaps, was there such sincere unanimity in glorifying a Catholic priest. Wherever a journal was printed, this greathearted man's death, the man clothed with leprosy, was announced. His stirring prowess broke all records. He was big news. Thousands of articles told — with emotion — of his heroism and martyrdom. In a few months, Father Damien was famous the world over.

Glory is capricious; and at times it is hard to explain. Sometimes it is partial, ephemeral; sometimes it is well deserved. Did Father Damien's renown come from the fact that he was a pioneer? The public, not too much given to admiring the same exploit twice, has neglected his imitators. There is also the spectacular side of a unique adventure. People could hear the heart-rending cries of those outcasts of humanity, forcibly thrust on this island in the ocean. They admired the man who voluntarily buried his youth among them. He did not fold his arms and mouth platonic consolations. He could have allowed himself to be fired with a flame of heroism that would be quickly snuffed out. On the contrary, they saw him there in that living graveyard, serious, solid, willing, positive, paying the price with his very own person; he did not allow himself any letup during the innumerable minutes and interminable days, poignant in their incessant renewal of a sixteen-year sojourn. He was as ardent on the last day as he had been on the first. And thus did he take his place among the purest heroes of history and legend. Finally, people were touched to learn that after so many years of pain and work, the poison of leprosy had taken hold of him in turn; and that five years were enough to make this sturdy man into a knotted, wasted, corrupted ruin, "of two hundred lepers, the most hideous of all"; and yet paradoxically, that he had simply blessed God for his lot.

Thus it was that he was esteemed outside the cloister of the leprosarium, even unto the remote confines of the world. Hundreds of books and pamphlets, in every language, have described his life. Statues have been erected in his memory. Poets and musicians have composed odes and oratorios in his honor. His name has been given to streets, publications, colleges for the preparation of future missionaries, various movements founded and still operating for the lepers. His popularity has spread everywhere. The radiance of his life is ever on the increase. He is known and spoken of throughout the leprosy-stricken islands of Oceania and of the entire world.

His memory, is strongest, however, in the Anglo-Saxon world where it has taken its rightful place among men of renown. You will find the name "Damien de Veuster" listed in encyclopedias and books of famous men. This leper Catholic priest is mentioned in the works dedicated to the great benefactors of humanity.

Legends are appearing, created by oral tradition and the popular imagination. "Why is it that Damien has such popularity rather than others who are as deserving?" The marvelous exploits of Father Conrardy did not cause the same sensation. Other missionaries have died, lepers and martyrs, yet their names have remained unknown.

Yet, no one will claim that his glory was usurped. He deserves to be revered as a real disciple of Christ and a man who is a credit to humanity. Up to his time, people tended to forget that lepers were human beings. His example inspired shame for the continued neglect of essential duties toward them, and for the cruel egoism practiced toward them. Since his time, lepers are no longer treated as pariahs. The world has been brought to realize that they have as much right to help as other suffering persons. Humanity no longer has to blush over spurning those most worthy of pity, because they were at one time the most miserable of its children.

Two months after the leper priest's death, the future Edward VII, then Prince of Wales, summoned the Committee of the Leprosy Fund to his palace and, as its head, delivered a discourse. Part of it follows:

> The heroic life and death of Father Damien has not only roused the sympathy of the United Kingdom, but it has gone deeper. It has brought home to us that the circumstances of our vast Indian and Colonial Empire oblige us, in a measure at least, to follow his example. And this not for foreigners and strangers, but for our own fellow subjects.
>
> India . . . and our colonies with their unnumbered but increasing victims to a loathsome disease that has hitherto baffled medical skill, have a far stronger claim on our aid than the poor natives of the Hawaiian Islands could ever have had on the young Belgian priest, who has given his life for them.

To mark our debt to him, as well as our sympathy with his noble self-sacrifice, I have to propose to this Committee a memorial scheme that embraces a three-fold object: (1) A monument to Father Damien at Molokai; (2) The establishment of a leper ward, probably attached to some London hospital or medical school, to be called the Father Damien Ward, and the endowment of a travelling studentship or studentships, to encourage the study of leprosy; (3) A full and complete inquiry into the question of leprosy in India, one of the chief seats of the disease, and where there are no adequate means of dealing with the disease.

This program was carried out. A large, white granite cross was dedicated at Molokai, September 11, 1893. On it is a sculptured head of Father Damien and the inscription: "Greater love than this hath no man, that he give his life for his friend."

In December, 1894, the Belgians erected a bronze monument at Louvain to their fellow countryman. On that occasion, the president of the Council said that the government's duty was to be present at this manifestation of national recognition and pride.

"This statue," Georges Goyau said more specifically, "symbolizes in one magnificent movement, the double gesture of charity: Clasping the crucifix to his breast, you would say that the missionary wants to enflame his heart from the very Heart of Christ crucified; and right beside him, resting against him, taking shelter under his compassionate gesture, is a leper whom his human charity cares for and consoles, a reflection of divine charity."

In 1935 the Governor General of Hawaii signed a law, adopted by the Parliament, which set up an annual gift of $3,000 to assure the preservation, as a national monument, of that part of Molokai where are located Father Damien's church and the graves of Brother Dutton and heroic lay Brothers who worked there for so many years.

Out of respect for the dead man's wish, Father Damien was buried at Kalawao. Yet, it seems as though the piety of the living did not remember that wish too well, since he no longer rests among the lepers of Molokai. Those who had every reason for visiting his grave, to pray there, miss him. Hundreds of patients who have passed through Molokai since 1936 have wept over the removal of his remains.

In 1936, the Belgians wanted to bring back Father Damien's body to his homeland. At the request of King Leopold III, President Roosevelt assisted in the project and helped to bring it to a successful conclusion.

Hawaii, however, still remains rich with memories of Father Damien: the Cathedral of Our Lady of Peace, where he was ordained deacon and priest; some of the churches erected by him, the most precious of all, St. Philomena on which he worked with his leprous hands at Kalawao; his tombstone under which he rested for forty-six years; the monument at Kalaupapa erected by the English in his memory; and, above all, the present leprosarium, a model of its kind.

When the body of Father Damien was exhumed, the remains were found to be in a remarkable state of preservation; the body was darkened but intact save for the joints of the fingers and some toes that had been destroyed by the disease. His hair remained, black mixed with gray. His priestly vestments — chasuble, alb, stole, and maniple — were covered with mold, the embroidery dull.

Lepers present at the disinterment spontaneously gave expression to their grief in doleful Hawaiian chants, in which were mingled old funeral songs of the warriors of the great Kamehameha I. The farewell song, *Aloha Oe*, was heart-rending.

At the beginning of February, 1936, while standing

about the grave where flowers were always kept growing, the lepers watched the white U. S. Army Airforce plane take off over the water and rise into the sky, bearing their treasure away — a fitting symbol!

Solemn ceremonies at Honolulu marked the first stage of the trip. The highest dignitaries were present, government, civil, military, naval officials, members of the diplomatic corps, representatives of religious orders, and a huge crowd of people of all religions and classes of society. The wood of the casket was of *Koa,* Hawaiian acacia, reserved for members of the royal family. To the music of the 20th Artillery Regiment, the remains of Father Damien were carried under military escort to the U. S. Army transport *Republic.* He was given the honors the U. S. Army reserves for its heroes. Overhead eight bombers flew.

At San Francisco, at the request of Archbishop Mitty, again Father Damien was honored.

The Belgian Navy training ship *Mercator* was waiting for Father Damien's remains at Panama to take him home — to Belgium. They arrived at Antwerp on May 3.

Meanwhile, Eugene Cardinal Pacelli, then Secretary of State for Pius XI, whom he succeeded as Pope Pius XII, sent the following message:

> The Vatican
> April 25, 1936

His Holiness has felt a keen and paternal consolation in learning that the entire people of Belgium, with their noble Sovereign, their Episcopate and Government, is preparing itself to render national homage to one of its most glorious sons, Father Damien de Veuster, whose precious remains his homeland will soon receive with unanimous sentiments of admiration and piety.

The sublime devotion of this religious, consuming his life on the far-off Islands of Hawaii in the service of the

lepers, to whom he abundantly gave all spiritual and
corporal comforts, will remain *one of the most beautiful
examples of apostolic activity of our times.*

Already, His Holiness has been pleased to give the
work of this valiant missionary a choice place in the
Lateran Ethnological and Missionary Museum. But, He
does not the less praise the glorification that Belgium
intends to reserve for this hero of charity. At the same
time, He wishes to bless all who will take part in it; and,
above all, the Religious Family that can justly glory in
having given Christian civilization a pioneer as deserving as Father Damien.

(signed) E. Cardinal Pacelli

This humble priest's return to his homeland was a real
triumph. The homage of the people was moving and magnificent. The King, the government, the hierarchy, surrounded by innumerable throngs of the faithful, awaited
his arrival. When, accompanied by festooned ships, the
Mercator dropped anchor, the trumpets sounded . . . can-
nons boomed . . . all the bells of Antwerp began to peal
. . . and the soldiers lifted their arms in salute to the returning hero. The casket was placed before the platform
on which stood Cardinal Van Roey, Primate of Belgium,
members of the episcopate, and the King with his cabinet.
A thrill passed through the crowd as they saw His Majesty
King Leopold III step from his place and salute the humble son of a Tremeloo peasant. Father Damien must have
been smiling.

Then, a hearse, drawn by six white horses, carried his
body to the Cathedral where a solemn pontifical Mass was
celebrated with magnificent ceremonies in the presence of
the highest civil and religious personages of the land.
Eulogies were pronounced by the Primate of Belgium and
by the renowned orator, Father Rutten, O.P.

Late in the evening, a hearse slowly began the journey

to Louvain. In this manner, under the myriad stars, did Father Damien once again traverse the Tremeloo countryside so familiar to him when he was a boy. About midnight, he arrived at the place which he had left seventy-three years before to go to his destiny.

The remains of the humble missionary were again laid to rest in a crypt of St. Joseph's Chapel, a national shrine dedicated to Father Damien's patron, and directed by the Fathers of the Sacred Hearts. Under a beautiful black sarcophagus, he awaits the resurrection; and, perhaps also, the honors which the Church may bestow upon him in the not too distant future.

"Father Damien," as Msgr. Cruysberghs has stated, "will ever be a living argument. The question of his sanctity has been raised. It must be resolved. Damien the hero can only be explained by Damien the saint."*

* *Panegyric on Father Damien*, delivered by Msgr. Cruysberghs at Louvain, May 4, 1936. Published in pamphlet form.

Epilogue

The Legacy of Father Damien

by Raphael Brown

ALL of the biographies of Father Damien which we have examined end with his death or with the removal of his body to Belgium in 1936, but they do not give their readers any specific information about the marvelous development after 1889 of the world-wide Catholic leprosy apostolate which was so dear to the heart of the saintly Flemish priest. Yet the influence of his example on that great movement, even when it was only indirect, has certainly been profound and enduring.

It is an undeniable and a glorious fact that Father Damien's sixteen years of self-sacrifice on Molokai opened the eyes of the world to the suffering of millions of victims of leprosy and stirred thousands of generous persons to support leprosy work by their prayers and financial contributions.

Perhaps the most important aspect of Father Damien's role in the modern battle against Hansen's disease lies in the selfless decision which his example inspired in the souls of hundreds of young men and women to devote their lives to this noble apostolate. Although documentary evidence is often lacking, we can be sure that most Christian leprosy workers of the past seventy years—both

Catholic and Protestant — would gladly testify that Father Damien was a primary factor in their own vocations.

Since their work was a continuation and an extension of his, a brief outline of the evolution of the modern world-wide Catholic apostolate for victims of leprosy forms a fitting epilogue for this comprehensive biography. Unfortunately, no thorough history of that dramatic epic has yet been published in English, although plentiful materials are available in the files of the mission magazines.

The subject lends itself to a twofold division: (1) the expansion of the work in the field by the missionaries, and (2) the chronicle of successive organized efforts made in Europe and America to implement their work.

While we are concentrating on the contribution of the Roman Catholic Church to the world-wide campaign against Hansen's disease, we should not fail to note in passing the admirable share of the total effort which has been made since 1874, even before Father Damien became famous, by the British Protestant Mission to Lepers, and, beginning in 1917, by the Protestant interdenominational American Leprosy Missions, as well as the excellent work of such secular groups as the British Empire Leprosy Relief Association (BELRA), and the Leonard Wood Memorial, and the International Leprosy Association.

THE FIELD AFAR

We should not imagine that Father Damien was the first Catholic priest and that the Franciscan Sisters of Syracuse, New York, were the first nuns to volunteer to take care of victims of leprosy in foreign lands. After the almost complete disappearance of the disease in Europe in the sixteenth century, the Church's missionaries nevertheless frequently encountered it on their path in Latin America and in Asia. Until the history of this little-known period is studied, we have only a few scattered references to the care given to leprosy patients by priests: Franciscans in Macao and Manila as early as 1570, in Japan some years later, in China in 1693; a Jesuit Father died with leprosy there in 1722. During the seventeenth and eighteenth centuries, a number of leprosaria were founded under the auspices of the Church in Spanish and Portuguese America; Havana (1667), Rio de Janeiro (1763), and Costa Rica (1826).

The honor of creating the first modern Catholic mission leprosarium belongs to Blessed Anna Maria Jahouvey, foundress of the Sisters of St. Joseph of Cluny, who in 1833, at the request of the French government, took charge of the Acarouany hospital in French Guiana. Fifteen years later French priests opened a leprosarium in Pondichery, India, and then in Reunion (1852) and Maurice Islands (1858). Catholic Sisters were employed as nurses in the government hospitals of Tracadie, N. B., Canada, in 1864, and Trinidad, British West Indies, in 1868.

It is interesting to note that the French Dominican chaplain in the latter institution, Father Etienne Brosse, not only corresponded with other chaplains in Pondichery and Tonkin — and with Father Damien — but also in 1879 wrote a book with the striking title *La Lepre Est Contagieuse (Leprosy Is Contagious)*, probably the first book on leprosy by a Catholic priest in modern times, in which he refuted, largely, from the observations of missionaries, the thesis of a British Colonial Secretary's report of 1865 contending that the disease is not infectious.

When Father Damien died in 1889, there were probably not more than half a dozen leprosaria outside of Latin America in which Catholic priests and nuns were engaged in full-time work. Barely ten years later, 1898, such was the impulse given to this apostolate by his heroism that the magazine *Les Missions Catholiques* published an editorial stating that "almost each mission considers it an honor to

open asylums. . . . Everywhere our missionaries are opening homes for leprosy patients."

In 1896, the Rev. L. W. Mulhane, pastor in Mount
Vernon, Ohio (the home of Brother Dutton's divorced and
deceased wife), as a result of his friendship and correspondence with Brother Dutton, published a valuable book
entitled *Leprosy and the Charity of the Church*, which is
the first modern survey of Catholic leprosy work. This book
vividly describes the apostolate of priests and nuns serving
in leprosaria which had been founded since Father
Damien's death in Colombia, Japan, China, Indo-China,
India, Burma, and Madagascar.

A powerful new stimulus was given to the cause by
Mother Mary of the Passion (1839-1904), the foundress of
the Franciscan Missionaries of Mary. During her years in
South India, she had seen and treated victims of leprosy.
In 1896, after she had organized her new order, she received the first of many appeals to provide Sisters for leprosy work. "I will never refuse a leprosarium," she declared. When she sent a circular letter to all her Sisters
asking for six volunteers for the first two hospitals, over
one thousand of her valiant nuns applied for the assignment. Mother Mary of the Passion called the list of their
names "my Golden Book." Pope Leo XIII gave the six his
blessing in a private audience and called them "true consecrated victims." In 1902, twenty-one Franciscan Missionaries of Mary left Europe for service in the new Catholic
leprosaria of Mandalay and Rangoon in Burma, Biwasaki
in Japan, and Marana in Madagascar. In 1914 and 1921,
respectively, their order was asked to staff the two large
government hospitals of Hendala and Mantivu in Ceylon.
In 1953 it was giving care to 5360 patients in 16 private
and government institutions. Only the Daughters of Charity of St. Vincent de Paul are found in more leprosaria
(21), while the Marist Missionary Sisters have the honor

of assigning one-fifth of their total membership to leprosy work.

At least seven important Catholic leprosaria were founded during the sixteen years following Father Damien's death, or an average of one nearly every other year. After the foundation of the French Capuchin colony at Harrar in Ethiopia in 1905, there was a lull until after World War I, during which only two large mission hospitals were established.

One of them owed its inspiration directly to Father Damien, as it was founded by his intimate friend and helper, Father Louis Lambert Conrardy, one of the most interesting figures in the entire history of leprosy. A former Belgian parish priest and missionary among the Indians in Oregon, Father Conrardy left Molokai a short time after the death of Father Damien in order to found a leprosarium in South China, where several hundred thousand victims of leprosy were living in a condition of cruel neglect and need. First, however, he had to secure a doctor's degree and some substantial funds. He therefore took a full course of medicine at the University of Oregon and then began a prolonged begging tour of Europe and the United States. His stirring sermons and appeals sowed the seeds of many future missionary vocations, including that of Maryknoll's heroic Bishop Francis X. Ford. In 1912, Father Conrardy finally succeeded in opening St. Joseph's leprosarium on the island of Shek Lung, between Hong Kong and Canton. With the coming of the Canadian Missionary Sisters of the Immaculate Conception, his foundation was able to survive his death in 1914. For many years this hospital with its 700 patients was the largest Catholic leprosarium in the world.

Since the Chinese Communists took over Shek Lung in 1952, that honor belongs to the Sacred Heart Leprosy Home in Kumbakonam, South India, which was founded in 1916 by the heroic and saintly Sister Caroline of the Tabernacle, who was herself a patient there until her death in 1933.

The thirty years between 1920 and 1950 saw the creation of about fifty major Catholic leprosaria in various parts of Africa, India, Burma, Indonesia, Indo-China, and China, with Catholic Sisters becoming nurses in over a hundred government institutions. Statistics covering missions under the jurisdiction of the Sacred Congregation for the Propagation of the Faith give the following totals for both private and official leprosaria:

Year	Leprosaria	Patients
1927	90	10,000
1935	108	12,700
1940	127	13,200
1950	174	17,600

However, in order to have a clear picture of the precise contribution of the Church in this field, it is necessary to differentiate between the purely private leprosaria (with or without a partial subsidy) and the government hospitals in which Sisters are employed as nurses and which may or may not have a resident Catholic chaplain. *The World Survey of Catholic Leprosy Work* supplies the following figures for the year 1951:

97 Catholic leprosaria with 25,000 patients;
122 government leprosaria with Sisters nursing 46,500 patients;
total: 219, private and government hospitals with 71,500 patients;
leprosaria of both types having Catholic chaplains: at least 135.

In addition, it must not be forgotten that many mission

dispensaries in Asia and Africa give out-patient treatment to uncounted thousands of victims of leprosy.

A comprehensive study of the world-wide leprosy apostolate of our missionaries reveals three striking features: (1) the numerous discouraging hardships which impede their already difficult work, ranging all the way from hurricanes and invasion of ants, locusts, or bats, to epidemics of yellow fever and the bitter hostility of human neighbors; (2) the remarkable longevity of many priests and nuns engaged in this field: it would not be hard to draw up a list of two dozen who have served in leprosaria for 25 to 40 years; and (3) the grateful official recognition which their selfless service has evoked from public authorities: at least a dozen have been awarded special medals and honors by various governments.

The number of Catholic orders of priests and nuns who are today continuing Father Damien's work is indeed striking; no less than 130 in all. Besides the secular clergy, there are 42 orders of priests and 2 of Brothers, while the orders of nuns amount to 86. Moreover, there are also 4 groups of lay apostles. It is unfortunately impossible to mention in this brief sketch more than a tiny representative minority.

Finally, the world total of Catholics who are afflicted with Hansen's disease is estimated at over 175,000, of whom 150,000 are in Latin America. Most of the patients in Catholic leprosaria in Africa and Asia join the Church before they die, largely due to the powerful example of Christian joy in suffering which they observe in their fellow patients.

THE HOME FRONT

Here too the influence of Father Damien has been profound, even if it cannot always be accurately measured.

We can mention briefly only some of the Catholic groups and personalities who have played leading roles.

During Father Damien's lifetime, the Very Rev. Charles Emile Lesserteur (1841-1916), a Paris Foreign Missions Society priest who became superior of the famous mission seminary — France's "Maryknoll" — advocated the use of a Chinese drug named *Hoang-nan* as a specific remedy for leprosy. He wrote a book on the subject, published in 1879 (and reprinted in 1896), which shows that he was corresponding with a number of chaplains in leprosaria.

The Franciscan Missionaries of Mary, and Father Damien as well, must share with St. Francis of Assisi the honor of having inspired the work of Miss Kate Marsden, the extraordinary convert foundress of the St. Francis Leper Guild of London. Miss Marsden, "a quiet, retiring, Victorian lady," became intensely interested in victims of leprosy, whom she observed in her travels in Palestine and Turkey in the 1880's. Hearing that several hundred patients were in dire need in far-off Siberia, she won the powerful support of Queen Victoria and of the Russian Tsarina, and proceeded to journey across most of Russia by train, carriage, sleigh, and horseback, until she found the neglected sufferers near Yakutsk, and on her return organized relief measures for them in Russia and England. After this exciting expedition, which she described in a memorable book, Miss Marsden joined the Catholic Church, became a Franciscan Tertiary, and in 1895 founded, under the patronage of Cardinal Vaughan, the St. Francis Leper Guild. In the past sixty years the Guild has distributed nearly £100,000 to Catholic leprosaria in 25 countries. In 1953 it sent £10,665 to 61 leprosy colonies. The Franciscan Missionaries of Mary have served as secretaries of the Guild since 1922.

In 1893, Dom Joseph Sauton, a monk of the famed Benedictine Abbey of Solesmes who was also a physician, received permission from Rome to undertake a field study of leprosy. With the encouragement of Louis Pasteur, he made a trip around the world, visiting as many leprosaria as he could. In 1901 he published a book of nearly 500 pages, *La Leprose*, which is (as far as we know) the only medical treatise on Hansen's disease ever written by a Catholic priest. Dom Sauton presented a lengthy memorandum on "Assistance to Victims of Leprosy at the Present Time in France and Abroad" to the International Congress of Public Assistance and Private Benevolence in 1900, in which he announced his plans for a model St. Martin Sanatorium for French patients. Unfortunately, due (as so often happens) to the bitter prejudices of the local inhabitants, the institution was never built. Before he died at the Abbey of Liguge in 1916, Dom Sauton also contributed a learned article on leprosy to the great French biblical encyclopedia, *Dictionnaire de la Bible*.

The ideal of an international Catholic leprosy aid society was formulated by Mother Mary of the Passion, F.M.M., in these prophetic words:

> I would like to see a leprosy aid society founded, not only for our Order but for all the leprosaria and victims of leprosy in the world. . . . Certainly nothing would be greater utility than this society, which could be, beside the Propagation of the Faith, that of charity; and perhaps God will one day bring forth a chosen and generous soul who will have the gift of awakening in the hearts of our selfish and sophisticated twentieth century that touching compassion for victims of leprosy which ennobled the centuries of faith and enriched them with the most charming episodes.

As early as 1896, a Jesuit Father in Shanghai had reported to Father Mulhane that Father Conrardy "has now, it seems, undertaken the direction of leper missions all over the world," adding "I don't know whether he received the charge from Rome, or was prompted to undertake it by his own zeal and devotion."

In 1923, an Italian physician, Dr. Vincenzo d'Amato, apparently set out to fulfill Mother Mary of the Passion's ideal and prophecy, for he organized an international Franciscan Association Pro Leprosis in Rome, the aim of which was to provide assistance to all mission leprosaria and to undertake scientific research. The great "Pope of the Missions," Pius XI, "warmly favored the society's aims" and wisely "desired that the organization be built on the broadest possible foundations." Unfortunately it ceased to function within two years, due to the founder's insistence that it retain a special link with a particular religious order. During its all too brief span of existence, it published a beautifully illustrated quarterly journal entitled *Charitas-Scientia*.

Nevertheless, this idea of a world-wide Catholic leprosy aid society was again advocated in 1936 when Father Damien's remains were transported to Belgium. Dr. Georges Mensaert, O.F.M., a distinguished Belgian missiologist, wrote:

Only the organized cooperation of Catholics in leprosy work can make a more intense program of activity possible. Besides, would not the creation of a special fund for leprosy patients be evidence of that cooperation among Catholics which is so much desired? It too would make its way around the world, and like the Association of the Holy Childhood, it would become a real power, a universal apostolate of Catholic charity.

Noting that Dr. D'Amato's Association "was unable to obtain the necessary cooperation," Father Mensaert concluded:

Let us hope and pray that Catholics may become more and more conscious of their duties so as to make possible at last a society which would organize the Catholics of the whole world in favor of our most unfortunate brethren, the victims of leprosy. Such an organization would be the finest monument that could be erected in the memory [of Father Damien].

The National Office of the Society for the Propagation of the Faith in New York is, we believe, the only organization of its kind which makes an annual Christmas appeal for victims of leprosy. Since 1937 it has maintained a separate fund for that cause. Distribution of the fund is made to over 219 leprosaria by the Holy See. In addition, designated gifts distributed by the National Office to leprosaria between 1937 and 1953 amounted to $533,417.

In 1938 a French Missionary Sister of the Holy Ghost, Soeur Gilbert (Genevieve de Colonjon), wrote a masterly doctoral dissertation for the degree of doctor of medicine on "The Struggle against Leprosy; the Work of the Catholic Missions in the French Colonies."

A movement under Msgr. Fonteny in 1931-1932 to create an international leprosy center in France to give medical assistance to mission leprosaria did not produce any immediate results. However, in 1942, Msgr. Joseph Lavarenne, director of the Lyon Central Council for the Propagation of the Faith, founded a small leprosy research laboratory. And on December 7, 1948, His Eminence Pierre Cardinal Gerlier inaugurated the Clinique du Saint Redempteur in Lyon, primarily for missionaries with Hansen's disease. The laboratory and hospital have been organized by the present director, Msgr. J. Maury, into an Association Medicale Missionnaire which also supplies information about leprosy and courses of instruction and training for missionaries planning to work in leprosaria.

It is in this all-too-small laboratory in Lyon that the Marist Sister Marie Suzanne, after 24 years of service in the great British government hospital of Makogai in the Fiji Islands, has in recent years been conducting experiments which have attracted the favorable attention of the foremost leprologists in the world, particularly at the International Congress of Microbiology in Rome and at the Sixth International Congress on Leprosy in Madrid, both in 1953. A retired French missioner, Father Chauvire, who found that he had Hansen's disease ten years after leaving Africa, volunteered to remain without treatment so that specimens of his infected skin could serve as material for research. After six years of disappointing tests, Sister Marie Suzanne succeeded in developing a culture of a new bacillus which may become the long-awaited vaccine for leprosy. A fellow scientist named this bacillus *Mycobacterium Marianum* in honor of the Marist Order.

We can therefore say with Msgr. Maury: "It is good for us to know that the Church is remaining in the advance guard of scientific progress." Msgr. Maury wonders too whether in time "there will not be established a semireligious, semi-lay organization for generous souls who feel that they have a vocation to fight against leprosy and to relieve its victims, without becoming members of a religious order? Divine Providence, which is always attentive, and which has made possible the foundation of what now exists, will certainly assist in extending its benefits."

Among the various independent Catholic groups active in leprosy aid work which deserve mention are the Catholic Medical Mission Board of New York, which supplied several million sulfone tablets to leprosaria, and two lay organizations, the Damien-Dutton Society of New Brunswick, New Jersey, and The Friends of the Lepers of San Francisco. In Latin America there is the Patronato de Leprosos Internacional which, while not professedly Catholic, naturally has a large majority of Catholics among the members. It is especially active in Argentina. In Brazil the Federation of Societies for Assistance to Leprosy Patients, founded by an apostolic Protestant lady, Mrs. Eunice Weaver, has "eight thousand loyal Catholic women (members), many of whom," according to Mrs. Weaver, "are like Father Damien" in their zeal. Brazil has the most outstanding record of any country in the world in the number of sanatoria for patients and especially in the number of model preventoria for children of patients which have been built in the past twenty years, many of which are staffed by Catholic Sisters. Spain and Portugal also have excellent modern institutions for patients and children organized by the State and the Church.

In France special credit must go to M. Raoul Follereau, a distinguished attorney and founder of L'Ordre de la Charite, for his extraordinary efforts on behalf of victims of leprosy. In recent years M. Follereau has visited most of the leprosaria in the French possessions in Africa, Asia, the Pacific Islands, and Central America, bringing them generous gifts of funds. He has been admirably successful in stimulating widespread public interest in the leprosy apostolate, which has resulted in the establishment of special annual leprosy collection days in France and its colonies. Moreover, his moving appeal to the United Nations for a charter of human rights for the world's victims of leprosy was unanimously endorsed by all political parties in the French General Assembly.

Recent years have witnessed a renewal of interest in the noble leprosy apostolate of the Church, which has been manifested in the publication of books such as Father Momenico Rosconi's *Sole nei Villagi dei Lebbrosi;* M. Follereau's *Tour du Monde chez les Lepreux;* Father Patrick Myers' *Uplifted Hands, The Story of Leprosy;* and the *World Survey of Catholic Leprosy Work.*

The *World Survey* was based on approximately 150 detailed answers to a questionnaire which was sent to Vicars Apostolic in all areas in the world which have Catholic leprosaria. Besides providing statistics on Catholic leprosy work in those areas, the replies revealed several startling conditions which govern Catholic leprosy institutions:

1. The great majority of leprosaria reported that only from 3 per cent to 25 per cent of the thousands of victims of leprosy in their area are receiving any medical treatment at all;

2. Most of the mission leprosaria are in serious need of expansion.

Moreover, an overwhelming majority of chaplains and nursing nuns working in leprosaria expressed their conviction that the efficacy of their work would be greatly increased by the creation of a central Catholic leprosy information office and by the publication in several languages of a Catholic leprosy information bulletin or newsletter. This project, which undoubtedly has the blessing of Father Damien, is now under study by the proper authorities.

The *World Survey* also disclosed that the number of "other Damiens" — Catholic missionaries who, like him have contracted Hansen's disease — is at least 145; 80 priests, 9 Brothers, and 56 Sisters. Of the total, 67 are still living: 28 priests, 5 Brothers, and 34 Sisters. But the point to be stressed here is that these figures represent only 7 per cent of the number of Catholic missionaries (1000) that are estimated to be engaged in this work.

The only living member of the hierarchy who has Hansen's disease, the Most Reverend Tomas Aspe, O.F.M., Bishop of Calinico, wrote in a stirring "Message to Catholic Leprosy Workers" which was included in the *World Survey*, that "leprosy is the only sickness which turns its victim into a pariah — the only pariah of the civilized world." Bishop Aspe emphasized that "society has evolved a conception of this disease that is as deadly as it is false and that lacks a basis in truth to the extent of ninety-five percent. . . . For in the immense majority of cases, leprosy is not the most painful nor the most fatal nor the most contagious nor the most incurable of diseases." His Excellency "with heartfelt emotion" gives his blessing to the project of an international Catholic leprosy information office and bulletin, and makes its early foundation a special intention of his prayers and sufferings.

The year 1954 saw the appearance of the only comprehensive history of Catholic leprosy work which has ever been written: *Esperance pour les lepreux* by the Abbé Pierre Prenat (Paris, Le Rameau — Editions du Vieux Colombier, 287 pp.) with a preface by Msgr. Jean Maury; based on research in old mission journals by the Marist Sister Marie Suzanne, Father Prenat's excellent book gives a detailed outline of the splendid apostolate of our missioners throughout the world for victims of leprosy. It forms a welcome and indispensable addition to the growing collection of literature on this subject.

Finally, what can be said of the future of Father Damien's legacy?

The answer to that question lies in another question: What would Father Damien say and do today if he were alive and faced with the present drastically improved outlook in the leprosy field?

Today, as in his time, it is a tragic but universally admitted fact that *90 per cent of the world's four million or more victims of Hansen's disease are still without any care or treatment whatsoever.*

Yet today the astounding new fact is that one leprosy patient can be given a treatment with the sulfone DDS which will effect a probable cure and an almost certain major improvement in appearance, general well-being, and morale — *and that treatment costs only one dollar for one patient for one year.*

However, not only the dollar is needed, but also the well-trained medical missionaries — doctors and nurses — who will administer the health-giving treatment. The need for human volunteers is at least as great as the need for funds.

And so we come back to the challenge of Father Damien; who will continue his work, which is still so far from being finished?

We conclude with an eloquent tribute to Father Damien and his followers by the late Mahatma Gandhi, who took personal care of a leprosy patient and who loved to visit leprosy hospitals:

If to help persons suffering from leprosy is so dear to the missionaries, especially to Catholic missionaries, it is because no other service requires a greater spirit of sacrifice. To care for persons with leprosy demands the highest idealism and most perfect abnegation.

The political and journalistic world can boast of very few heroes who compare with Father Damien of Molokai. The Catholic Church, on the contrary, counts by the thousands those who after the example of Father Damien have devoted themselves to the victims of leprosy.

It is worth while to look for the source of such heroism.

BIOGRAPHICAL NOTE: Raphael Brown, the author of this Epilogue, is senior reference assistant, General Reference and Bibliography Division, Library of Congress, Washington, D. C. Mr. Brown received his education in private schools in Switzerland and France and at Harvard. He is contributing editor of *Damien-Dutton Call* and *Our Lady of the Cape Magazine.* He has written articles for *Catholic Digest, America, The Shield, The Star,* and other magazines. He is the author of *The Life of Mary as Seen by the Mystics* and translator of several works. His *World Survey of Catholic Leprosy Work*, on which this Epilogue is based, was published by The Mission Press of the Divine Word Fathers, Techny, Illinois, and is the most comprehensive work of its kind. The editors are grateful for Mr. Brown's fine contribution to this book.

Appendix

The Congregation of the Sacred Hearts

THE CEREMONY OF PROFESSION
OF VOWS

THE members of the Congregation of the Sacred Hearts take simple vows of poverty, chastity, and obedience; first, for three years, called "Temporary Vows," and then for life, called "Perpetual Vows."

To understand Father Damien's reference to being "covered with a funeral pall the day of my religious profession," it is necessary to know something about the ceremony and its significance.

All members of religious orders and congregations take vows. By so doing they bind themselves to a life of the pursuit of perfection according to the so-called "evangelical counsels" enunciated by Christ: "If thou wilt be perfect, go, sell what thou hast, and give to the poor, and thou shalt have treasure in Heaven; and come, follow me" (Mt. 19:21). The taking of vows is not an end in itself, but a means to an end, which is sanctity or holiness of life. The vows act as a stimulus to the practice of virtue; and at the same time remove three great obstacles to the total dedication of one's self to the service of Christ, namely — the seeking after and use of money and property, removed by the vow of poverty; the cares and responsibilities of raising a family, removed by the vow of chastity; and self-will, removed by the vow of obedience.

Because of the importance and responsibility attached to the taking of the vows, called "profession of vows," or "religious profession," great solemnity marks the occasion. In the Congregation of the Sacred Hearts, the profession of perpetual vows is surrounded by solemn rites of deep significance, calculated to make a profound impression on the candidates and spectators alike. Father Damien never forgot the occasion and referred to it in several of his letters more than 25 years later.

The ceremony of profession of Perpetual Vows is as follows: The candidates enter the sanctuary of the chapel or church carrying lighted candles, while the choir sings Psalm 121, "I rejoiced when they said to me: 'Let us go to the House of the Lord' "; the officiating priest, usually the Provincial Superior, then intones the hymn, *Veni Creator Spiritus (Come, Holy Spirit, Creator blessed)*.

Following the sermon, the celebrant sits next to the table on which is placed the open book of the Gospels. Handing his candle to an assistant, the candidate places both hands in the hands of the celebrant and pronounces the following formula, the same one used by Father Damien: "I, ... [*here the name of the candidate is inserted*] in accordance with the Constitutions, Statutes and Rules, approved and confirmed by the Holy Apostolic See, make forever, into the hands of our Very Reverend Father Superior General, vows of Poverty, Chastity, and Obedience, as a Brother of the Congregation of the Sacred Hearts of Jesus and Mary, in Whose service I purpose to live and die. In the name of the Father, and of the Son, and of the Holy Ghost. Amen."

The celebrant then sprinkles the newly professed with holy water. After this the professed places his hands on the opened book of the Gospels, while kneeling before it, and says: "So help me God and His Holy Gospel."

Now comes the impressive part of the ceremony to

which Father Damien referred. It symbolizes the death of the religious to the world and his awakening to a new life. The ceremony parallels part of that used in a funeral service. It begins by the newly professed prostrating themselves before the altar. A funeral pall, a large black cloth, held by four professed priests, is spread over them; while four other professed stand at their side, each holding a lighted candle. The celebrant, standing, intones Psalm 50, the well-known *Miserere (Have mercy on me, O God)*.

At the end, he sprinkles them with holy water and sings certain prayers the second of which is particularly significant when applied to the life of Father Damien at Molokai. Translated freely from the Latin, it runs as follows:

Almighty and eternal God, who commands that we die to the world to live in Christ, direct Your servants along the way of eternal salvation. May their life be hidden in Christ, so that, with Your help, they may not only desire the things that are pleasing to You, but with all their strength may do them. Through the same Christ Our Lord, Amen.

ASSOCIATION OF THE SACRED HEARTS

IN ONE of his letters Father Damien writes that he had succeeded in establishing Perpetual Adoration among his patients; no mean feat, considering the difficulties under which he labored.

The privilege of sharing in the adoration of the Fathers, Brothers, and Sisters of the Congregation of the Sacred Hearts is one of the principal aims of the *Association of the Sacred Hearts*. The Association, which is not a Third Order, has functioned since the inception of the Congregation and is made up of men and women who wish to associate themselves with the main work of the Congregation, namely, Perpetual Adoration — hence the title, "Associates of the Sacred Hearts."

Their principal obligations are: a daily half-hour of adoration before the Blessed Sacrament, or at least weekly (an obligation that can be fulfilled if necessary by assisting at Mass); daily recitation of the "Hail, Holy Queen"; and monthly Holy Communion of reparation.

It was probably this Association which Father Damien set up at Molokai among the patients. Through it he instilled in the hearts of his flock a great love for the Blessed Sacrament and the spirit of reparation for those Catholics, who, though more fortunate than they, still were indifferent to the Holy Eucharist. So great was this desire to make reparation, that on the First Friday of the month, according to one of the old missionary Brothers who worked at Molokai for many years, many of the patients voluntarily abstained from all food the entire day, taking something only at sundown.

BROTHERS OF THE SACRED HEARTS

IN COMMON with other religious congregations, there are three classes of members within the Congregation of the Sacred Hearts. They are: priests, students for the priesthood, and the Brothers. These latter are variously designated, according to the custom of each community. They are known as lay Brothers, working Brothers, missionary Brothers, coadjutor Brothers, or just plain Brothers. In any case, they constitute a distinct branch, an important branch, of every congregation and order.

So far as the essentials are concerned, Brothers are just as much religious as are the priests. They take the same vows, live by the same rule, wear substantially the same habit, and fulfill the same essential duties. In the Congregation of the Sacred Hearts, these duties are, primarily, and in essence, "to practice and propagate devotion to the Sacred Hearts and to make perpetual adoration of the Most Blessed Sacrament." In this respect they are on the same level with the priests. It is true, they do not offer the Holy Sacrifice, nor perform strictly priestly functions, but they assist the priest in every possible way both at home and in the missions. By the exercise of perpetual adoration, by their prayers and the offering of their labors, they are effective missionaries even though they may never go to the missions. In the mission fields, they are invaluable, whether it be for constructing chapels or catechizing, working in a dispensary or raising foodstuffs. But it is especially by the sanctity of their daily life, often hidden and unknown to men, that they constitute the backbone of every religious congregation. These humble men of God draw down countless blessings on the work of the priests, and there is no doubt this is the reason Father Damien was anxious to have them at Molokai.

"I have always believed," Brother Dutton states, "that Father Damien desired to have a brother at the settlement but could not get one." Actually the Brothers came in November, 1895. Their unselfish devotedness to often unpleasant duties over long periods of time constitute one of the most inspiring pages in the annals of modern missionary activities. Among these unsung heroes are Brother Louis, who spent 46 years at Molokai; Brother Liborius, 31 years; Brother Materne, 28 years; and Brother Jules, now in the Sacred Hearts Seminary, Washington, D. C., who was there for some 14 years. From 1895 until 1951, the Brothers had been in charge of the Baldwin Home for boys. They were withdrawn in the latter year by mutual agreement between the religious and territorial authorities, due to changing conditions that no longer necessitated their presence at Kalaupapa.

In the United States a training school for Brothers, under the patronage of St. Joseph, has been opened at the Sacred Hearts Seminary, Wareham, Massachusetts.

Index

492